ADAPTING FOR INERTIA

DELIVERING LARGE GOVERNMENT ICT PROJECTS
IN AUSTRALIA AND NEW ZEALAND

ADAPTING FOR INERTIA

DELIVERING LARGE GOVERNMENT ICT PROJECTS IN AUSTRALIA AND NEW ZEALAND

GRANT DOUGLAS

Australian
National
University

ANU PRESS

Australian
National
University

ANU PRESS

Published by ANU Press
The Australian National University
Canberra ACT 2600, Australia
Email: anupress@anu.edu.au

Available to download for free at press.anu.edu.au

ISBN (print): 9781760466091
ISBN (online): 9781760466107

WorldCat (print): 1395054467
WorldCat (online): 1394969572

DOI: 10.22459/AI.2023

Cover design and layout by ANU Press

This book is published under the aegis of the Public Policy editorial board of ANU Press.

Contents

List of illustrations

Boxes

Figures

Tables

Abbreviations

APS	Australian Public Service
ATO	Australian Taxation Office
CIO	chief information officer
DBC	detailed business case
DTA	Digital Transformation Agency
EPDP	Education Payroll Development Program
EPL	Education Payroll Limited
ICT	information and communications technology
IQA	internal quality assurer
IT	information technology
LMBR	Learning Management and Business Reform
MoE	Ministry of Education
NSW	New South Wales
NSW DoE	NSW Department of Education
NT	Northern Territory
NZ	New Zealand
PBO	project-based organisation
PID	Program Initiation Document
PMI	Project Management Institute
PMO	project management office
RCF	reference class forecasting
SAFe	Scaled agile framework

SSC	State Services Commission
Tas.	Tasmania
UK	United Kingdom
US	United States
Vic.	Victoria

Acknowledgements

I would like to acknowledge the outstanding guidance throughout my research from John Wanna (Emeritus Professor, School of Politics and International Relations, The Australian National University, and former Sir John Bunting Chair of Public Administration, ANZSOG Head of Research), Professor Helen Sullivan (Dean, College of Asia and the Pacific, The Australian National University), and Professor Karl Löfgren (Head, School of Government, Victoria University of Wellington). Without their support and advice, not only throughout my PhD, but also in the adaptation of the PhD thesis into this book, I am not sure where I would have finished up. With their very different styles, they collectively steered me down the path with a mixture of extensive experience in research and publishing, compassionate support (a nod to Helen), and very direct but correct advice: 'That's rubbish!' I am very fond of and thankful to each of these people.

The Australian National University was a wonderful place to undertake research and share experiences. A special nod to Christiane Gerblinger: we started our research at the same time and shared an office for a period. Christiane recently published her book (*How Government Experts Self-Sabotage: The Language of the Rebuffed*, ANU Press, 2023) and her support to me in finalising this book was constant. ANU Press were instrumental in making this book possible, and thanks to Andy Kennedy, the ANU Press Publication Subsidy Committee, and the whole ANU Press team for their support and encouragement.

I would also like to acknowledge and thank all the individuals across Australia and New Zealand who agreed to participate in my research, either as interview participants or by providing information and documentation. Without that participation, this book would not have been possible. A special thank you to Marg McLeod (Ministry of Education, New Zealand) for initially rallying the New Zealand troops and then introducing me to the New Zealand participants.

One of the goals of this book was to—while meeting the necessary academic requirements—make it easy to read and comprehend, perhaps even enjoyable to read, and to do so by telling the stories of the individuals involved in these large government ICT software projects. At The Australian National University, I attended a small work group by a visiting US political scientist named Katherine J. Cramer, the author of a book called *The Politics of Resentment: Rural Consciousness in Wisconsin and the Rise of Scott Walker* (University of Chicago Press, 2016). Cramer stated she used to write in a very prescribed manner to meet the demands of political science journals and defended political arguments through quantitative methods. However, she took a new approach when writing her book. Cramer wanted to address academic criteria but also write in a style that would communicate to a group wider than other academics and demonstrate that qualitative research can be applied effectively to political analysis. This was important as Cramer wanted to tell the stories of rural voters, what mattered to them, and why. It is a particularly good book. While I am certainly not comparing my book with Cramer's work, she did inspire me. I hope that when people read this book, it communicates the message clearly. For those involved in these projects, the narrative documented throughout will be relatable to many— at times, painfully so.

Finally, a dedication to my amazing mother, who put her five children before everything and still believes it is her role to make sure we are okay. In turn, I owe her everything.

Preface

For many decades, worldwide and across sectors, large information and communication technology (ICT) software projects have experienced poor outcomes, with industry research indicating that almost all will fail to deliver to original expectations—some spectacularly so. There is much existing research on the causes of both public and private sector project failure, such as poor project management. Despite all this learning and research, the problems continue.

To address an identified gap, this book differentiates itself from the literature in several ways. First, it focuses on the Australian and New Zealand public sectors, for which, it is argued, there is a dearth of targeted research. Second, these large projects operate within frameworks that provide the rules, guidelines, and controls, collectively forming their institutional governance. Given that the Australian and New Zealand public sectors have historically developed institutional frameworks but continue to have poor outcomes, there is something amiss. The puzzle is, therefore, how effective are these institutional frameworks in providing the governance for large ICT software projects?

To address this puzzle, this book further differentiates itself from the existing literature by applying an institutionalist's lens. To obtain the data, a qualitative, interpretative, and comparative research design was applied. Seventy-five elite interviews were conducted with stakeholders who have direct involvement in such large projects and therefore a personal perspective on the institutional frameworks. This is effectively a collaborative exercise to discover from those most impacted their perspectives on institutional governance.

The narrative that emerges is that the institutional frameworks are in a state of inertia; they are failing to adapt due to various institutional factors. Change is costly and not prioritised politically or organisationally.

The frameworks 'stick' to a historically implemented path. Governance is imposing structure over agency. Governance leadership is failing to collaborate. Finally, there is a culture of forgetting from one project to the next. All have public policy implications.

There is also a perception that this state will continue. Therefore, the dominant perspective is to reduce project complexity: stop undertaking large projects as traditionally planned, for which a 'superhuman' capability is required, and break them into a series of smaller component-based projects. Actors with agency and entrepreneurial skills have done this successfully; however, they succeeded by circumventing the institutional frameworks to address their weaknesses. Such entrepreneurs are rare.

To address the rather sad perspective of interviewees that nothing much is likely to change, and that success will remain dependent on chance, a more practical proposal was identified: undertake at the initiation stage a brutal independent assessment of the likelihood of a project to deliver as planned. The assumption is that, given poor outcomes are likely, the forecast is just a guess and the agency/project must explain how they will address this. If you have planned a single large project, you cannot start. If you do not have a skilled, trained, and committed sponsor, you cannot start. If you do not have the project management capability and capacity required, you cannot start.

The logic is simple: if you do not have the ability to enable successful delivery, it is better to stop the project at the initiation stage and work on a revised plan until you determine how you can deliver. Project funding must also change to support this approach, to be iterative and progressively based on results, delivery, and revised forecasts for each stage.

In effect, there must be an acknowledgement that if there is difficulty in changing the capacity to govern, the nature of what is to be governed must change.

1

Governance doesn't seem to be working too well

At the heart of my findings is a conclusion that, notwithstanding the work undertaken to-date, the current model of weak governance of ICT at a whole-of-government level … leads to sub-optimal outcomes. (Gershon 2008: iii)[1]

[Earlier reports] identified significant shortcomings in the public sector's management of such [ICT] projects and included numerous recommendations. Despite this, there has been little sign of lessons learnt and ICT projects such as myki, HealthSMART and LEAP, were regularly in the newspapers for the wrong reasons. (Victorian Ombudsman 2012: 1)[2]

The [negative] impacts of the well-publicised Novopay[3] failures have reverberated across New Zealand. Every state and state-integrated school in the country has been affected … [I]t is clear to us that important lessons from the past … should have been learned but were not. (Jack & Wevers 2013: 1)

Rarely has the need for change been demonstrated more clearly than through the failure of the Asset Management System project. To spend around $70 million dollars only to make the system worse is clearly unacceptable … [and] further demonstrates that action to

---

1   This report was the result of a review of the Australian Government's use of ICT.
2   This report from the Victorian Ombudsman was the result of an investigation of ICT-enabled projects in the Victorian public sector.
3   Novopay was a large payroll project within the New Zealand Ministry of Education. It is one of the case studies in this book and was the subject of a ministerial inquiry.

improve the management of ICT projects is required to not only get
better levels of service provision but also to avoid crippling waste.
(Public Accounts Committee 2014: 5)[4]

The above quotes are from reports into the poor outcomes of large
information and communications technology (ICT) software projects in
the Australian and New Zealand public sectors. They either reference or
allude to a failure in institutional governance and a failure to adapt that
governance based on past learnings.

They resonated with me due to my professional life as a long-term NSW
Government employee. For the past 20-plus years, I managed various
government ICT software and infrastructure projects and programs. My final
responsibility was managing components of the Learning Management
and Business Reform (LMBR) program within the NSW Department of
Education (NSW DoE). The LMBR was an exceptionally large program
of work, attempting multiple organisational transformations: a new financial
system; a new student administration, learning, and management system;
and a new human resources/payroll system. For an organisation the size of
the NSW DoE, any one of these was a huge undertaking and to attempt all
of them together under the umbrella of one program was delusional.

The LMBR became a political and organisational hot potato and was the
subject of much negative media interest.[5] Yet throughout, the program
complied with the NSW Government's governance arrangements for
a large ICT software project. These arrangements did not seem to help the
program; instead, they arguably pushed planning down a path that increased
the likelihood of a poor outcome.

I was aware of and at times engaged in another example: a large, much
troubled NSW Government ICT software project (which I will anonymise)
that underwent several planning revisions to reset and start afresh, with
a new and weighty business case prepared. It was a governance requirement
in New South Wales that for projects of this size a business case in a standard
format was completed and a gateway review undertaken before formal
approval. The review resulted in complimentary feedback from the gateway

---

4   This emerged from a Northern Territory Government review of the management of ICT projects
by government agencies.
5   The then education minister, Adrian Piccoli, was interviewed for this book. His perspectives on this
program and other issues have been included.

panel, the project team was congratulated, and the business case, project, and funding were approved. The project was to span several years, was complex and had many organisational-change challenges and dependencies.

However, once the project began, the business case was immediately challenged, and on completion, it bore no relation to the eventual approach. It was an all but irrelevant historical document—one completed due to and reviewed via a formal institutional governance requirement. On completion, the project was wildly over time and budget, yet it had been continually approved to progress. What was the point of the business case other than complying with the governance rules? The forecasts in the business case for time, cost, and scope proved to be incorrect. The project budget in the business case was at best misleading, yet this was how the project was assessed as viable, and then funded and approved. Is this an appropriate means of approving and funding such large complex projects? What was the point of funding such a project in full upfront when the business case was simply a guess? The agency did not have the project management capability to undertake the program of work; it was not their core business, yet they prepared the business case and took ownership of the program. Why was this allowed?

Finally, this capability issue extended to the project assurance. The project was praised for the quality of its planning, yet that planning proved to be unsuitable for the task. What was the value of the gateway review that effectively endorsed an approach that failed? Did it have the capability to challenge these plans? Were there alternative governance approaches available that would have been more suitable and aided the project in its objectives? These questions challenge the effectiveness and appropriateness of the NSW Government governance framework for large ICT software projects.

Working within the LMBR program and other ICT projects provided extensive exposure to the factors that can impact on them—from the political and environmental influences to the maturity, capability, and capacity of government agencies to undertake a large and complex program of work.

At the completion of my final LMBR role, I left the NSW DoE, and indeed the NSW public sector, partly due to the LMBR's continued failure to deliver the final product. I had no confidence that the organisation would adapt, do things differently, and not repeat the same mistakes. It was, however, also time for a break and to find new challenges.

After leaving, I had time to reflect, not just on the NSW DoE but also on the government sector in general and why these large ICT software projects continue to have so much trouble achieving success and learning from the past. The governance did not seem to be adapting as required. Not once in my working life was I asked to provide feedback on the governance of these projects; the expectation was to follow the controls and guidelines imposed by central agencies and deal with events independently.

I was curious to put my views aside and find out what others felt. I believed the puzzling issue of governance effectiveness for these large projects would make an excellent research topic—both interesting and important. Hence, I moved into student life again and began a PhD at The Australian National University to research this governance puzzle and to try to somehow measure effectiveness. This book reflects the outcome of that research.

I should also point out that the NSW DoE and its Information Technology Directorate have and continue to deliver excellent products and were a wonderful place to work. I have seen and been part of projects that were rightly classified as great successes. The staff are skilled, dedicated, and committed to providing an excellent service, and this is true for the public sector generally, and is confirmed by the many elite interviewees who participated in this research. The puzzle addressed in this book relates specifically to large ICT software projects. The distinction between outcomes for operational and smaller projects and those for large ICT software projects was also made clear by the interview participants.

The puzzle

Within each jurisdiction across the Australian and New Zealand public sectors all large ICT software projects are subject to governance frameworks at the jurisdictional level. While there is no universal definition of governance (Frederickson et al. 2003: 224; Meuleman 2008: 9), a 'minimalist' explanation is that governance 'is the capacity to get things done and to have services delivered' and is likened to 'steering a boat' to achieve a desired outcome

(Peters 2012). Governance is also defined as 'patterns of rule' such as the systems, institutions, and norms by which organisations are directed and controlled (Bevir 2007: 365). The goal of effective governance is to create the 'conditions for ordered rule and collective action' (Stoker 1998: 17).

Taking these definitions into account, for the purposes of this book, the institutional governance of large ICT software projects can be defined as the collective policies, rules, guidelines, and so on that control their multilevel operations. It also provides the strategies to build the required capability and capacity for these projects.

This institutional governance is quite different to governance within a project. Institutional governance is all-encompassing for every project and is the reason a project is initiated, approved, and continues. Within a particular project there will be 'project governance', such as a project board or steering committee, to steer the project through its course. The requirement for the project to follow PRINCE2 and have a project board would be mandated by the institutional governance. This book focuses on the governance that stipulates the use of PRINCE2 and other methods and guidelines within a project.

The puzzle is that despite these historically developed governance frameworks, poor outcomes for large ICT software projects continue, and the same issues keep arising. Is this an indication that the governance is ineffective, that it is failing to create the 'conditions for ordered rule'? It is difficult to answer this question, for two reasons. First, little research on the institutional governance of such projects across the Australian and New Zealand public sectors has been undertaken. Second, measuring governance effectiveness is tricky.

Effective governance can be defined as 'the extent that the actual performance matches the desired outcomes' (Baekkeskov 2007: 258): Did you achieve what you set out to do? But how can governance effectiveness be measured? It is not readily quantifiable as obvious measures are few— and when governance is multilevel, this becomes even harder (Besancon 2003; Bevir 2007)—or the measure may focus on one set of criteria to the exclusion of others (Baekkeskov 2007). To add to this dilemma, McConnell has argued that public policy has had difficulty coming to terms with outcome determination and disputes about whether a policy has 'failed' are commonplace and open to varying perceptions and political point-scoring (2015: 222). These factors often lead to an 'endless debate' about the outcome (Bovens & 't Hart 1996; Baldry 1998).

If a measure of effective governance for large ICT software projects was to be purely empirical and quantifiable, one possibility would be a traditional assessment of the project outcome. This is where real outcomes are compared with the forecast outcomes of time, cost, and scope (Chua 2009; Al-Ahmad et al. 2009; Bolin 2012; Fabricius & Büttgen 2015; Hughes et al. 2016)—a measure commonly known as the 'triple constraint' (Zwikael & Smyrk 2012: S7) or 'the iron triangle' (Budzier & Flyvbjerg 2011: 2). Did the governance framework enable the project to deliver on the forecast?

Aligned to the earlier arguments about the dilemmas faced in measuring governance and public policy in general, measurement of a project's outcome against this 'iron triangle' has received similar criticism (Standing et al. 2006; Goldfinch 2007; Thomas & Fernández 2008; Stoica & Brouse 2013; Lehtinen et al. 2014; Fabricius & Büttgen 2015). Therefore, while those factors are important parts of project control, they 'should certainly not be confused with measuring success' (de Wit 1988: 164). Projects can be classified as successful even if time and costs are exceeded (Wateridge 1998; Thomas & Fernández 2008) as the priority is to deliver a solution that effectively transforms how an organisation does business (Rothstein & Teorell 2008; Budzier & Flyvbjerg 2011). For these reasons, a quantifiable measure has not been selected as the method of measuring the effectiveness of governance for large ICT software projects. In addition, quantitative studies typically focus on the specific, are narrower in scope, and identify a handful of measures, whereas the research in this book is quite broad and more holistic—an approach more aligned to a qualitative study (Mertler 2016: 108–10).

Nonetheless, a measurement of governance is important—indeed, critical—for this book, as it is central to the puzzle and the resulting research questions. This book is interested in the perspectives of the key stakeholders, the chosen experts (Besancon 2003) with proximity to operational decisions, the actors in these projects who are expected to operate these projects within the institutional governance framework. Do they perceive that the governance assists them in achieving the desired outcomes? From their perspectives, a narrative will emerge that will be the measure.

To assess this 'effectiveness' there are two research questions. The first aims to address the 'effectiveness' puzzle. The second is related to a core concept of governance: the need for continual fine-tuning of the 'fitness' of the governance arrangements (Schneider 2012). Governance must adapt and evolve based on learnings. This clearly should be the case with the governance arrangements of large ICT software projects as there is much past learning. Has this been happening and, if not, why not?

The two research questions are:

1. What is the perceived effectiveness of governance in the Australian and New Zealand public sectors for large ICT software projects in achieving desired outcomes?
2. What, if any, are the perceived challenges to adapting governance for large ICT software projects in the Australian and New Zealand public sectors?

Background

In 2015, the Australian Government commissioned a report titled *Learning from Failure: Why Large Government Policy Initiatives Have Gone So Badly Wrong in the Past and How the Chances of Success in the Future Can be Improved* (Shergold 2015: i), which was referenced as 'an independent review of government processes for implementing large programs and projects, including the roles of the ministers and public servants'. While the Shergold report is not specifically about large government ICT software projects, its findings are applicable as they largely relate to improving good government through project governance—a principle founded on 'good policy' (Shergold 2015: iii). In short, the report proposed developing governance to support robust decision-making, enhancing the project management discipline, improving collaboration, and embracing adaptive government and governance (Shergold 2015: iii–xi). The proposal to adapt is referenced in the title of the report, as it found weaknesses in governance and was making recommendations to learn from those.

The problem, however, is that many of Shergold's findings can also be found in numerous other reports, within and external to the Australian Public Service (APS); they are neither new nor unique. For example, an earlier Australian Government report, *Review of the Australian Government's Use of Information and Communication Technology* (Gershon 2008), also concluded that governance was weak and was contributing to poor outcomes. It acknowledged the need to adapt by recommending the establishment of a process for developing whole-of-government ICT policies and strategic visions to support 'the achievement of the Government's outcomes and wider policy agenda' (Gershon 2008: 3). Rather disturbingly, according to a review of the documents and the elite interviews, there is no evidence that anything concrete has eventuated from either the Shergold or the Gershon reports.

Of course, this issue is not restricted to the Australian Public Service. There has been a multitude of other reports produced within Australia and New Zealand, and internationally, into why large government ICT projects have failed to meet expectations, and recommending adaptations to improve outcomes.

In the Northern Territory, the *Management of ICT Projects by Government Agencies* (Public Accounts Committee 2014) was prepared after a series of poor project outcomes. The New Zealand Customs Service commissioned Deloitte to undertake a 'lessons learned' report into the troubled Joint Border Management System (Deloitte 2017). The New Zealand Controller and Auditor-General (OAG 2012) identified several key lessons from a review of six public sector projects, while the Victorian Ombudsman (2011) presented a report titled *Own Motion Investigations into ICT-Enabled Projects* after looking into a series of troubled projects in that sector.

These reports and others have similar findings, such as the need to improve the project management discipline in the public sector. The Victorian Ombudsman's report—like the earlier comment on the Gershon report's recommendations—found that the government had failed to learn from past mistakes and adapt governance accordingly (Victorian Ombudsman 2011). In each of the 2011, 2013, and 2017 annual *Lessons Learned* reports produced by the New Zealand gateway review teams after assessing projects across its public sector, factors such as addressing jurisdictional capability in key project areas were identified as major issues (SSC 2011, 2013; The Treasury 2017).

Several observations can be made from these reports. While they acknowledge governance failures and make recommendations to 'improve governance', they do not measure governance effectiveness, nor do they take a collaborative approach to identifying governance effectiveness or opportunities for adaptation. They generally identify the cause of a problem, such as the lack of project management capability, and recommend that this be addressed. What they fail to address are the underlying institutional challenges that cause these governance issues to continue over an extended period.

The reports have also been prepared after the event, generally take an audit-like approach, and then hand down findings. They can fall victim to being 'a tick in a box'—a reaction to a crisis—and are not followed through. For example, in media coverage of a 2017 parliamentary inquiry (Senate Finance and Public Administration References Committee 2018b) into the digital delivery of APS services, it was reported that the status of the 2008 Gershon recommendations remained unclear (Se Eun 2018). When the committee asked about progress, it was told that agencies did not collect such data. In addition, the Chief Digital Officer of the APS's Digital Transformation Agency (DTA) was quoted as saying that while the Gershon report was important, the 'world has moved on'. The DTA also admitted that issues in ICT governance would continue and many of Gershon's recommendations may never be implemented (Se Eun 2018).

This book seeks to address these issues by attempting to measure governance effectiveness and to identify what, if any, institutional challenges exist that impede governance adaptation. This research was undertaken in a collaborative manner by engaging with stakeholders who are impacted by governance frameworks.

In conclusion, the following quote from an APS elite interviewee, in response to a question about the Gershon report and whether they were consulted for it, indicates a consequence of not collaborating and then handing down recommendations:

> Finance, the central agency, here is a pattern for you, same with the DTA. They had these propeller heads, up there in the clouds, and know it all. Well, they do not bring in people that have runs on the board that are practical, pragmatic with big service delivery systems. You have to build a relationship; it is not 'Oh, I am smarter than you and I can do this and move over'. It is not like that. How? How can I work with you? Because I need to learn about what you are doing and why. What is your context? I will share my story and then jointly we will work out the how. So, you have a mix of people in AGIMO [Australian Government Information Management Office] that are away with the pixies, [and] had no respect in operational agencies. They never come out and talk to you, never tried to learn about what you did. That Gershon, that was a money grab. (Person AB, Senior project officer, APS)

Research scope

The research in this book focuses on institutional governance in the Australian and New Zealand public sectors for large government ICT software projects, and on the people and processes of governance, but not the technical aspects. This is because an organisation needs effective and capable people and processes to implement and use—indeed, even decide on—the technical elements (Bhargav et al. 2008). Governance frameworks arguably concentrate on the people and process aspects.

There is a focus on the Australian and New Zealand public sectors as there is a gap in targeted research on the institutional governance of large ICT software projects across these sectors. While there is much research on large ICT projects, it tends to concentrate on a specific theme—for example, the impacts of project roles and disciplines (Crawford & Helm 2009; Williams & Samset 2010; Kwak et al. 2014; Joslin & Müller 2015; Kloppenborg & Tesch 2015; Flyvbjerg et al. 2016; APM 2018; Marcusson 2018; AIPM & KPMG 2022)—or it is international (IPA 2018), related to a particular Australian or New Zealand jurisdiction or project (Gershon 2008; KPMG 2012; OCIO 2013; Shergold 2015; Senate Finance and Public Administration References Committee 2018b), investigates projects in general rather than ICT specifically (Dobbs et al. 2013; Lind & Brunes 2014; Siemiatycki 2015) or a particular project approach (Hodgkinson 2019), is related to public policy and its application (Wanna 2007, 2021; McConnell 2015), or to governance in general (Edwards et al. 2012).

Academic research into public sector institutional governance of large ICT projects is harder to find and, again, is not specifically targeted at large ICT projects, particularly those in Australia and New Zealand—for example, a study into the governance of large ICT healthcare reforms in Europe (Ulriksen et al. 2016) and research into the governance framework of public projects in Norway (Volden & Andersen 2018). Joslin and Müller (2016) have tried to quantify internationally the relationship between governance and project success but have a narrower focus. There was an Australian study of interest identified, albeit for a particular APS agency (Caravel Group 2013); however, there was none that took a holistic view of the institutional governance of large ICT projects across the Australian and New Zealand public sectors.

In addition, the results of the above research and other studies identified throughout this book cannot be generalised to the research undertaken here, or vice versa. Qualitative research academics (Freidson 1975; Maxwell 1992; Flick 2004; Creswell 2009) argue that you should not generalise findings from one context to another. The focus of this book is firmly on the context of the elites involved in large ICT software projects in the Australian and New Zealand public sectors and, while there is similarity with other research findings that assists in comparative analysis, the results should not be generalised. The perspectives of the elites interviewed in this book are specific to their context.

The historical, political, and governmental similarities between the Australian and New Zealand public sectors also make them suitable for combined research. Both have stable governments and societies and both were British colonies and transplanted the Westminster system. They also share common institutional specifics such as being parliamentary democracies and having a professional public service (Kumarasingham & Power 2015). One final argument for a focus on Australia and New Zealand is that due to their geographic isolation and the similarity in size of some jurisdictions, they could be experiencing similar challenges in the governance of large ICT software projects. This could lead to synergies between the two countries and across jurisdictions, such as currently exists in organisations like the Australia and New Zealand School of Government (ANZSOG 2018: 6), which aims to jointly 'enhance the capability of public servants' in both countries.

The focus on large government ICT software projects is due to three factors, the first of which is size. There is a long and consistent history globally of 'failed' large ICT software projects across all sectors and industries, and the evidence indicates that the larger the project, the worse the outcome. The Standish Group report (Goldfinch 2007: 917) in the United States found that the success rate for ICT software projects was 55 per cent for those valued at less than US$750,000, but for those with budgets exceeding US$10 million, it was zero. In a later report (Standish Group 2015: 3), the success rate for large projects had moved to a hardly acceptable 2 per cent. These studies assessed outcomes as comparisons between the actual and the planned time, cost, and scope of the project. Failure in these large projects, as measured against these criteria, is almost habitual. Large projects for the purposes of this book are defined as those with a budget exceeding A$10 million.

The second factor is government, for while large government ICT software projects share many commonalties with private sector projects, such as project management techniques, there are distinct environmental and institutional issues that differentiate them and make them more complex and therefore worthy as an area of research. These include their political environment and the susceptibility and uncertainty this can bring to long-term projects. Government projects can have numerous stakeholders with competing expectations; they also have mostly intangible goals and, unlike the private sector, are not primarily driven by financial benefits (Campbell et al. 2009; Kwak et al. 2014; Shergold 2015).

The final factor is the specific focus on ICT software projects. ICT is defined as all aspects of a technology solution, from the software and hardware to the communications devices and services utilised to plan and implement solutions (Beckinsale & Ram 2006: 848; Cardona et al. 2013: 110; BCS 2013; QGCIO 2019) that deliver and transform the operations of government (Department of Finance and Deregulation 2012: 4). Software is the application that supports business processes and the means of interfacing with users and the driver of a project such as a new payroll solution. However, among other dependencies, software must reside on hardware and be delivered over communication devices, hence the need to include all aspects of ICT in the definition.

A project is defined by the Project Management Institute (PMI 2013a: 1) as a 'temporary endeavour' to create a product with a distinct beginning and end. However, ICT software projects have certain characteristics that differentiate them from others, making them more complex, and increasing their likelihood of producing poor outcomes. These include factors such as overambition, unrealistic expectations of technology, hidden complexity, and uncertainty of requirements, particularly when related to business requirements (Al-Ahmad et al. 2009: 93).

A detailed report by the Royal Academy of Engineering and the British Computer Society (2004) into the challenges of large ICT software projects detailed some of the differences between these and typical engineering projects. Engineering projects are restricted by physics and materials; ICT software projects are not, and there is therefore a perception they can do anything, but they cannot. This creates issues with visualising the product and enthusiasm about dreamt-of possibilities. Like engineering projects, it is possible for an ICT software project to produce a product, but the problem in ICT is finding a common expectation of what is to be produced and for what need (Royal Academy of Engineering & BCS 2004).

In summary, while all projects are susceptible to poor outcomes—as, regardless of project type, size and innovation add risk—the complexities, intangibility, and often ambiguities of a large government ICT software project increase this likelihood.

A large ICT software project requires many roles and disciplines, each of which can impact on the outcome and can often work in 'conflicting and complex ways' (Remler & Van Ryzin 2011: 26). It was not feasible, or necessary, in this book to undertake research on all the project roles and disciplines. Therefore, a specific focus was required (see Figure 1.1), on three roles/disciplines that are critical to good project outcomes: the sponsor role, the project management roles and discipline, and the forecasting discipline. The research focuses on the institutional governance of these three and provides comprehensive and relevant analysis. If any of these is governed poorly, poor project outcomes are all but assured. These three roles/disciplines are the subject of a review in Chapter 2, where they are defined and their importance discussed, providing a reference point for the later analysis of each.

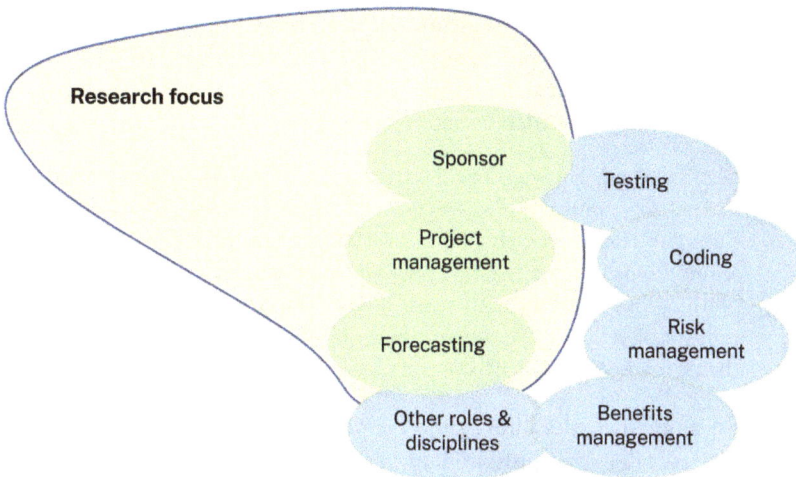

Figure 1.1 The roles and disciplines in a large project that provide the research focus
Source: Created by author.

Finally, this research is significant for several reasons. First, it addresses a gap in the literature by uniquely analysing the effectiveness of governance for large government ICT software projects from the perspectives of many elite interviewees—actors who have been participants in these projects and are therefore impacted by their governance. Their unique views and stories, and the resulting narrative, will document a group 'reality' of governance.

Second, to add to the uniqueness, the research focuses on the institutions of governance for these projects. Whereas much existing research has focused on procedural issues, this book is concerned with the overarching governance framework for projects and measuring it. Measurement is important for governments in adapting governance and for long- and short-term policy developments (Besancon 2003).

Third—and adding to the relevance and potential use for adapting governance—it was quite common in the elite interviews for the participants to state that the reason for their participation was the hope that it would drive change. This is the essence of new or good governance: collaboration and adaptation. Two quotes provide examples:

> [W]e cannot say enough that things like this help the public sectors on both sides of the Ditch. Obviously, for me as a current public servant, I think you have to give back, and if we all believe that we can do things better and differently and save taxpayer money to deliver other programs, then it is incumbent upon us to do it. So, whatever you publish, I hope public sector agencies pick it up and say, 'Yeah, we can learn from these lessons, and let us do it better and save taxpayer dollars.' (Arlene White, Chief executive, EPL)

> My final comment would be, I started out as an analyst programmer in 1980 at [company]. Projects were failing in those days for exactly the same reason that they are now: poorly defined requirements, scope creep, not the right people, and poor project management. Nothing has changed in 40 years. If what you do adds value to one sponsor on a large government project in Australia or New Zealand then it has been of benefit. (Person C, Senior internal quality assurer)

Last, and aligned to the above, any adaptation in governance to improve project success has the potential to result in better financial outcomes. In government, when large ICT software projects have poor outcomes there can be severe negative impacts on the use of taxpayer funds. In the United Kingdom, more than £12 billion was spent on the National Health E-Records System before it was scrapped (Martin 2011)—a truly gobsmacking waste of public money. In Canada, a new government payroll system was scrapped after C$1.6 billion was spent (May 2019; Marrs 2019). Within the Australian and New Zealand public sectors—the focus of this book—there are also examples. The New Zealand Police's Integrated National Crime Information System (INCIS) project, with a budget of NZ$100 million, was much troubled from the beginning, labelled a fiasco (Gauld & Goldfinch 2006: 83–98), and subject to a ministerial inquiry (Small 2000). The NSW Department of Education's LMBR program was completed in 2018, four years late and A$265 million over original forecasts (Hendry 2018). In the Australian Public Service alone, the value of ICT projects in 2017–18 was estimated to be A$7.76 billion (DTA 2018a: v). Given the level of investment, any research that can assist in improving outcomes and preventing financial waste, even marginally, is significant.

The governance dilemma

There are two accepted approaches to governance. The first is a state-centric approach, in which, through power, there is authority to force or at least attempt to gain compliance (Peters 2012). This has been labelled '*impositional*' as it is imposed hierarchically (Richardson 2012). This is a structural approach to control the behaviour of individuals, yet it is then subject to individual agency for compliance (Peters 2012).

The second approach—and the one aligned with the modern principle of 'good governance'—is more interactive and collaborative and, through engagement, seeks to build trust in governance and boost compliance (Rothstein & Teorell 2008; Peters 2012) as a means of bringing agency into governance. This has been labelled '*consensual*', with an emphasis on governing through consultation with the relevant interest groups and/or actors. This is classified as a contemporary style of governing (Richardson 2012)—a change from a fixed pattern of rule to one in which the patterns of rule 'are changing practices arising from interactive processes' (Bevir 2007: Introduction). This change from a control-focused 'push' model to a collaborative-inclusive 'pull' model also highlights a change in required leadership style. Executives are required to let go of control and allow collaboration to drive governance (Sullivan et al. 2012: 45). This is the dilemma between the old and the new practices of leadership for governance (see Figure 1.2).

The dilemma: letting go

Old leadership in governance		New leadership in governance
Control	→	**Collaboration & inclusiveness**
Push model		Pull model

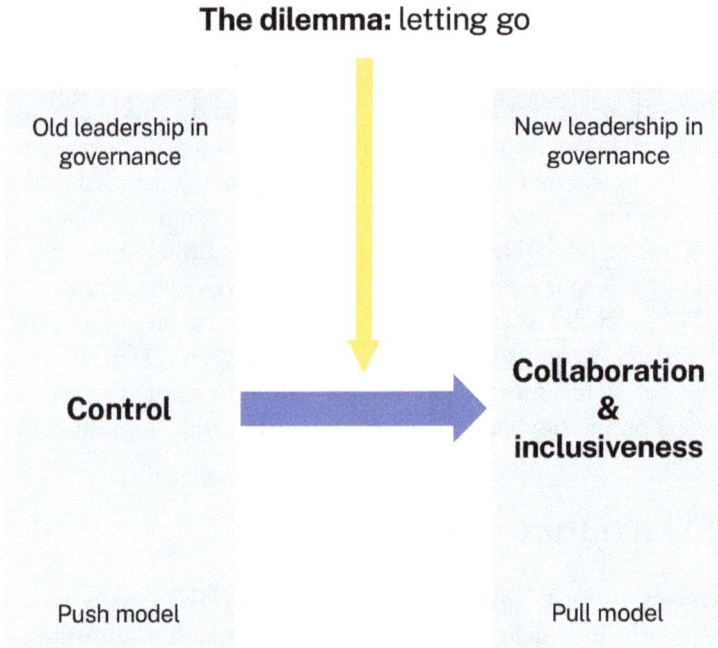

Figure 1.2 The governance dilemma
Source: Created by author.

This dilemma will be an important part of answering the research questions. Is governance being 'imposed' from the top down with disregard for the actors involved in these large ICT projects and their experience, or is it 'consensual', with the governance adapting from the bottom up? Perhaps the Australian and New Zealand public sectors are being impacted by this dilemma and this could help to explain any lack of governance adaptation.

The governance dilemma in action … Keep this in mind as you read

Since the completion of my research, I have given several presentations on the findings to government agencies. At one of these—to a large agency about to enter a major business transformation project—I was asked a question that highlighted the governance dilemma. One of the agency's heads challenged me, saying: 'Surely you are not suggesting people ignore governance when you say they succeed by stepping away from governance arrangements? Do you mean you found that people don't want governance?'

Initially, I was taken aback, as I thought I had failed to get a key finding across to the audience. However (with a spoiler alert to later findings), I said no, this is not what I found, what I found in fact was the opposite. I found that the actors in these projects want and understand the need for governance, but need it to be effective and to assist them in achieving good outcomes. At the moment, they perceive governance as focusing on top-down control and not adapting to the learnings of those involved in these projects. Therefore, when I said some projects had succeeded by stepping away from governance, it was not to avoid governance but rather to address its shortcomings—a dilemma for all involved.

I gave to my audience an example highlighted in the Education Payroll Development Program (EPDP) case study (Chapter 7, this volume). Traditionally, project audits occur after the completion of the project or at major milestones. This is fine, but of what relevance and help to the project and its stakeholders are retrospective audits? The EPDP sponsor, while acknowledging the importance for governance of independent audits, saw this retrospective model as being of little benefit to the project. The audit team was instead heavily involved in a process of continual review throughout the progressive delivery of the products. Findings were actioned almost in real time, with learnings applied to future components, and so on.

The sponsor did not hide this alternative approach from anyone; in fact, she was keen to share. The audit team and the project were recognised with a national audit award. The central agencies acknowledged the effectiveness of this alternative approach. Excellent drivers for change, you might think? But no, when asked what change had occurred in New Zealand governance as a result, the answer was 'nothing'; the learnings remained localised within the agency. When the project's audit team was asked why, other than a shrug of the shoulders, the argument was that the central audit agencies perceived this as letting go of control and independence of the audit function. Surely, a process that improves the project's outcomes should be the goal rather than maintaining control over a historical process.

I mention this now as it is useful for the reader to keep this in mind as they read and relate to the perspectives of those involved in the research. It is not an argument against governance; it is a plea for good governance and for change. Perhaps my questioner highlighted the dilemma of letting go in achieving this change.

The research framework

To answer the research questions, there had to be a structure that would provide applicable data and a framework to analyse and interpret those data. It is appropriate to explain this approach so readers can understand how the data were gathered and interpreted. The framework employed in the research is represented diagrammatically in Figure 1.3.

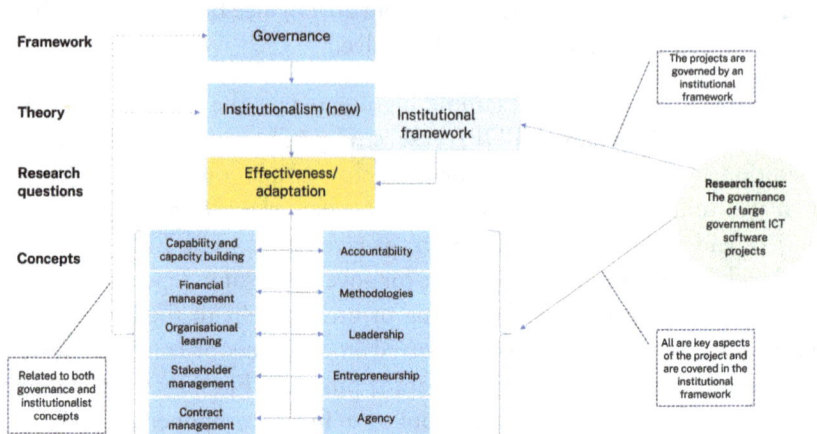

Figure 1.3 The research framework
Source: Created by author.

Earlier we defined governance as 'patterns of rule' such as the systems, institutions, and norms by which organisations are directed (Bevir 2007: 365), and that the goal of effective governance is to create the 'conditions for ordered rule and collective action' (Stoker 1998: 17).

An institution is not a thing as such; rather, it 'is a collection of rules' (March et al. 2011: 239; Steinmo 2015: 181) or 'humanly devised constraints that shape human interaction' (North 1990: 3). Ferris and Tang (1993: 7) argue that institutions constrain activities through rules and that actors adhere to rules as it is in their best interest to do so. It is important to acknowledge this relationship, as it provides meaning, structure, and stability to behaviour 'through routinisation and prior determination of acceptable and non-acceptable interactions' (Timney 1996: 101). The institution provides direction and boundaries.

New institutionalism is concerned with not only institutions but also the relationship between the institution and its actors (March & Olsen 1984; Koning 2016; Lowndes 2018). This is key to answering the research questions in this book. The research is seeking to measure how the institution influences the behaviour of the actors in these large government ICT software projects and how they interact with the institution.

Therefore, the term 'institutional governance' used throughout this book can be thought of as how the behaviour of actors is influenced by the institution and how the governance is influenced by the behaviour of actors—that is, the formal interaction between the two.

The system or collection of formal rules, guidelines, procedures, roles, and informal norms that shape both actions and behaviour is classified as an institutional framework (North 1994). This classification is important to this book. Each jurisdiction within the Australian and New Zealand public sectors has an institutional framework that shapes the behaviour of the relevant agencies in the operation of large ICT software projects. Their purpose is to provide a 'stable structure' in which all agencies and actors can operate and to ensure consistency. However, North's (1994) argument that stability does not equate to efficiency is central to this book and its research questions.

It is also pertinent at this point to briefly, albeit simply, explain how a large ICT software project is typically structured within the Australian and New Zealand public sectors, and how the institutional framework—the collective institutional governance arrangements—interacts with and influences these projects.

Projects begin with a catalyst of some sort—perhaps an idea, a political initiative, or the need to replace an ageing system. They may also be part of a portfolio of planned work. From that moment, detail is progressively added to provide all the information required for the project to be approved. The project then begins along the path of development and implementation, through to assessment of outcomes. Before, after, and at every stage in this process the institutional framework has an impact— for example, jurisdictional strategies to build the required capability and financial guidelines (see Figure 1.4). The point is that the institutional framework has a major influence on the governance of these projects; they do not operate in isolation, they are controlled. So, back to North's argument and the research questions: How effective is the governance via these institutional frameworks?

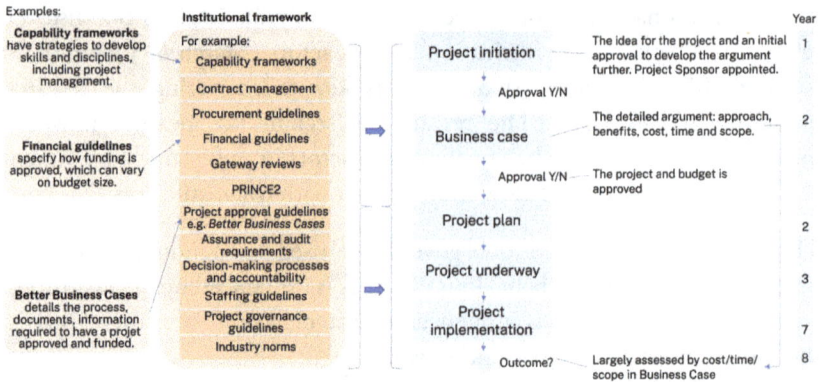

Figure 1.4 How the institutional framework influences large ICT software projects

Source: Created by author.

The lowest tier of the research framework is that of the concepts, which are described as 'the points around which research is conducted' (Bryman 2015: 151). They provide a focus for data analysis. This book therefore identified 10 concepts of institutional governance to analyse, which relate to practices and dilemmas in governance (Bevir 2011) and collectively provide an institutionalist perspective on governance. They are covered within the various institutional frameworks for large ICT software projects as each is a key factor in the operation and management of these projects. These concepts, together with a description and their relevance to the research, are detailed in Appendix 1. It is important to note this here because Chapters 3–7 include an analysis of each as part of their findings.

Solving the puzzle through listening

The research questions ask: What is the 'perceived' effectiveness of governance for large government ICT software projects in the Australian and New Zealand public sectors? In addition, what, if any, are the 'perceived' challenges in adapting this governance? Earlier in this chapter, there was a discussion of the difficulties of 'measuring' governance and public policy outcomes in general, and how it was important—indeed, critical—for this book that an appropriate measure is applied.

As a preface, the following quote attributed to nineteenth-century Danish theologian and philosopher Soren Kierkegaard is used to highlight the intent of the research design: 'Life is not a problem to be solved but a reality to be experienced.'

The research in this book aims to look at the 'reality' of life in these projects from the narratives of the actors involved and, through those personal experiences, to try not to 'solve' life in these projects but to highlight experiences. The measure will be the actors' perceptions: How has the governance helped them in their objectives?

Figure 1.5 is a diagrammatic representation of the research approach. With the puzzle in mind, I reviewed past and current research on my three focus areas (sponsor, project management, and forecasting). Key factors were identified for each (for example, the sponsor is a critical role) and from that emerged my research questions (for example, does the organisation understand the importance of the sponsor's role).

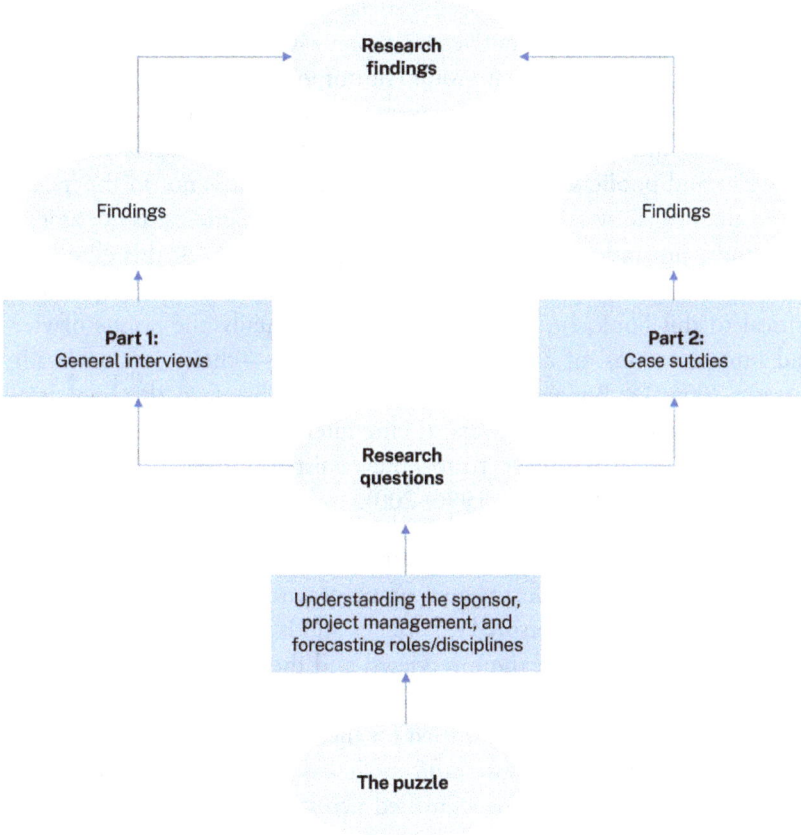

Figure 1.5 Research roadmap
Source: Created by author.

A two-part analysis was undertaken to provide the data to answer the questions. Part one (Chapters 3–5) provides a general collection and interpretative analysis of data related to the governance of large ICT software projects across the Australian and New Zealand public sectors. I conducted extensive interviews with key stakeholders and experts with experiential involvement in large ICT software projects. Part two (Chapters 6 and 7) provides case studies of two large ICT software projects. From the interpretation of these data, findings are made for each part. In the closing section, the findings from parts one and two are compared (Chapter 8), an overall narrative emerges, various implications are identified, and a conclusion is made.

Elite interviews were the primary source of data. Dexter (2006: 19) argues that elite interviews target a specific social group, comprising 'influential' or 'well-informed' representatives or those with some special knowledge garnered by being part of that group (Bottomore 1993). In the case of this book, the group is those actors who were, or still are, important stakeholders in the management of large ICT software projects across the Australian and New Zealand public sectors. That means the interest is not in the 'person' but in their capacity as an elite in the group, and the interest is not as a sole case study, but rather what they add as representatives of this elite group (Flick 2002). The elites will provide the interpretative knowledge that is critical to this book. Interpretative knowledge entails 'the points of views and interpretations' of the actors in these groups—their view on 'reality' (Dexter 2006: 18; Bogner et al. 2018: 658–59). Therefore, this book is not seeking 'right' or 'wrong' answers, as elite interviews by their nature do not seek to establish a positivist 'truth'; they assist in interpreting a situation from the narratives (Richards 1996: 200).

The interviews sought to elicit from the elite group their personal interpretations of the effectiveness of governance in large ICT software projects based on their personal experience and is information not available elsewhere. The data from the interviews, and their interpretation, provide the critical information to answer the research question. Part one (general) interview participants were identified for their involvement as key actors in large government ICT software projects. It was a key aim of the research to ensure that these actors were identified across jurisdictions and agencies, with an important stake or role in large government ICT software projects, that this was not restricted to ICT professionals, and that the research was not ICT-centric.

A total of 57 interviews for part one were completed (see Appendix 2 and Table 1.1). This number was effective for reaching the saturation point— one large enough 'to allow for discursive repetition and recurrent patterns of argumentation to emerge' for further analysis (Nikander 2012: 406). A similar process was undertaken for the case study interview participant identification, except that the targets were direct stakeholders in the project. The total number and category of participants interviewed for the case studies was 18 (see Appendices 3 and 4; Table 1.1).

Table 1.1 Summary of elite interview participants

	Exec.	CIO	Ass.	SPO	Pol.	Cons	Acad.	Union	DCom	T2	Total
Part 1											
NZ	3	5	3	4							15
APS	2	2	2	2							8
NSW	2		3		1	1					7
Vic.		3	3								6
NT	4		6	2							12
Tas.	1		1	1							3
Anon.	1										1
Private sector		1		1			3				5
Subtotal	**13**	**11**	**18**	**10**	**1**	**1**	**3**	**0**			**57**
Part 2											
NPay	2	1		3				1	1	2	10
EPDP	1		2	5							8
Subtotal	**3**	**1**	**2**	**8**	**0**	**0**	**0**	**1**	**1**	**2**	**18**
Total	**16**	**12**	**20**	**18**	**1**	**1**	**3**	**1**	**1**	**2**	**75**

Exec. = Executive
CIO = Chief information officer
Ass. = Assurance officer
SPO = Senior project officer
Pol. = Politician
Acad. = Academic
DCom = Datacom
T2 = Talent2
Anon. = Anonymised
NPay = Novopay
Source: Compiled by author.

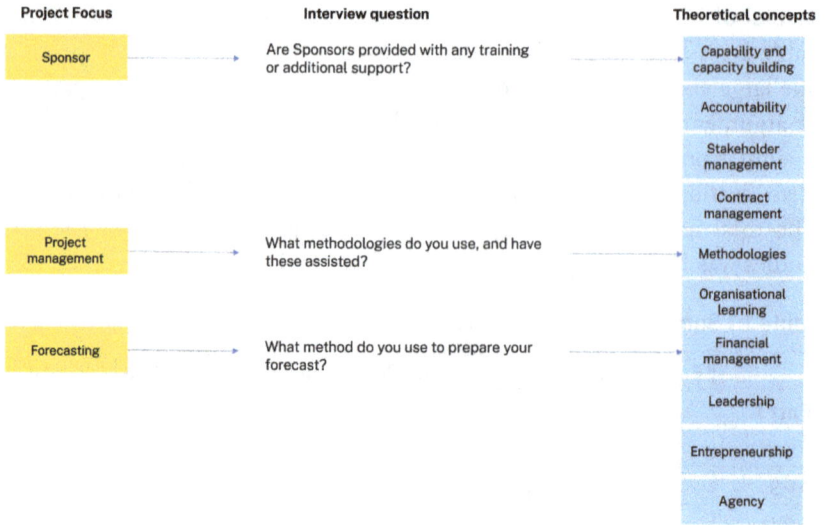

Project Focus	Interview question	Theoretical concepts

Figure 1.6 Aligning questions to theoretical concepts
Source: Created by author.

Part one interview questions were open-ended, semi-structured, and aligned to the roles/disciplines that were the project's focus—sponsor, project management, and forecasting—and to the concepts identified in the research framework section, such as financial management, and capability and capacity-building (see Figure 1.6). In the interviews, each participant provided their personal perspective; the semi-structured approach provided flexibility. While the interview may have started with a defined question, the conversation flowed naturally and allowed for additional information and perspectives to be provided, and some great quotes to be captured. This is an advantage of the semi-structured approach, as the interviewer can 'come away with all the data intended but also interesting and unexpected data that emerges' (O'Leary 2010: 195). However, while semi-structured interviews enabled this flexibility, they also provided the structure for consistency and commonality in questioning required to aid the later analysis and thematic coding of the data (Flick 2002).

As with those in part one, the elite interviews in part two were semi-structured, with questions targeted to the research focus roles/disciplines and theoretical concepts. The difference was that instead of the questions seeking general perspectives based on the participants' experiences with various projects, the part two questions related to the case study project. The intent was to gain a personal perspective based on the participant's role as an actor in the case study project.

One of the strengths of elite interviews is that they enable actors from a 'cluster' to be compared (Liu 2018)—an acknowledgement that these elites may have different perspectives on some matters. Aligned to this, elite interviews—particularly when they are semi-structured—while allowing the actors to tell their own story, also provide the opportunity for the interviewer to ask additional questions where perspectives differ (Sabot 1999; Hochschild 2009). One of the assumptions before the interviews was that there would be contrasting perspectives among the elites, potentially according to jurisdiction, and there would be a need to analyse why this was so. However, as will become evident, one of the findings was the great consistency in the perspectives of all the elite interviewees, regardless of jurisdiction or role; the governance issues identified were common to all.

For the case studies, a comparative approach was adopted. The use of two case studies was intended to provide a 'systematic comparison' (Kaarbo & Beasley 1999: 377) between the two. The case studies are two large ICT software projects in the New Zealand public sector. Intensive study and observation of each allowed for the discovery of 'contrasts, similarities, or patterns' (Campbell 2010) across the cases that would not have been possible using just one case.

There is a final reason for utilising case studies and the comparative approach. As well as comparing the two case studies, the intention is to compare the case study findings with the findings from part one. Part one identifies general findings on the governance of large ICT software projects, while part two is a detailed examination of two such projects. To enable the comparison, an identical interview process was applied. Did the findings from part one match those from the case study and, if not, what could be the explanation? The comparative approach provides additional validity and rigour to the research (Eisenhardt 1989).

The research questions seek to assess the effectiveness of the institutional governance of large ICT software projects in the Australian and New Zealand public sectors, so an appropriate means of comparison is identifying two similar projects with different outcomes. This follows the principle of Mill's 'method of difference' or the related 'most similar systems design' logic that says that differences—in this case, project outcomes—can be explained by comparing similar cases with varying outcomes and can aid in the identification of the reasons for this (Meckstroth 1975; Van Evera 1997; Bleijenbergh 2010).

The case study projects have many similarities, but one major difference. Both were large ICT software projects that operated within the New Zealand public sector and were therefore governed under the same jurisdictional institutional framework. Both targeted the delivery of a payroll solution to the same customer base—namely, staff within the New Zealand school system.[6] Therefore, both should have encountered similar environmental and stakeholder management issues. The two also had a direct relationship, as one arose from the need to address weaknesses in the other. The difference is that, given these similarities, one was classified publicly as a 'disaster' and led to a national apology; the other project was cited as an 'exemplar' for its success. Why are the two project outcomes so different?

The two case study projects are:

- The New Zealand Ministry of Education's Novopay payroll project (2008–12), which was deemed to be an abject failure.
- The New Zealand Education Payroll Limited's Education Payroll Development Program (EPDP) (2017–20), which is cited as an 'exemplar'.

The comparative relationship of the findings for each case study and the part one general interview findings is displayed diagrammatically in Figure 1.7.

The third data collection method was the identification and collection of relevant documents, which were then reviewed, interrogated, and analysed (O'Leary 2010: 223) to form the third source of data for this book. This documentation was used to complement and interpret the data obtained from the interview and case study processes and to build on the literature review.

---

6   Person U, a senior executive in the New Zealand Ministry of Education (MoE), said the MoE is primarily responsible for school policy and funding, with the schools themselves largely autonomous entities. Each school has a Board of Trustees which employs the principal and teachers. Each school determines its own staffing based on available funding; however, the MoE retains responsibility for the staff payroll. The two case studies relate to the provision of that payroll service.

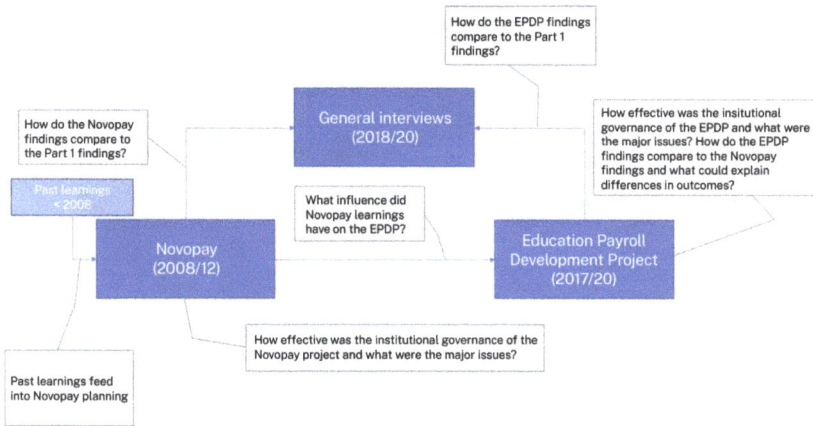

Figure 1.7 Case study comparative relationship
Source: Created by author.

Thematic analysis was utilised to interpret interview data. Thematic analysis is defined (Braun & Clarke 2012: 57) as 'a method for systematically identifying, organising, and offering insight into patterns of meanings (themes) across a data set'. Applying this definition to this book and the intent of the research design, the analysis is not focused on identifying what is unique within a single interview but is a means of identifying what is common across all interviews for the topics under discussion. It is about 'making sense of those commonalities' (Braun & Clarke 2012: 57) and identifying themes in the data (Castleberry & Nolen 2018).

An identical process was used for elite interviews in both part one and part two. A 'pragmatic' (Aronson 1995), simple hierarchy of thematic analysis was employed (see Figure 1.8). For each of the three research areas—sponsor, project management, and forecasting—interview questions and discussions focused on the theoretical concepts. Interviews were transcribed and entered into NVivo, where they were reviewed and thematically coded by identified common 'patterns' (Aronson 1995). This resulted in the identification of the core themes for each theoretical concept. From these findings an overall story emerged of the institutional governance of large ICT software projects in the public sector.

Project focus	Theoretical concepts		Themes (by project focus & theoretical concepts)
	Capability and capacity building	Accountability	
Sponsor	Financial management	Stakeholder management	Theme 1
Project management	Organisational learning	Contract management	Theme 2
	Methodologies	Leadership	Theme 3
Forecasting	Agency	Entrepreneurship	Theme 4 etc ...
Interview questions align to the theoretical concepts			For each theoretical concept thematic coding is undertaken to highlight core themes

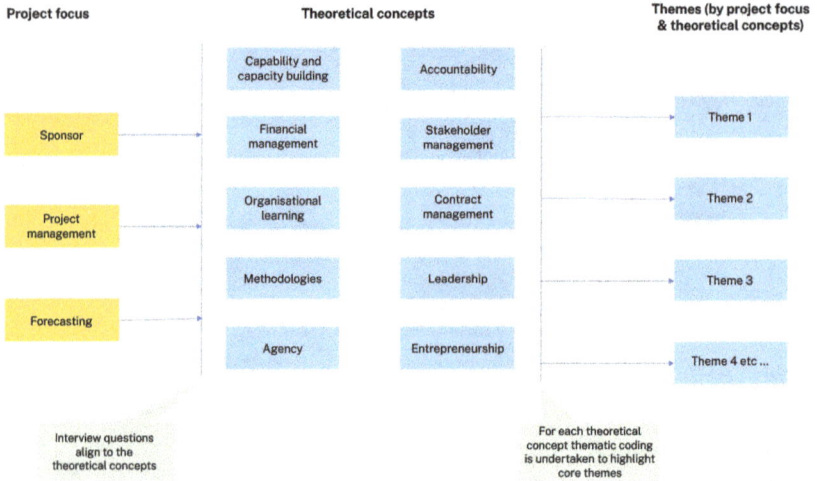

Figure 1.8 Thematic analysis hierarchy

Source: Created by author.

The thematic analysis approach to the interview data was also applied to document analysis. The documents were read and, if relevant, stored in NVivo, where text was coded using the same process as the interview data. This provided consistency and comparability of data and aided in interpretation and reporting, effectively creating a 'systematic procedure for reviewing and evaluating documents' (Bowen 2009: 27).

As a final note to this section, the willingness of public sector staff to participate in the interviews varied; most were supportive, and I am grateful to them all. However, almost all public sector staff wished to be anonymised and participated on that basis. Given the generalisation of most data, this was not usually an issue. However, in some situations, this did limit potentially important analysis. For example, an actor who was leading a much-vaunted political initiative to address ICT project governance was interviewed but revealed that, despite the media hype, not much had been achieved, nor was it likely to, as it was extremely hard to enact change. This could have been an excellent mini case study, but this was not possible without putting the interviewee at risk of exposure and its consequences.

Intended audience

This book is intended for a dual audience of policymakers and government ICT project practitioners. Its findings highlight the interdependence of the policy and the practical. The personal perspectives of the elites in these large government ICT projects provide a painful narrative of the impact of unsuitable policy on practitioners and the problems for policymakers of enacting change. So, what can be done both policy-wise and practically? The concluding chapter has specific, but related, findings for both audiences.

The governance focus and the research design of this book also provide a different perspective for the audience. This book highlights the fact that there is a plethora of research on large ICT projects but it is typically independent analysis of all the things that went wrong, with the findings related to 'lessons learned'. One interviewee equated this to someone coming in after a battle and stabbing everyone left alive.

I wanted to do something different and make the book personally relevant for the audience. Gauld and Goldfinch's *Dangerous Enthusiasms: E-Government, Computer Failure and Information System Development* (2006) is referenced in several parts of this book. I like their book because it provides a unique insight into several large New Zealand Government ICT project failures and identifies lessons for future projects.

However, when I asked my New Zealand interviewees what they had learnt from the book, I was taken aback by the derision and at times contempt expressed towards its authors. The criticism was that the authors had no experience of, and did not reflect on, what it was like to work on large government ICT projects day to day. The interviewees believed the authors had ignored the organisational complexities and frameworks in which such projects and staff operate, and concentrated on the lessons to be learnt, rather than the underlying institutional issues.

This book is not taking a detached, remote view, nor is it focusing on 'lessons learned' to add to the pile of existing reviews. It also does not focus on the minutiae of the project management tasks and outcomes—what was delivered and what was not. This book investigates the institutional framework in which these projects operated and how effective this was for those involved. How was the project approved to begin? Did the framework provide the capability required? How did the institutional financial management of these projects assist? If the framework was unsuitable, did actors make local adaptations?

In summary, this book differs from other research by analysing, from the very personal experiences of those involved in these projects, how institutional governance impacts on the operation of large Australian and New Zealand government ICT software projects. These findings are relevant and important for both policymakers and ICT practitioners.

Plan of the book

Chapter 2 explores the three project roles and disciplines that are the focus of the research. The importance and development of the roles and disciplines are discussed and reference is made to documents within the Australian and New Zealand public sectors that provide the institutional governance for large ICT software projects. This assists in providing a comparison of the literature and the institutional frameworks.

Chapters 3 to 5 document and analyse the data from many elite interviews for each of the three project roles and disciplines—namely, sponsor, project management, and forecasting. For each a narrative emerges and findings against the theoretical concepts are detailed.

Chapters 6 and 7 are case studies of two large ICT software projects that were similar in product and target stakeholder group, but different in outcome. The chapters undertake a detailed analysis of the projects using the same format as that utilised in Chapters 3–5, except that the findings relate specifically to the case study.

Finally, Chapter 8 details the overall findings and the narrative that emerges. A comparison of the findings from Chapters 3–5 with those of the two case studies (Chapters 6 and 7) is then undertaken. Theoretical, policy, and practical implications are highlighted and a conclusion is made, including answering the research questions.

2

Understanding the sponsor, project management, and forecasting roles and disciplines

Sponsor

The role of a project sponsor has not always been considered important in projects or as part of project management. It emerged and has evolved with project management. In the 1950s, it was typical for the project manager to have total responsibility for a project (Morris 1994; Stretton 1994). As projects became more institutionalised within organisations, the term project 'sponsor' started to emerge in the 1980s, and the role was initially described as the project manager's boss (Briner et al. 1990). The role arose from a need to have an organisational actor responsible for the project on behalf of the organisation and not abdicate that to the project manager (Kerzner & Kerzner 2013: 464–66).

The United Kingdom's Association for Project Management defines the sponsor as being 'accountable for ensuring that the work is governed effectively and delivers the objectives that meet identified needs' (APM 2019a). The Project Management Institute (PMI 2013a: 32) defines the sponsor's role as providing 'resources and support for the project' and being 'accountable for enabling success'. The sponsor must be the 'project champion, approve the business charter, [be the] business case owner, [be] accountable throughout the lifespan of the project and [for] prioritisation of the project within the organisation' (Alie 2015: 6). These views are summarised by Crawford and Brett (2001: 2), who state that the sponsor is 'responsible for the project on behalf of the organisation'. The sponsor can therefore be classified as the 'project owner' (Labuschagne et al. 2006). Within the Australian and New Zealand public sectors, largely due to the use of the PRINCE2 project management methodology, the term 'sponsor' is also known as the 'project executive' or 'senior responsible owner' (SRO).

Having an effective and capable sponsor is critical for project success (Bryde 2008; Kloppenborg & Tesch 2015; Pádár et al. 2017; Breese et al. 2020). In their 2018 global review of the project management profession and projects, the PMI (2018: 6–7) concluded that inadequate sponsor support was the number one cause of project failure, responsible for 41 per cent of all failures. As such, the PMI argues that project support by the sponsor is 'priceless' as it bridges a gap between the organisational influencers and the project implementers, boosting collaboration and support, and leading to increased project success. Given the increasing complexity of projects, the sponsor role and its business focus are even more critical (AIPM & KPMG 2018).

The role of a sponsor is often misunderstood and simplified as a result, but it is a complex and critical set of activities (Bryde 2008: 800). The sponsor role is not only multidimensional, it also spans the entire project lifecycle (APM 2019b). This includes aligning the project with organisational strategy (PMI 2018), owning the business case, defining the business requirements and benefits, specifying the project's priorities, defining success criteria, involvement in developing the strategy and objectives, monitoring progress, tracking benefit realisation, and accepting delivery of the project. It would also fall to the sponsor to either decide or recommend upwards to cancel a project (Briner et al. 1990; Turner 1993; Morris 1994; Bryde 2008; APM 2019b). The sponsor is responsible for securing the necessary financial and other resources (Crawford & Brett 2001; Helm & Remington 2005), ensuring proper project governance throughout, being the escalation point for and resolver of any conflict, and maintaining internal relationships and those with external partners and suppliers. For a project implementing a new software solution, the sponsor would also be responsible for driving organisational change (Labuschagne et al. 2006). This is quite a job—in fact, arguably, a superhero is needed, and therein lies one of the major organisational challenges.

Kloppenborg and Tesch (2015: 29) argue that the role of the sponsor changes as the project moves through its lifecycle. At the initiation stage, key roles are setting goals and selecting the project manager. Sponsors must ensure planning is effective and start developing key stakeholder relationships. During project execution, they must keep the flow of communication open and ensure the quality of solutions. In the final stage of the project, they must capture the lessons learned and benefit realisation (Breese et al. 2020).

If the project is to have every chance of success, it needs an effective sponsor in place for the duration. That means the sponsor must have organisation-wide credibility, be an effective change advocate, and, importantly, be able to commit time and skills to the role (APM 2019b). An Organisation for Economic Co-operation and Development (OECD 2001: 4) policy brief argues that unless a single senior officer 'has final responsibility and is held accountable for the success of a project, the project will most likely fail'. Its argument is that organisations must take the sponsor role seriously, and it must therefore be given recognition, priority, and status. A review of public sector documentation (QPSC 2009; DPAC 2013; PSC 2013, 2017, 2019; VPSC 2015; SSC 2016; Victoria Police 2016; Office of the Commissioner for Public Sector Employment 2022; QGCIO 2018a; OCPE 2018; SAES 2019; PSC 2020), such as capability frameworks, found no evidence of sponsor-specific initiatives, so the perspectives of the elite interviewees will provide a unique view on this issue.

There is also some debate about the difference between the terms project sponsor and project 'champion'. Some say they are one and the same (Crawford & Brett 2001; Helm & Remington 2005; Dalcher 2016; Zwikael & Meredith 2018), while others treat them as separate roles, with the sponsor as the project owner and the champion as the project advocate (Turner 1993), driving and selling the project within the organisation (Schibi & Lee 2015). Crawford and Brett (2001) posit that the best way to differentiate between the two is to understand that the sponsor is a formal role in the project, and there should only be one of these, while the sponsor can and should also be a champion, so a project can have many champions or advocates for change within the organisation. In this book, there is a mini case study involving the Australian Commissioner of Taxation (see Box 3.1), who undertook both the champion and the sponsor roles, with the project benefiting as the change was visibly driven from the top and resources could be secured. The Novopay case study (Chapter 6) is an example of a disconnected sponsor—one who was tapped on the shoulder and was not the champion of change—and a project that had very poor outcomes. The point is, regardless of whether the champion and the sponsor are the same person, commitment to the change is a critical role of the sponsor.

The sponsor is supported in their role by the project team itself, other organisational senior managers, and governance groups such as a steering committee; however, the sponsor remains the accountable officer for the project (Alie 2015; APM 2019b). This is key, as sponsors are not there to manage the day-to-day delivery of the project; for that, they rely on the project manager or director (Kloppenborg & Tesch 2015: 27). This is a key project relationship as the sponsor must provide the project manager and the project team with all the organisational support required to fulfil their roles (Bryde 2008: 801). While a sponsor wants and needs a good project manager, it also works in reverse (Pádár et al. 2017; Buttrick 2019): it is critical for the project manager, and the success of the project, to have the active support of the most appropriate person within the organisation.

While the sponsor and project manager have an interrelationship and co-dependency, it is important that each is clear about their own role and does not cross into the other's territory (Bryde 2008: 801); nor should one usurp the role of the other (Crawford & Brett 2001: 4). They should be compatible members of the project team (PMI 2012). The relationship between the sponsor and the project manager—and their roles at various stages in the project—is summarised by Breese et al. (2020), who argue that the sponsor addresses project issues that are above the control of the project manager and facilitates the transition of the project into the business of the organisation. The high-level focus of the roles at various stages of a project are highlighted in Table 2.1 and, while certainly not exhaustive, it indicates the importance of the sponsor at all stages of the project, whereas the major focus of the project manager is the planning and execution stages.

In a study of project managers' perceptions of sponsors, Helm and Remington (2005: 57) found that where there was 'inadequate support at the executive sponsor level', the project manager tended to mask this by 'using a complex range of tactics and behaviours' to deliver the project despite this executive ineffectiveness. Masking ineffective sponsorship is not organisationally beneficial and can lead to filtered communication between the project manager and the sponsor. These are further arguments for an effective sponsor, as they and not the project manager should be leading the change and making core organisational decisions; otherwise, the project risks losing its business focus and becoming a delivery project instead. The multidimensional role of the sponsor and the various relationships required are displayed in Figure 2.1.

Table 2.1 Changing focus of the role between the sponsor and the project manager

Project stage	Key sponsor responsibilities	Key project manager responsibilities
Initiating stage	• Take ownership of the business case development and planning. • Obtain funding. • Commit to the project and how the solution will be used. • Select and mentor project manager and establish priorities.	• On-boarded (selected by the sponsor). • Assist in developing the business case.
Planning stage	• Ensure planning is undertaken. • Develop relationships with stakeholders. • Provide clarity of purpose. • Demand objectivity and transparency. • Own the business case.	• Main contact for project activities. • Activity planning and sequencing. • Develop project approach. • Time and cost estimation. • Create and plan for required project documentation.
Execution stage	• Ensure adequate and effective communication. • Understand project management process. • Celebrate accomplishments. • Create a community. • Make decisions and obtain decision acceptance. • Solve problems. • Provide political and top management support for the project manager and their team.	• Apply project management disciplines. • Be accountable for the delivery of the project's outputs as per the approved project plan. • Manage risks and issues. • Monitor and report on progress. • Team leadership. • Quality control. • Escalate issues.
Closing stage	• Output realisation. • Identify and capture lessons learned to ensure capabilities and benefits are realised.	• Project closure functions.

Sources: Adapted from James et al. (2013); Kloppenborg & Tesch (2015); APM (2018); Zwikael & Meredith (2018); AIPM (2020); Breese et al. (2020).

The arguments above indicate the importance, relevance, and many dimensions of the sponsor role. It is not for the faint-hearted or to be treated lightly by organisations, yet research by the PMI (2012) indicates that 68 per cent of organisations do not have effective project sponsors.

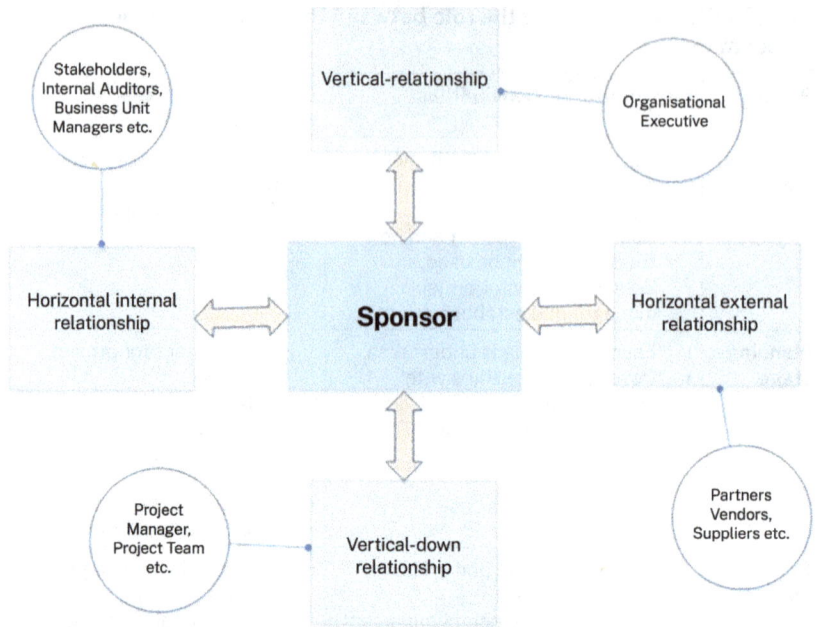

Figure 2.1 The sponsor's role and interrelationships
Source: Created by author. Adapted from Labuschagne et al. 2006.

To build organisational capability and capacity in this role, organisations must avoid two 'pitfalls in project sponsorship' (Crawford & Brett 2001: 4). First, if the role is not defined, recognised, supported, and visible in the organisation, problems will arise. Second, if the sponsor does not fully understand their role and have the skills required, they will be unable to carry out their functions. Therefore, guidance, support, and training are required (AIPM & KPMG 2018). Research undertaken by Crawford and Brett (2001: 5) found that this critical aspect was often neglected and the sponsor was left to fend for themselves. Australia-wide project research by the Australian Institute of Project Management (AIPM) and KPMG (2018: 14) found that organisations that provided training and support to sponsors almost doubled their success rates.

These are important points, as a survey (Chapman 2017) of senior executives across sectors and industries of their understanding of the sponsor role had some damning findings. Ninety per cent of senior executives did not know what the role involved and did not feel they were effective in the role. Unfortunately, of the remaining 10 per cent who claimed to know what they were doing, most did not, with less than 1 per cent having a good understanding. The AIPM and KPMG (2018: 16) research concluded that if organisations wanted to improve project success rates and get better returns for their investment, they must increase the focus on education and professionalisation of the sponsor role. This obviously links to the earlier point of the sponsor role being an organisational priority; if it is not, this will contribute to the lack of understanding of the role.

Often when organisations attempt to address the training issue, sponsors are given the incorrect skills (Chapman 2017). For example, while sponsors need an understanding of project management, they do not need to be trained as project managers; that is not their job. Rather, organisations should focus support and training on improving the disciplines 'associated with portfolio decision making and governance, particularly in the areas of defining and monitoring the realisation of project benefits' (AIPM & KPMG 2018: 16). Defining and addressing the support and training requirements of sponsors, given the multidimensional role they undertake, can be a challenge for organisations (Bryde 2008; Breese et al. 2020).

As sponsors are generally a senior executive within the organisation, it can be assumed that they are already busy people, which leads to the risk of them being unable to commit the required time to the sponsor role (PMI 2012). How the organisation and the sponsor structure their role and time is therefore critical. Should they step out of their day-to-day role for the duration of the project? Should they enlist support to build a 'sponsor support' team? What is not required is a 'disconnected executive whose main responsibility is to secure the project funds and then come in for the victory lap when it is all over' (PMI 2012). Other types of unwanted sponsors (APM 2018: 8–9) include the 'butterfly type, whose interest in the project waxes and wanes'; the 'reluctant sponsor', who does not want the role and is not tied to the benefits but feels unable to say no; and the 'incompetent sponsor', who simply has no idea of what the role requires. Interestingly, the research also indicates a growing trend in organisations for large projects to dedicate a full-time sponsor and treat this as a career development role (APM 2018).

Research on the institutional governance of the sponsor role in the Australian and New Zealand public sectors could not be identified; however, the jurisdictional frameworks and internal reviews offer insight. For example, with the introduction of PRINCE2 and gateway reviews in New Zealand and several Australian jurisdictions, the sponsor became an identified role and its importance was detailed (Tatnall et al. 2013: 53; Sharpe 2007: 205).

However, despite these institutional guidelines, there is evidence that while the sponsor role and its importance are documented, implementation is a different challenge.

A number of years after the introduction of PRINCE2, the Victorian Auditor-General (VAGO 2008: 8) concluded that project outcomes were negatively impacted by poor project sponsorship, with the sponsor not at the appropriate organisational level (p. 34), the sponsor's roles and responsibilities neither documented nor identified (p. 33), and methodologies to assist with the sponsor role not being used (p. 34). Three years later, the Victorian Ombudsman (2011: 5–8) reported that sponsors' roles and accountability were unclear and undefined, the responsible officers were reluctant to make decisions, and leadership from the top was required—much the same outcomes as the 2008 report. A follow-up report (Victorian Ombudsman 2012: 3) concluded that sponsors did not have the requisite expertise to undertake the role. In its audit of the A\$500-million-plus Learning Management and Business Reform (LMBR) program, the Audit Office of New South Wales (2014) found that the quality of project sponsorship had an impact. Gershon found that the Australian Public Service needed 'improved governance/management of projects through greater understanding by SROs of their responsibilities' (2008: 79). In New Zealand, the ministerial inquiry into the Novopay[1] project (Jack & Wevers 2013) clearly detailed a failure of project sponsorship as a key factor in the project's failure, and annual reviews of the gateway review process continue to identify sponsor-related issues (The Treasury 2017).

Another commonality is that many of the jurisdictions have capability frameworks that address organisational ICT and non-ICT roles, yet the project sponsor is not identified as a specific role (APSC 2010; Office of eGovernment 2011–13; Department of Finance and Services 2012, 2014; Department of Finance and Deregulation 2012; DPAC 2013; VPSC 2015).

This highlights a disconnect between the claimed understanding of the criticality of the sponsor role and the failure to incorporate this within the project management framework in the Australian and New Zealand public sectors. Bertsche (2014) argues that what is required is a strong organisational link between the sponsor's capability and role and the overall project management approach to build the notion of a project team working together and helping each other yet understanding one another's roles and

---

1   Novopay is covered in more detail in Chapter 6.

responsibilities and 'staying in their lane'. This means for the organisation to improve its project management capabilities and maturity, it must put in place strategies to integrate the role of the sponsor within its project management framework (Jones 2006). There is little evidence of that in the Australian and New Zealand institutional frameworks.

In summary, the literature indicates that the sponsor role is critical to project success, yet it remains largely misunderstood organisationally and there is no priority to address this as a required executive skill or to provide the necessary training and support to develop the skills. For a project to succeed it needs a capable and dedicated sponsor for its duration. While within the Australian and New Zealand public sectors there is evidence of recognition that the sponsor role is required and is important, there is little evidence that the necessary capabilities are being addressed institutionally.

Project management

Project management as a formal discipline 'was born in the middle of the twentieth century' with schemes such as the Manhattan Project to build the first atomic bomb (Shenhar & Dvir 2007: 8–9). The discipline and its guidelines and processes continued to develop and began to be recognised as a profession. Rules and procedures for use emerged and, in 1969, the Project Management Institute formed to develop global standards, with the PMI described as the premier global project management professional body (Shenhar & Dvir 2007: 8–9; Dinsmore & Cabanis-Brewin 2010).

The PMI, leveraging its other guidelines and project management standards such as the Project Management Body of Knowledge (PMBOK) and the Standard for Project Management, provided guidelines for organisations to use in improving their project management disciplines, the Organizational Project Management Maturity Model (PMI 2013b). The PMI argues that for organisations to successfully deliver in areas such as new product development, operational effectiveness, and customer services enhancement, the executive must focus on project management capability. This means building 'an environment for delivering individual projects and programs, while creating an organisational culture that treats temporary endeavours as projects' (PMI 2013b). This requires the organisation to understand what 'project management-related practices, knowledge, skills, tools, and techniques have proven consistently to be useful', including processes to compare against industry practices, the identification of capabilities, and 'the establishment of a roadmap for achieving improvements specific to the needs of the organisation' (PMI 2013b: 1.2). Organisational project management (OPM) is an integrated model to deliver organisational strategy/policy through project and program management. From organisational strategy, OPM evaluates and aligns initiatives to 'a set of programs and/or projects that yield the appropriate value decisions and benefits for the organisation'. These are delivered by a series of projects or programs through to the realisation of the benefits (PMI 2013b: 1.3). There is an important feedback loop that reviews, monitors, and adjusts projects/programs as necessary (see Figure 2.2). The key factor to note in this principle is that projects are not ad hoc; they derive from a strategy, assessed as part of an organisational portfolio of work, and delivered and monitored throughout. This is the result of the integration of knowledge, strategy, people, and processes (PMI 2013b).

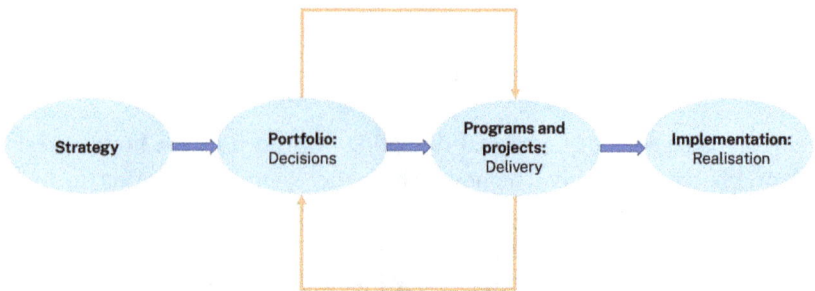

Figure 2.2 The organisational project management model
Source: Created by author. Adapted from PMI (2013b: 1.3).

'Portfolio' refers to the collective management of a group of projects or programs aligned to achieve organisational objectives. Program management is a collection of projects linked through a common outcome or type of collective capability. Program management has specific knowledge, skills, tools, and techniques that differ from the management of individual projects and has a focus on the interdependencies between the individual projects. Project management is the application of knowledge, skills, tools, and techniques to meet project requirements (PMI 2013b: 1.5.1–3).

A principal factor to note is that 'project management' does not refer to a particular position or role, such as a project manager. It is a discipline that encompasses the integration of the right processes (structure, guidelines, standards, rules, and so on) that can be actioned by the right people (organisational capability and capacity) to plan and deliver a coordinated series of projects/programs that realise organisational strategy; a project manager is supported in their role by the other integrated parts.

To assist in this process, mature project management organisations can have a project management office (PMO), which is a central organisational body that coordinates all projects or programs. A PMO is responsible for translating the organisation's strategy into a series of projects and programs (Altuwaijri & Khorsheed 2012: 39) and is responsible for organisation-wide distribution of project management best practices (Bolles 2002). The PMI argues that a PMO liaises between the portfolio, program, and projects, and monitors and reports on progress, and its primary function is to support the programs, projects, and key staff—for example, through initiatives such as training, communication, developing processes and templates, identifying methodologies, and the management of shared resources (PMI 2013b: 1.5.5). However, the structure and role can vary in each organisation.

Another indication of an organisation's project management maturity is whether they can be classified as project-based organisations (PBOs). A PBO is 'one which makes the strategic decision to adopt project, program and project portfolio management as business processes to manage its work' (Miterev et al. 2017: 481).

PBOs treat project management as a 'strategic competency' (Green 2005), which is evidenced by a 'strategic decision to adopt project-based working' and the formalisation of 'processes and structures to support that choice' (Miterev et al. 2017: 481). Developing and improving project management capability are therefore priorities of senior management in these organisations (Kwak et al. 2015: 1652).

In PBOs, people can 'spend a large amount of their time working in various types of temporary project constellations' (Bredin 2008: 567). That is not to say PBOs do not have permanent structures and processes; rather, temporary project structures are embedded in this permanent context. Organisational structures can also differ in PBOs, from the traditional top-down hierarchical structure to those more vertically and horizontally integrated to meld business and corporate strategy with project delivery (Thiry & Deguire 2007: 651–52). However, Bredin (2008: 567) argues that, regardless of these structures, a key feature of PBOs is that they 'retain a core group of employees for initiating, organising, and conducting' projects. Another emerging trend in PBOs is for project managers to take on senior organisational management roles (Thiry & Deguire 2007: 651) in recognition of their organisational importance.

These arguments about the importance of project management in the delivery of an organisation's strategy, and the need to integrate this within the organisation, lead to a discussion of where project management fits within an organisational structure and the importance placed on it by executives. Bolles (2002) argues that if an organisation wants to effectively deliver strategy, project management must be at the executive management level, otherwise 'how can a company ensure that projects are managed successfully across the organisation, and that strategic, mission-critical projects are given the best opportunity to succeed from the very start'. This includes executive acceptance of project management as an independent business function 'at the highest level of the organisation to enable the authority that is required to distribute, monitor, and control the distribution of the disciplines required to achieve enterprise-wide project management best practice capabilities'.

There have been many reviews of project management capability across the Australian and New Zealand public sectors that indicate that this executive priority is missing. In his extensive review of large APS projects, Shergold (2015) cites the lack of project management capacity and capability as a major factor in project failure. He found that the Australian Public Service lacked discipline in project management (Shergold 2015: vii), did not value the importance of project management skills, needed to recognise project managers as a community of practice within the public service (p. 6), and had no plan to address this deficiency.

The Victorian Ombudsman (2012: 5–7), following an investigation into large Victorian Government ICT projects, concluded that within the Victorian public sector there was a lack of skilled senior project managers and no effective strategy in place to address this, which remain factors in the ongoing problems within Victorian Government ICT projects. It was noted that in an attempt to manage projects internally, agencies had appointed unskilled public sector staff to manage projects with 'often disastrous consequences'. A review by the Northern Territory Legislative Assembly (Public Accounts Committee 2014: 15–19) into the management of public sector ICT projects concluded that a major factor in the continuing problems with project delivery was the lack of inhouse project management capability and capacity, inclusive of staffing, guidelines, methodologies, and standards. In their extensive study into large New Zealand Government ICT projects, Gauld and Goldfinch (2006: 132) concluded—tongue in cheek—that if the public sector wanted to increase the likelihood of failure, they should continue to 'rely on the advice and skills of contracted consultants, salespeople, and ICT suppliers, and do not develop your own project management' capability and capacity.

There is evidence within the various jurisdictions' capability frameworks that project management has been identified as a specific capability (APSC 2010; Office of eGovernment 2011–13; Department of Finance and Deregulation 2012; DPAC 2013; Department of Finance and Services 2012, 2014; VPSC 2015); however, as detailed in the literature, addressing project management capability and capacity is more than just having several project managers. There is little literature to indicate that Australian and New Zealand public sector agencies have addressed the integration of the project management discipline within organisations.

As evidenced in Chapter 1, regardless of sector and industry, large ICT software projects continue to have poor outcomes when measured against time, cost, and scope, regardless of how project management has been addressed within those organisations. Using data collected over many years, Shenhar and Dvir (2007: 5–7) argue that these poor outcomes do not necessarily mean that the project was poorly managed or the organisation had poor project management capability, as these 'failures' have occurred in many well-respected organisations, such as the US National Aeronautics and Space Administration (NASA). These projects had every reason to succeed but did not. The authors conclude that the common theme in the organisations and projects is that 'executives as well as project teams failed to appreciate up front the extent of uncertainty and complexity involved (or failed to communicate this extent to each other) and failed to adapt their management style to the situation' (Shenhar & Dvir 2007: 5–7).

Yet, size alone is not an indication of project complexity, nor is project complexity unique to size (Rolstadås & Schiefloe 2017), as every type of project involves some level of complexity (Hornby 1995). Defining complexity is a hot topic (Bakhshi et al. 2016). While the PMI defines project complexity as 'a characteristic of a program or project or its environment that is difficult to manage due to human behaviour, system behaviour, and ambiguity' (2014: 12), in an excellent article researching project complexity, Bakhshi et al. (2016) argue that it is challenging to provide a single accurate and comprehensive definition of complexity. This is because there are many factors in complex projects, with their literature review identifying 128 complexity factors. Hence, they argue that project complexity should be analysed according to seven dominant integrated elements: context, autonomy, belonging, connectivity, diversity, emergence, and size. In a slight variation, but certainly linked to these findings, Rolstadås and Schiefloe (2017) argue that all projects start with a set of 'generic complexity drivers such as ambiguity, uncertainty, unpredictability and pace', which are then influenced by the project's context, such as that of the political and the organisational, to determine complexity.

Therefore, while size alone is not a determinant of complexity, it has been argued that the complexity of large ICT projects has increased (Baccarini 1996; Ribbers & Schoo 2002; Hass 2008: Introduction; Bakhshi et al. 2016) due to the focus on business-driven change, to which the traditional information technology (IT) function has had to adapt. IT projects are no longer developed in isolation but with 'the overarching process of business transformation; the reach of change extends to all areas of the organisation and beyond to customers, suppliers, and business partners—making the complexity of projects formidable' (Hass 2008: Introduction). This complexity is increased as large-scale projects are long in duration and susceptible to changing environments and business needs. They can have far-reaching but ill-defined scope and poorly understood requirements, and often have rigid time frames and inflexible budgets. By their size alone, they will be organisationally important and therefore extremely visible, in the public sector politically charged, and with many varying expectations— a challenge for any organisation, regardless of its project management maturity. Therefore, Hass (2008: Introduction) argues that 'we must find new ways to manage large, complex projects' with a starting point being a 'more flexible and adaptive approach to project management'.

Due to these factors, where once project management was a focus on time and money, and achieving those targets in a linear manner, due to the complexity of large projects there is now a requirement for a more 'exciting' and adaptive form of project management (Morris 1998: 3). However, Hass (2008: Ch. 1) argues that the problem is that with more complexity impacting on projects, the common organisational response is to revert to the assumed control and rigidity of the traditional project management approach. Hass argues that to deal with this dilemma, a 'contemporary adaptive project management model is emerging'—one that acknowledges the unpredictability of large projects, and the resulting need to manage 'in a very different manner using complexity thinking, which teaches us to adapt to our environment for our very survival'. A comparison of the conventional and adaptive approaches to project management is provided in Table 2.2.

Table 2.2 Conventional versus adaptive project management

Conventional project management	Adaptive project management
Structured, orderly	Spontaneous, disorganised
Relies heavily on plans	Evolves over time as more is learned
Predictable, well-defined	Ambiguous, unique, unstable, full of surprises
Stable environment	Chaotic environment
Proven technologies	Unproven technologies
Realistic schedules	Aggressive schedule, urgency

Source: Adapted from Hass (2008: Table 2.1).

Organisations must find not only new ways of applying the project management discipline, but also a fresh style of project leadership (Hass 2008: Ch. 4). In recognition of this, and to address the complexity issues in the project management of large complex projects, the Australian Department of Defence has issued standards (ICCPM 2012) and describes requirements for adaptive planning and leadership. There is a series of special attributes, such as wisdom, action, outcome orientation, and the ability to create, lead innovative teams, be focused, courageous, and influential (ICCPM 2012: 93). While this is an excellent initiative, one criticism is that the literature indicates there are issues with obtaining capability and capacity in the public sector for 'conventional' project leadership; this requirement for an adaptive project management style ups the ante even further, as it will be a special person and team that have all those attributes.

The project management framework within an organisation should also address appropriate delivery methods. This is discussed at length by Hass (2008: Chs 6–8), who argues that, depending on the complexity of the project, different models are suitable.

One is the waterfall method, which has sets of distinct activities that are carried out sequentially—for example, gather your requirements, undertake the design based on those requirements, code, test, and so on (Royce 1970). Waterfall projects seek stability and predictability, are quite formal in structure, and require extensive documentation for managing stakeholder concerns, such as clearly communicating the expected results and approach to stakeholders at the start of the project (Thummadi & Lyytinen 2020; Fagarasan et al. 2021; Thesing et al. 2021).

Recent industry research has found that a waterfall approach is advantageous when the project has fixed roles and processes with clear responsibilities, team members with predictive capabilities and capacities, dependencies are known and can be predicted, it is possible to deliver reliable estimations of time, scope, and budget, and therefore the original planning will be relevant throughout (Thesing et al. 2021). However, therein lies the challenge for large long-term projects operating in a complex, changing environment: How can the stability and predictability required for the waterfall method be achieved? That question is perhaps answered by the disadvantages of waterfall, as highlighted by Thesing et al. (2021). Their research found that from a project management practitioner's perspective, waterfall led to inaccurate planning due to abstract specifications and an inability to detail all requirements at the beginning; the correction of errors as a result was costly and time-consuming; and, due to the rigid structure, flexible and adaptive approaches to address issues were limited. As a result, they argue that waterfall is suitable for small to medium-sized projects that have little room for change, have fixed scope and budget, and for which the product must be delivered in one piece (Hass 2008; Fagarasan et al. 2021).

To address these shortcomings, an alternative is to use an iterative approach, such as agile, the principles of which are simple: start with your goal, requirements, scope, and so on, but break the delivery into iterations. Complete iteration one and then fully review what was done, how it was done, how long it took, and so on. Then apply those lessons to iteration two and repeat, learning, adapting, and finetuning as you progress (Hass 2008). Agile differentiates itself from traditional methods like waterfall by placing more value on individuals and interactions than on processes and tools, on working software than comprehensive documentation, customer collaboration over contract negotiation, and responding to change rather than following a plan. It also has principles of early and continuous delivery of software, harnessing change, collaborative development between the business and developers, face-to-face communication, sustainable development with a cycle of continuous learning and improvement, and continuous attention to technical excellence and design (Beck et al. 2001; Aleinikova et al. 2020; Thesing et al. 2021).

It is claimed that agile has other advantages, such as rapid recognition of issues and requirements, flexibility to adapt to change, fast identification of errors, and lower risk of false developments (Aleinikova et al. 2020; Thesing et al. 2021). In addition, a study focused on the public sector found that agile can remove bureaucratic procedures and problems through its flexibility and adaptive culture (Aleinikova et al. 2020). However, industry research also found that, from a project management practitioner's perspective, there were disadvantages, including organisational cultural issues with the approach, dependence on self-organisation, communication issues across large, distributed teams, and increased testing requirements (Thesing et al. 2021).

Unlike waterfall, an agile method, it is argued, is suitable for any size project, but particularly for those where requirements are initially unclear and progressively emerge, the scope is likely to change, the project can begin with a 'rough order-of-magnitude budget', the product can be delivered in iterations, and there is importance placed on progressive customer feedback and end-user value (Fargarasan et al. 2021). Agile is now in wide use for software projects (Abrahamsson et al. 2009; Dingsøyr et al. 2013; Lappi & Aaltonen 2017) as it encourages creativity and rapid adaptation and has a customer focus (Thomke & Reinertsen 1998; Schwaber 2004).

For the most complex of projects, Hass (2008: Ch. 7) argues that a prototyping model is more appropriate. This is also iterative, but simplified, with the aim to build a prototype, review, validate, and then adapt, addressing design, technical, and stakeholder issues as you go (for a diagrammatic view of complexity and project delivery models, see Figure 2.3).

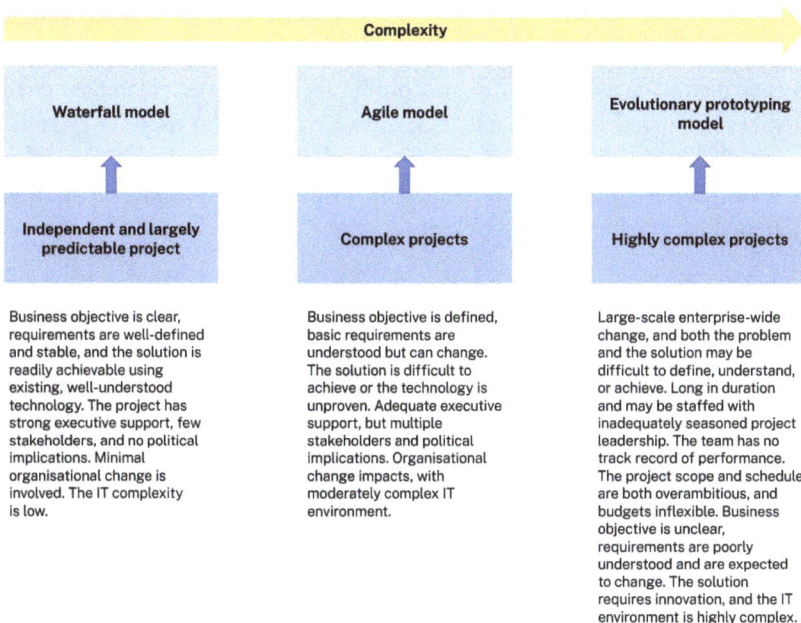

Complexity

Waterfall model	Agile model	Evolutionary prototyping model
Independent and largely predictable project	Complex projects	Highly complex projects
Business objective is clear, requirements are well-defined and stable, and the solution is readily achievable using existing, well-understood technology. The project has strong executive support, few stakeholders, and no political implications. Minimal organisational change is involved. The IT complexity is low.	Business objective is defined, basic requirements are understood but can change. The solution is difficult to achieve or the technology is unproven. Adequate executive support, but multiple stakeholders and political implications. Organisational change impacts, with moderately complex IT environment.	Large-scale enterprise-wide change, and both the problem and the solution may be difficult to define, understand, or achieve. Long in duration and may be staffed with inadequately seasoned project leadership. The team has no track record of performance. The project scope and schedule are both overambitious, and budgets inflexible. Business objective is unclear, requirements are poorly understood and are expected to change. The solution requires innovation, and the IT environment is highly complex.

Figure 2.3 Complexity and project delivery methods
Source: Created by author. Adapted from arguments in (Hass 2008: Chs 6–8).

It is also pertinent to note that there are differing views on the application of iterative models like agile to large projects. There is an argument that it is more suited to a project with low 'background complexity but high front-end interactivity' (Berger & Beynon-Davies 2009: 566), while another is that it can and has been applied successfully to a large complex ICT software project (Fowler 2005). The commonality is an agreement that the iterative approach helps break down complexity and how the organisation adapts its project management framework to support its use has a major bearing on its success.

There is evidence of a need for most Australian and New Zealand jurisdictional institutional frameworks to consider iterative project management options, such as agile, for large complex projects (Victorian Government CIO Council 2015; GCIO 2016; digital.govt.nz 2019; Digital.NSW 2022a; QGCIO 2018a). The issue for these jurisdictions is that organisations need the corresponding project management capability.

In summary, project management must be understood as a discipline, comprising many roles and skills, and supported by institutionalised guidelines, rules, processes, and the like. Mature project organisations integrate projects throughout their core business and support project management as an organisational priority. There is little evidence this applies to the Australian and New Zealand public sectors. Project management is further challenged in large-scale ICT software projects as they are classified as complex and therefore require additional skills. The argument is therefore to break down complexity by engaging in an iterative delivery method, such as agile.

Forecasting

In my career, the terms 'forecasting' and 'estimating' were used interchangeably when discussing the process of planning a project's outcome and deriving factors such as cost and time—something that the literature highlights is not quite correct.

A forecast is a prediction 'of what will happen based on evidence or assumptions' and is an approach to lessen uncertainty in the estimation process. This is undertaken by 'using past and present data, [and] analysing trends' and 'can be data-driven rather than shots in the dark'. Forecasting can help 'identify threats to achieving project timelines: particularly when you are managing a long-term, complex project' (AIPM 2021). In effect, forecasting is an estimation of future events, but one made by a deeper analysis of the past, using data and potentially data models to estimate the future.

Estimation is less structured and can be thought of as a considered guess— one possibly based on experience. Meyer (2016) argues that estimation is 'human involvement to create a forecast that considers past projects, personal experience, and industry-specific knowledge and techniques', but concludes, importantly, that 'the process of estimation is often subject to biases by the estimator'. In addition, Meyer states that these subjective guesses are open to optimism bias and the vagaries of memory and can be internally focused and exclude external factors. Forecasting aims to apply methods to address these estimation shortcomings for large complex projects. The progression from a pure guess to a data-driven estimation is displayed in Figure 2.4.

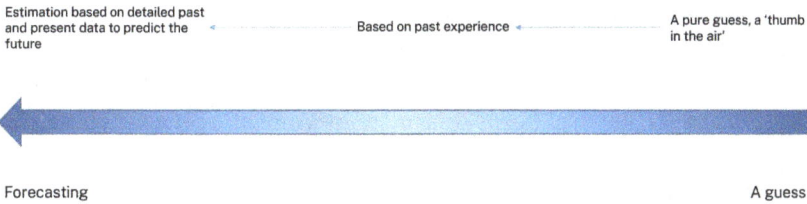

Estimation based on detailed past and present data to predict the future ← ⋯ Based on past experience ← ⋯ A pure guess, a 'thumb in the air'

Forecasting   A guess

Figure 2.4 The progression to a data-driven forecast
Source: Created by author.

Flyvbjerg (2013: 760) describes the forecasting process as the 'front end' of a project, as it is where alignment with organisational processes and resources to achieve that 'target' is made (Kwak et al. 2014: 41). Flyvbjerg (2013: 760) argues that many researchers cite this stage as critical to a good project outcome; in fact, they claim it is perhaps the 'most important stage in the overall project cycle in securing the success of projects or avoiding failure'.

The forecast establishes factors such as cost, time, the scope of work, and what benefits will be delivered, to whom and by whom. Forecasting provides criteria for the approval of the project and potentially for its approval over other projects. This means any unrealistic forecast 'corrupts the decision-making process' (Andersen et al. 2016: 171–72). It also sets the benchmark for assessing the project's outcome. Hall (1980: 4), in his study of great planning disasters, argues that these projects were evaluated as disasters based on 'forecasts that were later found [to be] inadequate and misleading'.

The organisation's project management maturity, capability, and capacity and the role of project management guidelines, practices, standards, forecasting methods, and particularly how the project manager applies these are crucial factors in the forecasting process (Caliste 2013; PMI 2013a). Given the importance of the forecast to gaining approval, and then throughout the project to implementation and evaluation, it must be, if not accurate, then relevant; it must have some efficacy. Both the PMI (2017) and the International Project Management Association (IPMA 2015: 6)[2] have codes of ethics and professional conduct that clearly indicate the responsibility for the project manager to undertake ethical planning and create a forecast that is reasonable, truthful, and accurate.

While professional bodies argue that there is an ethical requirement for project management to prepare relevant forecasts, there are two other factors widely documented in the literature that impact on forecast preparation for all large projects. Flyvbjerg (2008) argues that the first is excessive optimism or 'delusion' about what is to be achieved, how, at what cost, by when, and, importantly, what benefits will be delivered. This is largely the topic of the book *Dangerous Enthusiasms* (Gauld & Goldfinch 2006), in which the authors argue that New Zealand Government agencies, with great optimism and enthusiasm, initiated large projects that were simply beyond their capability and capacity and for which they were delusional to think they would succeed. This is not so much unethical as excessive—to the point of being dangerous—optimism.

The second and more sinister factor, unethical and difficult to prove, is 'deception' at the time of planning—for example, deliberately under- or over-forecasting costs and benefits to gain approval. The issue with this is that governments commit to the project at a cost to achieve those benefits and, if they are inaccurate, the premise for the approval is false. Both scenarios have a similar negative impact, as they set unrealistic and possibly unachievable expectations from the outset—a platform for failure that could be a factor in the current high failure rates.

---

2   According to the IPMA's website, it 'is a Federation of about 70 Member Associations (MAs). Our MAs develop project management competencies in their geographic areas of influence, interacting with thousands of practitioners and developing relationships with corporations, government agencies, universities, and colleges, as well as training organizations and consulting companies' (available from: www.ipma.world/about/).

The organisational, environmental, and especially political factors in the public sector can escalate this propensity for both optimism and deception. For example, when there is competition for limited project funding, an environmental condition is established for either optimism or deception in forecasting (Flyvbjerg 2008: 19): 'If the project cost is too high, I will not get the funds so I am sure we can do it for less and secure the money.' If the project contracts with a third-party vendor who by necessity must be involved in forecasting, this can be 'negatively impacted by the self-interest' of the vendor (Fukuyama 2004: 52) as they aim to secure the contract. Elder-Vass (2010: 4–5) argues that within organisations specific groups have social structural power and collectively 'emergent properties' that have causal impact. These factors in turn have implications for forecasting. This was discussed in a study for the UK Department of Transport (Flyvbjerg & COWI 2004: 37–38), which found that forecasting in the public sector is influenced by rational institutionalism as the administrative and political decision-making processes are influenced by 'actors that seek to maximise their utility in line with their interests within a rather stable institutional setting which impacts upon their behaviour'. These organisational influences impact on actors differently, depending on their own interests and personal stake in the project. The guide argues that, within the public sector—in this case, the UK Department of Transport—this means the various actors have either a direct interest or little interest in avoiding delusion and deception (see Table 2.3).

Table 2.3 Example from a transport agency of forecasting influenced by direct interest

Actors have no or little direct interest in avoiding cost overruns	Actors have a direct interest in avoiding cost overruns
Local transport authorities	Ministry of Finance
Local politicians	Department of Transport
Local economic interests	
Local civil servants	
Consultancies	
Individual Members of Parliament	

Source: Adapted from Flyvbjerg and COWI (2004: 48).

The implication is that actors such as local politicians have much to gain politically from a project proceeding in their constituency, hence optimism and deception prevail. However, actors such as the Ministry of Finance are more concerned that projects are accurately planned to ensure the best use of limited resources and to approve those projects that will provide the best outcomes. The challenge for the public sector is how to manage these conflicting interests.

The literature review highlights that there are methods to address both delusional optimism and deception in forecasting during project planning. As an example, Flyvbjerg et al. (2005) proposed a method called 'reference class forecasting' (RCF), based on the work of Kahneman and Tversky (1979) that earned them the Nobel Prize for Economics. The theory proposes that, due to organisational overconfidence, people generally underestimate factors such as cost, time, and risk, and overestimate factors such as benefits. This is called an 'inside view'. The theory therefore proposes an 'outside view', in which forecasts are made considering data available from similar initiatives (Flyvbjerg 2008: 18–19). The intent of RCF is to compare project forecasts with past similar projects to 'establish the most likely outcome for the specific project' (Flyvbjerg et al. 2016b: 2).

There are many other methods. Two methods common in the Australian and New Zealand public sectors, the PMBOK guide (PMI 2013a: 204–7) and the PRINCE2 guide (OGC 2002: 177), provide advice on a process and the details to be included—a forecast built on known and assumed details, which arguably is more of an estimate than a forecast. The PMI (2011) has a process of identifying inputs and required outputs, then estimating the tools and techniques required to meet these. In their books on forecasting, Jones (2007) and Laird and Brennan (2006) detail various methods and tools to assist in forecasting ICT software projects, such as bottom-up, top-down, benchmarking, object-oriented, and function-point analysis.

However, all these methods arguably fall victim to Flyvbjerg's argument of delusional or deceptive behaviour as the output is only a reflection of the estimates entered. Jones (2007: Preface) acknowledges this by arguing that within an organisation methodically produced estimates 'may be arbitrarily replaced by optimistic estimates'—a factor that remains 'troublesome'—and cites organisational pressures and environmental factors as key reasons. Laird and Brennan (2006: 79) simply state that forecasting 'has a long way to go'. In a nod to the arguments of Flyvbjerg and the RCF, Jones concludes that the only way to temper this is to keep historical data on past projects and compare forecasts against these—in effect, to learn from the past. The notion of 'learning from the past' is hardly a new insight. In 1905, George Santayana argued that 'those who cannot remember the past are condemned to repeat it'. To undertake such comparisons and learn from the past would require the public sector to have the data available, and there is no evidence that this is the case. In addition, the variances of and time between large projects in an organisation or sector are such that the application of past learnings to future forecasting is difficult (McMillan 1992; Liu et al. 2010: 230).

The other factor—as identified in the project management section—that negatively influences the ability to provide relevant forecasts for large ICT software projects is their complexity (Cooke-Davies et al. 2011; Herszon & Keraminiyage 2014). In their study of the impacts of complexity on forecasting, Herszon and Keraminiyage (2014) argue that traditional forecasting processes fail to deal with complexity and they identify 23 dimensions that impact on this, including the project size, organisational capability and capacity, political influence, environmental constraints, uncertainty, stakeholder interaction, and project management maturity. The argument is that all these add to the complexity of the project and challenge the ability to accurately forecast over the long term. Therefore, forecasts for large complex projects that have tried to predict the future are 'fanciful' and only 'guesstimates' that provided a starting 'target' and are simply 'unreliable' (Touran & Lopez 2006; Andersen et al. 2016: 172; Turner & Xue 2018: 783).

Within the Australian and New Zealand public sectors there is evidence from the institutional governance frameworks of efforts to enable more accurate forecasting. New Zealand has implemented extensive procedures for large ICT projects within the Better Business Cases framework (The Treasury 2019), including various forecasting methods and reference to optimism and how to address this. Victoria has the High Value High Risk (DTF 2018) assurance framework for large high-risk projects, which aims to improve both preparation and vetting of forecasts. It is not as though the public sector is unaware of the issue and its challenges and, to their credit, they are adapting processes. However, the question remains, for large complex projects with long time frames, how can this ever be accurate? It is arguably about applying more control from above, rather than looking at the issues only from the perception of actors involved in these projects.

Within the project management literature review, the recommended approach is to break down the complexity of large ICT software projects by moving to an iterative delivery model. A principle of this approach, such as in agile, is to do 'just enough' planning and forecasting to begin and then build knowledge and certainty as you progress. In effect, begin with knowing what you want to deliver and why, but not necessarily how long it will take or cost. This imposes conflicts on organisations used to traditional upfront forecasting, approval, and funding, including fluid versus specific delivery dates and costs, flexible versus fixed plans, and just enough versus total control. The conclusion is that organisations must adapt the funding process accordingly (Cao et al. 2013). This is perhaps easier said than done in the public sector, as evidenced by the fact that the institutional frameworks across Australia and New Zealand generally require the preparation of a full upfront forecast for a large project (DPAC 2008a; Queensland Treasury 2015; DoF 2015; DTF 2015, 2018; The Treasury 2019).

In summary, the literature indicates that relevant forecasts at the project approval stage and at implementation are vital for the allocation of limited organisational resources and for assessing the project's outcome. Various methods are utilised, but each is a complex task and dependent on data that may not be available. There are many environmental factors that add to the forecasting challenge. Political factors can also influence public sector forecasts—for example, through pressure to keep the forecast within a politically acceptable range. Delusional optimism and deception have been identified as factors that skew forecasts, rendering them irrelevant; acknowledging these behaviours exist is one thing, effectively controlling them is another. There is an argument that the complexity and multifaceted and unpredictable interdependencies of large ICT software projects make any expectation of a relevant forecast 'fanciful'. That leads to the question of whether the only point of doing them is to tick a box? New delivery methods such as agile conflict with traditional forecasting and funding processes in the Australian and New Zealand public sectors and, if these methods are to be used, the forecasting process must adapt accordingly.

3

The sponsor: The career-limiting role

It is career-limiting to damage your reputation with a big IT project.
(Person AH, CIO, Victoria)

Introduction

According to the analysis of all part one elite interviewees (see 'The puzzle' section, Chapter 1: Table 1.1), supported by vignettes from cited interviewees, there is a perception that governance via the institutional framework of the sponsor's role is ineffective. The dominant view is that no jurisdiction has the capability and sponsors do not fully understand the role and its responsibilities and accountabilities.

This is due to a senior executive failure to address the sponsor role and recognise its speciality and complexity; the sponsor remains organisationally a 'second-fiddle' role. As a result of this failure to address capability for a critical project role, the key lesson learnt by executives is a 'learned helplessness'—a belief that all large projects fail. Therefore, actors try to avoid undertaking the role and its resulting accountability as it is seen as career-limiting with little chance of success and with punishment awaiting—a role seen as the proverbial 'hospital pass'.

There was a small group of entrepreneurs who perceived the issue to be the complexity of large ICT software projects undertaken by traditional delivery methods. These projects require a very skilled, specialised, and experienced sponsor—one who, except by chance, does not exist in the public sector. Therefore, the argument is to change delivery methods, stop doing large ICT projects traditionally and look at component-based delivery to remove that specialised capability from the equation. This would improve the chances of success, lower the risk of failure, and provide the sponsor with some hope and encouragement, rather than fear. However, this would require an actor with the right agency and entrepreneurial skills, as they are in effect required to step outside the institutional governance framework. The problem is such actors are in short supply.

To support these findings, this chapter details the elite interviewees' perspectives on the governance of the sponsor role across the New Zealand and selected Australian jurisdictions. The interview questions were aligned to four categories identified in the review of the sponsor literature (see Figure 3.1). They are:

- Capability: Do the sectors have sponsor capability and is an assessment of this capability part of project planning and initiation?
- Role: How institutionalised is the sponsor role, its responsibilities, and accountabilities, and how well is this understood by the actors?
- Model: How are sponsors selected and appointed?
- Training and support: What training and support are provided?

For category, perspectives from the elite interview data are analysed, supported by vignettes from the interviews. These findings are summarised by various categories, followed by a short conclusion.

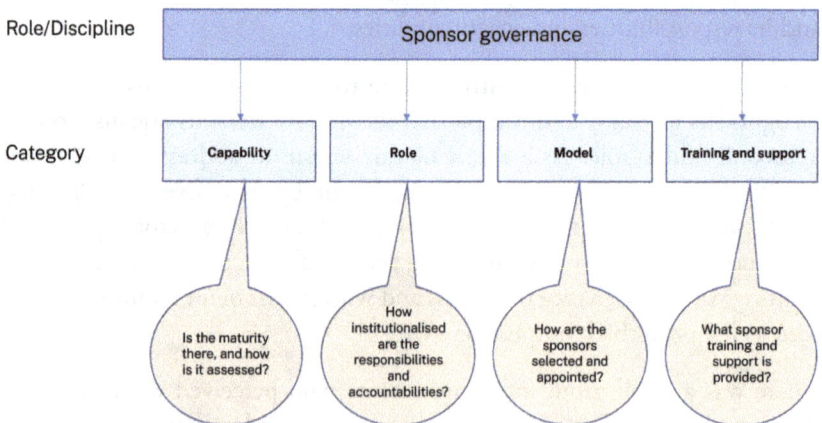

Figure 3.1 Categories for sponsor analysis
Source: Created by author.

The elite interviews

Capability: Is the maturity there, and how is it being assessed?

The elite interviewees were asked whether they believed sponsors within their jurisdiction had the required capability for a large ICT software project. It was a direct question that received direct answers, with the dominant perspective across all jurisdictions being that the capability does not exist, as evidenced by the following vignettes:

No, they don't have the skills. (Person AK, CIO, Vic.)

Ah, shit no. (Person AB, Senior project manager, APS)

[T]he sponsor would be the first to tell you they don't. (Person Q, ICT assurance, NZ)

I've rarely seen that [capable sponsor] to be the case. (Person AA, ICT audit, NSW)

The other consistent perspective was that there is a reliance on written guidelines to lift sponsor capability, with a supporting perspective that documentation alone is not enough. An APS CIO (Person G) summed this up: '[I]t is not just about reading. I can read all that, but if I have never done it before, gosh!'

Where there are exceptions to this lack of capability, the factors for this are consistent across jurisdictions. Capability can be present because of experience, chance, luck, or, in effect, it can be 'random' (Person AH, CIO, Vic.). The argument for experience as a factor is that these sponsors have learnt by doing the 'hard yards' and 'have the scars' (Person C, Senior IQA, NSW) to prove it. A senior ICT assurance officer (Person AG, Vic.) argued that, without this experience, sponsors are left floundering while they 'try to come to terms with what [the role] means'.

This was tempered by a senior executive (Person E, NSW), who argued that experience is no guarantee of improved capability, and depends on the actor learning from that experience. They cited an example of a sponsor who had not learnt and simply carried forward poor practices from a previous project to the new one. This was supported by the perspective of a CIO (Person O, NZ) that the ability to learn from past experiences 'has not been a skill always displayed by sponsors'.

Adding another twist to this perspective, a CIO (Person W, NZ) posited that sponsor capability has not improved, despite the volume of projects in the sector, due to ongoing poor project outcomes, which has resulted in senior executives wanting no involvement: the sponsors 'get so burnt and destroyed over them they will always refuse to do another one. So, there is never a lesson learnt because there is never an experience you take forward.'

Person W argued that this is an organisational loss of 'learned capability' and that there is a tendency to punish a sponsor instead of supporting them and saying: 'We understand what you have been through, it was hard, but you have learnt a lot, we value that experience and hope that you will now be a valuable organisational asset for future project capability.' As a result, the actor says 'not on your life'.

A final factor that can contribute to existing sponsor capability is when the agency is a project-based organisation[1] that has a 'demonstrable' (Person AF, Senior ICT assurance, Vic.) culture of running large projects. However, there was also a perspective across all jurisdictions that there are very few such government agencies. A senior ICT assurance officer (Person T, NZ) argued that private sector project-based organisations understand the difference between an operational role and a project-based role but the public sector does not. With the ability to compare sectors, a former Victorian Government CIO now in the private sector (Person AI) adds that private sector project-based companies have entrenched and mature project delivery capability and consequently sponsors understand what is involved and are more likely to have the capability required. They argued that things are different in the Victorian public sector, where 'the sponsor of that program, that's not really what they do, and so they do not really understand what is involved'.

The belief that jurisdictions fail to understand the sponsor role is not only a result of agencies lacking project-based maturity, but also related to the lack of senior executive–level commitment to acknowledging the sponsor role, its importance, and the need to have this as an organisational capability.

---

1   According to Thiry (2007), this is: 'An organisation that manages functions within a temporary project organisation setting. Firms that conduct the majority of their activities in project mode and/or privilege the project dimensions over functional dimensions in their structure and processes.'

One CIO (Person AK, Vic.) highlighted the sponsor as one of the top-three large project capability issues for the public sector to address, and argued that capability will only be addressed when 'there is genuine intent to have executive sponsorship as part of the organisational culture'.

A reason for this lack of organisational intent—one highlighted in other jurisdictions—was given by a senior executive (Person AN, NT), who stated that improving sponsor capabilities 'will always play second fiddle to day-to-day operations capabilities'.

The common perspective is that improving senior executive sponsor capability takes a back seat to operational capabilities. However, there were also views that this is not acceptable and entrenches the attitude. One CIO (Person AH, Vic.) argued that sponsor capability should be a prerequisite for all senior executives, part of their skill set, just as financial management is. This means claiming 'I do not know how to manage a technology project' would be akin to stating 'I do not know how to manage money'.

A consequence of this lack of organisational understanding of the breadth and diversity of the sponsor role and responsibilities is that jurisdictions focus on one skillset such as project management, instead of the full suite of required skills, believing this is a 'panacea' (Person AI, CIO, Vic.). Linked to this lack of organisational understanding was a popular perspective that actors undertaking the sponsor role have a misguided assessment of their own capability—or, as a CIO (Person S, NZ) stated, being capable 'in your day job does not mean you will be a capable sponsor'.

Person S argued that this is human nature as such executives are unwilling to admit 'that I do not know what I am theoretically supposed to know'.

Another CIO (Person O, NZ) summed this up: '[T]hey do not know what they do not know, they struggle and do not always have the humility to learn from people that have done that before.'

Despite these comments, interviewees made it clear that sponsors want the project to succeed; they do their best but simply do not have the capability or understanding required. For a personal perspective on this issue, a senior executive (Person AM, NT) who at the time of the interview was also the sponsor of a large ICT software project was asked about their capability to undertake the role. They stated: 'Whether I have all the knowledge and capability, I do not know, but we certainly put in the effort.'

Person AM will hopefully become an effective sponsor, but this reinforces earlier views that the sponsor role and required capability are not understood organisationally or jurisdictionally, so finding an effective sponsor is open to chance.

While jurisdictions were perceived to be failing to address sponsor capability requirements, several elite interview participants raised the spectre of the public sector being left further behind due to exogenous and endogenous changes in the way large ICT projects are managed. The issue is that while the public sector has not yet addressed the current capabilities, new ones have emerged. The two examples raised in several jurisdictions were agile development and digital transformation, both of which, it was argued, would lead to a change in approach, delivery, and project management. A senior executive (Person AD, APS) said that the Australian Public Service did not have a plan to address this and acquiring these new capabilities would not be a simple matter of 'flicking a switch'.

The interviewees confirmed a lack of awareness of the need to undertake a formal capability assessment of a sponsor before appointment. A CIO (Person O, NZ) argued that it is the responsibility of the agency's chief executive to ensure that a sponsor with the appropriate capability is appointed. There was agreement across all jurisdictions that a capability assessment should be a requirement and part of the selection process; in fact, if the capability does not exist, the project should not start.

However, there were two examples—one more advanced than the other—of jurisdictions starting to address the sponsor capability assessment requirement. In New South Wales, a senior executive (Person Z) in an ICT assurance group with jurisdiction-wide responsibilities said the need to uplift sponsor capability is now recognised as a key area in which they can assist agencies and projects. As part of this, the unit has implemented a capability review of the designated sponsor before appointment, and this will continue to be assessed throughout the project's lifecycle. In New Zealand, a senior ICT assurance officer (Person Q), also with jurisdiction-wide assurance responsibilities, said the assessment process was being discussed with a target delivery date of two years (from 2018).

In summary, there was much similarity among the elite interviewees and across jurisdictions in the perceptions of sponsor capability. At best, sponsor capability is dependent on experience or luck, not institutional governance. However, the capability is lacking, it is not an organisational priority to address the issue, and sponsor capability is not assessed as part of project initiation.

Role: How institutionalised are the responsibilities and accountabilities?

There was a clear understanding and agreement among the elite interviewees of the criticality of the sponsor role. A senior project manager (Person AB, APS) said the role is 'fundamental' to project success, while a senior executive (Person K, NZ) believed the role is a 'huge responsibility'. A CIO (Person L, NZ) described the sponsor as 'a key [project] role'. A senior project manager (Person BM, Tas.) argued that the sponsor is the project's champion and a project is reliant on the sponsor to ensure that everyone in the organisation is 'on board' with the project's aim. These perspectives were perhaps best summed up by another CIO (Person AI, Vic.), who said: '[A]nybody who has ever been on a project management course [knows] paragraph one on page one says the most important person in the project is the sponsor.'

While there was a general awareness of the sponsor's criticality to project success among the interviewees, there was also a common perspective that the actors—typically, executives—who fill the role do not understand this. They also fail to understand the full responsibilities and accountabilities of the role. It was the opinion of a senior ICT auditor (Person AA, NSW) that senior executives in the sponsor role see themselves sitting above the project as a figurehead rather than being an active and critical part of it. This was supported by a senior project manager (Person AB, APS) who argued that sponsors fail to manage project issues; instead, 'they fester', with negative impacts. Supporting this perspective, a senior executive (Person E, NSW) cited as an example an instance in which the sponsor failed to attend a project governance meeting that was to make a critical project decision. The sponsor was also the chair and the ultimate approver of the decision. According to Person E, not only did the sponsor not attend, but also '[n]o notice was given, and no apologies received'.

The meeting was leaderless and the project was left floundering. Person E believed this not only showed a lack of understanding by the sponsor of their responsibilities, but also was an avoidance of accepting responsibility for the decision. A similar story was provided by a senior project manager (Person N, NZ) for a troubled project in which, even with an institutional framework providing guidelines for sponsors—such as the need for a steering group and their role as head of this—the new sponsor stated upfront: 'I do not see why we have the need for steering groups.'

When this lack of understanding was discussed with a senior executive (Person K, NZ), they posited that 'there has been naivety by some sponsors in regard to their role'.

A senior and very experienced internal quality assurer (IQA) (Person C, NSW) with previous roles in many large government ICT projects supported these perspectives and added that in some instances sponsors had ignored advice and tried to transfer responsibility: '[S]ponsors did not really want to hear about problems, or they would just say to the program director, "You have to solve it somehow".'

As a result of these issues, a senior ICT assurance officer (Person AD, APS) with jurisdiction-wide ICT capability responsibilities acknowledged that there is a 'desperate need' for the sponsor to be aware of and fully understand their responsibilities. They posited that this lack of understanding, as in other jurisdictions, is sometimes due to sponsors seeing ICT projects as IT technical projects rather than business transformation projects, and therefore believe they can absolve themselves of the responsibility and 'let the IT guys deal with it'. Person AD added that there are plans afoot to form an APS 'community of practice' to address these issues. That seems prudent, as a CIO (Person A, APS) stated that within the Australian Public Service there needs to be greater clarity on the responsibilities and accountabilities of the sponsor to ensure jurisdiction-wide consistency.

The elite interviewees believed sponsors are unwilling to accept responsibility and be held accountable. A CIO (Person AH, Vic.) argued that sponsors use the history of poor outcomes for large ICT software projects as a reason to not be held accountable. Person AH argued that there is a 'bullshit construct' within the public sector that 'big IT projects always fail', therefore they are 'absolved of responsibility'—what could they possibly have done to change it? Another CIO (Person AI, Vic.) suggested that the avoidance of accountability by the sponsor in the public sector is abetted by government lifecycles that see large ICT software projects typically extending across government terms. Person AI believed this resulted in the agency and sponsor pushing a problem on to a new administration to be dealt with: '[A]ll I have to do is go slow this year and then it will be somebody else's problem.'

It was suggested that one issue for sponsors with this approach is that avoidance can become a trap. A senior executive (Person E, NSW), citing a large and troubled project, said that despite the best efforts of another senior executive in the sponsor role to be 'very removed' from the project and view it as 'somebody else's problem', ongoing problems simply moved 'closer and closer' to the sponsor; there was no escape. To address avoidance of accountability, a CIO (Person L, NZ) argued that it requires a sponsor 'brave enough' to take appropriate action, but then suggested that organisational factors such as a culture of punishment means finding a brave executive is difficult, particularly if that action is seen as career-limiting.

Interviewees across all jurisdictions consistently raised one responsibility as being poorly understood, accepted, and managed by sponsors: that of stakeholder management, particularly when a third-party vendor is involved. It was argued that it is common—in fact, the norm—to have a vendor or vendors as part of large ICT software projects either in delivering or as partners in delivering the solution, including providing the skilled resources required. The consistent perspective was that such vendor management is poorly understood and sponsors generally lack the capability to undertake this role, because, according to one CIO (Person O, NZ), 'they have never had to do it'.

Person O went on to argue that this capability means understanding the need to own the vendor relationship role, which means taking responsibility for contacting the vendor directly to highlight and address any serious issues.

Interviewees made several references to sponsors trying to abdicate responsibility for the project to the vendor. A CIO (Person G, APS) was clear on this, saying the sponsor is responsible for 'leading the project', even if delivery involves a third party. In those instances, vendor relationship management becomes key, as the sponsor cannot—even if they try—absolve responsibility or accountability to the vendor. Providing a vendor's perspective on this, a private sector CIO (Person AW, NT) with experience in large government projects argued that, from a vendor's perspective, relationship management is typically poorly done and the sponsor, rather than seeing this as a collaborative win-win arrangement, often sees it as an opportunity to 'screw the vendor', or thinks it is a strength to be seen to be tough on vendors.

Vendor relationships are of course not the only relationships to be managed by a sponsor in a large ICT software project. There are relationships internal to the project team and those with other internal and external stakeholders. As a positive example of a sponsor acknowledging the importance of this responsibility, a senior executive (Person AM, NT), currently a sponsor of a large program, said they were aware of the importance of engaging with stakeholders and clear that it was their responsibility to do so.

A final perspective concerned the role of the sponsor at the project initiation and planning stages. The argument was that this is a critical time in the project lifecycle that requires active sponsor involvement to undertake the responsibilities required. A CIO (Person G, APS) said this includes, but is not limited to, the project structure, contract, relationship management, governance structures, and funding. This view was supported by a senior executive (Person BL, Tas.), who said previous project successes were a result of having the sponsor's support and involvement from the initiation stage, at which they set realistic expectations for deliverables, budget, and time.

In summary, while there was a general perspective on the criticality of the sponsor role, there was also a common view that sponsors do not generally understand or accept their role, responsibilities, or accountabilities, although these are critical from the initiation of the project.

Model: How are sponsors selected and appointed?

As highlighted in the capability section, the sponsor selection process generally does not include a capability assessment of the actor's maturity to undertake the role. An experienced senior ICT auditor (Person AA, NSW) said they have never seen a sponsor chosen based on capability— a consequence of which, according to a senior executive (Person K, NZ), is that this immediately hands the agency and the project the challenge of equipping that person to undertake the role.

The elite interviewees perceived that, while not exclusively the case, the default across the Australian and New Zealand public sectors is to assign the sponsor role to a senior executive in the agency. For large ICT software projects, this typically is at the deputy secretary level with portfolio responsibility for the project outcomes. Ideas about why this is the default were also aligned: allocating the role to a lower organisational level would diminish organisational oversight and these executives have the authority to implement organisational change, can make decisions on factors such as budgets and resources, give the project visibility and importance in the organisation, and are accepted as an appropriate person to drive change. That said, there were also some elite interviewees, such as a senior executive (Person BM, Tas.), who acknowledged that this default option is not always the best or most appropriate selection method.

There was, however, a common view of who should not be a sponsor: an ICT representative such as the CIO—something that, according to an experienced NSW IQA (Person C), would be 'a waste of time'. This is because these types of large ICT software projects are business transformation projects and must be seen and recognised as such. The CIO may form part of the project with responsibility for technical delivery or the supply of other ICT services, but they do not own the business transformation outcomes. Selecting a sponsor from the business at project initiation was identified as the number one priority by a CIO (Person AI, Vic.), as the actor has a 'vested interest in the outcome of the project'.

A final perspective on sponsor selection is aligned with earlier views that there is poor organisational understanding of the sponsor role and it is not given priority by senior executives. There were arguments that, given these factors, organisations blindly follow a process such as gateway or PRINCE2, first, to select a sponsor, and, second, to ensure this is a 'senior officer'. A senior executive (Person E, NSW) argued that this represents not a focus on an appropriate selection process but rather a procedural step in initiating a project that typically leads to the wrong person being appointed sponsor— or, as they succinctly put it: 'All we look for is names [to fill boxes].'

Disturbingly, the consensus from the elite interviewees was that the sponsor role is one to avoid and there is a general reluctance among senior executives to take it on; or, as one CIO (Person W, NZ) said, they will refuse to do so. Another CIO (Person AI, Vic.) argued that even those who consider taking on the role choose not to once they find out what is involved. This reluctance stems from a view that the risks inherent in a large ICT software project are large while the upside is small: if I fail, I will be accountable, but if I succeed there will be no reward. For executives who have carefully established a career in the public sector with hopes or expectations of greater things, being the sponsor of a high-risk large ICT software project is seen as a possible end to that plan—or, as one CIO (Person AH, Vic.) puts it: 'It is career-limiting to damage your reputation with a big IT project.'

Interestingly, there was an argument that the various lessons-learned reports and project reviews produced to assist in improving outcomes for future projects in fact contribute to this reluctance to take on the sponsor role by planting a sense of inevitable failure in executives' minds. Person AH argued that the 2011 Victorian Ombudsman's (2011) report is such an example: '[E]ver since that report came out, really, senior executives in the VPS [Victorian Public Service] … have lost confidence that it is possible to manage these things.'

They went on to describe this as a 'learned helplessness': instead of taking the positives from the lessons learned, all they learn is that they are powerless to achieve good outcomes and they will be held accountable. Person AH posits that this can only be addressed by executives seeing a pattern of improvement in project outcomes to gain confidence and therefore become more inclined to support and sponsor projects. Their argument is that this can only be achieved not by undertaking large ICT projects but by breaking projects into less risky and less complicated components, under the logic that if large projects 'always fail, if the medicine kills the patient repeatedly, then doubling the dose is not the right thing. What you need to do is think about a different medicine'.

A political argument for this unwillingness to take on the role was also highlighted. A senior executive (Person BM, Tas.) argued that there is reluctance to be part of government-imposed initiatives, or 'brainwaves', as they can be seen internally as 'not important, not needed, and [at] high risk of failure'.

Person BM argued that in these instances sponsors fear they will end up 'carrying the can' for that political decision. Person BM suggested there are also cases where sponsors have been very willing, but these tend to be projects they classify as 'sexy', such as a new innovation that has wide internal and external appeal and the additional attraction to the sponsor of being associated with the outcome—a possible career-enhancing factor rather than a career-limiting one.

When discussing the resource model for the role, interviewees in all jurisdictions agreed that the default is that the sponsor role for large ICT software projects is undertaken part-time on top of the person's existing role. A senior executive (Person BL, Tas.) said this is typically because there is an 'underestimation of the time required to be a sponsor', so these executives believe they can manage the project 'from arm's length', although they soon discover this is not possible.

That arm's-length assumption was supported by another senior executive (Person E, NSW), who cited a large project that was having substantial challenges, yet the sponsor insisted on remaining in their senior substantive role. Issues continued to mount until jurisdictional executives acted and advised the sponsor to relinquish the substantive position and become a full-time sponsor. From this discussion, it is important to note that Person E was not being critical of the sponsor or suggesting they were uncommitted or the wrong person for the job; the argument was that for these large ICT projects the sponsor should have been full-time 'from day one' as such projects 'are not things that can be run on the side'. Not making the role full-time not only endangers the project but also is unfair to the sponsor, who is immediately challenged by the competing demands of organisational and project responsibilities.

Another senior executive (Person BL, Tas.), however, argued that some executives who undertake the sponsor role on a part-time basis due to an inability to relinquish their substantive position, such as a chief executive, have implemented an effective model. In these instances, the executive has realised the constraints and implemented additional project positions and roles that, while not removing accountability, relieve time constraints; this is a similar approach to that undertaken successfully by Michael Carmody at the Australian Taxation Office (see Box 3.1).

A final narrative concerned the timing and selection of the sponsor and, like earlier comments, the perspectives were clear that the sponsor must be selected at the time of the political mandate and must take on responsibility then, not after the project has begun. That is, they should drive the planning process from the project initiation stage.

In summary, the elite interviewees believe the sponsor selection process is flawed, as is the model under which they are engaged. An ongoing issue is a reluctance to accept the role for fear it will be career-limiting. The role comes with a reputation for little reward but high personal risk. Perspectives on the current selection process are perhaps summed up—if cynically—in the following quote from a CIO (Person W, NZ): 'I talked to one other government department who said one of the criteria for starting a project is that there is a passionate person in the business that is willing to lose their job over whether it succeeds or not, and you make them the sponsor for it.'

A model based not on capability or suitability but on being an enthusiastic risk-taker is perhaps not the best approach.

Training and support: What sponsor training and support are provided?

There was a consistent perspective across all jurisdictions that formal training for sponsors would be beneficial. A senior ICT assurance officer (Person T, NZ) argued that training for the sponsor before appointment should be mandatory—something another ICT assurance officer (Person R, NZ) claimed was the case in the United Kingdom. A senior executive (Person AD, APS) suggested a major and obvious benefit of sponsor training would be in providing the sponsor with the 'right skills upfront; they know what to do and [will] be aware of their role'.

Adding to this view, a CIO (Person A, APS) argued that sponsor skills can be taught, just like project management; the issue is this is not happening. There were also strong opinions that if a training course is to be developed it must be targeted at the sponsor role and the range of capabilities required for large ICT projects, not just, for example, gateway or project management training—or, as a senior project manager (Person P, NZ) stated: 'I do not mean just go and do PRINCE2 training or whatever it is, the flavour of the month for New Zealand Government methodology … [Y]ou cannot do that.'

However, some interviewees believed there would be a problem getting executives to, first, acknowledge they need training and, second, attend. One senior executive (Person BM, Tas.) felt senior executives are resistant to this type of training, believing they do not need it and do not have time for it. A senior project manager (Person AS, NT) claimed that getting a chief executive to attend sponsor training is 'never going to happen'.

Another senior project manager (Person N, NZ), based on experience with sponsors in government projects, said getting senior executives to participate in any training is a serious issue that has impacted negatively on projects. They gave an example of a jurisdictional initiative to provide formal training to sponsors on project governance that resulted in an uptake of about 50 per cent. The remaining half

> who were invited to it were horrified and insulted that it was felt that they needed this training. They go, 'I have reached level X in this organisation, therefore I understand governance', and in fact … they were the ones who needed it most. So, I think that was a problem with the culture of the organisation.

A review revealed that Victoria and New South Wales are the only jurisdictions with some form of sponsor training within their institutional framework. The Victorian course is not mandatory and runs for one and a half days. A senior assurance officer (Person AG, Vic.) said the Victorian course mainly discusses 'processes', which is not suitable on its own for sponsor training. Two Victorian CIOs (Persons AI & AK) supported this perspective, adding that it is not suitable to uplift capability to the required level. Person AK said the training 'does not guarantee an understanding and awareness of their obligations and role'.

The NSW course is also voluntary, and runs only for a half-day. Most NSW elite interviewees were not aware of the course, which could be because it was relatively new at the time of the interviews, commissioned by a relatively new jurisdiction-wide assurance team. A senior executive (Person Z, NSW) from that unit said the course was intended to provide a half-day 'sponsor masterclass' for senior executives; the course was more a 'conversation' about the role and what had been experienced in the past and providing some structure to this. It was also acknowledged that this is a starting point, with a plan to develop the training further.

There was evidence from several other interviews that the establishment of a formal sponsor training course had been raised, but all confirmed that to their knowledge it had not progressed. For example, in Tasmania, a senior executive (Person BM) said there had been some talk of developing a targeted course with the AIPM, but it seemed to have 'dropped off the radar'. In New Zealand, a senior assurance officer (Person Q) with jurisdiction-wide responsibilities confirmed that the need for such a course had been raised. When asked why this had not progressed, they said: 'I have been wanting to for several years, but again we have not had the support or the funding … I am doing what I can with this grant.'

The issues of capacity, funding, and support to address the sponsor training requirement were also raised in the Tasmanian interviews, and are arguably relevant to other jurisdictions. It was argued that the small size of the Tasmanian sector limited the ability to develop and maintain a detailed training course.

In summary, the elite interviewees believe training is important, and should even be made mandatory, but few options exist because of a lack of organisational priority or ability. There is a reluctance to undertake the training required and a view that this is unlikely to change until sponsor skills are recognised organisationally, as are other senior management skills.

There were similarities identified with sponsor support models across all jurisdictions, with some exceptions, including new initiatives in New South Wales. Commonalities were the inclusion of an internal quality assurer (IQA) in some guise, the use of gateway reviews and PRINCE2, documented guidelines, commissioning of independent external reviews, and the mandatory or optional provision of assurance services by a central assurance team. No interviewees identified any support process outside these approaches; it was their application that varied across jurisdictions.

As examples of some initiatives, two senior ICT assurance officers (Persons AG & AF, Vic.) said they review and assess a project sponsor's support structure, including the mandatory inclusion of an independent expert from industry or elsewhere to provide 'unencumbered advice'. A senior executive (Person Z, NSW) said they have compiled a 'highly experienced panel' of people to assist sponsors, while an APS senior executive (Person AD) with jurisdiction-wide assurance responsibilities said the main source of support is gateway reviews; however, they also acknowledged that this process 'is not really providing assurance to the government as an investor'.

Person AD added that, as a result, their unit is looking at how to improve support, but they could not 'pre-empt which way it is going to go'.

A more common view, however, was that it is the responsibility of the sponsor to seek jurisdictional assurance assistance rather than this being a mandatory part of the project structure. As an example of this, a CIO (Person S, NZ) said that while options exist within the New Zealand institutional framework to provide sponsor support, this is reliant on the sponsor asking for it, which is something senior executives are not always willing to do—that is, admit they 'need help'.

The Northern Territory has invested considerable effort in enhancing assurance for large ICT projects and deserves credit for that, but two senior assurance officers (Persons AS & AT) confirmed that it is up to the sponsor to seek advice. However, two other Northern Territory assurance officers (Persons AO & AP) said that as part of their role, they monitor the sponsor's performance and 'if we identified a sponsor as low-engagement or low-ability, we would raise that as an elevated risk and highlight' this upwards. Arguably, a better approach would be to assist before it reached that stage by providing support from project initiation.

As indicated earlier, and while the model varies, the use of IQAs as a support method for sponsors is common across all jurisdictions. These assurers are sourced from various places such as the large consulting firms like Deloitte and KPMG or are independent contractors. While the inclusion of an IQA is common across jurisdictions, it is not always mandatory to do so—for example, in Tasmania, a senior executive (Person BM) said it is up to the sponsor to decide. The New Zealand interviewees indicated that the use of IQAs is common practice within that jurisdiction; however, one CIO (Person W, NZ) argued that there is a tendency to bring assurers in after project issues arise, when they should already be there if they are to 'advance the project'.

There was also commonality across all jurisdictions that having an IQA was no guarantee that the sponsor would receive the support required, as the quality and engagement model of IQAs vary, as does the willingness of the sponsor to ask for, process, and accept that advice. At their best, IQAs are 'key in training a sponsor' (Person L, CIO, NZ), someone who 'creates value' (Person O, CIO, NZ), and someone who is willing to be truly independent and 'challenge' the sponsor when required (Person R, ICT assurance, NZ). At their worst, they are 'someone who goes into the battlefield after the battle and stabs anyone on the ground who is still alive' (CIO, Person O, NZ).

These were not arguments against having an IQA as part of a sponsor support model; the argument was that an IQA is just one part of a sponsor support structure and should not be the only part. The other argument is that to be effective the IQA's role and the timing of their engagement should be established early in the project. Looking from the outside in, a private sector senior IQA (Person C, NSW) talked about the challenges of providing external independent quality assurance to government sponsors, saying it is difficult to get the sponsor and the project team to accept that the assurer is there to independently help them improve outcomes, not to conduct audits. Person C said in a recent project, it took six months for the sponsor to understand this and to accept and trust them as an ally.

The provision of 'peer' support was an emerging concept among some interviewees. A CIO (Person G, APS) argued that it would be worthwhile for jurisdictions to identify actors, either internal or external, with sponsor experience who can 'buddy' up with new sponsors. Person G claimed this would provide a positive role model and a timely and relevant-sounding board, so the buddy could say: 'This is what I did in my role.'

The interviewees believed such as model acknowledges that a training course alone is not effective and a buddy/mentor provides consistent support to the sponsor throughout the project. A senior executive (Person X, NZ)—a sponsor themselves—supported this view, saying that while training is beneficial, 'having someone coming alongside us in the workplace would be more valuable'.

The provision of a buddy/mentor is already incorporated in Victorian and NSW support models. In New Zealand, an ICT assurance officer (Person Q) said they had been investigating such a model due to feedback from past sponsors, but the idea had lost internal priority and stalled. In Tasmania, it was argued, jurisdictional size had advantages in providing peer support, with the smaller size enabling informal support networks to develop quickly and easily (Person AM, Senior executive, Tas.).

In summary, the elite interviewees indicate that while support is available in guidelines, it is variable in quality and effectiveness, not always mandatory, and often left to the agency and sponsor to establish. This is a problem given the sponsor does not have the capability; a suitable support option is therefore critical.

The findings and their conceptual relationship

Interviewees believed the Australian and New Zealand public sectors do not have the sponsor capability to initiate and plan large ICT software projects. They also argued that if the capability is not there, a project should not commence; however, assessment before initiation is not common practice, nor is it a decision point. Additionally, chance or luck is likely to be the major capability factor, with the agency by chance having an experienced, capable sponsor available or lucky in their sponsor being motivated, willing, and able to learn as the project progresses. By implication, being 'lucky' means the project begins without a capable sponsor.

It was argued that while sponsor capability is lacking, the advent of digital and agile delivery brings a requirement for new sponsor skills. This means 'letting go' to encourage innovation and fast delivery while maintaining responsibility and accountability. This is not only a new skillset but also a cultural shift and, given the public sector has failed so far to address capability, there is a distinct new challenge in addressing emergent skills.

Sponsors are not selected and appointed based on their capability or suitability. The default is to select a senior executive who is organisationally aligned to the project outcomes. The problem with this is the actor is generally unsuitable as they do not have the experience and do not understand the role. They are not capable of undertaking the role but receive a 'tap on the shoulder' regardless.

Institutional frameworks across the Australian and New Zealand public sectors include sponsor roles and responsibilities, albeit in varying detail. These are generally documented roles and responsibilities, some dot points, and guidelines for the sponsor to read. This is not enough to either address capability or transfer the required knowledge to the sponsor. Reading some dot points is unsuitable on its own as a capability-building strategy.

There are generally no training options available to sponsors before their appointment, yet there is collective agreement that this would be beneficial and, arguably, should be mandatory. While the need has been acknowledged, it has not been prioritised and funded accordingly, and there is little evidence that this will be addressed soon. There are exceptions in Victoria and New South Wales, but while these are better than nothing, they arguably are too brief to cover anything like the range of skills required to undertake the sponsor role. Part of the problem is that establishing such a training option requires a lot of effort and cost, which for jurisdictions like the Northern Territory and Tasmania is simply not an option; arguably, this is a factor across all Australian and New Zealand jurisdictions.

It was argued that, regardless of available documentation and training, or even experience, it is critical that the sponsor has an effective support structure in place—this has not always happened. There was no preferred way to provide sponsor support, rather there was a range of options based on the needs of the sponsor and the project. There is growing support for the provision of 'buddies' as capable and experienced peers with whom sponsors can talk openly; however, this would require a cultural change across the jurisdictions.

For leadership, addressing sponsor capability was perceived to be lacking in organisational priority and executive understanding of the role. The organisational culture requires change to acknowledge sponsor capability as a core senior management capability, similar to the requirement for financial management capability, rather than as a 'second-fiddle' capability.

Arguably the greatest example of a lack of senior organisational understanding of the sponsor role is the resource model utilised. Sponsors are generally expected to do the role on top of their substantive organisational position and fail to understand that it requires commitment from project initiation through to completion; this model sets the project and the sponsor up for failure.

Sponsors do not fully understand or accept the roles, responsibilities, and in particular the accountability of the position. Sponsors must champion and drive business change throughout a project, but they are failing to do so, instead taking a hands-off, figurehead approach, and the project falters as a result. There is a tendency to not hold the sponsor to account for outcomes, one of the reasons for which is a mindset at the executive level that these ICT projects always have problems, so 'what could I do'. However, despite attempts to avoid accountability, either deliberately or naively, if the project fails, there are cases where the sponsor has been held accountable to their very personal cost. It is best to understand and address these issues upfront.

A key sponsor role is managing the internal and external stakeholders, which has been done poorly and sponsors have failed to understand this is their responsibility. They have also failed to demonstrate the capability to manage these relationships, with vendor management highlighted as an issue. The lack of vendor management capability has led to a focus on hard negotiations—a 'screw the vendor' approach—rather than looking to develop a win-win collaborative partnership. It was perceived that this was due to vendor management being a role that many public sector managers have never had to do. Unfortunately, the sponsors' response has been to try to abdicate responsibility for the project to the vendor, rather than understanding it always remains with the sponsor.

The sponsor role is seen as one to avoid because of a 'learned helplessness'. The litany of poor outcomes for past and ongoing large ICT software projects, understandably, situates the role as extreme risky and potentially career-limiting. Therefore, avoidance of the role becomes a strategy: 'I quite like the job I have and would like to keep it.' There is therefore a perception that sponsor capability is not increasing as lessons learnt are not taken to a future role, meaning there is an organisational loss of learned capability.

In PRINCE2, the sponsor role ('senior responsible officer' in PRINCE2 terminology) is a requirement in the methodology. The sponsor is a key, if not the most important, role in the PRINCE2 organisational and governance structure, and it recommends appointing a senior officer in the role. Interviewees perceived this as 'ticking a box' in a methodological process rather than a considered selection. They believed there was a misguided organisational belief that the sponsor role had been addressed, typically resulting in a sponsor without the capability, role awareness, or time to undertake their responsibilities.

A mini case study of a sponsor for a major APS ICT software reform program is provided in Box 3.1, in which the word 'serendipitous' is used as the sponsor's capability assessment and selection did not follow the ideal approach. In fact, you could argue that the program began without a capable sponsor—untrained, no experience, and maintaining their very senior permanent role on top of the sponsor role—yet the sponsor garnered much praise from within the program and the program itself was considered a success. However, the argument is that this outcome was due to the agency of the individual—someone who displayed excellent leadership, personal awareness, and entrepreneurial skills—and was the result of chance, not institutional governance or the institutional framework.

Box 3.1 Intuitive sponsor skills: A serendipitous counterexample

Michael Carmody was the Commissioner of Taxation with the Australian Taxation Office (ATO) from 1993 to 2005, CEO of the Australian Customs Service from 2006 to 2009, and CEO of the Australian Customs and Border Force Service from 2009 to 2012.

At the ATO, Carmody drove a large ICT reform program to implement the delivery of e-government services to ATO customers. This was a major undertaking—a program of many interrelated projects spanning more than 10 years—and was considered a success. His role as the champion and sponsor of this program was praised by interviewees. He was cited as an exemplar, with one assurance lead on the program (Person AB) describing Carmody as an 'amazing man'.

I interviewed Carmody, told him of these positive comments, and asked about his approach.

> Interviewer: Why did you take such a visible, strong leadership role from the start?

> Michael Carmody (MC): Well, it was about the future of the Tax Office and tax administration. I guess it comes back to the fact of what I wanted to achieve ... I wanted to take the opportunity to ... change the experience with taxpayers ... [T]he biggest thing that I did and that committed me to it was to talk about the outcomes we were going to achieve, [and] what was going to be the difference in the experience of people dealing with the Tax Office ... [T]hat is about the whole of the Tax Office, so, if I was not going to take leadership, who should? It was really as simple as that.

Interviewer: And what would be the risk of you not doing that?

MC: The risk of me not doing that is … [the project] would languish. If people do not see the person at the top of the organisation committed and enthusiastic about what they are being asked to do then it makes a complete difference to their commitment to their work.

This leadership, sponsorship, and championing from the top by the commissioner and the success of the program as a result support a finding that the higher the level of the sponsor in the organisation with an interest in the outcome, the greater is the chance of success (Graham & Englund 1994; Buttle 1997, cited in Crawford & Brett 2001: 3). There was no one higher in the ATO than the commissioner.

There were positive comments from interviewees about Carmody's approach to relationship management, particularly between internal staff and the external implementation partner, and the independent support process he instigated.

Interviewer: How did you as the sponsor go about setting up an appropriate program governance structure?

MC: The project teams had their steering groups, [a designated ATO officer] met with them regularly … and then, on a regular basis, I chaired a meeting which had all the major project managers and [implementation partner] people there, [at] which we went through where we were at according to the plan and what were the barriers we had. But important to that … we also engaged another company … to sit in on those meetings and deliver their perspective of how the project was actually going. So, I was not just hearing from the people engaged in the projects, I was hearing from what would be judged as independent reviewers and that gave me a lot more confidence. I mean, there was a bit of tension created by that, I will not kid you.

Interviewer: That is natural.

MC: Yeah, but I thought it was a particularly valuable way of going about it.

Person AB said that Carmody chaired a meeting twice a month right through to the end of the project:

So, you have that drive from the top, that ownership at that top executive level … [H]e wanted the people in the room that could help advise him … [T]hen he would call people in … bring them in for those [hot] topics/issues … [I]t is mind-blowing and works well.

A senior project manager (Person F) explained:

For big program changes, we would not have gotten as far as we did without the absolute commitment from the commissioner … [He was] 100 per cent behind it … [H]e also ensured the organisational resources were made available. I cannot overstate how significant this was to the program, otherwise the program would have … fallen apart due to all of the pressures.

This indicates the sponsor model Carmody employed, as the most senior executive: he was the sponsor and project champion, and a very visible and involved one at that. However, as he was not full-time in the role, he released a senior executive on a full-time basis to manage, for the ATO, the day-to-day role reporting directly to him. He then engaged a third-party firm to provide both specialist capability and capacity and, as additional support, separately engaged an independent advisor to report directly to him. Carmody maintained a relationship management role with all parties and religiously attended all meetings. Compare this with comments from New South Wales citing the sponsor who did not attending critical decision-making steering committee meetings.

Carmody was not a formally trained sponsor and he was asked about the capability of public sector staff to undertake a sponsor role for a large complex ICT software project.

> MC: I cannot comment on other organisations, I can only comment on what I experienced in the Tax Office … I don't know anything about coding or the technology or whatever … but if you can focus on what you are trying to achieve in a real business sense then it gives you something to measure your success by and gives the stakeholders a reason to be enthusiastic about it.

> Interviewer: Do you think that providing more training, support, and guidance for people in these leadership roles on large ICT software projects is of any benefit?'

> MC: Oh, of course it is.

This mini study highlights the fact that, despite Carmody not being an experienced or trained sponsor, he was aware of his limitations in the role and implemented strategies to provide the support and capability required. While he did not release himself full-time to undertake the role—which was understandable given he was commissioner—he did assign a full-time second-in-command. Despite this, he never abdicated accountability, he led from the front, was a visible champion of change, gave the project priority and resourcing, and had a clear focus on outcomes that he instilled across the organisation. Carmody arguably addressed the key issues identified in the earlier analysis; without any real reference to an APS framework, he built his own. The issue for the public sector is that not every agency will have a Michael Carmody; therefore, a framework to address the sponsor role remains central.

Interviewees argued that the only way to improve acceptance of the sponsor role is improving project outcomes instead of the litany of disasters and the fear that instils in senior executives. This, coupled with an ongoing lack of sponsor capability, led to the argument that the solution is to de-risk these projects by breaking them into components rather than undertaking them as a single large project. This enables the progressive delivery of products, increasing the likelihood of success and decreasing the risk of failure.

The conceptual findings are summarised in Table 3.1.

Table 3.1 Summary of the sponsor role conceptual findings

Concept	Sponsor role key findings
Capability and capacity	• The Australian and New Zealand public sectors do not have the required capability or capacity. • There is no assessment of sponsor capability prior to project approval and commencement. • Having a capable sponsor is a matter of chance or luck. • The advent of agile and digital technologies introduces a new sponsor requirement/capability. • Sponsors are not selected based on suitability or capability; they receive a 'tap on the shoulder'. • Roles and responsibilities are generally dot points in a document; this does not address the capability issue. • There are no or extremely limited and unsuitable training options for sponsors; they are expensive to establish and the executive support does not exist. • The support options available to sponsors are inadequate and largely left to the individual to structure.
Leadership	• There is no organisational priority to address sponsor capability. • A sponsor remains an organisational 'second fiddle'. • Sponsors are generally required to undertake the demanding role on top of their substantive role, demonstrating a lack of executive awareness of the demands and importance of the role.
Accountability	• Sponsors fail (sometimes to their severe detriment) to understand or acknowledge the accountability associated with the role. • Sponsors are failing to drive business change. • There is a belief among sponsors that large IT projects always fail, so 'what could I do?' • Accountability, and the potential cost of this to the sponsor, is not being made clear at the project's outset.
Stakeholder management	• Stakeholder management is poorly undertaken and a missing public sector capability. • Sponsors have failed to understand their responsibility for stakeholder management. • Vendor management is particularly poorly managed, with a failure to understand the need for a workable win-win relationship: a partnership.
Organisational learning	• Executives view the sponsor role as one to avoid at all costs. • Given the perceived high likelihood of poor outcomes, they fear for their future if held accountable.

Concept	Sponsor role key findings
Methodologies	• While the sponsor role is mandatory across sectors and its importance is highlighted in governance documentation, creating and filling the role are seen more as 'ticking a box' than addressing the capability issue.
Entrepreneurship	• The only way to encourage good sponsors is to improve acceptance of the role by improving the organisation's project outcomes. This can be done by breaking down the complexity of large ICT projects, to lower the risk, and to increase the chances of good outcomes.

Source: Compiled by author.

Conclusion

The perspectives of the elite interviewees for the various sponsor themes indicate there is much commonality across the Australian and New Zealand jurisdictions. Institutional governance for the sponsor role was perceived to be ineffective, misunderstood, not organisationally prioritised, and to be avoided if possible. Large complex projects magnify these issues; therefore, there was a growing perception that the solution is to avoid large projects.

In conclusion, these findings can be compared with the key points in the review of the sponsor literature (see Table 3.2). While this is a simplified summary, it highlights a disconnect between what the literature argues is good governance for sponsors and the perceptions of the elite interviewees on the effectiveness of institutional governance for sponsors in the Australian and New Zealand public sectors.

Table 3.2 Comparison of literature review and findings

Literature review (Chapter 2): Key points	Interview findings
The sponsor role has evolved and matured to be the critical organisational project role (Briner et al. 1990; Morris 1994; Stretton 1994; Kerzner & Kerzner 2013).	The public sector has not evolved in sync.
Sponsors must be accountable and responsible for the project objectives (Alie 2015; APM 2019a).	Sponsors do not fully understand the role and its responsibilities and therefore the resulting accountability. Many sponsors also try to dodge accountability.
The sponsor role is critical to good project outcomes (Bryde 2008; Kloppenborg & Tesch 2015; PMI 2018; AIPM 2020).	There is no organisational priority given to addressing sponsor capability.

Literature review (Chapter 2): Key points	Interview findings
The sponsor role can be misunderstood and simplified (Bryde 2008; PMI 2018; APM 2019b).	In the public sector, the complexity and extent of the role are not understood and therefore not given organisational priority.
The sponsor role and its focus change as the project moves through its lifecycle, and the sponsor adapts accordingly (Kloppenborg & Tesch 2015; AIPM 2020; Breese et al. 2020).	Linked to a misunderstanding about the role, sponsors fail to adapt their focus throughout the project, with many taking a hands-off, 'figurehead' approach and abdicating key tasks such as vendor and benefits management.
The sponsor must be capable and able to commit time and skills to the role (OECD 2001; APM 2019b; AIPM 2020; Breese et al. 2020).	Sectors lack the required capability and sponsors generally underestimate the time and skills required.
The relationship between the sponsor and the project manager is a critical and co-dependent one (Bryde 2008; Bertsche 2014; Alie 2015; Kloppenborg & Tesch 2015; Zwikael & Meredith 2018; APM 2019b; Breese et al. 2020).	Too often sponsors abdicate key roles and responsibilities to the project manager and fail to provide the executive support necessary.
To build sponsor capability, organisations must avoid two pitfalls. First, the executive fails to recognise, support, and make the role organisationally visible. Second, a lack of understanding by the sponsor of the role renders their contribution ineffective (Crawford & Brett 2001; AIPM & KPMG 2018).	The public sector does not avoid either of these pitfalls.
Sponsor training is ineffective when it focuses on the incorrect skills and not on the breadth of disciplines required (Bryde 2008; AIPM & KPMG 2016; Chapman 2017).	Sponsor training is either non-existent or limited in its range.
Projects do not need a disconnected or reluctant sponsor (PMI 2012; APM 2018; AIPM 2020).	Executives see the sponsor role as one to avoid.
Sponsors can fail to commit time to the role due to other organisational demands, which is also related to a failure to understand the time demands for sponsor roles over an extended period (PMI 2012; APM 2018; Breese et al. 2020).	The normal process is to assign an already busy senior executive to the sponsor role, on top of their substantive role, so they simply cannot provide the focus required.

Source: Compiled by author.

4

Project management: Superhumans required

For transformational programs, if you think that you are going to be able to develop and retain people inhouse, and they are going to sit around waiting for a once-in-15-year project, you are absolutely dreaming. (Person Q, ICT assurance, NZ)

Introduction

Analysis of all part one elite interviewees (see 'The puzzle' section, Chapter 1: Table 1.1) and selected vignettes reveal that the governance of the project management discipline and roles via institutional frameworks is ineffective. This is reflected in the dominant view that the capability for large ICT software projects does not exist in any jurisdiction. Like the findings in the previous chapter on the sponsor role, it is argued that this is due to a lack of organisational priority in addressing project management capability, with senior executives failing to provide leadership.

There was a distinction made between capability for small projects and that required for large ICT software projects. Capability was deemed to be better for smaller projects; however, even here there has been a focus on improving project managers' skills rather than addressing the broader requirements of the project management discipline. It was argued that the public sector need not maintain inhouse the skills required for large, complex, and specialised generational-type projects; they can be sourced externally as and when required.

Theme

Category

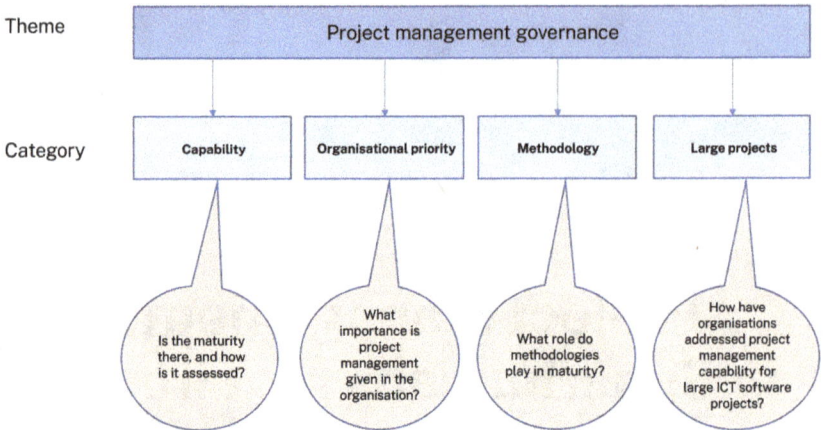

Figure 4.1 Categories for project management governance
Source: Created by author.

There were also arguments—albeit not universal—that the best way to address project management capability and capacity issues for large ICT software projects is to stop doing them, which removes the challenge and risk from the equation. The proposal was to treat them as a series of smaller component-based projects that have reduced capability demands, more inhouse options, and the potential for continuous learning. Where this has happened, it has been due to the agency of an individual actor rather than the result of the institutional framework. An alternative proposal is to form a 'talent pool' of experience and proven capability within or across jurisdictions that can be moved from project to project; however, this would require a major cultural shift.

To support these findings, this chapter details the elite interviewees' perspectives on the governance of the project management discipline and roles across the New Zealand and Australian public sectors. The interview questions were aligned with four categories[1] identified from the project management literature review (see Figure 4.1):

- Capability: Do the sectors have project management capability, and is an assessment of this capability part of project planning and initiation?

- Organisational priority: What importance is project management given in the organisation?

---

1   It is acknowledged that the discipline, roles, and functions of project management are many and diverse—too many to be covered in this section.

- Methodology: What role do methodologies play in maturity?
- Large projects: How have organisations addressed project management capability for large ICT software projects?

For each category, the perspectives from the elite interview data are analysed, supported by vignettes from those interviews. These findings are summarised and aligned with the theoretical concepts, followed by a short conclusion.

The elite interviews

Capability: Is the maturity there and how is it assessed?

Before analysing the elite interviewees' perceptions of project management capability within the Australian and New Zealand public sectors, it is apt to recap what is meant by capability. The PMI (2013b) defines an organisation's project management capability as the maturity and effectiveness of its framework to execute project, program, and portfolio management, supported by organisational practices than can effectively produce better performance and results. This framework is a combination of talent, processes, and knowledge. Does the organisation have the project management framework that provides people with skills and experience, supported by effective governance processes?

The elite interviewees felt the capability for large ICT software projects does not exist within the Australian and New Zealand public sectors. No interviewee argued otherwise. Responses to the question 'Does your jurisdiction have the project management capability to undertake large ICT software projects?' were generally a short and sharp 'no'. The following quote sums up these views: '[I]t is lacking. We do not have the skills' (Person E, Senior executive, NSW).

The interviewees were asked whether they believed this lack of capability had been a factor in poor outcomes and the universal perception was yes. Responses included the following:

> [A]bsolutely a factor, it is a major factor. (Person C, IQA, Private sector)
>
> Couldn't agree more. (Person AD, Senior ICT executive, APS)
>
> I have to agree. (Person S, CIO, NZ)

There was little awareness among the elite interviewees of a jurisdictional requirement for a project management capability assessment to be undertaken before a project began, or a means to do so; at best, there was vagueness. As an example, a senior ICT assurance officer (Person AE, APS) said it was probably best to ask the Department of the Prime Minister and Cabinet: '[T]hey do have sort of whole-government-wide kind of initiatives and capabilities, so they are probably best to answer that question, because I am not sure what is in place around that.'

This was a little disconcerting given this person's role. Another APS senior ICT assurance officer (Person AD) recalled that several years earlier there had been a portfolio, program, and project management community of practice forum operating in the Australian Public Service that also undertook informal maturity assessments, but this had now stopped. They argued that while this was operating, there was evidence of improvements in project management capability. Most interviewees argued that such an assessment should be mandatory before a project begins and a project should not start if the maturity and capability are lacking.

However, interviewees made a clear delineation between project management capability for large ICT software projects or programs of work and the capability for smaller projects, such as business-as-usual projects, which it was claimed is better. This was because teams and processes have been established over time to support smaller projects, with past learnings applied. The teams have been specifically developed to support these types of projects, not the large generational type. However, there was a common view that, even for smaller projects, this was a result not of strategies within the institutional framework but of initiatives within individual agencies. An APS chief executive (Person AY) claimed that, within the Australian Public Service, this was necessary as there was no jurisdiction-wide capability development program. There was a similar perspective in New Zealand, with a CIO (Person L) arguing that project management capability development was 'being left to individuals' within agencies to act as 'there is no overarching approach to address the issue'.

While there are independent initiatives to address project management capability for smaller projects, the interviewees claimed capability for large ICT projects is being addressed separately at the time of the project. An example of this was provided by a CIO (Person S, NZ): '[W]e have an inhouse team of reasonably capable people that are all well qualified in

PRINCE2 and those things. Where my internal team tends to peter out is when we have large-scale business change initiatives … so we tend to complement that with some external [expertise].'

The use of external staff—typically contractors—is common across jurisdictions. These resources are typically used to either supplement existing or provide new capability and capacity, such as one large agency, where the senior project manager (Person N, NZ) stated: '[O]ur whole team has been contractors.'

This mix varied across jurisdictions and even between agencies within a jurisdiction, but a common argument for this approach is the flexibility that contractors provide in being able to readily increase or decrease capacity based on organisational factors and project complexity. A senior ICT assurance officer (Person AT, NT) stated that 'our resource pool is predominately external contractors; this gives us the ability to scale up or down as required'.

Tempering this approach of employing contractors were two common perspectives: first, that contract resources can be itinerant and lack loyalty to the agency, which can result in high staff turnover. A senior project manager (Person N, NZ)—themselves a contractor—suggested this was because contractors have flexibility and can 'move with the money', 'follow the interesting projects', and 'leave difficult projects'.

Second, being a contract resource is a guarantee not of capability, only of availability—that is, agencies can become focused on capacity (headcounts) at the expense of capability. These factors could compound the capability gap, as argued by a CIO (Person AI, Vic.): '[U]sing capacity in lieu of capability … leads to suboptimal outcomes.'

A common issue with these strategies is a tendency to concentrate on building a collective of capable project managers rather than addressing the wider project management governance requirements, such as the culture, tools, processes, structure, assurance, support, and training across the agency or jurisdiction. A former public sector CIO now in the private sector (Person AI, Vic.) said that in their private sector role the entire organisation was project-focused with the supporting project management governance and resulting capability, whereas in the public sector role they had seen 'very few, if any, people in the organisation with that capability' or awareness.

Finally, there was a perception that agencies with an effective project management office (PMO) are likely to have better organisational project management capability. However, interviewees struggled to identify examples of effectively implemented PMOs and, where they did, the outcomes were variable. The Centrelink PMO was cited as one exemplar (Person G, CIO, APS). A senior ICT assurance officer (Person R, NZ) claimed that existing PMOs fail to provide a quality service. A senior executive (Person B, NSW) argued from experience that NSW agency PMOs tend to concentrate on financials rather than aiding the overall dissemination of the project details to stakeholders and working collaboratively with the project team.

In summary, the perception was that project management capability does not exist for large ICT software projects; however, it is better for smaller projects. Capability-building is largely the result of individual initiatives rather than jurisdictional efforts, but this has concentrated on project managers rather than the broader organisational integration of the project management discipline. There is also a lack of awareness of the need to assess capability before initiation of a large project, yet there is agreement that this should happen.

Organisational priority: What importance is project management given in the organisation?

There was a clear understanding from the interviewees that project management is not unique to the public sector; it is a global discipline. According to Professor Ofer Zwikael, Associate Editor of the *International Journal of Project Management*, because the knowledge exists, the public sector does not have to 'reinvent the skills'; they are transferrable between sectors and industries.

Given the discipline and skills are well defined, the common perspective on the public sector's failure to address project management capability is that it simply is not an organisational priority. Reasons for this varied, but some vignettes from the interviews include the following:

> I do not think we as the public sector have recognised that project management is a core [organisational] capability. (Person A, CIO, APS)

> [Executives believe] that project management is easy, and any sensible person can do it … [I]t is not undervaluing; it is not understanding. (Person C, IQA, Private sector)

> The focus I saw in the organisation was the business of government … fulfilling the priorities that the government of the day has established, and therefore [little priority is given to the role of project management in delivering these]. (Person AI, CIO, Vic.)

> At a senior organisational level there is a lack of experience in driving organisational change, which leads to issues with recognising the discipline of project management and implementing strategies to address skills gaps. (Person L, CIO, NZ)

Like perspectives in the sponsor chapter (Chapter 3), it was argued here that this lack of priority was because public sector organisations were not project-based organisations. In Victoria, two senior ICT assurance officers (Persons AF & AG) claimed that project management capability varied across agencies due to their project-based culture or lack thereof, with VicRoads[2] being quite mature, as road-building projects are a core part of its business, whereas this project culture is not the case in other agencies. Even here, however, there were cautionary perspectives. A program director (Person F, APS) with experience in projects across the Australian Public Service argued that, despite some agencies touting maturity in project management and being project-based, this in fact did not meet the requirements of the project. A private sector and former public sector CIO (Person AI, Vic.) argued that their current employer was an example of a project-based organisation for whom projects were critical to the delivery of their services and infrastructure, hence internal capability was a priority. They said this was never the case during their time in the public sector.

Also like the sponsor role, there was a common perspective that senior executives fail to understand the project management discipline and its organisational role, leading to a lack of executive commitment to drive change. Two senior ICT assurance officers (Persons AF & AG, Vic.) claimed there was 'no recognition upstream that project management is a discipline and [that there] is a current gap'.

A CIO (Person G, APS) argued that executives are aware of project management needs but fail to prioritise them as they do not perceive any professional gain in addressing the issue; they therefore prioritise other organisational issues that they deem will provide greater personal benefit.

---

2   According to its *Customer Charter*, 'VicRoads is a statutory corporation within the Victorian Government. Our purpose is to manage a safe, reliable and sustainable arterial road system as part of an integrated transport network' (available from: www.vicroads.vic.gov.au/about-vicroads/our-customer-charter).

It was further argued that senior executives still assume that a skilled staff member can adapt to a project management role. A senior executive (Person E, NSW) claimed this is evidence that senior executives do not understand the discipline, believing it is 'easy and pretty much a lot of sensible people can do it'.

Aligned to this perspective was a claim by a senior executive (Person X, NZ) that, in their experience, agency project management staff are in these roles by default, with resulting negative impacts on projects: '[P]eople would morph into project management through sort of a leadership section head-type route and some of them had never had formal project management training, but just learned by doing ... [Those ones are] very obvious to us ... as opposed to the professional project managers.'

A CIO (Person A, APS) argued that this instant 'rebadging' of staff as project managers is a major organisational failing. Aligned with this there were perspectives that until project management capability is an organisational prerequisite for career advancement, the capability will never be addressed. Another CIO (Person G, APS) suggested that the status quo will continue and project management capability will not gain senior executive buy-in until it is a 'prerequisite for me to get to the next level'.

There was also a belief that this senior executive failure to understand project management is a legacy of viewing ICT projects as IT projects rather than the business-change projects that they are. A senior executive (Person E, NSW) posited that being a technically competent IT manager is a different skillset to 'running a business project' and the public sector still does not understand this. This leads to organisations appointing the CIO as the project manager/director. As evidence that this remains an issue, a CIO (Person W, NZ) confessed that they had recently taken on the sponsor role of a large ICT project in their organisation. They admitted that this was 'wrong', as it was a business project not a technology project; however, they justified it by saying that the capability did not exist elsewhere in the organisation.

Interviewees suggested differences between public and private projects were another factor in making project management capability an organisational priority. Private sector projects are driven by a market imperative, delivering core services, and leading to a culture of developing project management capability to support this, while this imperative is missing in the public sector. This organisational priority is reflected in the lack of appropriate funding to support capability development initiatives, as evidenced in the following quote from a senior ICT assurance officer (Person Q, NZ), who, when asked about organisational capability development initiatives, said: 'Although we have an appetite for it, when money is scarce, capability is the first thing to go … [R]eally the only capability things that we do here are running communities of interest, which are largely self-help.'

As a counter to this common perspective is an acknowledged need to address prioritisation at a jurisdictional level. A senior executive (Person AD, APS) claimed that when it was created, the Digital Transformation Agency (DTA)[3] was to take a central role in addressing this capability across the Australian Public Service. However, at the time of writing, there was little evidence of what had been achieved, nor were any of the other APS interviewees aware of DTA initiatives in this area.

The other issue highlighted is that the successful implementation of capability initiatives is challenging and requires continuous organisational commitment over an extended time frame—factors that could impact on the DTA's plans. A CIO (Person G, APS) stated that these initiatives can happen while so much other change is under way, so 'fatigue' sets in as it becomes 'administratively burdensome', and the initiatives then become victims of organisational capacity constraints. There was also a perspective that leaving agencies to independently implement a strategy to address capabilities leads to a disparity between how it is applied and even prioritised within the agency, which then does not address jurisdictional capability. A senior executive (Person BM, Tas.) said that 'approaches vary across the jurisdiction due to agencies largely tackling the issue independently, not [in] a consistent approach'.

Meanwhile, a CIO (Person G, APS) said: '[Y]ou could have quite a disparity in terms of what is applied … [W]hat one agency may see as B-level quality could be a C or even less for another … [You must be] looking at whole-of-APS capability.'

Political influence was perceived as an additional organisational factor limiting the ability to address capability—for example, the jurisdiction's staffing policy could vary within as well as between government terms. One government may support the use of contract staff rather than a permanent headcount, the next may not. There could be caps placed on permanent

---

3   According to its website, the DTA oversees 'significant ICT and digital investments, assurance policy and framework, and the whole-of-government (APS) digital portfolio' (available from: www.dta. gov.au/about-us).

or contract recruitment, or both. The perception is that this makes long-term capability planning and retention difficult. A senior project manager (Person N, NZ), citing experience in resourcing a team for a large project that ran across government terms, said:

> The National [Party] government, they reduce the public sector headcount right down. So, anything that is project linked, they will not have permanent jobs for it. They will just bring in contractors as and when they need them. Then once we changed to a Labour government, it goes the other way.

The impact of such policy changes is that agencies that have carefully built up a capable team of contract project managers may lose this capability and capacity overnight. The other political factor raised is that agencies and their executives prioritise a focus on political initiatives in delivering the business of government, which can come at the expense of addressing the capability required to deliver those outcomes. This is perhaps best summarised by a CIO (Person AI, Vic.), who argued that a focus on political initiatives has led to a lack of organisational focus on the 'mechanics of running the organisation that needs to underpin that capability'.

The assumed cost of project management capability is also an organisational limitation. An external consultant specialising in large government ICT projects (Person C, NSW) argued that the norm is to expect project management to account for about 20 per cent of a project's costs. They said, in their experience, agency senior executives considered this overhead unacceptable and it was therefore reduced, resulting in less capacity and capability, which inevitably led to poor outcomes and their resulting costs, neither of which were factored into the executives' logic.

Interviewees in all jurisdictions, except the Northern Territory, raised as a factor in addressing capability the public sector's limitations on pay scales, grades, and their relationship with hierarchy. It was argued that this limits the ability to compete with the private sector to obtain and retain senior and experienced permanent project management capability. A CIO (Person S, NZ) said in their experience this has and will always be a factor in obtaining the most capable project management resources as no competent contractor in a market short of supply is going to take a '$100,000 pay cut' just to join the public sector. A perspective on this issue from a former NSW Government minister (see Box 4.1) highlights the fact that this is an issue not just for project management capability, but also for the public sector in general.

Box 4.1 A problem with getting the required capability: A minister's perspective

Adrian Piccoli was the NSW Education Minister from 2011 to 2017, resigning from parliament in late September 2017. Shortly after this, he was appointed Director of the University of New South Wales's Gonski Institute for Education. During his time as minister, Piccoli was responsible for the exceptionally large Learning Management and Business Reform (LMBR) program. In an interview with Piccoli, the problems of addressing project management capability for the LMBR and other large ICT software projects were discussed.

Interviewer: Does the public sector have project management capability for these large ICT software projects?

Adrian Piccoli (AP): I never saw a lack of trying, I never saw they took it less seriously, I just do not know [whether] they have the capacity to get the people they need … [W]hat does KPMG pay for an IT guru? More than $300,000, which is more than the maximum salary band for an IT guru in the public sector.

Interviewer: How can the public sector build and maintain these skills internally, particularly when even large private firms may not have these people sitting in the organisation?

AP: [T]hey [have] tried to get people, with varying degrees of success. People came in and people went out. It just got too much. It does not just apply to IT; the head of finance is a deputy secretary on a $300,000 salary running a $12 billion organisation. Is it any wonder they cannot give you an accurate monthly finance report at the right time? They try their best but … the constraints of the public service are part of the reason this does not happen … [I]f you are the CEO of Health and [are] getting paid $350,000, people who run Snowy Hydro get paid more than that. Hospitals have bigger budgets than Snowy Hydro … [T]his is a genuine problem … [I]f you want these public sector organisations to run like businesses, you have to pay to compete.

Interviewer: Do you think the public sector will ever resolve this limitation?

AP: It is a genuine question. You are asking the CFO [chief financial officer] of an organisation to look after a $12 billion budget and you are offering $350,000, so she/he is not in it for the money. They are absolutely vulnerable to public scrutiny … [T]his goes to that capacity issue. What capacity do you have to manage a big IT project like that when you cannot compete to get resources, when you are competing against whoever, such as [software company] SAP, to get the same resource? They have lots of money and of course they are going to do you over in negotiations.

This highlights the limitations across roles—of which project management is one—in the public sector being able to compete with private sector remuneration rates. The size and complexity of many public sector organisations and their projects are greater than many large private sector organisations that offer greater remuneration without the political complexities.

In an interesting anomaly, there was one exception to this organisational issue, and that was in the Northern Territory. The Northern Territory interviewees claimed that its size and geographic location have resulted in ongoing difficulties in attracting skilled project management staff, so the usual approach is to source from outside the territory, using incentives. This has led to the Northern Territory paying its skilled project management staff rates above those in other states or, as a senior assurance officer (Person AQ, NT) said, these people can 'simply name their price'.

However, a private sector executive in the territory (Person AW) argued that while this strategy may initially attract resources, it has failed to address the long-term retention of those skills. Money is attractive in the short term, but gaining commitment to stay in the Northern Territory is more difficult; hence capability and capacity ebb and flow. To address this, the NT Government has a program called the 'Welcome to the Territory Incentives' that provides monetary rewards for relocation to the territory: A\$7,000 initially and another A\$7,000 after five years (Department of Tourism, Industry and Trade 2018). ICT project managers and staff are in the highest priority skillsets.

In summary, interviewees believe the public sector does not prioritise, support, or fund the development of project management as a core organisational discipline and has a focus on a role rather than the discipline. In addition, it is left to agencies to independently address the issue, leading to disparities within and between jurisdictions. There is a reliance on skilled external staff, but even then, capability and capacity are hard to obtain.

Methodology: What role do methodologies play in maturity?

The widespread implementation of project management methodologies or practices such as PRINCE2 across the Australian and New Zealand public sectors was surprisingly topical, with some interviewees becoming agitated about the issue.

The interviewees understood PRINCE2 to be a series of processes or steps that a project should have so that certain products/artefacts are progressively delivered. The common view was that the implementation of PRINCE2 has led to an organisational uplift of project management capability. However, the elite interviewees' argument was that PRINCE2 does not manage a project, with all its tasks, daily challenges, personal and vendor relationships, twists, and turns—all of what the discipline of project management encompasses—so there is no corresponding uplift in project management maturity. Some relevant vignettes are:

> [A]s soon as [someone says PRINCE2 says this or that] … those are warning signs … my alarm goes there, because that means someone is trying to hide behind a methodology. (Person E, Senior executive, NSW)

> We pay too much attention to methodology … [I]t is almost like we are paying lip-service rather than genuinely applying project management disciplines. (Person R, Senior ICT assurance, NZ)

> [S]ometimes people get too caught up on the methodology as opposed to the basics—basics meaning, how do you put the controls in place to monitor and deliver a project as opposed to following PRINCE2? (Person AF, Senior ICT assurance, Vic.)

> [P]eople do not do it well; they do not know how to do project management. And the number of people who will tell you that they are PRINCE2 trained, well, PRINCE2 training has a lot to answer for. (Person J, Program director, NZ)

Maintaining these methodologies, it was argued, requires specific expertise. An APS program director (Person F) said their jurisdiction lacks expertise in how best to apply PRINCE2 to large complex ICT projects. A senior executive (Person E, NSW) argued that while PRINCE2 is supposedly mandatory in New South Wales to apply consistency, this is not the reality and there is no consistency across projects. They said PRINCE2 practitioners trained even within the same organisation would 'apply the methodology in a very different way': 'I'm saying it [the methodology] is irrelevant.'

The use of gateway reviews also came in for criticism as a method for addressing project management maturity. Like the comments on PRINCE2, the argument was clear: gateway reviews are an assurance process that can be valuable, but cannot provide the organisation with project management maturity on their own. A senior project manager (Person AB, APS) with extensive experience in APS projects, when asked about gateway reviews and their effectiveness in addressing project management maturity, put their head in their hands, sighed, waved their hands, and, through gritted teeth, answered: 'No. Bloody gateway reviews.'

In summary, the argument is that methodologies alone cannot uplift project management capability; they do, however, assist in project assurance.

Large projects: How have organisations addressed project management capability for large ICT software projects?

The elite interviewees' perspective on the selection of the project or program manager/director for a large ICT software project was clear and consistent. Projects such as payroll implementations are generational, occurring once every 10 or 15 years. Therefore, these projects have particular skillsets, gained not only from formal training and qualifications but also from vast experience, including in vendor management. An IQA (Person C, NSW) with decades of experience in providing an assurance role for large government projects suggested:

> [M]ost agencies will only ever do those [large projects] once every 10 years. So, when they are about to start it, who inside the agency has any experience in running a project like that? Probably no one. So … the smart agencies go and get an experienced contractor, or some heavy-hitting program director who has done it before.

No public sector interviewees believed their organisation had these skills inhouse and, revealingly, none believed they should have them. It was argued that because these are specialised skills, what is this person to do in the 10 to 15 years between each project if they are employed inhouse? Supporting this view, a senior executive (Person AM, NT) said they had recently hired an external resource for a large new project as they 'could not sustain a person like that in a normal office environment'.

A CIO (Person AH, Vic.) argued that it is not practical to have such resources inhouse, as retention becomes a problem. They defended this argument by stating that 'the idea you could spend years training people to be ready for something that might happen in two or three years' time is good in theory but unlikely to happen in practice. The very people you have invested in are unlikely to still be there'.

A senior ICT assurance officer (Person Q, NZ) said it was not only impractical to have such a resource inhouse, it was also delusional: '[F]or transformational programs, if you think that you are going to be able to develop and retain people inhouse, and that they are going to sit around waiting for a once-in-15-year project, you are absolutely dreaming.'

The common argument was that these skills should be purchased externally when required. An APS program director (Person F) argued that the Australian Public Service would 'never be big enough to have the skills required' and therefore needed to look externally for such expertise. They also posited that this was not an approach specific to the public sector and that many large private firms follow the same approach for the same reasons.

It was also argued that even with the many commonalities of the project management discipline, not all large ICT software projects are the same and, depending on the solution, the experience and skills required may differ. Therefore, buying in experience specialised to the project is an advantage over any notion of having these skills inhouse. As an example, it was argued that the project management skills and experience required for an SAP payroll replacement differ from those for an Oracle financial solution and, by buying capability, there is the advantage of purchasing capability targeted at the solution. Additionally, buying in a resource with up-to-date skills removes the need for the organisation to maintain the currency of those skills internally. A senior executive (Person E, NSW) with extensive experience in large ICT projects supported these perspectives: '[T]hat is why you do not deal with that; you buy that experience.'

However, there was also a common belief that this approach is not always applied. Examples were cited in the interviews of an agency continuing to appoint an internal resource even though that person was deemed to lack the capability, and this was done despite the risk being acknowledged. A CIO (Person AK, Vic.) expressed the view of many interviewees about this approach: 'Giving someone internally an opportunity can set the project, and that person, up for failure.'

It was claimed this was done largely as a cost-saving measure, as the purchasing of specialised skillsets and expertise is expensive, and agencies have baulked at the cost, resulting in the use of internal resources or cheaper external options, both of which ignore the capability requirement and represent a false economy. The cost of failure is severe compared with the cost of a capable project manager. These perspectives were supported by an IQA (Person C, NSW), who stated that in their experience, 'those guys and girls cost money and agencies can baulk at paying that sort of money for people ... [They then] try to keep those roles internally and get into trouble.'

New Zealand interviewees agreed this remains an issue, with senior executives and government not supporting the engagement of a suitable and capable resource, which one CIO (Person O, NZ) posited was out of fear that the media will find out the cost and 'splash it across the front page of a paper'.

Instead, they claimed, projects are forced to engage a cheaper, less capable option, immediately endangering the outcome, with executives and politicians simply not understanding the cost benefit that capable resources bring to a project. Another CIO (Person L, NZ) added that the willingness to pay can 'depend on the mindset of the organisation and leadership' at the time and reflects their understanding of the importance of these skills.

The consensus from the elite interviewees is that it is a simple fact that for large complex ICT software projects the project management team will be a mixture of external and internal capability and capacity. A senior executive (Person BL, Tas.) said that all projects with which they had been involved had a mixture of internally and externally sourced staff.

Another senior executive (Person AD, APS) claimed this was just the 'nature' of these projects and there would always be a need to supplement internal resources with those from outside. Two CIOs (Person AI, Vic., & Person S, NZ) claimed their agencies concentrated on developing and maintaining capability to support core business processes and always brought in external resources for larger projects. Private sector elite interviewees also used this sort of blended process; however, unlike the public sector interviewees, they stressed the importance of internal project management resources retaining responsibility and accountability for the project and typically filling the project/program manager role internally. David Boyle, a former CIO of the Commonwealth and National Australia banks, described his approach:

> I prefer to put a blended team together of existing people who know the existing environment and augment them with skills and capabilities around the targeted [system] ... But, invariably, I like it to be led by somebody who [is not going to] pick up stumps and leave at the end of a so-called delivery day.

Several reasons were given for the use of a blended team, the first of which is capacity, as large projects often require a major capacity boost across a wide range of tasks. Second is the capability to provide the specialised project management discipline, with one program director (Person F, APS) saying that this is an acknowledgement of the different capabilities required for 'project and program expertise'. The model successfully employed by

Michael Carmody for the ATO change program (see Box 3.1) is an example of an agency realising it had neither the capability nor the capacity to undertake the project and forming a blended team to fill the gaps.

As was the case in the chapter on sponsors, jurisdictional size was raised as an issue. Across all jurisdictions there were perspectives that finding a suitably qualified and experienced external project or program manager within the jurisdiction may not be possible and the only option is to source from another state or even internationally. This was argued as another factor in why any notion that the sector should have this capability inhouse is flawed. Jurisdictional size could also impact the ability to obtain the required project management capability and capacity to fill the roles on large ICT projects. The New Zealand interviewees confirmed that all agencies there struggle to find the required capability and capacity. Because Wellington is a small city with heavy demand, New Zealand Government agencies must fight for the same resources. One undesired outcome of this reduced talent pool is that agencies end up with less-than-capable project management capacity. New Zealand agency interviewees said that to counter this, once they find a good contract resource, they try to keep them from other agencies. One CIO (Person W, NZ) also claimed that, given this demand for contractors, it is extremely hard to attract people to a full-time permanent position, which reinforces the need to rely on contract staff.

This is an interesting conundrum; regardless of jurisdictional size, a large ICT software project will have the same demands, complexities, and resource requirements wherever it is undertaken. The Northern Territory is the jurisdiction with the smallest population, of 245,000 people (DTF 2022); Darwin is remote from all other major centres and, as identified earlier, attracting the required project management capability and capacity to the territory is a major challenge. The impacts of this on planning for large ICT projects in the Northern Territory is discussed further in Chapter 5. The Tasmanian interviewees said this was also an issue for them, with a senior executive (Person BM, Tas.) claiming they constantly encountered capability and capacity constraints, which was why large organisations such as Deloitte were engaged to meet requirements.

When asked whether there are solutions to this problem, there were lots of shoulder shrugs, although a small number of interviewees suggested an internal or cross-jurisdictional 'talent pool' is a viable option. For the Australian Public Service, the notion of an internal jurisdictional capability pool was not supported by one CIO (Person A, APS), who argued that given this capability was lacking service-wide, looking to gain expertise from another APS agency was not an option. A CIO (Person O, NZ) with previous jurisdiction-wide responsibilities argued that any notion of public sector agencies building 'a cadre' of highly skilled project managers would not work well in Australia or New Zealand. They suggested that none of the jurisdictions across either country would be large enough individually to warrant such an effort, nor was there a culture of collaboration across or even within jurisdictions. Person AA (Senior ICT auditor, NSW) is uniquely placed to provide a perspective on this issue (see Box 4.2).

Box 4.2 An ICT auditor's reflections: Scheduling delivery and repurposing project management capability

A NSW ICT auditor (Person AA) has extensive experience in auditing large government ICT software projects, which has provided the advantage of seeing many similar projects being run in the same jurisdiction. SAP financials has been implemented in several NSW agencies. While there are organisational differences in each agency, in essence, it is the same solution. Assuming these agencies need to do this at the same time or with some crossover, each must form its own team, finding the internal and external project management capability. This means they are competing for already limited resources and each team must go through its own learning curve.

As has been identified in the interviews, capability is uplifted by experience. Therefore, as projects progress with their own degrees of success, the team builds that experience of implementing SAP financials in a NSW Government agency. Person AA used an example of a successful implementation in one agency after which the team disbanded and the knowledge left. At the same time, a new project was starting and they recruited a different project management capability, who had to learn from scratch and in turn encountered many of the same issues as the previous project but had poorer outcomes.

Reflecting on this, Person AA posited that project management resources engaged for a project in one agency who successfully delivered that solution could be repurposed and moved on to the next. That obviously requires some asset replacement planning and scheduling within the jurisdiction; however, with foresight, experience and capability can be built on and retained, coordinating across the jurisdiction rather than agency by agency to establish an approach of 'doing the best you can with what is available'.

This thinking aligns with a proposal by Mayhew et al. (2013: 6) following research into the New Zealand public sector that the sector spends time building up capability for a project—'often at a painful cost'—and then lets them go, meaning organisational capability is not improved. They argue for the creation of a central New Zealand organisation to improve long-term capability.

Interestingly, this notion of retaining the services of a skilled and experienced project management capability for large ICT projects also found support from a very experienced and senior executive (Person AL) from a firm with vast experience in providing project management capability for large government ICT software projects. Person AL argued that one strategy to provide consistent and proven capability and experience for these types of projects is for government, whether jurisdictional or national, to create a contract pool, 'ring-fence them', and have them move between projects. The argument is that this maintains capability and an ongoing incentive to remain part of that pool. A New Zealand senior executive (Person K) argued that there is also a case for Australia and New Zealand to address this together and share resources. However, given earlier interviewee perspectives that cooperation and collaboration within jurisdictions is hard enough, the implementation, management, and maintenance of a cross-national/jurisdictional team would arguably add a whole new layer of complexity.

To solve these issues, a perspective raised in the sponsor chapter was also present in the project management capability interviews—that is, avoid doing large projects and think of other ways to deliver. A CIO (Person AH, Vic.) said that by undertaking smaller component-based or agile[4] project delivery, their organisation had been able to build project management capacity and capability, which had resulted in the successful delivery of multiple projects, with no failures. They classified this as 'compounded organisational learning' and used the example of a school savings program: when children save a dollar a month, at the end of 12 months they have $12 and have learnt the value of compound saving (learning), and are not required to put in $12 at the end of the year. If this is applied using several small, agile projects, rapidly completed using project teams and managers, the capability to deliver is compounded and capacity builds accordingly. It was argued that capability would be iteratively developed as would be awareness of the project management discipline and the agile approach in the organisation. An example of an agency successfully using agile delivery is provided in Box 4.3.

4　The PMI's website provides a definition of agile approaches: 'Agile approaches to project management aim for early, measurable ROI [return on investment] through defined, iterative delivery of product increments. They feature continuous involvement of the customer throughout the product development cycle' (available from: www.pmi.org/learning/featured-topics/agile).

> **Box 4.3 A successful agile experience in the Victorian public sector**
>
> This example is provided from a paper written by Dr Stephen Hodgkinson (2019), the CIO and Executive Director of the Business Technology and Information Management (BTIM) branch within the Victorian Department of Health and Human Services (DHHS).
>
> In 2014 in response to low IT project capabilities, poor project outcomes, internal frustrations with IT, and inadequacies in traditional project management and development methods, a different approach to project delivery was developed, called Platform + Agile. This was trialled on a new online system for social housing applications, and won industry awards. The second project, relating to family violence, was successfully delivered within nine months. Since these early successes, the approach has continued to evolve and has been applied to other DHHS projects such as the Victorian Health Incident Management System and the Personal Hardship Assistance Program. Dr Hodgkinson claims this has lessened the capability required for traditional 'large' projects by breaking the project into manageable components, enabling the successful delivery of more than 40 new business systems over three years. In addition, there is evidence of ongoing learning and capability development within the DHHS/BTIM as each project progresses.

The use of agile delivery is not restricted to Victoria. There is evidence from other jurisdictions, such as a senior assurance officer (Person AE, APS) who confirmed its 'use was growing' within their agency. A senior ICT executive (Person AD, APS) with jurisdiction-wide responsibilities said they review proposals for projects and look for evidence of alignment with digital strategies, such as agile delivery options. The other factor public sector interviewees claim is common to this approach is that an initiative is agency-driven and not the result of a jurisdiction-wide initiative, such as the Victorian examples cited earlier. There was also common agreement on the benefit of undertaking projects via agile delivery rather than as a single large project, helping to de-risk obtaining and retaining resources for large projects. Smaller, component-based projects, where the project management capability is largely inhouse, improve loyalty, interest, commitment, and retention (Person AH, CIO, Vic.).

In summary, the dominant perception was that project manager/director capability for large ICT projects does not exist internally within the public sector and it does not need to; it should be sourced externally. The project team requires a blend of internal and external resources to temporarily boost capability and capacity. Problems with acquiring and retaining resources exist in all jurisdictions. To negate these issues, component-based, agile delivery was suggested as an alternative.

The findings and their conceptual relationship

Interviewee perceptions are that the Australian and New Zealand public sectors do not have the project management capability to undertake large ICT software projects. It was argued that if the capability is not there, the project should not begin; hence, agencies should be assessed before commencement. While capability for the less complex smaller projects is better, this is not due to a coordinated jurisdictional focus. Capability varies within a jurisdiction as it is largely left to agencies or individuals within agencies to prioritise. Even for smaller projects, however, there is a heavy reliance on contract staff so that the permanence of that capability and capacity is always at risk. In addition, these strategies have largely concentrated on project manager capability rather than addressing the full suite of project management skills.

Second, it was perceived that politics and government policy have impacted, and will continue to impact, on the ability to address project management capability, particularly when there is a focus on capacity as a prime strategy in uplifting capability. Policies on permanent and contract staffing levels can change almost overnight, leaving capability initiatives unsupported and carefully established capability walking out the door.

Third, capable project management resources, particularly for large ICT projects, are in high demand but short supply, and are therefore expensive. The public sector is not willing or able to compete on price, leading to the engagement of less-capable resources who fit a price range or the use of internal resources. These cost-based decisions put the project at risk of failure, with the extraordinary financial and organisational costs of failure being ignored.

Fourth, a distinct perspective is that the public sector need not have the project management capability and capacity for large ICT software projects inhouse. These large projects come along only every 10 to 15 years. They require not only specific experience, but also a specific skillset, as well as a substantial boost in capacity for the duration of the project. To expect these skills to be available in numbers within an agency and the currency of those skills to be maintained during this period was described as 'crazy'. While agency project management staff form part of the project team, the required project management capacity and capability should be sourced externally for the duration of the project.

Last, and to put a slight damper on the preceding paragraph, interviewees across all jurisdictions said they have trouble meeting capability and capacity demands for large ICT software projects. The size and geographic location of jurisdictions were factors, particularly in smaller jurisdictions such as the Northern Territory. These problems are compounded by the issue of retention, as external resources tend to 'abandon ship' when a project gets tricky, leaving the project exposed.

Like the findings for the sponsor role, the perception is that uplifting project management capability across all disciplines is not an organisational priority as it is misunderstood by senior executives. This has meant executives fail to identify, target, support, and fund initiatives to address capability. They also fail to understand that project management is an integrated system of roles, skills, processes, and guidelines that collectively form capability. This has led to a tendency to concentrate on the role of the project manager at the expense of the others. Due to all these factors, there is an incorrect executive belief that skilled organisational staff can be 'rebadged' as project managers, which sets the person and the project up for failure. In summary, the executive leadership necessary to drive this change is missing and will remain so until senior executives recognise project management as a core organisational capability requirement.

There was a belief among interviewees that agencies are using the application of methodologies such as PRINCE2 as evidence of project management capability and maturity, which is naive, wrong, and further evidence of an organisational lack of awareness of the project management discipline. PRINCE2 and initiatives such as gateway reviews are assurance tools, not methods of improving project management capability across the diverse disciplines required. It was suggested that this is akin to an executive saying, 'Oh, we have a project manager, they will follow PRINCE2, and we will do a gateway review as well, so we have project management covered'!

In terms of entrepreneurship, it was argued that large ICT software projects are complex and high risk, even when they have substantial and specialised capability. These projects are dependent on external resources to meet the capability demands, at serious cost. Therefore, there is an argument to remove both the risk of large projects and the demands for extensive external capability and capacity by breaking them into smaller components/projects, using agile delivery and a reduced mix of inhouse and external resources. Capability would be continually improved with each deliverable, leading to progressive learning.

Given the similarities between many government projects, there were suggestions to form a 'talent pool' of resources within a jurisdiction, nationally, or internationally, creating a team with proven capability that can move from one project to the next. Such an initiative would require substantial cultural change in all jurisdictions.

There was a proposal that if jurisdictions planned for asset replacement, such as a financial system, a schedule could be developed that enabled the team to move from one project to another to retain capability. The perceived problem, again, was that this would require substantial cultural change and an improvement in portfolio planning processes.

There was evidence that within jurisdictions, agencies have not undertaken large ICT software projects in the traditional manner and instead have broken them into smaller component-based projects, delivered via an agile approach. These lessen the capability and capacity demands and risks of a large ICT software project and provide continuous learning benefits; however, this has only happened because of the agency of the initiating actor. For example, the change program in the Australian Taxation Office (see Box 3.1) was driven by the commissioner—someone with the volition to drive and support the initiative.

The conceptual findings are summarised in Table 4.1.

Table 4.1 Summary of the project management conceptual findings

Concept	Project management key findings
Capability and capacity	• The Australian and New Zealand public sectors do not have the capability to undertake large ICT software projects. • Agencies should be but are not assessing the capability to undertake projects before they are approved. • Capability to manage smaller, less complex projects is better than that for large projects. • Capability improvements are not the result of a coordinated jurisdictional change but are left to agencies to deal with independently. • Politics and government policy continue to negatively impact on long-term initiatives to uplift capability. • While there is evidence that agencies have resourced capability externally, they tend to put a priority on cost rather than the best resource. • The public sector should not have the project management capability and capacity for large ICT software projects inhouse for generational change projects; resources with the current skills must be engaged externally and blended with an internal team. • The challenge of meeting the capability and capacity issues for large projects is even more complicated in smaller and remote jurisdictions.
Leadership	• Uplifting project management capability across all disciplines is not an organisational priority. • There has been a concentration on increasing project manager numbers to the exclusion of addressing wider project management needs. • There is a belief that staff can be 'rebadged' as project managers.
Methodologies	• Methodologies such as PRINCE2 have been used as evidence of improved project management capability, but this is naive, wrong, and a further indication of the lack of understanding of the project management discipline. • These methodologies, while useful, are really assurance tools and not methods of improving overall organisational project management capability.
Entrepreneurship	• Due to the elevated risk and high capability demands of large ICT software projects, and the fact the capability does not exist in the public sector, a preferred approach is to break down large projects into less complex components to which capability is aligned. • Agencies within and across jurisdictions undertake similar projects (for example, a SAP financial implementation), leading to a proposal to form a talent pool of resources to move between projects; this would be dependent on cultural change and coordinated cross-jurisdiction planning.
Agency	• Agencies have begun to look at alternatives to planning a single large project, moving to component-based delivery methods such as agile. However, this largely occurs through the entrepreneurship of an actor with the agency to do so, and not as a change in the institutional governance framework.

Source: Compiled by author.

Conclusion

Like the findings in Chapter 3 on sponsors, there was much commonality in perspectives across the Australian and New Zealand public sectors, with no wild divergences.

These findings can be compared with key points in the literature review (see Table 4.2). While this is a simplified summary, it does highlight a disconnect between what the literature argues is good governance for project management and the perceptions of the elite interviewees on the effectiveness of institutional governance for project management in the Australian and New Zealand public sectors.

Table 4.2 Comparison of literature review and findings

Literature review (Chapter 2): Key points	Project management findings
Organisational project management capability requires the organisation to understand what 'project management-related practices, knowledge, skills, tools, and techniques have proven consistently to be useful'. This includes processes to compare against industry practices, the identification of capabilities, and 'the establishment of a roadmap for achieving improvements specific to the needs of the organisation' (PMI 2013b).	The public sector does not understand the 'discipline' of project management and its integration within the organisation. An example is a focus on 'project managers' that excludes the framework in which they operate.
Organisational project management requires the evaluation and alignment of initiatives to 'a set of programs and/or projects that yield the appropriate value decisions and benefits for the organisation'. These are then delivered via a series of projects or programs through to the realisation of the benefits (PMI 2013b).	The public sector is poor at portfolio management, with large projects typically resulting from an 'urgent' need, such as to replace an ageing payroll solution.
Organisations mature in project management can be classified as project-based organisations (PBOs) (Miterev et al. 2017) in which the organisation 'makes the strategic decision to adopt project, program and project portfolio management as business processes to manage its work'. PBOs therefore treat project management as a 'strategic competency' (Green 2005). Developing and improving project management capability are therefore priorities of senior management in these organisations (Kwak et al. 2015).	Public sector organisations cannot be classified as PBOs, nor is there an organisational push to address this. Large ICT projects are simply not the core skill or requirement of these organisations.

Literature review (Chapter 2): Key points	Project management findings
Even organisations with highly developed project management capability struggle to deliver large projects successfully (Shenhar & Dvir 2007), due to their complexity (Aucoin 2007: 132).	The public sector continues with large complex projects, the problems of which are compounded by a lack of project management capability.
Project management should adopt a more adaptive and agile approach to address the complexity issue (Fowler 2005; Hass 2008).	The public sector should stop undertaking large projects as traditionally planned, although this is not supported within institutional frameworks.

Source: Compiled by author.

5

Forecasting: A 'ridiculous nonsense of a process'

I think everybody knows how to game the system.
(Person A, CIO, APS)

Introduction

In Chapter 2, it was claimed that forecasting is the most critical stage in a project (Flyvbjerg 2013) as it sets a baseline for the project's approach and assessment. A forecast is a prediction 'of what will happen based on evidence or assumptions' (AIPM 2021). This is important, as forecasting, while inevitably involving time and cost (Batselier & Vanhoucke 2017), has many other underlying factors to consider, including complexity, capability demands, capacity constraints, and the organisational and political environments. Forecasting can, and arguably should, also look at previous projects that are similar in nature, complexity, and environment. For example, if Organisation A took five years and $50 million to implement an SAP payroll that is similar in size, structure, and culture to what Organisation B wants, why does Organisation B believe it can complete an SAP implementation for less? What is different to justify this? This is what Flyvbjerg (2008) calls taking an outside view to reduce internal optimism—in effect, a reality check.

Forecasting is not an exact science, but it is an essential aspect of project management and is meant to lessen uncertainty. Forecasts also have a direct influence on project approvals as the basis of the assessment of their viability. The issue for an organisation is: What if the forecast is misleading? Would the project have been approved and funded if the cost and time frame were greater than the forecast?

Discussions about the forecasting discipline with the elite interviewees were the most animated; it was a hot topic. The analysis of all part one elite interviews (see 'The puzzle' section, Chapter 1: Table 1.1) and vignettes from cited interviewees suggest there is a perception that the forecasting governance via the institutional framework is ineffective. The overwhelming perception is that the public sector is forced to provide forecasts that arguably everyone knows are inaccurate, as accuracy is an impossibility, but they are done anyway and, despite this knowledge, projects are approved and irrelevant benchmarks established.

There is a false sense of security or even a sense of irony in this process: it is necessary to provide the minister or senior executives with some surety and to prevent projects being given a 'blank cheque'. It was argued, however, that initial forecasts provide uncertainty, not surety, and that projects, however they are funded, are never given carte blanche. Continued and additional funding are always subject to organisational approval, and organisational and political influences.

The interviewees argued for an end to large ICT projects and the 'nonsense' process of preparing full upfront forecasts, recommending instead that the body of work be broken into manageable components, reviewed and forecast progressively, and funded accordingly. The preferred approach was via agile delivery; however, frameworks and culture would need to change to support this. Without this change, individuals are acting independently.

Interviewees also cited the failure to treat ICT solutions as assets, fund their maintenance, and plan for their replacement as prime reasons for the continuing need to undertake large projects, as action is never taken until replacement becomes 'urgent'. Spending money on ICT asset maintenance can be politically and publicly unpopular, which presents a dilemma.

To support the findings, this chapter details the elite interviewees' perspectives on the governance of the forecasting discipline and roles across the New Zealand and Australian public sectors. The interview questions were aligned with five categories identified in the literature review (see Figure 5.1):

- Capability: Do the sectors have capable organisational resources and analytical practices to undertake the forecasting? Is the capability to undertake the task assessed before forecasting?

- Forecasting framework: How effective are the institutional frameworks that provide the guidance, processes, and rules for preparing and approving the forecasts?

- Organisational factors: Are the internal and external organisational factors that could impact on a project being considered when forecasting?

- Financial management: Do the organisation's financial maturity and financial frameworks have a direct influence on how projects are funded, and thereby on the preparation of forecasts? Does this aid or hinder the forecasting process?

- Large project dilemmas: The literature indicates that most large projects will be judged as failures when assessed against original forecasts. Therefore, there is a trend away from planning and forecasting such projects in the traditional manner. How is the public sector addressing the planning of large ICT software projects and are they supported by the frameworks in these initiatives?

For each category, the elite interviewees' perspectives are analysed and supported by vignettes. These findings are summarised and aligned with the theoretical concepts, followed by a short conclusion.

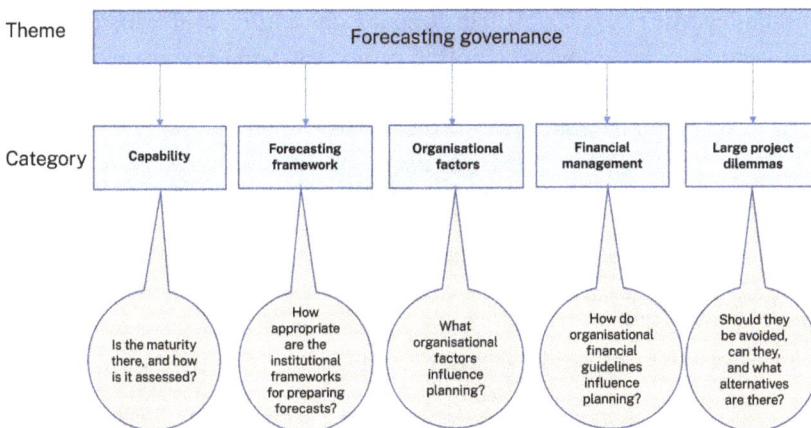

Figure 5.1 Categories for forecasting analysis
Source: Created by author.

The elite interviews

Capability: Is the maturity there and how is it assessed?

All interviewees believed the Australian and New Zealand public sectors do not have the analytical capability to prepare meaningful forecasts for large ICT software projects. A common response to whether this capability existed was that of a CIO (Person G, APS), who simply said 'no'; alternatively, a rating was provided, such as that by another CIO (Person L, NZ), who said that forecasting was done 'very badly'. Also evident from the interviewees was a perception that capability in project financial and contract management has a major influence on overall forecasting capability. Unfortunately, and adding to the risk of these projects, the capability in these disciplines is lacking.

Financial management influences how costs are forecast and approved. There is a perception that the financial management capability to support the forecasting of large ICT projects is a unique skillset and requires alternative guidelines to those for normal operational financial management—and this is what is lacking. It was argued that finance executives skilled in normal public sector financial management do not understand how large ICT projects work and are managed and that the roles are not transferrable. A senior partner (Person AL) in a major consulting firm with extensive involvement in large government ICT projects argued that the public sector 'cannot just take someone who is a finance manager in government and is used to yearly budgets and … put them into a program and expect success … [Y]ou need that project financial management expertise alongside project execution.'

This lack of financial management capability and its impact on large ICT software project forecasting were also raised by former NSW education minister Adrian Piccoli, who argued that even for operational financial management, the capability is lacking, citing the following example:

> When I became the minister, one of the KPIs [key performance indicators] was that we had to stay within our budget—fair enough. I said [to the agency] every month we needed an update; there is no good finding out in May that we are a billion dollars in the red, so they did. But every month it was not particularly accurate, it was always sort of a best guess. So [they were] very poor systems, so how can you make decisions on this data?

If the capability does not exist for standard operational financial management and reporting, the unique challenges of large ICT project financial management create another gap altogether. Financial management is discussed in greater detail later in this section.

Contract management can have a critical impact on forecasts. A senior executive (Person E, NSW) stressed the importance of the contract at the initiation stage as it establishes the relationship, roles and responsibilities, deliverables, schedule, and costs for the project's duration, and if it is wrong, 'you have a major problem'. A CIO (Person G, APS) agreed that the initial contract negotiation is critical to the project, as this is when expectations are set between the project and the vendor. Another CIO (Person L, NZ) likened the contract between the agency and the vendor to a 'recipe' in which each knows what to do at what time and for how long. However, the elite interviewees' views on this critical capability were consistently negative, with one CIO (Person AI, Vic.) arguing that it is yet another critical skill that is missing.

It was argued that this is the case even for large agencies with many commercial arrangements, with a senior executive (Person E, NSW) suggesting they should have 'absolute experts', but 'they do not'. A senior ICT assurance officer (Person AD, APS) said it is a capability for which 'there is room for improvement'. There is a perception that this gap puts agencies and/or projects at a disadvantage to vendors at the contract negotiation stage. From a vendor's perspective, a senior partner (Person AL) in a large consulting firm said that contract management capability and focus are always a priority for their firm when involved in large government projects, and it is important for there to be a 'corresponding relationship' within the agency/project, but this is not always the case.

There was evidence that agencies have acknowledged this gap and taken steps to address it, largely with a mixture of central agency involvement and external expertise. The Northern Territory uses interstate legal experts for complex projects (Person AN, Senior executive). A New Zealand senior assurance officer (Person Q) stated that a pool of specialists exists for agencies to embed within a project, while another option is for the project to recruit a commercial manager, which they claim 'had worked well in the past'. In New South Wales, a senior ICT assurance officer (Person Z) said the procurement process is subject to a stage gate review by a panel of experts.

Regardless of these approaches, there was a perception that the agency or project should retain substantial contract management responsibilities, such as in the Australian Public Service, where a senior ICT assurance officer (Person AD) confirmed contract negotiation is an agency/project responsibility. Similarly, two Victorian senior ICT assurance officers (Persons AF & AG) said that while their unit provides support at various stages, it is up to the agency/project to undertake and manage the contract process.

Another common perception is that the default position taken by agencies/ projects during contract negotiations is not a focus on a collaborative 'win-win' outcome, but a more aggressive stance in which it is seen as a win if they can 'screw' the vendor. A CIO (Person O, NZ) argued that this reflects a government mindset that vendors are 'bad' and 'are always trying to put one over on us', which ultimately negatively impacts the project.

Implicit in all this is the cost of the contract and its relationship to the project's forecast. The interviewees argued that predicting the future for long-term projects is an impossibility as there are so many unknowns, yet when long-term contracts are negotiated at the same time, the same logic applies, so immediately a major cost component is unclear. Following a similar theme, it was argued that this commercial uncertainty and risk could be reduced by not undertaking large projects. A senior ICT assurance officer (Person R, NZ) argued that iterative delivery, with contracts to match, enables each project to forecast, measure outcomes, and progress with less complexity.

As with both the sponsor and the project management capability findings, interviewees were unaware of any requirement to undertake an assessment of the organisation's capability to plan and forecast for a large ICT software project. David Boyle, former CIO with the Commonwealth and National Australia banks, said the first step in forecasting is always to undertake an analysis of the organisational capability to prepare a forecast and manage such a project. If that capability is not there organisationally, the recommendation should be that the project does not proceed as a large complex undertaking. If the project were to proceed, other planning and delivery approaches would need to be investigated to reduce risk.

In summary, the dominant perspective is that forecasting capability does not exist for large ICT software projects, nor is this assessed before project initiation. This is not aided by the public sector also lacking the required project financial and contract management skills.

Forecasting framework: How appropriate are the institutional frameworks for preparing forecasts?

All jurisdictions have planning guidelines for large ICT software projects within their institutional framework, a commonality of which is that an upfront forecast for the entire project, including cost, time, and so on, is a requirement. The interviewees believed this was why so many large projects were assessed as failures, and claimed that the process was not appropriate for large ICT software projects.

A senior ICT auditor (Person H, NSW) argued that the current guidelines force projects to plan 'too big', with the resulting risk and uncertainty. A CIO (Person AH, Vic.) argued that requiring people to plan for a big IT project is a major failing as there is an assumption or expectation that it is possible to define something of great complexity in detail at the start and at some time in the future it will be correct. This perspective found support with a senior ICT assurance officer (Person T, NZ), who agreed that it is not feasible to plan for large ICT projects that forecast 'five years into the future'. They clarified that this does not mean you cannot have a five-year vision, but doing a single detailed and accurate one-off forecast upfront is unrealistic.

The political factor was used to defend the requirement for a full upfront forecast: 'We have to do it this way as that is what the minister requires; anything else is too abstract.' To assess this perspective, Adrian Piccoli was asked (Piccoli, Pers. comm., 22 June 2020) whether he would require a full upfront estimate for a large ICT software project. His answer was 'yes', because of his ultimate accountability:

> Ministers want greater certainty over something like an ICT upgrade that are notoriously expensive—i.e. if something goes wrong or it is a massive cost, it is the minister who cops it, not the public servants. So, yes, I would have wanted to know what it would cost. I also cannot imagine that any organisation would just provide a blank cheque for an ICT upgrade.

There was a perception among interviewees that this requirement has a negative influence on the relevance of the forecast: because actors are aware of the financial guidelines and what is required to have a project approved, they deliberately under or overestimate. Actors are also aware of financial limits in the approval process. A senior executive (Person E, NSW) argued that the process leads to 'people just playing with numbers'.

A CIO (Person AI, Vic.) said it led to people 'sandbagging' their estimates, while a program director (Person J, NZ) had a similar perspective, arguing that people 'game around the margins, particularly when there is a boundary'.

An IQA (Person C, NSW) argued that this was because if the true time and cost of the project were known upfront, 'the project may never have started'.

Finally, a CIO (Person A, APS) argued that the forecasting requirement is being exploited to document an outcome that is acceptable rather than realistic, saying: 'I think everybody knows how to game the system ... [T]hey know if they go over a certain money amount, they will incur more scrutiny, so they limit themselves and they know once they are 90 per cent of the way through, people will be unlikely to stop it.'

As another CIO (Person L, NZ) argued, these factors lead to a forecast that is forced to meet a figure, rather than being an outcome calculated on project tasks. This can also lead to some 'culling' of project costs. Paul Barratt, former secretary of the Australian departments of Primary Industries and Energy and of Defence, cited an example where, at the behest of the minister, the forecast for a multi-billion-dollar project was arbitrarily reduced as 'Cabinet would not accept a larger figure'. A senior ICT auditor (Person AA, NSW) cited an example in which to meet monetary limits, the project's risk budget was simply reduced; there was no reduction in scope or risk, nothing changed other than an arbitrary reduction in dollars to bring it within a limit. A senior executive (Person E, NSW) cited an example of a project that did not include the substantial cost of the hardware necessary to support the software because excluding it made the business case more palatable. Of course, the need remained and had to be funded from somewhere. A senior project manager (Person P, NZ) cited an example of a decision to remove the replacement cost of internal staff required for a project to reduce it to within funding limits. The problem of course was that those resources were still required, as was the cost; they were simply now undocumented and unfunded. Person P concluded: '[W]e write it [the forecast] in a way that will get us the money.'

It was also argued that the forecast requirement leads to deliberate overestimation—a view common across jurisdictions—because at the planning stage you do not know the total cost with any accuracy, but you know the project will be assessed against it. There is therefore a tendency to add a contingency. A CIO (Person AH, Vic.) said:

[T]he way I think about that is if you ask me how much something that is ill-defined will cost, I will give you a very big number because I do not want to trap myself by not having enough money, because I know that you will criticise me for overrunning the budget. So therefore, you have trapped me into a game … where I have all the incentives on me to overinflate all of the estimates. If I think I could do it for $10 million, I will ask for $50 million. That would be fine if I then had a series of motivations to deliver at $10 million and give you back the $40 million, but the problem is, as soon as everyone knows it is a $50 million project, because it is published in the budget papers, everyone manages it as if it was a $50 million project, even if it could have been delivered for $2 million. So, it is a ridiculous nonsense of a process.

Other interviewees, such as a senior ICT auditor (Person H, NSW), argued that the 'one-off' funding process contributes to the view that one should 'get the money now or you may not get it later'.

It is difficult not to consider this under or overestimation as anything other than deception, yet despite the above vignettes, this was not the general perception of most interviewees, who took a kinder view. A senior ICT auditor (Person AA, NSW) argued that these are 'good people' and 'they want to do the right thing'; they place accountability on the framework that forces people down this path. This was a view supported by a CIO (Person L, NZ), who claimed the framework 'encourages optimism'. However, a senior project manager (Person N, NZ) argued that this optimism meets a rapid reality check once the project starts, leading to a realisation of 'my god, how did we end up in such a terrible space?'.

The literature and the data from the elite interviews indicate that delusional optimism is almost a natural reaction when so much is unknown, and there is then eternal optimism that 'we can do it'. Citing more than 20 years of experience on large government ICT software projects, an IQA (Person C, NSW) argued that this has always been the case. Regardless of how many times people have done it before, they 'always come up with a time less than it will take, and always come up with a cost of less than it will cost'.

A CIO (Person G, APS) argued that in preparing forecasts people are 'overly optimistic, ill-informed, or not informed, really, just [going on] a gut instinct'.

I was challenged by several interviewees about overoptimism, as they argued it is important to be enthusiastic and optimistic. However, as a senior executive (Person BM, Tas.) noted, the problem is when optimism loses touch with the reality of the task ahead.

The interviewees were asked whether they utilised a specific method when preparing forecasts. Two senior ICT assurance officers (Person Z, NSW, & Person AE, APS) and a CIO (Person G, NZ) argued that there is no jurisdictional standard for preparing forecasts, with these largely developed independently within agencies. A senior project manager (Person N, NZ) claimed that, in the absence of any formal jurisdictional method, the default is 'past experience'. Part of the problem with this approach, according to a senior ICT assurance officer (Person T, NZ), is a dependency on such 'experience' when it is not widespread: 'I have been doing this for 17 years in the public sector, we just do not have enough experienced people.'

A senior executive (Person B, NSW), who was involved in the planning and forecasting for a major human resources (HR) replacement program, claimed that the process is not 'sophisticated' and is undertaken to provide a figure within a time frame rather than investigating all aspects before making an estimation. One senior project manager (Person M, NZ) said they generally utilise 'brainstorming' sessions, while another (Person P, NZ) claimed that when forecasting ICT projects, agencies are simply 'left on their own' to work out how to do it.

Interviewees claimed that where vendors were involved, their propriety tools were utilised; however, there was also some evidence that agencies/projects had utilised various industry standard forecasting methods. These included quantitative risk analysis[1] (Person R, Senior ICT assurance, NZ), investment logic mapping[2] (Person P, Senior project manager, NZ), and the Monte Carlo[3] simulation method (Person O, CIO, NZ). Tempering

---

1   According to Meyer (2015), there are 'three risk elements that concern project management: Schedule—will the project be completed within the planned time frame? Cost—will the project be completed within the allocated budget? Performance—will the output from the project satisfy the business and technical goals of the project? Where possible, these risks should be quantified to enable the project team to develop effective mitigation strategies for the risks, or to include appropriate contingencies in the project estimate.'
2   'Investment Logic Mapping (ILM) is a technique to ensure that robust discussion and thinking is done up-front, resulting in a sound problem definition, before solutions are identified and before any investment decision is made' (The Treasury 2021).
3   'Monte Carlo simulations are used to model the probability of different outcomes in a process that cannot easily be predicted due to the intervention of random variables. It is a technique used to understand the impact of risk and uncertainty in prediction and forecasting models' (Kenton 2022).

this, a CIO (Person S, NZ) argued that effective use of these methods required extensive experience and represented another missing capability. Additionally, a senior executive (Person E, NSW) claimed these methods commonly require past metrics to be useful, but these have not been kept, so in effect 'nobody even knows if they have been getting it wrong for the past 10 years'.

A CIO (Person AH, Vic.) argued that formalised forecasting methods in ICT have 'never worked' as there are too many organisational factors that vary in cost and complexity, so reference class forecasting (RCF) is unsuitable. Supporting this perspective, a senior ICT assurance officer (Person AF, Vic.) argued that the use of RCF on large ICT projects is impractical because of the difficulty of identifying similar projects given these organisational variances.

There was one consistently expressed perspective: regardless of the forecasting method employed, it remains an inaccurate science and is influenced by individual perceptions, organisational factors, and the data entered, meaning the models can be played to create a figure (Person G, CIO, APS). For a final word on the application and suitability of forecasting methods, Ofer Zwikael, academic and Associate Editor of the *International Journal of Project Management*, claims there is no common agreement on the effectiveness of methods and tools, nor is there sufficient evidence to support their effectiveness. Zwikael concludes that, given the effort required, 'for governments to take this on in earnest, they will need evidence that it actually will provide benefit'.

The interviewees were asked whether they sought collaboration when planning, either internally or externally. The prevalent response was that collaboration is uncommon and impeded by competitiveness between jurisdictional agencies. Attempts by Tasmania to collaborate with larger jurisdictions such as New South Wales were resisted and the latter acted in an elitist 'big brother' manner (Person BM, Senior executive); as a result, Tasmania tended to liaise with other small jurisdictions. A senior project manager (Person AB, APS) described collaboration within the Australian Public Service as almost non-existent and said the APS is 'fractured and becoming more fractured'. They cited an example of where they thought their project team was being proactive by approaching another APS team beginning a similar project and offering to help, 'just to share experiences', but the response was 'they didn't want to know, [and] in effect, told us to piss off'.

The only regular, though independently initiated, cross-agency collaboration came from Tasmania and the Northern Territory, for which it was argued that due to their small size they tended to reach out to other agencies as a matter of course, with a Tasmanian senior executive (Person BM) saying this is something they always do in planning.

However, there is some evidence that limited collaboration external to the jurisdiction has been employed, generally with positive impacts. The Australian Taxation Office used collaboration with other tax offices internationally to good effect in planning (see Box 5.6). Stats NZ participates in a collaborative quartet with the Australian, UK, and Canadian statistics agencies in which they discuss issues with their respective censuses to aid future planning. For example, the Australian team shared experiences from the troubled 2016 Census that were then factored into New Zealand's planning for its next census (Persons X & Y, Senior executives, NZ). A Tasmanian senior executive (Person BM) cited a current project implementing a service-specific software for which they approached several other Australian agencies because of commonality to understand what went wrong and right and learn from that experience. They claimed these agencies were supportive, the lessons were applied in Tasmania to great effect, and it was planned to keep this collaboration permanently as a form of user group. All these initiatives, however, were the result of independent actions rather than a standard guideline or process.

The literature review highlighted the importance of seeking an 'outside' view to provide a comparison when preparing forecasts. The interviewees were asked whether this method was utilised. In the Australian Public Service, a senior ICT assurance officer (Person AD) said that one of the recommended Gershon (2008) reforms was the introduction of IT benchmarking, but this had fallen by the wayside. A senior project manager (Person P, NZ) said this was 'not normal' and '[w]e would be lucky to look outside the [agency], let alone outside the sector'.

A senior ICT assurance officer (Person T, NZ) claimed that the resistance to looking for external comparisons is due to a view that the public sector, or even an agency, is 'unique in some way', so there is no point looking elsewhere for comparisons as they will not be of benefit. They stated that this insular view 'takes away some ability to think outside and think about all of the potential value you can capture from other views'.

There is isolated evidence of individuals implementing such strategies. A senior project manager (Person M, NZ) stated they had engaged the services of a 'big five' company on a previous project to independently review estimates based on their experience with similar projects. A senior executive (Person BM, Tas.) said that as part of the planning process they went to an international event attended by many organisations using the same solution and met with many to discuss their experience, which was freely provided. These learnings were then incorporated effectively into the forecast. In New South Wales, a senior ICT assurance officer (Person Z) claimed there is intent to include an independent expert on a review panel—for example, for a payroll project, they will include a payroll specialist to provide an outside view.

Lessons learned (LL) reports are a common requirement, usually at the completion of projects, within both the Australian and the New Zealand public sectors. An LL report is also a PRINCE2 requirement to enable an organisation to learn and reduce the chances of these issues being repeated.[4] There is a history of these or similar reports being produced throughout the public sector, typically including lessons from the planning and forecasting processes. The elite interviewees were asked about their use of LL reports and their effectiveness for future projects. The common perspective was that they have not been effective, nor have they had a positive influence on forecasting.

There was a view that LL reports are prepared to comply with a methodology but there is no organisational process to put them to effective use in future projects. A CIO (Person AI, Vic.) said they were 'simply a tick in a box [or a] bureaucratic necessity'. They said even the agency that produces the report is unsure of 'what they are going to do with it'.

A CIO (Person AK, Vic.) argued that while there may be an intention to apply the lessons to planning for future projects, it simply 'does not happen'. They said the primary reasons for this were the lack of a single source of information and the fact the reports were seen as a project artefact rather than a tool for future projects.

---

4   'Lessons Report', *PRINCE2 Wiki*, available from: prince2.wiki/management-products/lessons-report/.

A senior ICT auditor (Person AA, NSW) 'was certain' that LL reports are not utilised in planning and no one makes a 'serious effort' to do so. They cited instances where a recent project's LL report was simply a replica of several previous ones, all highlighting the same issues. That view was supported by a senior executive (Person K, NZ), who stated that 'people do not look at past reviews', as evidenced by the same mistakes being made repeatedly. To support these perspectives, Table 5.1 highlights key lessons learned from planning and forecasting by three large New Zealand ICT projects spanning 17 years, in which there is much commonality.

Table 5.1 Comparison of New Zealand lessons learned over 17 years

INCIS lessons learned (Small 2000)	Novopay lessons learned (Jack & Wevers 2013)	JBMS lessons learned (Deloitte 2017: 11–12)
Assurance (pp. 147–48): The timeliness and applicability of assurance advice should be critically reviewed in total by monitoring agencies.	Assurance (p. 71): Did not encompass the entire project and was not provided continually.	Assurance: Plan and monitor the effectiveness of assurance.
Planning (pp. 55, 207): There was a lack of long- and short-term planning, and of an integrated technology and business change plan.	Lifecycle planning (pp. 39, 43): Neither the ministry nor the vendor recognised the impact of the organisational change as the project progressed and both were ill prepared for the expertise required. Sectoral readiness was poor.	Lifecycle planning: Plan how your methods, processes, skills, and resources must change as you move through program phases.
Contract (pp. 53, 140): A fixed or capped price contract for the whole of a large IT project should normally be avoided. The level of sophistication in the contract dictated a need for a formal, clear, and separate contract management function within New Zealand Police.	Commercials/contract (pp. 36, 67): The ministry did not have the commercial experience to manage the project. There was poor practice in the management of project schedules and deliverables.	Commercials: Agree on a contract that allows you to regularly monitor progress against business outcomes.
Requirements (pp. 29, 133–34): Business process re-engineering was critical to obtain INCIS benefits. The process was poorly managed and the budget did not reflect the cost of the changes.	Requirements (p. 37): The gathering of user requirements was poorly managed and there was no appreciation of the requirements.	Requirements: It is vital to fully understand the scope across every agency and agree on business outcomes and requirements before procuring, designing, and building the solution.

INCIS lessons learned (Small 2000)	Novopay lessons learned (Jack & Wevers 2013)	JBMS lessons learned (Deloitte 2017: 11–12)
Delivery (p. 80): The life of the project should normally be limited to one year. Any project planned to take longer must be in modules and, on the completion of each module, a decision can be made to modify technology to meet the position.	Delivery (p. 39): The decision to remove a staged rollout was ill advised, counter to good practice, and exposed users to serious risks and issues.	Delivery methodology: A phased delivery should be considered to effectively mitigate scope and delivery risks.
Leadership (p. 109): Projects are more likely to suffer if the chief executive does not oversee the governance and management of the project.	Leadership (p. 81): No evidence of the sustained and focused attention on the project from the ministry's leaders that would have been expected.	Leadership commitment: It is vital for strategic transformation efforts to be actively led from the top.

Notes: The Integrated National Crime Investigation System (INCIS) was a New Zealand Police project. Novopay is the name given to the project to implement a payroll solution and services for the New Zealand Ministry of Education and is the subject of a case study in Chapter 6. The Joint Border Management System (JBMS) was a project for the New Zealand Customs Service.

Source: Compiled by author.

Perspectives from the Australian Public Service are interesting as the APS has been the subject of two major reports into large projects—by Gershon (2008) and Shergold (2015)—with each making recommendations for how to improve planning. Hence, APS staff were asked about these reports and how they were factored into future planning. In summary, it seems they were ignored. A senior ICT assurance officer (Person AD, APS) argued that Gershon 'was done and dusted' and there was no monitoring of the reforms, and concluded that 'some might say we have actually gone backwards since'.

A CIO (Person AI, Vic.) with both public and private sector experience compared the use of LL reports in each. In their private sector role, LL reports are completed after a major incident, analysing it and identifying causes that must be addressed in future projects. Person AI said this was not their experience in the public sector. A senior partner (Person AL in a large consulting firm agreed that a team reviews all aspects of each project, including how effective their estimating tools were in the planning stage; these are adjusted accordingly and applied to future projects.

Another common perspective was that written LL reports are ineffective on their own, as there is a reliance on the project to independently locate and interpret the findings. A senior ICT assurance officer (Person AS, NT) argued that 'it is very difficult to put [experience] down on paper'.

Person AS stated they therefore tend to encourage verbal communication and explanation of the issues among the project teams. This was also the case in Tasmania, where a senior executive (Person BM) said experiences and learnings are typically verbally communicated as this provides for better interaction and interpretation. This approach was supported by a senior project manager (Person AA, APS), who argued that the true value of lessons learned is when that experience is passed on via verbal collaboration with the project team; however, this was tempered by their perspective that this practice is rare. However, there is evidence of initiatives to address this issue, with a senior ICT assurance officer (Person Z) from New South Wales stating that their unit, with jurisdiction-wide responsibilities, is 'harvesting this information' with the intent to eventually 'systemise' and share it.

For a final word on the failure of LL reports, former bank CIO David Boyle argued that they are typically produced at the end of a large project as part of a post-implementation review, which can be many years after the project started and largely reflect what went wrong. Boyle argues that they do not aid a project at all, nor the many others that may have started in the interim, as the horse has already bolted. He said this reveals another benefit of agile delivery: learning is continuous and timely with each component.

There was also a belief that the customisation of packaged software has a major impact on the ability to forecast with accuracy. A CIO (Person S, NZ) argued that the cost of customisation is rarely considered or understood in detail during initial forecasts, so the future costs of support and upgrades are also generally ignored. Hence, while the project starts with an 'intent' to implement a standard software package and adapt organisational processes to suit, it in fact morphs into software to suit existing processes. The problem in these instances for the project and the organisation is that the initial forecast is made against the original intent. A senior ICT auditor (Person AA, NSW) added to this perspective by arguing that customisation is really only changing technology—at additional cost and complexity and 'certainly reducing if not completely decimating any benefits'. Piccoli argued that customisation was one of the major issues with the LMBR program:

'That is probably the mistake they made. They are making an IT system fit a complex system instead of simplifying the system and then bringing in an IT system that would fit this.'

To address this issue, a senior ICT assurance officer (Person T, NZ) suggested the organisation should 'standardise' processes as much as possible upfront, before the project starts, so that customisation is reduced. However, other interviewees indicated that while this is logical, it is difficult to implement. A CIO (Person AH, Vic.) said that while everyone acknowledges the need to minimise customisation, it is difficult as organisational change must happen within a time frame suitable to the project. Citing their involvement in a HR/payroll project, a senior executive (Person B, NSW) cited these time constraints as one reason so many customisations are made: '[I]t is easier to tack it on than change the organisation.'

However, a CIO (Person S, NZ) argued that it is possible to address customisation impacts, and alternatives, if there is executive support. They gave an example of an existing, heavily customised integrated business package being replaced with a 'pure-vanilla' alternative package. This was 'a bit tricky', as some processes and existing features 'disappeared', and the business had to learn to operate with the new solution, but it was successful. There was evidence from Tasmania that customisation impacts are managed. A senior executive (Person BM, Tas.) cited a project where the customisation of the solution was discouraged from the outset and a change to business processes was pursued. Where this could not be done, a configuration option was the next alternative. Only if no alternative was possible was customisation considered, and this was kept to a minimum. These were the only two examples cited of successfully dealing with organisational change instead of customisation.

A final perspective on the unintended consequences of customisation is the impact not on the organisation, but on the project vendor. A senior executive (Person B, NSW) argued that part of the problem is that at the planning and forecasting stage neither the organisation nor the vendor has full knowledge of the processes in the legacy system. Processes are integrated over decades, resulting in many unplanned changes and the flow-on of impacts to cost and schedules. An IQA (Person C, NSW) cited an example where the software provider had more than 300 people engaged just to deal with changes to the solution required by the agency/project. The project eventually collapsed under this weight and the vendor walked away, happier to pay a financial penalty than to continue.

While there was evidence from the elite interviewees of an assurance process for the business case/project plan and its forecasts, there was also a common perception that this is poorly undertaken—for several reasons. First, organisational factors influence not only the preparation but also the assurance of forecasts. In a discussion with a senior partner (Person AL) of a large international consulting firm, an example was raised of the great effort a firm had put into planning and estimating for part of a large project involving many hours of work and a detailed summary of time, resources, and cost. It was peer-reviewed within the firm, as was normal practice, and within the project team and was praised for its detail. On presentation, the program's general manager, after a quick glance at the total cost page, pushed the document back across the table, saying: '[I]t is too expensive, change it!' The trouble was the same outcome was still required.

Second, the detail required in a plan for a large ICT software project is part of the problem in effectively assuring forecasts. An IQA (Person C, NSW) asked how anyone could be expected to thoroughly review a 'six-inch-high document' and clearly understand all of the complexities and interdependencies, risks, what is to be delivered, and the cost and time frame.

The third reason was the effectiveness of gateway reviews. These are a common, though not universal, assurance process across the Australian and New Zealand public sectors and are a much-hyped initiative. It can be argued that the New Zealand and Victorian sectors are world leaders in the implementation of gateway reviews. The interviewees' perspectives on these reviews and their effectiveness as an assurance tool, particularly at project approval, were varied, with a senior ICT assurance officer (Person T, NZ) saying the 'feedback had been mixed'. The general perspective is that while gateways serve as an external review method, their effectiveness in the assurance of large ICT project forecasts is doubtful. A CIO (Person S, NZ) argued that part of the problem is that assurance of forecasts provides feedback based on the assumptions and information provided by the project team. Person S sums up this limitation: '[T]here is a reasonable check … but it is only as good as the information that is on the table on the day.'

Last, the role and effectiveness of jurisdictional central agencies in the assurance process vary, as does understanding of the central agency's role and initiatives. In New Zealand, this role is clearly understood; however, in the Australian Public Service it is not so clear. A senior ICT assurance officer (Person AD, APS) said that one role of the DTA is to provide a third-party independent review on plans and forecasts and give 'frank and fearless advice'. It is of some concern that no other APS interviewee highlighted the DTA's role as an assurance provider. The second issue with the effectiveness of central agency assurance here is aligned to the earlier assurance problems. How can anyone accurately review a forecast for a large program of work that spans many years with many unknowns and much complexity? This dilemma impacts on central agencies just as much as on the project team, gateway reviews, and independent reviews.

In summary, the forecasting framework is seen as a major contributor to past and ongoing poor project outcomes. The common requirement to provide an accurate forecast for a large ICT software project upfront and in full for the entire process is misguided, as this is impossible to do with any accuracy. Therefore, the benefit of doing so was challenged and it was deemed to be just another factor setting the project up for failure.

Organisational factors: Are organisational factors considered during planning?

The interviewees were asked for their perceptions of how organisational factors—such as geographical issues, capability and capacity, industrial climate, award structures, and culture—are considered when forecasting and are factored into planning. This will have direct impacts on planning and the resulting forecasts. For example, if there is a dependency on major industrial reform to coincide with the development and implementation of the initiative and the organisation is heavily unionised, there may be resistance. Therefore, a forecast based on active participation and acceptance ignores the organisational reality of a challenging path and could be classified as optimistic or delusional.

A senior partner (Person AL) in a large consulting firm with extensive experience of providing services to large government ICT projects described this requirement in planning as 'fundamental'. However, a senior ICT auditor (Person AA, NSW), citing experience, stated: 'I cannot think of a single example at the minute where I have ever seen an organisational, cultural assessment factored into planning … [I]t is certainly a huge factor.'

A NSW Auditor-General's report on the LMBR program found that the business case did not reflect the project's costs, that the 'complexity of the project was not factored into costing', and that impacts on departmental resources were not identified and in fact were classified as 'unknown', yet this business case had passed internal and jurisdictional reviews (Audit Office of New South Wales 2014: 16). In another example, a senior executive[5] cited the case of a project from which all change management responsibilities and the budget were removed to reduce complexity, time frames, and costs. The problem was the project simply shifted the responsibility and cost to another business unit, which—not unreasonably—had not planned for this. A CIO (Person G, APS) claimed this is common in planning. A senior executive (Person B, NSW) and key business stakeholder in a major enterprise resource planning project, when asked about their involvement in the planning and consideration of these factors, simply stated: '[W]e did not do that.'

Within the New Zealand institutional framework, the Better Business Cases (The Treasury 2019) document provides extensive guidance to agencies on project planning and forecasting, including examples of organisational factors to consider. However, interviewees had contrasting views about the adherence to and implementation of these guidelines. A senior project manager (Person P, NZ) argued that 'everybody knows you need' to consider organisational factors in planning and forecasting and, supporting this view, a program director (Person M, NZ) stated that it is 'absolutely' common for planners to take these factors into account. However, others disagreed, with both a senior executive (Person K, NZ) and a CIO (Person L, NZ) stating that it does not usually happen, and another New Zealand CIO (Person O) claiming there is no jurisdictional standard; it is dealt with independently by each agency/project. Person P said it is 'evident' through all stages of the business case development that these organisational factors are not considered in planning. For a final New Zealand perspective—and rather disappointingly—a senior ICT assurance officer (Person T, NZ) claimed that even when projects go through an exercise of identifying the organisational factors to be incorporated within forecasts, once the impacts are added up and assessed for scope, time, and budget, financial shock means requests are made for certain aspects to be removed from the plan. This is further evidence that institutional frameworks, and the best intentions of the project team, can be overridden by other organisational factors. Another example of this dynamic is provided in Box 5.1.

---

5   The identifier and jurisdiction have been kept confidential to avoid identification.

Box 5.1 Having planning guidelines is one thing, applying them is another

At the time of interview, a senior executive (Person BQ) was in the midst of planning for a large ICT project in their jurisdiction. The jurisdiction had recently 'strengthened' its institutional framework to support better planning practices. Person BQ arrived 15 minutes late for the interview, looking flustered, and apologised that they had been in a meeting with the executive leadership. The following is an extract from that interview.

> Interviewer: When planning, what organisational factors such as geography, resources, capability, culture, etcetera, are considered upfront and allowances made for?

> Person BQ: [Laughing] [At t]he meeting I have just walked out of it has been decided a paper will go to the minister this afternoon advising them of the cost, resources, and scope of the project. I stated we are not ready for that yet. We need to do research and investigation upfront first. The answer was no, it will be ready this afternoon. I know from experience whatever figure I put on paper we will have to live with. That is how planning is done and that creates a problem at the back end.

Having guidelines in this instance was of little use; the organisational and political imperatives overruled these and were perceived as immediately exposing the project to risk.

Note: The interviewee's jurisdiction has been kept confidential to reduce the likelihood of identification.

The literature indicates that one of the differences between large ICT projects in the public and the private sectors is that public sector projects operate in a political environment. The interviewees indicated this was indeed a major factor in following proper forecasting disciplines, as politics could overrule any effort to plan and forecast for the best outcome.

A senior executive (Person BL, Tas.) argued that political factors are rarely included in forecasts and wondered whether control is even possible. A CIO (Person G, APS) posited that the driver of the project itself has a major organisational influence on planning. The example used was a project that was part of a 'political agenda' with imposed expectations, meaning the time frames would be imposed rather than carefully planned and calculated. A senior executive (Person E, NSW) argued that political influence leads to projects being planned for an outcome and time frame that are politically beneficial, rather than on an assessment of whether it is a 'good project'. Two senior ICT assurance officers (Persons AF & AG) claimed a Victorian project in progress had 'a very aggressive' delivery time frame that was imposed by the government and not an outcome of planning. They indicated as part of an early review that this would create 'a serious risk of delay' to the project, and 'sure enough, a delay has happened'.

A CIO (Person O, NZ) described a political requirement to see results quickly, with no regard for what is required to achieve results effectively.

Governments can also have an influence by changing their agenda. As a program director (Person F, APS) posited, if the government changes superannuation legislation and imposes a date for the change to be in place, agencies such as the Australian Taxation Office must simply do their best to accommodate this. A change of government can also bring a change in priorities, and one CIO (Person K, NZ) argued that 'this can become a real problem for the public sector in long-term planning'.

A senior ICT assurance officer (Person R, NZ) said the impact of this was being unable to develop a strategic vision for the next five years with any confidence as the government of the day was focused on short-term deliverables. Political priorities can also be influenced rather quickly by the media, immediately impacting on projects and planning. A senior project manager (Person N, NZ) cited an example of being in the middle of a high-priority project when carefully laid plans were unexpectedly jettisoned. The minister had been doorknocked by a journalist who informed them of a glitch in another system, and the next day the directive was to stop the project work and 'fix it'. Paul Barratt argues this is symptomatic of the 'modern' politician for whom 'instant gratification' is required, leading to the situation where 'bright ideas' override historically developed processes.

Interviewees also raised the role of the public sector and agencies in challenging these political directives. A senior ICT assurance officer (Person T, NZ) argued that agencies have a role in explaining to ministers 'what is required to achieve the outcome', providing that 'frank and fearless' advice. Person T acknowledged that while it may not work, that is no excuse for not trying. Barratt, however, recommends putting advice in writing— something Shergold (2015: iv) also stressed.

There was no misunderstanding among interviewees that these large projects operate within a political context, as it is the nature of the sector. The challenge is how to plan for politics. How can you prepare for what is coming when large projects can be de-prioritised or defunded overnight?

Box 5.2 The Northern Territory's CCSRP: Is it possible to make accurate long-term plans for capability and capacity?[6]

In 2017, the Northern Territory began the Core Clinical Systems Renewal Program (CCSRP), a $259-million health system project of considerable size and complexity that would have been a challenge anywhere in the world. With the territory's known issues in attracting the required capability and capacity, developing an upfront plan with a forecast based on the timely acquisition of these resources is fraught with risk.

Relevant Northern Territory interviewees were asked about this issue in 2018. One senior ICT assurance officer (Person AS) said it was already proving a challenge, while another (Person AV) stated that it was the 'critical' issue for the project. A program director (Person AU) said it was starting to impact 'terribly' and that, despite interstate marketing, there was still a shortfall.

In the early stages of the project, the resourcing issues were already impacting on schedules. There is little publicly available documentation on progress since the interviews, other than a 2019 update stating that the design phase is complete (Digital Territory 2019), but there is no reference to progress against schedules, costs, and so on.

I can only wish the Northern Territory the best with this project; they were very welcoming to me and participated willingly and openly in the research, and they were a very dedicated team. However, attracting resources to the Northern Territory is a wicked problem. How can they accurately forecast over an extended period when the team will achieve the required capability and capacity? Arguably, the answer is they cannot. Perhaps they should instead look at alternative delivery models to reduce the risk?

Jurisdictional size and geographic location were again raised as organisational factors to be considered in planning, particularly their impact on obtaining the capability and capacity required. This issue was raised as a factor in all jurisdictions, not just the smallest or most remote. For example, in Victoria, two senior ICT assurance officers (Persons AF & AG) claimed that for one major project, there had been early slippages in schedule due to delays in obtaining a skilled program director. An IQA (Person C, NSW) argued that this highlights a common failure in government planning for large projects—that is, there is an assumption that projects 'will be singing

---

6   'In May 2017, the Northern Territory Government (NTG) funded $259 million over five years to support the Core Clinical Systems Renewal Program (CCSRP). CCSRP is developing a single, secure, Territory-wide, electronic patient record that integrates multiple systems currently used in NT Health, and replaces current aging clinical systems' (NT Health 2017).

from the outset'—an assumption on which forecasts are based. Instead, experience shows that it takes time to acquire capacity and capability and that it 'takes anywhere from six months onwards for a large project to find its rhythm'.

As detailed earlier, the Northern Territory has problems attracting the required capability and capacity for large complex ICT projects because of the double complication of small size and remoteness. Box 5.2 discusses the impacts of these factors on planning and forecasting large projects in the territory.

In summary, organisational factors have major impacts on the ability to forecast accurately over the long term. These factors are not always included in project forecasts and, even when they are, it is impossible to foresee the political and organisational conditions.

Financial management: How does organisational financial management capability influence forecasting?

The financial management guidelines across the Australian and New Zealand public sectors generally require an upfront forecast for the entire project. An earlier finding was that this is a flawed and inappropriate process. When applying a project financial management lens to this requirement, the overriding perspective is that financial management practices have not adapted to improve forecasting for large ICT projects; rather, they continue to have negative impacts.

The first factor several interviewees raised was that although projects may forecast for the duration upfront, and the budget is approved on that basis, this does not equate to the money being granted in full at the beginning of the project. Typically, projects are funded by fiscal year, based on the forecast, up to the total budgetary limit. This, as argued by a CIO (Person S, NZ), leaves the project, somewhat ironically, exposed. The framework requires a forecast for the entire project and a budget approved on that; the project commences, yet there is no certainty that the approved funding will be available. Like large ICT projects, which have many future unknowns, much can change in a few years with government finances. Economic times or the government can change. Therefore, although a figure of, say, $100 million is approved in the business case, there is no guarantee this amount will be available. If you have planned your project via a traditional waterfall delivery, this could leave the agency or project with a half-finished product.

A second factor raised is the focus within the framework on cost, rather than benefits or viewing the project as a long-term strategic investment. In New Zealand, a CIO (Person O) argued that the Treasury takes a very 'myopic view' of large ICT projects and becomes fixated on 'cost' rather than future benefits. A senior executive (Person E, NSW) argued that, unlike the private sector, in the public sector the emphasis is on trying to justify a project on a financial rather than an investment basis. Some projects should be treated as investment strategies and funded on that basis, not on a simple assessment of forecast cost and how this will fit within funding guidelines for approval. These perspectives were supported by a CIO (Person A, APS) with both private and public sector experience, who claimed that the public sector focuses on the financial, unlike the private sector, where 'scope drives everything'.

The third factor raised is the frequency with which additional project funding is requested due to the inaccuracy of the initial forecast and budget. There were varying perspectives on how these requests are managed. A senior executive (Person E, NSW) argued that these decisions are generally not based on solid financial and project management disciplines. The propensity for troubled projects to be provided with additional funding— perhaps multiple times—was described by a senior ICT auditor (Person AA, NSW) as 'non-stoppable inertia'.

Other interviewees had the view that the public sector does not consider the 'stop option' (Person H, Senior ICT auditor, NSW), 'people do not want to say stop' (Person R, Senior ICT assurance, NZ), even though projects can be planned with stage gates as nominal off-ramps. It was claimed that there is a mindset that stopping is an acknowledgement of 'failure', so they 'flog that dead horse' and hope to make up the lost ground in the next phase (Person S, CIO, NZ). Deciding to stop is not simply about having the power to do so, but also about having fortitude and an awareness that this is the best option.

The alternative perspective is that there are valid reasons to provide additional funding and to let the project progress and this is in fact an informed decision rather than 'unstoppable inertia'. This is an important perspective as it was argued that a funding correction is an acknowledgement that the initial forecast was insufficient to deliver the outcome and, even with a revised budget, the project remains supported. There are other organisational factors that influence the provision of additional funding. A private sector CIO (Person AD, Vic.) argued that even in the private sector decisions to stop funding large ICT projects are rare as they are typically delivering an important asset. Therefore, the cost of stopping and starting again, without an alternative, is a key factor as you 'end up spending more time restarting and remobilising later'.

An example of this scenario in the public sector is provided in Box 5.3.

Box 5.3 Ministerial support and additional funding for a much-troubled project

Adrian Piccoli was the NSW education minister during part of the LMBR program. This program received much negative media coverage due to its time and cost overruns, with the ongoing provision of funding part of the narrative. Piccoli was asked about his support and the reasons for additional funding.

Interviewer: Why did you continue to support the project in the face of such public criticism?

Piccoli: We came into government in 2011; LMBR had been problematic for the previous government as well. [There were c]ost blowouts, time blowouts, and principals were complaining. We spent a fair bit of time thinking about what we did. They had already spent $300 million. What do you do when you are halfway through a tunnel, do you stop and flush $300 million down the toilet or do you try and make it work? We decided, based on the advice from the department and others such as Treasury, to make it work.

Interviewer: Did those potential benefits to the schools remain a big driver for your continuing support?

Piccoli: Yes, we needed to have a system, it was not a matter of just stop and stay with the system we have. We could not do that … Even if we said forget about it, we would have had to go and design something else, so spend another $500 million on something that was equally unpredictable.

In a recurring theme, the use of component-based iterative delivery such as agile, supported by appropriate financial management processes, was raised as an alternative. A senior ICT assurance officer (Person AD, APS) with jurisdiction-wide responsibility said they were working closely with a central agency on alternative funding models based on component-based delivery. Future funding would be dependent on the successful and progressive delivery of benefits at each stage of the project. Person AD admitted there are organisational challenges ahead if this is to be achieved:

[H]ow do you marry that world [traditional funding] with a world that says, 'No, we are only going to give you a little bit of money and you have to come back and show us'? That is the heart of the challenge we face, so as someone from finance put it to me, cabinet ministers are not going to want to sign off on something that is open-ended. They are going to want to know, roughly speaking, what they are committing to … [I]f you turn around and say, 'Sorry, I cannot tell you because I do not know what the thing is going to look like until we start', it is difficult. We have these two worlds that are colliding, we have the structural budget world that forever has worked around [the idea of] make your business case, tell Cabinet what you want, we will give you your money, and away you go—that world versus the world where we are seeing the pace of change and technological evolution and [the] need for user focus, much more agile, chunked down delivery and the two are colliding. We have not worked it out yet. We have not worked it out.

As an example of this dilemma, another senior assurance officer (Person AE, APS) argued that forecasts must cover the entire project because the issue is 'making a good investment decision'. They claimed that an agile delivery approach could still be utilised by breaking deliverables into 'tranches' but projects cannot be given a 'blank cheque'. This need for an overarching plan covering all project deliverables and total cost, even when agile delivery was proposed, was an approach identified in Victoria by two senior ICT assurance officers (Persons AF & AG). Person AF argued that agile is simply a means 'to a predefined deliverable' and a 'way of getting there', but projects are still required to submit a full and detailed plan; projects cannot operate on a basis of 'we are not sure where we are going or how we are going to get there'.

Person AG argued that in the absence of a solution to the traditional funding approach and the agile funding model, the 'staged funding' model, as part of an overall plan, 'is probably the next best thing'. However, a CIO (Person AH, Vic.) was damning when asked how they manage their preferred agile approach when the Victorian guidelines require full upfront forecasts and funding:

That is a real problem, and that funding process is the biggest single risk to IT projects that governments create. Governments knowingly create the risk factors which cause most IT project failures, and the reason is because of the budget process that forces you to try and estimate the total cost of something that you do not know anything about and lock it in and then hold you to account for that.

Box 5.4 A private sector funding approach

David Boyle, former CIO of the Commonwealth and National Australia banks, said that in the private sector for large projects using a waterfall method, stage gate funding is employed. Boyle was a member of a committee that oversaw the entire portfolio of organisational projects and he explained the process:

> [D]epending on the risk profile of the project, that committee would maybe just give out funding for the next phase of work and ask for a checkpoint as to the learnings out of that phase. Or, if it was a more modestly scaled project with a very low risk profile from when the team had done that sort of stuff five times before, we might give them two stage gates worth of funding or the entire funding envelope.

The project would have an overall plan and estimated budget, but ongoing funding was provided on a staged basis pending outcomes of that stage and impacts on future stages. However, when an agile model was employed, the stage gate approach moved to a 'funding envelope' model,

> where we say, look, in our digital team or in our payroll team, we have a backlog of work to do … [R]ather than make a business case for all of it, why don't you deliver the first two months worth of work? Come back and show us for that level of funding what business benefits you have and, if you have a good backlog and even more value to create, we might increase your envelope. Or, if you are starting to dry up in terms of your backlog, we might reduce.

> And so that creates a much more iterative governance model over the funding than the rather binary yes or no, you have your funding for your project, or you do not. And a lot of change in [the company] and the businesses I work with can be done that way. And it is really an artificial construct to be grabbing a bunch of scope and putting it into a project model for getting funding, and if you unbundled it from that model and put it in an envelope, you get a lot more benefit earlier.

A private sector perspective of funding large projects using a traditional waterfall and a component-based method is detailed in Box 5.4. It indicates some similarity with the Victorian stage gate funding, the major exception being that this was not isolated but was part of an organisational investment portfolio of projects.

Person AH (CIO, Vic.) described their approach as providing 'seeding money', where you say to the project team: 'Okay, you have this idea, but we are not giving you $100 million. We will give you a small amount now for you to investigate further and then we will revisit and see where we are up to.' The agency also treats this as part of a 'multiyear investment strategy' with the money provided from internal agency funds set aside for that purpose. They set aside budgets to address ICT initiatives. These initiatives (agile projects) are initially provided with seed money and then assessed for further funding if there is positive progress and a clear next step. That means it is not managed as an ICT project, but rather at the portfolio level, with a collection of projects that are funded on priority and progress, with the portfolio mapped out over several years. They do not generally ask for large external funding as this would be one-off funding, which is contrary to their preferred development and management approach. The CIO championed this approach within the agency. It was not the result of a jurisdictional initiative; in fact, it can be argued that the approach is due to the inadequacy of the institutional framework to support these initiatives. This is like the approach used by Michael Carmody to fund the ATO program (see Box 5.6).

The final financial management factor identified was asset management and its role in funding large ICT software projects. In the interview with Boyle, the issue arose of treating ICT organisational solutions as assets and amortising these appropriately. Boyle described this necessity as a 'real passion' and argued that the metrics in an organisation's asset portfolio are their health, maturity, and age. He claimed that experience has shown him that the longer assets are left to age, the 'more expensive the project becomes and the fewer options you have on how to attack the problem because of the looming end-of-life risk'.

Lack of asset planning leads to a lack of options. Boyle said by his organisation planning for ICT asset replacement, they can make more informed decisions on cost, when to spend, over what period, and where this fits in the replacement cycles of other ICT and non-ICT assets. He argued that, by doing this, the organisation is not living in 'la-la land' under a misguided belief that the ICT asset will 'survive in perpetuity'.

Another private sector CIO (Person AI, Vic.), one with public sector experience, confirmed that in their private sector job they treat ICT systems as assets and manage them accordingly; however, in their public sector job, they do not and cannot as the sector is not mature enough to cater for this. They additionally argued that governments treat physical infrastructure assets and ICT assets differently, and do not understand that ICT assets need the same attention and planning. As a result, they argue, government 'IT has suffered from underinvestment that goes back over a decade'.

When the public sector interviewees were asked whether their jurisdiction treats major IT systems as assets, amortises these, and plans for their replacement accordingly, the only response was 'no'. There were also some blank looks and questions to clarify what I meant. A CIO (Person AH, Vic.) argued that their treasury and finance agencies would find such a concept 'too, loosey-goosey'.

Two Victorian senior ICT assurance officers (Persons AF & AG) argued that there is a need to plan for these asset replacements as the current process leads to 'must replace this now' projects receiving priority, but there is no clarity on what else is out there, looming. In the Northern Territory, a senior executive (Person AM) said 'it is not done that way', but claimed it is in a state of 'evolution'. In New South Wales, a senior executive (Person E) argued that this lack of planning, depreciation, and amortisation for ICT asset replacements means that governments fail to 'reinvest naturally' in ICT infrastructure. This results in funding requests for large projects 'coming out of the blue' and, as one CIO (Person S, NZ) argued, this then forces agencies into undertaking a large project. This argument found support with a senior assurance officer (Person T, NZ), who argued that without an 'iterative investment cycle' in ICT assets agencies are forced down a major replacement path that can limit alternative delivery options.

In the Australian Public Service, a senior ICT assurance officer (Person AD) with jurisdiction-wide responsibilities said their agency is 'thinking about this a little bit' and acknowledges that the APS ICT investment strategy must be more 'strategic'; instead of isolated one-off bids, it should look at investment decisions across a portfolio and develop a 'roadmap' for future investments. However, they did admit that while this is where they would 'like to get to', it 'would not be an easy path' as 'government budgeting does not work that way at the moment'.

When Barratt was asked why ICT solutions are not treated as assets, he argued it was due to 'political laziness' and a failure by politicians to understand that 'if you want something like a high-quality education system, you need the systems' to support this, such as paying staff, and student systems.

There was evidence of jurisdictions trying to address this issue. In New South Wales, a senior ICT assurance officer (Person Z) with jurisdiction-wide responsibilities is looking at the development of a 10-year 'strategic roadmap' but admitted that 'it is early days' and it will require consultation with and cooperation from Treasury due to the changes needed in funding guidelines.

Political factors can influence the treatment of ICT systems as assets and their funding, limiting initiatives within a jurisdiction to address this issue. Interviewees suggested it can be difficult to secure investment in ICT maintenance over more publicly popular options (see Box 5.5).

Box 5.5 A political perspective on ICT asset management

Looking back on his time as NSW education minister, Adrian Piccoli argued that a lack of forward planning for asset replacement and maintenance was part of the problem with the LMBR program, as the agency was trying to 'do one update after 30 years of not doing anything', which resulted in a 'mess-up of planning'. However, Piccoli argued that there is a political factor that limits the ability to address this kind of issue—that is, the public's perception of the use of government funds:

> [T]he political problem runs into this issue of what the public's perception is [of] how money should be spent in health, transport, and education. [There is a belief that this money] should be spent on, you know, doctors and beds and teachers and trains and train drivers, so if you are spending half a billion dollars over 10 years on an IT system, the public perception is this is a waste of money. This is the historical reason there is a reluctance to get regular upgrades. There is budgetary stress, and our school needs a new hall, but you are spending $100 million on an HR system, what a waste of money; what we need is a new hall or science lab updated. That is where the political pressure comes from. A minister is tempted to say let us not do the IT upgrade, there is no political bang in an IT system, you know you cannot unveil a new IT system whereas you can unveil a new hall. Yes, so, it very much plays into that.

> Interviewer: What are the other impacts?

> Piccoli: One is they do not regularly get money to do IT upgrades. When you are in a competitive budget environment [it] is difficult because the political imperative is upgrading hospitals, upgrading schools; it is not upgrading IT systems. So, then, when they do … because it has been such a long period, it is much more complicated and one big lump of money [is required] instead of spending incremental amounts.

It can be arguably concluded that it is not only governments that treat ICT assets differently to infrastructure assets; it is also the public, and public perception has a direct political influence on how funds are prioritised.

In conclusion, a CIO (Person AH, Vic.) provided this brutal assessment of government negligence in ICT asset management, and proffered a solution:

> Government is the most negligent and irresponsible owner of infrastructure of [all] … because they do not fund sustainment of their assets and replacement of their assets. So, that means that the safest path is not to have any assets, is to be acquiring IT systems and infrastructure through software-as-a-service arrangements, and that is what cloud services are all about. That saves government from itself, because it turns IT systems into a binary thing, a binary decision.

This suggests governments will not change on this matter, so assets and their maintenance and upgrading should be removed from government responsibility. This option was also raised by a senior partner (Person AL) in a large consulting firm and a New Zealand CIO (Person S), who agreed that government investment in their ICT assets is insufficient and not a priority, so they should seek serviced-based solutions. They argued that this would provide 'more flexibility and would not be as disrupted by political events'.

In summary, the perception is that financial management processes for large ICT software projects have a direct negative impact on outcomes. The requirement for a full upfront forecast is flawed, as it provides neither surety of nor limitations to funding. The financial management processes have failed to adapt to support alternative approaches. Investment in ICT asset management and maintenance is missing, leading to large 'must have now or else' funding requests, and a failure to understand what other requests are looming.

Large project dilemmas: Should they be avoided, can they be, and what alternatives are there?

'Stop doing large ICT projects' is the message from former bank CIO David Boyle, who argues that the 'further you look into the future', the harder it is 'to estimate the target state'.

Boyle claimed this is because you cannot have certainty in long-term plans, as there is too much about the future that is unknown. A senior partner (Person AL) from a major consulting firm agreed that government planning for a large ICT project is 'no longer the best option', and they must look at alternatives such as component-based, iterative delivery. These views were not isolated to the private sector interviewees and were common among those from the public sector. A CIO (Person O, NZ) was just as emphatic: '[T]o me, the answer is obvious: do not do big projects! Do a collection of smaller projects.'

A senior ICT assurance officer (Person Z, NSW) stated that large ICT projects are 'hot topics' and New South Wales must 'adapt to new ways of delivery'. This means the jurisdiction is trying to move to a 'situation' where 'big monolithic programs' can be avoided. A CIO (Person AH, Vic.) burnt by previous large ICT projects said they 'never want to have anything to do with a large IT project again'. Furthermore, they argued that they do not need to as there are alternatives.

A senior ICT assurance officer (Person AD, APS) cited a government initiative driven through the DTA to address large ICT software project planning, saying there is an intention to not have 'big five-year projects that are funded with $1 billion off the back of a 400-page business case that then becomes shelf-ware, and no one ever looks at the project again until it gets to the end and [they] realise none of the benefits has been delivered'.

They said 'the government's mood' is to break things into smaller components, but 'it is a work in progress, we're not there yet'.

A program director (Person F, APS) involved in the Australian Taxation Office's 10-year change program stated that the pace of technological change was at the centre of their planning. This directly contributed to the project following an iterative component-based delivery approach, and they argued that this was necessary because if they did not deliver quickly, they could be 'left with nothing'. Piccoli argued that this was a factor in the LMBR program, as planning was completed in 2007 and solutions chosen soon after, yet they were still going in 2015, during which time iPads had emerged for use in schools. In addition, SAP enterprise resource planning (ERP) may not be the choice if a review was done today. However, as one CIO (Person S, NZ) noted, you do have to make a final technology choice, as you cannot continually wait for the latest technology to emerge.

The overwhelmingly favoured alternative to the large project approach is agile delivery, which can address the impossibility of preparing a relevant forecast at the initiation of a large ICT software project. A CIO (Person AH, Vic.) noted that agile can address this long-term impossibility and is a 'methodology designed to deal with uncertainty in scope and quality'.

Another CIO (Person AI, Vic.) added that the agile approach allows uncertainty to be replaced with certainty as the project progresses; it is agile by name and by nature and can be adapted to the circumstances. A third CIO (Person O, NZ) argued that agile is evidence that the large project world 'has changed' for the better and governments must embrace this, as agile and component-based delivery are 'a much more organic and sustainable way … than the mega projects of the nineties and noughties'.

A private sector CIO (Person AC, Vic.) claimed that agile delivery enables large complex projects to be broken into discrete deliverables, allowing the project to 'walk before they could run'. Person AC claimed that in their experience the use of agile in large projects 'significantly outperformed the waterfall-based approach'.

There are other benefits from the use of agile delivery and the resulting improvements in forecasting, such as those noted by a CIO (Person AH, Vic.), who claimed that it can lessen the risk in procurement of services, which for traditional large ICT projects is high, requiring expensive upfront definition and ongoing contract management, and adding capability requirements to the project. Person AH claimed this type of upfront long-term all-of-project procurement is '[e]vil, immoral, and dangerous'.

There were perceptions that agile delivery is meeting resistance within the public sector because of organisational factors such as culture and traditional roles. A CIO (Person AI, Vic.) said this is due to a culture in which it is unacceptable to tell a minister that you do not know yet what the cost, time, or final deliverables will be, and 'until you can get comfortable with the idea that you are not going to make a commitment on day one, you cannot do agile'.

On a similar theme, Boyle argued that without organisational change across several functional areas, agile developments will struggle in the public sector to deliver on time and budget as they are caught up in red tape and organisational hierarchy. This is because this method requires agile decision-making and trust at higher levels for lower levels to make project decisions. Boyle stated that agile needs an organisation that enables 'rapid decision-making rather than slow and bureaucratic decision-making'.

Herein lies the barrier to agile delivery in the public sector: current institutional frameworks are not supportive of this method. A senior assurance officer (Person R, NZ) claimed that New Zealand guidelines such as the Better Business Cases and gateway reviews are not designed to cater for projects delivered via agile. Person R argued that the mismatch between the framework and agile options has been discussed 'quite a lot' and there is a common belief in New Zealand that change is required. Preparation of the business case at the initiation stage is seen as one area that must adapt, because 'the Better Business Cases framework does not support agile as well as it could do, because if you are spending 12 months doing a Better Business Cases, the world has already moved on'.

There were a few dissenting views on the use of agile as an alternative delivery method for large ICT projects, dismissing it as just another ICT fad. A senior executive (Person AN, NT) summed up these minority perspectives by stating:

[Agile] is fashionable at the moment … This whole concept of get a bit of money, and do a bit of scoping, and build a bit, and then see where it goes and get some more money, I am really uncomfortable with that. I think it is a slippery slope, I really do. To me, that is just insane, and it is code for lack of rigour and not doing your bloody homework upfront.

While there was much talk about avoiding large ICT software projects through agile delivery, the elite interviewees were asked whether it would always be possible to do this. A program director (Person J, NZ) argued that it 'may not always be possible' to avoid large ICT projects, with a New Zealand colleague (Person J, Senior project manager) providing support by arguing that for a project like Novopay, 'you could not have done it any other way'. A CIO (Person AK, Vic.) argued that large ICT projects are 'unavoidable', so the emphasis should be on agencies 'addressing the capability issues' to undertake the projects. Another CIO (Person AH, Vic.), a strong advocate for agile, mused that it 'may be not possible' but they would look at all avenues to 'de-risk' a project.

Others, such as a senior ICT assurance officer (Person AD, APS), believed regardless of size and complexity, it is always possible to break a large project into smaller deliverable components. An example of this was provided by Piccoli, citing the LMBR program, who claimed that the project made an initial mistake in planning the implementation of new finance, HR/payroll, and student management solutions across the school and TAFE sectors as one program. He argued that each should have been treated separately. A senior ICT auditor (Person H, NSW), when discussing the LMBR, agreed and, regarding planning the work as one super project, mused: '[W]as that really the only option?'

In summary, the overriding perception is to not undertake large ICT software projects via traditional delivery methods and instead look at alternative iterative component-based delivery methods such as agile. These allow the project and agency to break down both the complexity and the risk. Alternatives to planning as a large project always exist and should always be investigated.

The findings and their conceptual relationship

The dominant perception among interviewees was that the public sector does not have the capability to forecast large ICT software projects, the major problem being the guidelines within the institutional frameworks. It is impossible to forecast in full upfront, as is the standard requirement, for a long-term, complex large ICT software project with any accuracy or relevance. There are just too many future unknowns, regardless of the method used. However, agencies and projects are being forced to do exactly this, meaning the forecast will be a best guess based on known facts, experience, and capability—all of which are in short supply. This process was described as 'a ridiculous nonsense of a process' as everyone knows the figure is a best guess, yet it becomes the basis on which the project is approved and funded, and sets a benchmark against which the project will be assessed. It creates a situation in which 'I was forced to provide you with a forecast when I did not want to, and told you it was wrong, yet now I am being judged against it'.

Second, it was argued that guidelines that set boundaries on project approval lead directly to forecasts made to fit a guideline and gain approval, rather than reality. While there may be optimism that the project can stay within that limit, there is also a culture of thinking, 'If I need more money, I will probably get it, as once I have started it is unlikely the project will be stopped'. This leads to overestimation and the attitude that 'I'll get as much as I can' just in case. The guidelines encourage either deliberate or delusional optimism, adding to the perceived 'ridiculousness' of the process.

Third, every project operates within an organisational context and many factors can impact on the project, so addressing this should be part of the forecast, yet this does not always happen. It is also impossible to predict these impacts with any accuracy over a long period; how can you possibly know with any certainty what will happen in five years?

Fourth, because of the above, the interviewees felt there is a certain amount of irony in the requirement to fully forecast upfront for a long-term large ICT software project. While ministers and the jurisdiction need 'certainty' about future costs and cannot provide a blank cheque, given the impossibility of forecasting accurately or even with any relevance, all that is gained is future uncertainty—the thing they are trying to avoid.

Last, while assurance processes to review forecasts are common practice, they are also impossible because of the difficulty in upfront forecasting. The agency or project will defend its case, argue the variables, describe organisational complexities, and the assurance team can question and fine-tune based on that advice, but the impossibility remains. The assurance team will face the same challenges as the project team.

There was a dominant perception that the public sector does not have the financial management capability and maturity for large ICT software projects. There is a focus on cost to the exclusion of investment. Funds are allocated in a single large payment on request and not as part of portfolio management, and the funding guidelines reflect this. It was also claimed that decisions to continue funding projects are not always made following financial or project management disciplines.

Second, ICT solutions are not treated as assets so there is inadequate investment in their maintenance—something not helped by a lack of political priority to fund work that is not publicly appealing. It was claimed that at a jurisdictional level, the life expectancy of these assets can be a major hidden impact. The lack of an asset management process is another factor in forcing agencies down the path towards an 'urgent' large project to replace redundant systems.

For contract management, cost is a major part of a project's forecast. When this is negotiated and costed upfront as part of the full project forecast, it creates the same problem as project forecasting—that is, it is impossible to do with any accuracy and leaves the project and the vendor exposed. If the vendor feels they are trapped, they may walk away, as was evidenced in the interviews.

The interviewees stated that there is much organisational learning from past projects detailed in copious documentation, yet the same issues keep arising, which suggests that written records are ineffective. The preferred option is to sit down and discuss learnings with someone who has been through this before. It was also acknowledged that there is much experience within and outside the public sector that can enhance learning; however, collaboration across jurisdictional agencies is rare or even deliberately avoided because of the culture of public sector agencies. On a positive note, it was claimed that where there has been collaboration, it has been effective.

It was a common claim among interviewees that large ICT software projects require organisational change, so in forecasting there is an assumption that the organisation will adapt its processes to the new solution. However, it was noted that as a project progresses, the intent to change is not matched by organisational action or willingness, meaning the approach morphs into adaptation of the solution, as it is 'quicker' and 'easier'.

The interviewees argued that when leadership does not take on this organisational change, the solution becomes heavily customised, which is not part of the original forecast and the impact of which is twofold. First, there is an impact on the project cost and schedules to undertake the work. Second, there is a cost to provide ongoing support that was not part of initial planning.

The desired approach to address entrepreneurship issues in forecasting for most interviewees is to stop undertaking single large ICT projects. Organisations should look at alternatives when planning, even for work that would typically be regarded as only achievable as a large project, such as payroll delivery. The argument is that there are alternatives to an approach that is known to almost always produce poor outcomes.

The dominant option among interviewees is an agile delivery method: delivering solutions in components, with short-term forecasts and funding, improved in each cycle with lessons from the past, and the ability to quickly adapt to changing circumstances. Jurisdictions must change their processes and culture to enable this type of delivery method, although working out how to fund these could be a challenge. Actors are finding ways to manage this locally due to the lack of adaptation in the frameworks.

There were two major perceptions about the role of agency in forecasting. First, the political factor is a powerful force in project planning and forecasting. There may be solid guidelines, planning, and forecasting with the best—if optimistic—intentions; however, a minister may ignore these and impose a solution: a cost and time frame based on political needs with scant regard for whether this is achievable.

Second, where agencies and projects have decided not to undertake a large project and to implement strategies such as an agile component-based approach with alternative funding arrangements, this is usually due to the agency of a single actor. Box 5.6 provides an example from the Australian Taxation Office's change project.

Box 5.6 Mini case study: The ATO, an early adopter of component-based delivery

Chapter 3 detailed a successful 10-year ICT software change program within the ATO, with then Commissioner of Taxation Michael Carmody as sponsor (see Box 3.1). When interviewed, Carmody was asked about the planning and forecasting process within the ATO and its capability given the extent and duration of the work. He acknowledged that the ATO lacked the capability and capacity to plan and deliver the work so Accenture was engaged to fill that gap on an outcomes-based contract. Its staff were integrated within the project teams with internal staff in a successful and long-term relationship. We discussed the forecasting process.

> Interviewer: When preparing forecasts, did you base these on your outcomes?
>
> Carmody: Yes.
>
> Interviewer: How did you work out how you were going to do that and calculate a time frame and cost?
>
> Carmody: I tried to front-end some early deliverables so … [stakeholders] could have a bit of confidence … so that people can see inside and outside the organisation that we were actually delivering on this project … Then there was the hard slog of breaking down … the outcomes … how you deliver that, what time frames would be needed.
>
> Interviewer: So that was a progressive process?
>
> Carmody: Yes.
>
> Interviewer: You did not say it is going to take me 10 years and cost X million dollars?
>
> Carmody: That is not how it started. It started from delivering some earlier deliverables and then learning from that.
>
> Interviewer: So, you were progressively gaining knowledge and experience for the next phase?
>
> Carmody: Yes.
>
> Interviewer: Did you think that was a better approach than a guess upfront of X years and X dollars? Is it better to break it into components and build on that?
>
> Carmody: From my actions, you can see where I thought the advantage was.

Carmody and the ATO were delivering the project as a series of distinct mini projects and employing component-based delivery methods for each. I was curious how Carmody funded and gained approval for this method.

> Interviewer: The funding of such an approach is not always supported by the current project financial guidelines.

> Carmody: Rightly or wrongly, we took a decision that we were going to fund this ourselves, we were not going to government. Now, that put a bit of burden on the organisation, but it also freed us up to do things the way we wanted to do it.
>
> Interviewer: How did you balance your planning against potentially overly optimistic forecasts?
>
> Carmody: Timing of projects of that magnitude is inevitably difficult and I guess you have to be careful in leading these that you do not force people into overly optimistic outcomes.
>
> Interviewer: Is that another reason for breaking it into components?
>
> Carmody: I certainly say it would be, yes ... We went in a staged way but then eventually we had a full plan. It is not as if we did not have a full plan to deliver but we went through it in a staged way to get there and that gave us a better opportunity to understand what was involved.

It is important to note that the staged component-based planning did not occur in isolation; there was an overarching plan. Carmody highlighted the difficulty of making accurate forecasts for long-term projects, but argued that breaking this planning into components added relevancy and reduced factors like optimism bias. The advantage of this planning approach was supported by a senior project manager (Person AB) in this project, who said that findings from the first phase of the project were used to enhance the second phase, and so on, and each phase became more defined and relevant than the last. Person AB argued that this approach supported good contract management with Accenture and, after two phases, a fixed-priced method for the respective outcomes drove commitment between the parties to deliver and confidence that delivery within the boundaries was possible.

Carmody was also asked about seeking external collaboration as part of the forecasting process.

> Interviewer: Did the ATO ever work with other tax offices?
>
> Carmody: Yes ... we did work closely with a lot of tax administrations around the world. We pinched some of their ideas ... [I]t was [from] that sharing of ideas with international organisations ... that we got some of the ideas that we wanted to press, and they were open in sharing their experience and how they achieved it and the difficulties they faced.
>
> Interviewer: Do you think the public sector has a culture of collaboration and cooperation on some of these things?
>
> Carmody: I did not see a lot of sharing; that is the only way I could answer that.

Carmody was asked about the future of large government ICT projects given the poor outcomes.

Interviewer: Why does the public sector continue with large projects? Can they be avoided? They are problematic and the outcomes are being challenged all the time. What is the answer?

Carmody: That depends on what you are trying to achieve as to how you frame a project … [O]ften these projects get out of hand because they do not have a clear outcome that they are trying to achieve, and they just grow upon themselves.

Interviewer: Such as the public sector adapting some of its rules to better deal with component-based, agile development, changing the way funding happens?

Carmody: Yes.

Carmody was also asked about internal learning to improve planning and whether the choice of a staged component-based delivery was a factor in organisational learning.

Interviewer: What about learning? When you used your component-based method, I presume from each of those you would learn something—almost a cycle of continuous learning?

Carmody: Yes.

Interviewer: The reason I am asking is that projects typically do lessons learned reports for future use, however, they can end up in a drawer.

Carmody: Yeah, you could do all of that, but I think the way you do that is if you have a good group of project managers, all working on their projects but working as a collegiate group, that is when you get the real transference of experience and learning rather than reading something.

In summary, Carmody reduced forecasting complexities and increased the relevance and accuracy of those forecasts by breaking a large complex program of work into a series of smaller, less-complex, progressively delivered components. Carmody acknowledged a lack of internal capability to undertake this planning and engaged Accenture to provide specialised services, developing a strong relationship with that vendor to mutual benefit. Carmody looked externally to seek collaboration, gain ideas, and improve planning. The component-based delivery also enabled a progressive cycle of internal continuous learning. In addition, the plan had a set of tangible outcomes to work towards and be assessed against. Carmody also decided to prioritise funding of the component-based delivery from internal sources rather than through APS channels, the funding guidelines and requirements for which could have been at odds with the approach employed.

There is much to admire about Carmody and the way he led and supported the planning of this extensive body of work. He was a trend-setter, possibly without knowing it.

The conceptual findings are summarised in Table 5.2.

Table 5.2 Summary of the conceptual findings on forecasting

Concept	Forecasting key findings
Capability and capacity	• The Australian and New Zealand public sectors do not have the capability to forecast for large ICT software projects. • The institutional frameworks are a major problem as they require projects to provide a single upfront forecast of time and cost — something that is impossible to do with any relevance. • The data, skills, and processes to forecast are not available, meaning the estimates are guesses rather than data-driven. • The requirement for upfront forecasts was therefore described as a 'ridiculous nonsense of a process' because everyone knows the 'guess' is wrong, yet it is approved and then becomes the basis against which the project is assessed. • Project forecasts are being made to fit the guidelines and funding approvals, 'gaming the system'. • Organisational factors are generally ignored in forecasting. • The current guidelines exist to obtain surety over costs and time, yet what is delivered is a set of irrelevant figures. • Most institutional frameworks include an assurance process (e.g. gateway reviews), but these have failed because assurers face the same challenges as forecasters.
Financial management	• The public sector does not have the financial management capability and maturity to manage investments in large ICT software projects. • There is a focus on cost to the exclusion of investment. • The public sector does not treat its ICT solutions as assets so there is a lack of investment in maintenance, which leads to 'urgent projects' rather than planned and staged projects as part of a larger portfolio of work.
Contract management	• It is expected that full contract costs will be known upfront and included in the forecast, which is impossible for a long-term project with so many unknowns, leading to conflict with the vendor.
Organisational learning	• Despite much learning, the same issues keep arising. • Written records are ineffective, with real-time verbal interaction preferred. • Cross-agency and cross-jurisdiction sharing of learnings is rare, and there is evidence it is deliberately avoided.
Leadership	• Many large projects are meant to drive or enable organisational change; however, as the project progresses that intention is not matched by organisational action or willingness. The project then morphs into a customised solution to avoid major change.

Concept	Forecasting key findings
Entrepreneurship	• The way to close the forecasting capability gap is to stop undertaking large ICT projects as traditionally planned. • The public sector must look at alternative planning approaches to reduce complexity and enable progressive delivery through component-based planning, which will increase forecasting relevance. The problem is that public sector institutional frameworks do not support such an approach.
Agency	• Politics is a powerful force in the public sector and when it comes into play, the best governance guidelines can be ignored. • Agency is positive when used to address or bypass governance guidelines that increase the likelihood of poor outcomes.

Source: Compiled by author.

Conclusion

Once again, the perspectives of the elite interviewees across the various forecasting themes indicate that there is much commonality across the Australian and New Zealand public sectors.

These findings can be compared with key points in the literature review (see Table 5.3). While this is a simplified summary, it does highlight a disconnect between what the literature argues is good governance for forecasting and the perceptions of the elite interviewees on the effectiveness of institutional governance for forecasting in the Australian and New Zealand public sectors.

Table 5.3 Comparison of literature review and findings

Literature review (Chapter 2): Key points	Forecasting findings
Unrealistic forecasts 'corrupt' the decision-making process (Andersen et al. 2016).	Forecasts are being made to be approved rather than realistic.
Unrealistic forecasts set a benchmark for how the outcome will finally be assessed (Hall 1980).	The public sector is failing to address the issues with forecasting, resulting in unrealistic expectations.
There is a requirement for ethical planning — a forecast that is reasonable, truthful, and accurate (IPMA 2015; PMI 2017).	Actors are 'gaming the system'.

Literature review (Chapter 2): Key points	Forecasting findings
Forecasts are open to optimism bias, both delusional and deliberate, and organisations need strategies to manage this (Flyvbjerg 2008).	Optimism bias is not being effectively managed.
Project complexity increases the likelihood of poor or 'fanciful' forecasts (Cooke-Davies et al. 2011; Herszon & Keraminiyage 2014).	The forecasting process is 'ridiculous'; however, full upfront forecasts remain the norm in the institutional frameworks.
Component-based agile delivery is a means to break down complexity and improve forecasts, including changes to the funding of these projects (Cao et al. 2013).	The institutional frameworks do not support funding of large projects through a series of iterative smaller projects.

Source: Compiled by author.

6

Novopay case study: Alone and set up to fail

[T]he triumph of hope over reality, cross your fingers. I think that is the essence of it. (Person BD, MoE senior executive)

Introduction

The Novopay project to implement a new payroll service for the New Zealand Ministry of Education (MoE) went live in August 2012, and immediately encountered severe operational issues. This caused major embarrassment for the government, with extensive and prolonged negative media coverage. In 2013, the New Zealand Government commissioned an inquiry into Novopay that produced the *Report of the Ministerial Inquiry into the Novopay Project*[1] (Jack & Wevers 2013). The following statement was included in the report:

> The impacts of the well-publicised Novopay failures have reverberated across New Zealand. Every state and state-integrated school in the country has been affected. Dealing with the aftermath has distracted schools' staff, principals, boards of trustees, the Ministry of Education and Ministers from other important concerns. This state of affairs and the wider disruptions that were caused were avoidable. (Jack & Wevers 2013: 1)

---

1   The original *Schools Payroll Revised Stage Two Business Case*, November 2007 (Novopay), was not publicly available. Therefore, as noted in various sections of this chapter, information about the contents of the business case was obtained from references to it within the ministerial inquiry report.

However, while the report argued that the Novopay issues were 'avoidable', the narrative from my elite interviewees provided a different perspective— that is, the project was doomed from the outset, with the outcome not avoidable, but inevitable. As distinct from the argument of Gauld and Goldfinch (2006) that New Zealand agencies enter large projects with excessive optimism, in the case of Novopay, this was not the common perception. The MoE interviewees indicated an acceptance of responsibility, an awareness of the challenge, but also a feeling of isolation and abandonment by others who feared becoming too involved in a project that had a stench of death.

It was acknowledged at the time of project initiation that the MoE did not have capability in the various disciplines required for something as complex as Novopay, yet they received central approval and funding to do so. The MoE then became heavily reliant on institutional governance to steer and support them through the project—which failed. They adhered to the governance and it led them towards failure. From the outset, there was a huge gap between the way the delivery of Novopay was planned and the capability of the MoE to deliver. Novopay required a team of superhumans, but the MoE team were babes in the woods, on project management learner plates. There was also organisational amnesia, both within the MoE and jurisdictionally. The MoE had major problems with the implementation of the previous payroll, yet by the time Novopay began, that knowledge and experience had gone, meaning mistakes were repeated—indeed, magnified. Novopay is an example of the failure of institutional governance.

In this chapter, a brief history of the Novopay project is provided, followed by sections in which the perspectives of all the Novopay part two elite interviewees (see 'The puzzle' section, Chapter 1: Table 1.1) are analysed, supported by vignettes. These findings are then summarised by various categories, followed by a short conclusion.

There is one point readers should bear in mind. While both Novopay and the Education Payroll Development Program (EPDP), discussed in the next chapter, were complex cases, it is not the intention of this book to be an audit of the products delivered, benefits gained, and so on. Rather, our focus is on the institutional governance in these projects and its impact, as perceived by those involved. Did the institutional framework assist the projects in achieving positive outcomes or did it prove ineffective in providing the support and structure required? It is this focus on institutional governance and its impact that differentiates this analysis of the Novopay and EPDP cases from other literature.

Novopay project history

The Novopay project was a complex and ambitious undertaking, with the ministerial inquiry noting that the vision was to replace the existing MoE Education Service Payroll[2]

> with a modern, technology-based solution that would provide greater functionality, a better user interface and more useful information about the national schools' workforce. A new online payroll system was expected to increase efficiency through automation, improve consistency through standardised business rules, and improve payroll accuracy. (Jack & Wevers 2013: 32)

Key parts of this vision were to move from a manual paper/fax-based processing method to automated online transactions and to develop and implement a revised and efficient outsourced service delivery model (Jack & Wevers 2013: 26–27).

The achievement of this vision was dependent on many interrelated tasks (Jack & Wevers 2013: Ch. 2). The MoE needed first to procure suitable core payroll technology; however, the real complexity lay elsewhere— in the challenges of making the technology effective within the MoE (for example, paying the correct amount to the right people at the appropriate time), designing and developing a new service delivery model, contract management, vendor management, stakeholder management, all the change management tasks necessary to ensure sector readiness for use of the solution, and last but not least, the project management capability to undertake these tasks. It was the combination of these factors that added to the project's already significant complexity. It was not solely about delivering new technology; it was a major organisational change project requiring specialised capability.

---

2   The MoE's Education Service Payroll is the largest payroll in New Zealand, paying NZ$3.4 billion to more than 120,000 employees across 2,500 schools (MoE 2012b: 7).

The origins of what was to become the Novopay project began in September 2004 when the MoE issued a request for proposal (RFP)[3] as an initial step in replacing its Datacom payroll solution. However, technology upgrades negated the claim of urgency to replace the Datacom solution and the MoE in 2006–07 changed its approach to a purportedly more beneficial business process outsourcing (BPO)[4] model, which was approved by Cabinet in November 2007 (MoE 2012a). It was at this stage that the cost forecast was set and Talent2 was selected as the preferred BPO supplier[5] for both the core payroll technology and the service delivery, with contract negotiations completed in May 2008 (MoE 2012a).

The project was named Novopay and officially commenced in October 2008, with a planned staged implementation from May 2010 (MoE 2012a; 2012b: 16). In November 2008, it was reported that Talent2 was on schedule and within budget (MoE 2012c: Meeting #88); however, one month later, Talent2 was reporting schedule slippages (Meeting #89). The project board's meeting minutes for August to December 2009 (MoE 2012c: Meetings #97–100) highlighted a series of escalating issues—new and old—that were impacting on project deliverables and schedules. Nevertheless, it was reported in January 2010 that the system would go live in the first week of July 2010 (MoE 2012c: Meeting #101). While the project board was reporting this, an independent external review was reporting that 'all indications are that the original transition dates are not achievable' (Extrinsic 2010: ii). On 1 March 2010 (MoE 2012c: Special Board Meeting), a revised go-live date of 18 October 2010 was proposed. In May 2010, approval was given for the go-live date to move to no later than 30 June 2011 (MoE 2012b: 8). Importantly, this included a change from a staged implementation to a big-bang approach. By February 2012, there were further slippages and the project's baseline plan was again realigned, with Cabinet approving a revised go-live date of 14 August 2012. This effectively signified the death of any fallback options involving the Datacom system (Jack & Wevers 2013: 42).

---

3   According to the New Zealand Office of the Auditor-General, RFP is 'a formal means of seeking proposals from the market for goods or services where the public entity is open to supplier innovation—that is, where the outputs and outcomes are important, rather than the process the supplier follows to deliver them' (available from: oag.parliament.nz/2008/procurement-guide/glossary).

4   BPO is 'an overarching term for the outsourcing of a specific business process task, such as payroll' (Overby 2022).

5   The software solution/package to be provided and managed by Talent2 to meet the requirement was based on an ALESCO application built in Oracle Forms and PL/SQL, using an Oracle database (Deloitte 2013: 18–19).

In mid-August 2012, with a substantial number of defects remaining and awareness of issues with call centre readiness, the project board granted conditional agreement for the go-live (MoE 2012d: Issue 12). On 15 August 2012, all project board members—including those from the State Services Commission, independent members, and PricewaterhouseCoopers participants—supported a go-live decision (Jack & Wevers 2013: 49). On 17 August 2012, MoE secretary Lesley Longstone and project sponsor Anne Jackson gave final approval for a 20 August go-live date, despite testing cycles being incomplete (Jack & Wevers 2013), saying that outstanding defects would be treated after going live and any unidentified defects would be managed as business-as-usual issues (MoE 2012d: Issue 13). Novopay was officially live on 20 August 2012 (MoE 2012a).

Shortly after the go-live and before the first pay run, there were 3,200 unresolved issues (Jack & Wevers 2013: 50). After the first payroll, there were 5,000 underpayments and 700 overpayments, some of which were substantial (Jack & Wevers 2013: 49). Data entry was blamed, with Talent2 saying there was no 'systemic failure' (Jack & Wevers 2013), but the problems continued into subsequent payroll runs (MoE 2012d: Issue 17). The New Zealand Principals' Federation said it could not think of a year in New Zealand education when things had gone so badly (Drummond 2012).

In January 2013, the *National Business Review* quoted education minister Steven Joyce saying steps were being taken to address the outstanding issues. Joyce was also quoted as saying that while the problems were unacceptable, it was expected they would continue to arise. The minister announced the terms of reference for the ministerial inquiry into the Novopay Project (NBR 2013). The inquiry's report (Jack & Wevers 2013) was released in late June 2013 and identified a systemic lack of capability within the MoE to undertake the project. The MoE's secretary, deputy secretary/sponsor, and CIO resigned.

A Novopay technical review was also commissioned and its report was presented in February 2013. It concluded that the current platforms were not stable and correction would require a sustained effort and improved capability in both the MoE and Talent2. In addition, the software functionality did not always support the business process and a review of the solution design was needed, which would require strengthening of the current remediation effort (Deloitte 2013).

In 2013, the New Zealand Post Primary Teachers' Association (PPTA) filed a class action against then acting education secretary Peter Hughes over the Novopay 'fiasco', claiming he had failed in his statutory duty to pay teachers. While the PPTA stated that monetary outcomes would be part of the case, like the Deloitte findings, they also said the focus should be on fixing the issues with Novopay (APNZ 2013b).

The remediation efforts continued (and continue to this day). In July 2014, Talent2 reportedly paid NZ$22 million to remove itself from the payroll (Cowan 2014). Aligned to this outcome, the minister announced the formation of the Education Payroll Limited (EPL). Ownership and management of the school payroll service were transferred from Talent2 to this government-owned company, with the transition completed on 17 October 2014 (EPL 2020a). This marked the total failure of Novopay to implement the BPO model that was the centrepiece of the original business case.

Table 6.1 outlines milestones in the Novopay timeline.

Table 6.1 Novopay timeline

Date	Milestones
30/9/04	MoE issues RFP for new school payroll system.
28/2/05	MoE selects Synergy/Talent2 consortium as preferred vendor.
2/5/05	Cabinet approves Synergy/Talent2 approach.
31/12/06	MoE considers (during 2006) changing to a full BPO approach.
11/6/07	MoE agrees to change to a BPO approach.
8/7/07	Initial Cabinet approval for BPO approach.
5/9/07	Return on investment calculation for BPO approach issued.
7/11/07	Cabinet approves MoE business case with BPO as the preferred option.
12/12/07	RFP for BPO services issued to shortlisted firms.
22/4/08	Talent2 chosen as preferred vendor from the RFP.
11/8/08	Education Minister (Chris Carter) signs off on BPO/Talent2 agreement.
6/10/08	Official start date of Novopay.
31/5/10	Go-live date changed to 30 June 2011.
12/11/11	Go-live date changed to no later than 3 July 2012.
31/5/12	Go-live date changed to August 2012.
17/8/12	MoE approves go-live date.
20/8/12	System goes live.
19/12/12	MoE secretary (Lesley Longstone) resigns.
9/2/13	Peter Hughes starts at MoE, begins remediation plan and review.

Date	Milestones
19/3/13	Deloitte's Novopay technical review completed.
11/6/13	MoE deputy secretary (Anne Jackson) resigns.
30/6/13	Report of ministerial inquiry into Novopay released.
31/7/14	Education Payroll Limited (EPL) established to take over school payroll services from Talent2.

Source: Compiled by author.

Sponsor role analysis

From the initiation of Novopay until after the go-live, MoE deputy secretary Anne Jackson was the project sponsor. Jackson resigned shortly after Novopay went live, citing her responsibility, and was quoted by Radio New Zealand (RNZ 2013) as saying she was 'truly sorry for the additional stress put on teachers, staff, and pay administrators'. Jackson declined to be interviewed for this book. Her personal perspective would have provided a comparison with the views of others assessing her capability. It is the intention of this chapter not to be critical of Jackson's performance, but to assess how the institutional framework supported her in this role.

The initial discussions with interviewees focused on Jackson's capability to undertake the role. They believed that while there was an organisational assumption that Jackson was capable of the sponsor role, she was not, and the project was set up for failure. The appointment was also contrary to the institutional framework guidelines at the time (Synergy International Ltd 2001), yet the central monitoring agencies seemingly allowed this to happen. The following vignettes support these findings.

An MoE senior executive (Person U) said: 'Anne was a smart person … and she ought to have known' what to do. Vendors' views were harsher, with a Datacom executive (Person BA) saying that Jackson 'was completely clueless' and 'out of her depth'. Person BA argued, however, that this was a failure of the MoE, as Jackson did not have the required sponsor experience, and they questioned why the agency assigned her to the role, saying 'they were setting her and the project up for failure'.

Another MoE senior executive (Person BD) agreed with this perspective, stating that it was wrong 'to assume that someone in the policy area can just take on an IT project in a sponsor's role where you have these varying responsibilities and relationships which you may not have known about, just not had much experience. You are setting yourself up for a bad time'.

No interviewees were aware of any formal sponsor capability assessment before Jackson's appointment. Neither the report of the ministerial inquiry (Jack & Wevers 2013) nor other documentation such as the review of the role of the State Services Commission (SSC) (Thorn & McMahon 2013) make mention of this. However, the *Guidelines for Managing and Monitoring Major IT Projects* (Synergy International Ltd 2001: 23–24) state that the sponsor 'should have had prior experience in large [IT] change projects' and central agencies have a responsibility to ensure this is so.

Discussion then focused on how aware Jackson was of her responsibilities and accountability. Without interviewing Jackson, it is not possible to know what, if any, process was undertaken to ensure she understood the sponsor role and its responsibilities. Only one elite interviewee had any direct knowledge of how Jackson was made aware of the role, and this was via institutional framework guidelines and procedures—that is, by reading documentation. This person, an MoE senior project manager (Person AZ), stated that

> there was very definitely a role description that Anne Jackson signed up to that had … delineated what you would expect the sponsor role to have. It was captured in a number of documents that she signed off on. So, I do not think that she could claim that she did not understand that.

An MoE senior executive (Person BD), who in addition to a Novopay role had been the sponsor of an earlier large MoE ICT project, was asked about their awareness of the role. Their response indicates a vagueness about the role and a feeling of being left to fend for themselves:

> Interviewer: Did you know what the role of a sponsor of an ICT project was?
>
> Person BD: [W]hether I fully understood or not is probably a debatable question … [N]otionally, I thought I knew what it was, whether I had the right idea of what it was is questionable … [I thought it was] exercising governance to some extent … I had some concept, but I certainly would not say I had a deep knowledge or understanding.
>
> Interviewer: Did the SSC provide advice on the sponsor role?
>
> Person BD: No, nothing terribly specific.

Asked whether they thought Jackson had the awareness required, Person BD argued that she was not clear on the role, that it had not been fully explained to her, and that this should have been a jurisdictional responsibility before her appointment. Interestingly, the guidelines (Synergy International Ltd 2001: 38) indicate this is exactly what should have happened as it was a central agency responsibility to ensure at the project's outset that there was 'clarity around the sponsor's role and responsibilities'.

The other elite interviewees could only offer their perspectives on how well Jackson undertook the sponsor role throughout the project, such as a Talent2 executive (Person BG), who stated that Jackson was 'pretty hands off with the vendor' and it was 'almost as if Anne didn't understand where the responsibility was'. However, the future management of the role cannot be causally related to a lack of understanding of that role and its responsibilities. In summary, the perception was that Jackson was reliant on reading written documentation to understand the role. There was no evidence of central agencies undertaking their own responsibilities to ensure Jackson had absolute clarity about her role.

Without Jackson's input, it is also impossible to say whether her ultimate accountability—which was career-ending—was understood. Many of the interviewees had strong opinions about this and, in reflecting on the project's failure, believed Jackson was correctly held accountable. An MoE senior executive (Person BD) stated that this accountability 'comes with the job and should not have been a surprise'. An MoE senior project manager (Person P) believed 'it was correct for Jackson to lose her position' and a Datacom executive (Person BA) agreed that Jackson 'deserved to be fired'.

Another interviewee (Person BH), a senior representative of the teachers' union, the New Zealand Education Institute, stated that while Jackson may have suffered, the Novopay shortcomings impacted substantially and negatively on many others—the very people the system was meant to be looking after: '[W]e talk about the personal cost to Anne; there were people in the front line of schools' administration [for whom] the cost was very personal.'

Another interviewee had a different perspective. An MoE senior project manager (Person BC) suggested that looking for and punishing a fall-guy did not help the MoE or the New Zealand public sector in addressing sponsor capability. They argued that punishing Jackson did not address the real issue: the fact she was appointed to the role in the first place given her

lack of experience. Person BC said the MoE 'felt that she was just a scalp …
then they could wash their hands of it and say, "Now we are into a new era.
Those people that caused all that trouble have gone", and of course it was
not that easy'.

In the New Zealand parliamentary system, while Jackson as sponsor
had accountability for delivery of Novopay, the ministers responsible
for education had ultimate accountability for the system. However, the
ministerial inquiry (Jack & Wevers 2013: 88) found the ministers 'were
not always well served by the quality of advice' and effectively cleared them
of accountability. Several interviewees provided a different perspective,
claiming that political influence was downplayed in the inquiry to
avoid ministerial accountability. One New Zealand CIO (Person L)
recommended that, when reviewing the report's finding on accountability,
one should '[k]eep in mind it was written for the minister'.

These comments lead to another obvious question: if Jackson was not
capable and had little awareness of the role and her accountability, why
was she selected for and appointed to the position? Most interviewees were
unaware of how Jackson was selected and assumed it was because of her
seniority in the organisation. However, an MoE senior project manager
(Person BC) and a senior ICT executive (Person BE) were adamant that
Jackson's selection was due to her being the MoE deputy secretary with
line responsibility for Novopay deliverables, which they said was and still is
the de facto approach in New Zealand.

Jackson took on the sponsor role in addition to her substantive
responsibilities as deputy secretary that included school policy, teacher
supply, industrial relations, curriculum, and school infrastructure, which
was found to be a 'very large workload' (Jack & Wevers 2013: 81). An MoE
senior executive (Person BB) stated that, at the time, Jackson was also
responsible for 'big educational reform programs' that were under way.
Another senior executive (Person BD) and sponsor on a previous large MoE
ICT project was asked how they were selected and the model utilised:

> Interviewer: Were you given the role as a full-time position or on top
> of what you were already doing?
>
> Person BD: On top of everything else I was doing.
>
> Interviewer: Anne Jackson was given the sponsor role on top of her
> normal job and she was doing several large reforms. Do you think
> that was a good model?

Person BD: No, it is a significant learning … Secondly, my background was policy … and Anne's the same. We might have a bit of common sense but none of us has the detail. We end up running these things, [being] ultimately responsible, without adequate preparation or background.

Other interviewees argued that this was not an appropriate model, with a senior ICT executive (Person BE) stating that it put Jackson in a 'very difficult position'.

An MoE senior project manager (Person BC) posited that appointing Jackson as the sponsor was evidence of the ministry's 'immaturity' in these large projects. Perhaps the perspective of an MoE senior executive (Person BF) sums up these views best:

[T]hose deputy secretary roles are crazy anyway. They are massive, massive. They completely consume your life … [Y]ou just end up spending 14 hours a day dealing with crisis after crisis … Anne was responsible for so much. She had the National Standards debacle, she had the NCEA [National Certificate of Educational Achievement].[6] There were masses and masses of really large, high-profile policy and implementation work that she was responsible for. She would have had to have been Superwoman.

From a vendor perspective, a Datacom executive (Person BA) argued that while the sponsor should not have been a part-time role, the real issue was that Jackson was not the right person for the job and the MoE should have appointed someone with the necessary capability, experience, and available time. A former MoE senior executive (Person BF), now working externally, stated that in their current organisation:

[W]e would never do that. You would never say, 'Oh well, because this person is deputy director, that person is responsible for', and so on … You need to put people in charge with the skills, the time, and the focus … [T]he hierarchical default is crazy. It is just foolhardy.

Person BF argued that the creation of a temporary deputy secretary role with full responsibility for Novopay delivery would have been a better option, and this could even have been someone outside the ministry with the required capability. This is like the option employed by the Australian Commissioner of Taxation for a large project (see Box 3.1).

6   According to the New Zealand Qualifications Authority: 'The National Certificate of Educational Achievement (NCEA) is the main national qualification for secondary school students in New Zealand' (available from: www.nzqa.govt.nz/ncea/understanding-ncea/how-ncea-works/).

Finally, the elite interviewees were asked, if Jackson and the New Zealand public sector in general were lacking in capability, what training and support were provided to address this discrepancy? One of the reasons it would have been valuable to interview Jackson would be to confirm what training and support were provided or would have been beneficial to her in undertaking the role. No evidence was found of Jackson being offered training before her appointment, presumably because, as one MoE senior executive (Person BD) stated, 'none existed'.

Given the lack of training, Jackson would have been reliant on an effective support model, such as Novopay's project governance structure. An MoE senior executive (Person BB) stated that this was important as at the time of Novopay's initiation, the MoE was not mature in ICT capability, leaving the project reliant on external support and advice, such as from central agencies. However, the effectiveness of the agencies themselves was questioned by an MoE senior project manager (Person BC), who argued that the central agencies such as the SSC did not have the required experience or capability to advise on large projects. The quality of support and the impact on Jackson were also raised by an MoE senior executive (Person BD), who argued that the reliance on and trust in independent advice left Jackson exposed:

> [T]here is no central capability so where do you go … [T]here is a myriad consultants running around all over the place … [A]n additional challenge is to know who to believe and who not to believe, [and] how to use them … [T]hat leaves you exposed, too …. [Jackson] did not get a lot of help to know which help to take notice of.

The Novopay support structure did, however, comply with the requirements of the guidelines (Synergy International Ltd 2001) and was approved accordingly (Jack & Wevers 2013: 58). The ministerial inquiry found that this was inappropriate, ineffective, and resulted in 'misplaced confidence' (Jack & Wevers 2013: 71).

In conclusion, the elite interviewees' perspectives on sponsor capability were clear: Jackson did not have the required capability and was selected due to her position as a deputy secretary with line responsibility for Novopay. There is no evidence of any capability assessment before her appointment, despite this being a requirement in the institutional framework. To compound this, Jackson was not provided with training, the centrally approved support structure failed to fulfil its own role, and Jackson was expected to undertake the sponsor role on top of her existing, substantial duties. This is an inappropriate model, as one interviewee claimed Jackson would have had to be 'Superwoman' to make it work. It was a commonly held view that all these factors set the project and Jackson up for failure from the outset.

While there was consensus that Jackson was rightly held accountable for Novopay's shortcomings, there were two other perspectives on accountability that varied from the findings of the ministerial inquiry. First, it was argued that punishment was not the only option and did nothing to encourage future executives to put their hand up for the sponsor role. Second, it was argued that the role and influence of the minister/s in Novopay were underplayed in the inquiry.

Project management role/discipline analysis

None of the interviewees believed the MoE possessed the required project management capability to undertake Novopay, with one senior executive (Person BI) saying the ministry lacked any 'project management structure'. An MoE senior project manager (Person BC) simply said: 'No, oh no, no way, no.'

An MoE senior executive (Person BB) said the ministry was 'not a sophisticated business organisation, it was a policy shop' and its capacity to run a large project 'was unbelievably immature'.

The Talent2 and Datacom interviewees argued that this lack of capability led to many of the later problems when basic project management principles were not followed at key decision points. A Datacom executive (Person BA) summarised these views: '[In the] project command group, none of them actually knew anything about the payroll or project management.'

In an interview with the *Education Review* (2013a), Peter Hughes, the Secretary of Education, supported all these perspectives by stating that his ministry was 'not set up for a project of that scale and complexity'.

An MoE senior executive (Person BD) argued that the ministry had been left to fend for itself and simply had to 'cobble together' a team as best it could. Another senior executive (Person BB), who held a senior Novopay role, argued that this was not just an MoE issue, as there was no such capability across the New Zealand public sector, which meant agencies had to deal with issues independently. This was supported by Mayhew et al. (2013) in a study of Novopay, who argued that the entire New Zealand public sector lacked the comprehensive project management capability to undertake a project like Novopay.

No interviewees were aware of any assessment of project management capability before initiation and approval, nor was this identified in documentation. Yet, the guidelines (Synergy International Ltd 2001: 38) specify central agency responsibility for assessing 'the level of experience the department has had with major IT initiatives and whether there are adequate in-house skills for project management'.

It is again unclear what happened to this monitoring role. The later impacts on the project of this capability gap are well documented in the ministerial inquiry's report (Jack & Wevers 2013: 41, 45, 63, 97). A Deloitte (2013) report also found that the lack of project management capability contributed to project issues. An example of this is the go-live decision-making process, which is discussed in Box 6.1, which explores how the political factor compounded this lack of capability.

Box 6.1 Go-live decision-making compounded by political pressure

The ministerial inquiry found that the decision to go live with Novopay despite a range of outstanding issues, such as incomplete testing, was the result of not using the correct disciplines and poor project governance (Jack & Wevers 2013: 43–51). This was supported by a senior ICT executive (Person BE), who argued that the go-live decision reflected the MoE's low project management maturity and poor governance.

However, some elite interviewees with involvement in or close knowledge of the process presented a different perspective—of political influence on the go-live decision. An MoE senior executive (Person BF) who was aware of this stage of the project argued that ministerial pressure to implement the solution was 'central' to the final go-live decision. This pressure led to a myopic focus on the date or, as a senior project manager (Person AZ) stated, a view that 'we [had] to do something, we cannot delay it again, let us just bite the bullet'.

An MoE senior executive (Person BD) argued that this reflected a collective mindset in which no one was quite 'brave' enough to speak up, so the result was 'the triumph of hope over reality, cross your fingers. I think that is the essence of it'.

Person BF was the most direct about ministerial influence and argued that people are simply 'so afraid' they will not speak up. When asked to clarify this in terms of the actors responsible for making these decisions in Novopay, the following conversation ensued:

> Interviewer: There were decisions made that were found not to follow solid project management processes, such as the go-live decision. What makes a collective of senior people do this?

> Person BF: [P]ublic servants have pressure on them [from ministers], and this is high pressure. People are on fixed-term contracts, they lose their jobs, they get yelled at, they get treated really, really badly, they get humiliated. It is awful. It is an awful, awful environment [with] bullying and abuse, and they are told to come up with a [decision] ... People are fearful about their own careers.

> ... [T]hat political dimension was appalling ... Ministers—many of them are very capable—but they are not experts in large-scale IT systems ... They are just not in the best position, and they are driving. They want to reduce the cost ... [T]hose political imperatives to reduce cost and to drive through the change are just the wrong ones ... [and] that environment is not conducive to good decision-making. You produce the answer that the politicians want to hear, rather than the actual answer ... They wanted to deliver good news.

When the challenges of 'speaking up' at these times were discussed, it was posited by several interviewees that, when it comes to going live, the decision should be independently reviewed by a capable and qualified party to remove all extraneous influences—something akin to the accounting principle of separation of duties/responsibilities. An MoE senior project manager (Person BC) describes this as: '[Y]ou should not have the people who have a gun to their head having to make that [go-live] decision.'

It was argued that the separation of responsibilities is a means of removing the need for courageous decision-making. Excluding arguments over its effectiveness, a gateway review is normally undertaken at this stage, but this was not done for Novopay. The idea proposed is a step beyond gateways and implies total organisational and political independence.

There was a discussion with the elite interviewees about what importance project management was given within the MoE and the perception was that, at the time of Novopay, this capability was not a priority. The organisational focus was on educational initiatives—a view supported by a Datacom executive (Person BA), who stated that the MoE executive and senior management team were 'really good-hearted, well-meaning people who have good, solid principles. They are good people, but ... they are not actually really imbued in ... project management'.

That perspective found support in the ministerial inquiry's report, which highlighted cultural issues within the MoE that led to poor practices in project management (Jack & Wevers 2013: 82–83). There was also a view that at the time of Novopay this was not just an issue in the MoE but was common across the New Zealand public sector. An MoE senior executive (Person BB) argued that the MoE and the Novopay team were left to fend for themselves: '[T]he whole of government was not acting as a whole of government at the time; it was acting as independent departments, so that [seeking government support] was more of a fantasy solution than a real solution at the time.'

Person BB argued that, like the sponsor appointment, this resulted in the appointment of MoE executive staff to senior project management roles for which they did not have the capability. Person BB admitted they were appointed to a senior Novopay role based not on capability but on organisational seniority and availability, and said they 'learnt as they progressed'.

At the time Novopay began, PRINCE2 was being implemented in the MoE (Jack & Wevers 2013: 58), but the elite interviewees believed the MoE lacked the structure and maturity to manage the process and to provide guidance on its use. An MoE senior project manager (Person AZ) directly impacted by this initiative stated: 'It was the first time the MoE had used PRINCE2' and because there was no project management office, 'its application varied'.

Another claim was that PRINCE2 was used almost as a front for project management maturity, with a Datacom executive (Person BA) saying they had been told by the MoE that PRINCE2 would help improve project management capability, which they believed was 'naive' as it would not and did not. An MoE senior executive (Person BD) argued that the use of PRINCE2 made people 'feel better' but it was merely 'cosmetic'—that is, it was seen as an act of compliance rather than being effective.

These perspectives had support in the ministerial inquiry, with a finding that while the Novopay governance structure complied with PRINCE2, it was not of sufficient quality (Jack & Wevers 2013: 63). The guidelines (Synergy International Ltd 2001: 4) indicated that it was up to the MoE to 'make their own decisions about which proven project management tools and techniques' would be used. Therefore, the MoE—acknowledged to be lacking in project management capability—was left to make these decisions independently.

It was interesting to discuss how the MoE addressed this capability gap at the initiation and planning stages. An MoE senior executive (Person BB) with a senior project role stated that the ministry's capability and capacity were sourced from internal full-time resources for some roles, but 'we contracted people predominantly [as] there was not much [capability] inside the ministry'.

Project managers were among those sourced externally; however, Person BB stated that the MoE did not identify the need for an experienced and capable payroll specialist to lead the program management of Novopay. This role seemingly sat with the MoE executive appointed to the business owner role, with the senior project manager/s reporting to that person. An MoE senior executive (Person BD) stated that the business owner was responsible for these recruitment decisions. Talent2 was responsible for its own project capability and capacity, which, again, was a mixture of internally and externally sourced resources.

An MoE senior executive (Person BF) said that, where external contractors were used, the numbers were limited during Novopay due to both budget and capacity caps. They argued that if one wanted to hire an 'A-team', capacity requirements would not be met as the headcount had to 'fit within a budget'. The alternative was to engage less capable but cheaper resources: quantity over quality.

Perhaps as a result, a later independent review (Change Dynamics 2011) found Novopay lacked project management capability and capacity at all levels. The ministerial inquiry found that issues with the project management team's structure were a key factor in many of the problems (Jack & Wevers 2013: 65). However, the guidelines (Synergy International Ltd 2001: 57–58) indicate that there is a monitoring agency responsibility at the initiation and planning stages to review the project team's structure and resourcing, before commencement. There is no evidence this occurred.

A key part of the project management discipline for a large project involving a third-party solution and provider is vendor management. The MoE and Talent2 had a critical interdependency; therefore, without vendor management capability, the project was arguably doomed. A Talent2 executive (Person BI) stated that, from the outset, the MoE approached the project 'combatively rather than collaboratively'.

Another Talent2 executive (Person BG) said the MoE project manager had advised them at the outset that their role was to 'kick the vendor', and when they raised this 'aggressive approach' with the MoE project owner, they were 'brushed off'. There was also a view among the Talent2 interviewees that the company had been too compliant, to their detriment. Person BG stated that '[o]n reflection, Talent2 said yes too much', but this was so they did not 'rock the boat'.

The MoE interviewees mainly focused on the souring of the relationship with Talent2 as the project progressed—arguably a reflection of the impact of the lack of vendor management capability. The one exception was a senior ICT executive (Person BE), who argued that the MoE's approach from the beginning was to focus on the commercial aspects and this got in the way of 'common sense and pragmatic decisions'.

This view was supported by the ministerial inquiry report, which found that the MoE did not have the capability to manage vendors in a project as complex as Novopay (Jack & Wevers 2013: 67). There was also evidence supporting Talent2's perspective that the MoE took an aggressive approach. It was claimed that Talent2 had attempted to implement a formal change management process but was told by the MoE that this 'would significantly affect the relationship' (Jack & Wevers 2013: 66), so it was not pursued. The assessment of vendor management capability is not mentioned in the guidelines (Synergy International Ltd 2001).

In conclusion, the perceptions of the elite interviewees on project management capability are again clear: the MoE did not have the required capability to undertake Novopay and it was left to address this gap independently as best it could. Project management was not an organisational priority and was misunderstood, with the MoE focused on education policy priorities. Despite institutional framework guidelines to the contrary, the New Zealand Government approved the MoE to undertake the project. It did not end well.

The MoE addressed resourcing capability and capacity for Novopay largely through external suppliers; however, it did not engage a highly skilled and experienced payroll system project management expert to sit across the project and be a key support mechanism for the sponsor. This role was filled by an inexperienced MoE senior executive, which led to decisions being made that were contrary to project management best practice. The critical vendor management, particularly with Talent2, was also poorly managed by the MoE.

Forecasting role/discipline analysis

This section focuses on the preparation of the original business case[7] from which the project was forecast and approved.

Without access to the business case, it was not possible to identify who prepared the document, nor could I find any reference in the ministerial inquiry's report; however, the elite interviews did shed some light on this. An MoE senior project manager (Person BC), who was involved in early parts of the business case development, said the process was driven by the MoE Policy Unit, which, they argued, did not have the expertise required. An MoE senior executive (Person BB) involved in this process said there was an understanding within the ministry that it did not have the capability to prepare the business case, so it engaged a local project management consultancy firm,[8] one of whose consultants was cited as the lead with overall responsibility for preparing the document. This was seemingly due to individual initiative rather than an identified process within the guidelines (Synergy International Ltd 2001: 25–32).

Although the ministerial inquiry highlighted various weaknesses in the business case (Jack & Wevers 2013: 32–33), it was prepared and approved following the processes identified in the guidelines (Synergy International Ltd 2001: 30), which require the inclusion of costs for the entire project, even when this is 'scheduled to cover several years in duration'. The business case complied with the 'part two' requirement that the document be the 'final consideration of the business case, [with] fully developed costs and benefits'—that is, the MoE was required to prepare a full upfront forecast for the entire project.

The elite interviewees were asked about this requirement and how it was possible to forecast Novopay with any accuracy. An MoE senior project manager (Person AZ) simply replied that 'you cannot'.

---

7   Ministry of Education, *Schools Payroll Revised Stage Two Business Case*, November 2007 (cited in Jack & Wevers 2013: 32).

8   The name of the consultancy firm has been kept confidential. The consultant who was cited as the lead in preparing the document was approached for an interview but did not answer any correspondence, hence this claim by MoE staff could not be validated with the firm or the individual, nor was there any way of questioning that consultant's experience or approach in forecasting for such a large government ICT project.

An MoE senior executive (Person BD) stated that it was 'not possible' to forecast future Novopay impacts, evidence of which was the project later discovering 'so many things', resulting in 'more and more' work. This specifically related to being unaware of the complexity of the project at the initiation stage, and the tasks only becoming clearer as the project progressed. Person BD claimed that because of the initial upfront forecast and subsequent budget approval, which did not include estimations for these newly discovered complexities, the MoE had to live with impossible budget limitations or, as they put it: '[Y]ou get locked in, so you have to make it work.'

This impossibility was a common theme—for example, an MoE senior project manager (Person BC) who had knowledge of the Novopay forecasting process said the problem was that, in the business case forecasting stage, the MoE had 'no idea of the scale' of what it was entering and how to achieve the outcomes, and the plan and forecast ultimately reflected that. Eppel and Allen (2020: 250) supported this when they argued that the MoE was from the outset 'blind to the outcome it was trying to achieve'.

The forecasting requirement also impacted on Talent2, with one of its senior project managers (Person BI) stating that there were concerns about the complexity and lack of clarity on requirements, which made it difficult to forecast with accuracy. However, they said these concerns were overlooked as there was optimism within Talent2 that they could deliver to the plan. Person BI stated: 'Optimism certainly comes into it. We really believed we could do a great job, but then reality hits as the project moves on and these things come out of the woodwork.'

Person BI argued that Talent2 should have pushed for a 'proof of concept', not only to validate the solution, but also to enable both the MoE and Talent2 to better plan and forecast for the remainder of the project. Instead, they guessed—badly and blindly—upfront.

Given the engagement of and reliance on Talent2, the contract component of the forecast was critical to its relevance. During the week-long contract negotiation, the MoE engaged an external negotiator (Jack & Wevers 2013: 35). The contract was then prepared by an external legal firm and was reviewed internally by the MoE's legal team, but there was no requirement for the government or a central agency to view the contract.

Like a dark cloud hovering, there was a critical limitation imposed on the contract negotiation. The business case with the full upfront project forecast, including the forecast contract cost, was approved in November 2007, yet the negotiations with Talent2 were not completed and signed off until August 2008. According to the ministerial inquiry report, the contract was then negotiated within this 'funding envelope' (Jack & Wevers 2013: 35). This was confirmed by a Talent2 senior executive (Person BG), who said that at the beginning of negotiations, they were informed by the MoE that it had a set amount of funding so the contract must stay within that amount—an imposed outcome to which Talent2 agreed.

The contract negotiation style was criticised, with an MoE senior project manager (Person BC) claiming that the ministry took a hardball, adversarial approach, which they described as a 'typical ministry thing' in which there is a belief that they have won if they have 'put one over the supplier'.

Person BC said that sense of victory was short-lived, and no one won as a result. The 'ministry thing' seemed to be confirmed by a comment from an MoE senior project manager (Person AZ), who stated that Talent2 'had signed the contract saying they were going to do these things for this much money, and I was damned if I was going to let them change it'.

The guidelines (Synergy International Ltd 2001: 51–52) highlight the criticality to the project of the contract and contractual relationship and stress that the contract negotiation must be a 'win-win' for both parties. Based on the interviewees' comments, this requirement seems to have been ignored.

The ministerial inquiry found that the contract negotiations were not suitable for the long-term nature of the project and there was a misguided emphasis on a 'fixed price' that later exacerbated problems (Jack & Wevers 2013: 36). It also expressed surprise that Talent2 would agree to the contract given the many unknowns of the project. This surprise was shared by an MoE senior project manager (Person AZ), who 'struggled to understand' why Talent2 signed a fixed-price contract for something so complex, and posited that if they had argued for a staged delivery contract, it 'would have been a more viable option for everybody'.

The idea that Talent2 entered into a contract that was commercially unsustainable was supported by others from both within the MoE and within Talent2. An MoE senior executive (Person BB) reflected:

> I do not think the people in Talent2 board level who signed off on the project had the faintest clue what the people who sold the project to us had signed up for, and that became very clear down the track … I think their eyes were bigger than their brain, to be honest.

That perspective was spot on, according to a Talent2 senior project manager (Person BI), who stated that the contract was negotiated by Talent2 sales staff and was not at a viable price, saying the sales approach was 'a fundamental mistake, and it set [the project] up for failure at that point'.

A Talent2 senior executive (Person BG) stated that at the start of negotiations, once the MoE identified the funding limit, Talent2 'did consider walking away from the contract at this stage'.

They posited that the decision to stay was influenced by wanting to 'have the prestige of the client' and optimism that they could pull it off. There was also an admission that at this stage Talent2 was 'a bit naive' and 'most definitely' underestimated the culture of the MoE. Person BG said they enjoyed working with Talent2 as there was a strong supportive culture in the organisation, but this had proved insufficient to deal with 'the challenges of Novopay' and the MoE. It is also interesting that, according to Person BG, at the contract negotiation stage, Talent2 was aware of the 'adversarial relationship between Datacom and the MoE' and was concerned that a similar approach would be applied to them. That turned out to be a valid portent as the project progressed. Person BG concluded by arguing that 'any vendor would have had the same issues':

> In hindsight, Talent2 should have walked away early when MoE would not accept responsibility and ownership of the project. We were never going to win in the MoE–vendor relationship. Talent2 have done this previously, where they decided it was just too much risk and a misfit of cultures to enter into a partnership with a government organisation and they pulled out.

This is exactly what Talent2 did in 2014—to their financial and reputational cost. It was reported (Cowan 2014) that Talent2 paid NZ$22 million to buy themselves out of any further Novopay responsibility. The Talent2 CEO was quoted as saying this move 'settles a flawed contractual arrangement between the parties'.

Given the above issues with capability and vendor and contract management, the elite interviewees were asked about the methods employed to make the forecast. An MoE senior project manager (Person BC) said it was developed by undertaking a series of workshops with a mixture of participants. The elite interviewee with the most direct involvement, an MoE senior executive (Person BB), indicated that the business case forecast was a 'best guess' from what was known at the time, and a relevant forecast could not really be made until Talent2 provided information: 'It would be unrealistic to have expected the ministry at that point to have known without Talent2 [involvement] how long you are going to take.'

However, the obvious and rather worrying problem with this argument is that contract negotiations occurred eight months after the business case and its forecast had been approved. As evidenced in the contract management section, the contract was therefore made to fit a monetary limitation rather than reflecting the work to be undertaken—an outcome that Talent2 accepted.

The guidelines (Synergy International Ltd 2001: 31) did not mandate a method to be used when preparing the forecast and left this up to the agency (p. 4). However, they do provide advice on the factors to be included, such as any direct or indirect project costs and contingencies, and an explanation of how these should be calculated (Synergy International Ltd 2001: 31). The ministerial inquiry ultimately found the methods and frameworks utilised by the MoE were 'weak' (Jack & Wevers 2013: 64).

The MoE elite interviewees had no recollection of any outside view being utilised; however—interestingly—nor did Talent2 when bidding for and planning the project, according to a Talent2 senior project manager (Person BI). Person BI said this was the result of optimism as Talent2 'had never had a failure before' so it was 'naive' about the task ahead and did not make external comparisons.

There was also the potential to incorporate into the planning and forecast lessons from the 1996 Datacom payroll project—the solution Novopay was replacing—which was also problematic (Jack & Wevers 2013: 30). The ministerial inquiry report noted that the MoE had implemented strategies in its planning to address these lessons (Jack & Wevers 2013), which was confirmed by two interviewees with knowledge of the planning process. An MoE senior project manager (Person AZ) stated that the ministry wanted to 'avoid the disaster' of the 1996 payroll and 'had incorporated some of those lessons into the plan'.

An MoE senior executive (Person BB) confirmed this, stating: 'We were particularly alert to the Datacom experience in our planning.'

Person BB went on to cite a story of when a Datacom executive met with MoE senior staff and recounted the implementation issues, the resulting political fallout, and how this impacted on project staff, such as '[b]eing called to the minister's office [late at night] in your pyjamas to sign manual cheques to pay people'.

Despite these statements by MoE staff, the ministerial inquiry report on page one states: 'It is clear to us that important lessons from the past, in particular those arising from the 1996 education payroll implementation difficulties and the INCIS experience in 2000, should have been learned, but were not' (Jack & Wevers 2013: 1).

The same issues encountered with the previous payroll implementation were repeated—and, in fact, magnified—with Novopay. There were claims that the institutional framework under which Novopay was planned was influenced by, and reflected lessons learned from, the Integrated National Crime Investigation System (INCIS) project for New Zealand Police (Jack & Wevers 2013: 19; Synergy International Ltd 2001: Preface). However, a selective comparison of three findings from the INCIS inquiry (Small 2000) and the related Novopay findings is displayed in Table 6.2, revealing that not much was learnt.

Table 6.2 Comparison of INCIS and Novopay planning and forecasting

INCIS lessons learned (Small 2000)	Novopay ministerial inquiry (Jack & Wevers 2013)
Contract (p. 157): A fixed-price contract for the whole of a large IT project has a high level of risk; a more flexible form should be used, requiring delivery in stages.	Contract (p. 36): The parties took an approach to the negotiations that was not suitable for the long-term strategic relationship that was being entered. There was too much emphasis on the total fixed price.
Contract (p. 157): Off-ramp and layby provisions are important means of risk control. Where they are in a contract, they must not be forgotten but kept under proper assessment.	Contract (p. 8): The contract was developed without a 'discrete stage gate and off-ramps' — for example, the development of requirements before 'commitment to the full solution'.
Requirements (pp. 29, 133–34): Business process re-engineering was critical to obtain INCIS benefits. The process was poorly managed and the budget did not reflect the cost of the changes.	Requirements (p. 37): The process of gathering user requirements was poorly managed and there was no appreciation of all the requirements.

Source: Compiled by author.

While there was an attempt to include past lessons, many of the same issues were repeated.

Within Novopay, there was extensive unplanned customisation of the software (Jack & Wevers 2013: 10). A Talent2 executive (Person BG) laid the blame for this squarely on the MoE, saying that 'there was a 100 per cent unwillingness for the MoE to change their ways—the worst I have ever seen. This led to heavy customisation of a core package that drove many of the later issues'.

Person BG argued that this was symptomatic of the way Novopay moved from being a planned business-change project to taking a technical focus— 'do what is required to make it work technically'—so that the human aspect was 'lost in the mess', as were the future impacts on the MoE. Person BG said the result was 'the product morphing from a package they bought, into almost a replica of the previous solution and the MoE seemed to not acknowledge what impact these decisions had on the project's time, costs, effort, and future impacts on support and upgrades, etcetera'.

The MoE's perspective was slightly different, with a senior project manager (Person AZ) arguing that part of the problem was it was an Australian product built around Australian legislation, so some change was inevitable and necessary; in fact, they stated, 'the ministry did not have any choice' but to make changes in those areas. However, they also admitted that the customisations made went beyond the necessary and changes were made to fit the solution with current processes rather than changing the business. Another MoE senior project manager (Person BC) argued that this was an example of a lack of 'maturity' within the MoE, which failed to understand the impact on the project of those changes.

The guidelines (Synergy International Ltd 2001) do not provide guidance on customisation and the resulting forecasting and planning considerations within large ICT projects. It was not possible from the interviews or the ministerial inquiry report to identify how much customisation was factored into the original plan and forecast. However, the interviews indicated this went beyond initial expectations, and the inquiry report stated that the changes 'compromised the original intent' of the solution (Jack & Wevers 2013: 10). Suffice to say, the extent and impact of the customisations could not have been included in the original forecast.

As identified in earlier chapters, another key aspect to include in forecasts are the organisational factors that could impact on plans, either time-wise or financially. A senior Datacom executive (Person BA) was emphatic about an initial planning mistake: the MoE failed to engage with or understand the impact on schools—the primary user group. Person BA claimed that instead of taking the stance of a partnership with schools, the ministry took the line of 'telling the schools what the schools were going to do'.

They argued that this was a fundamental planning failure because the MoE did not have this authority within the New Zealand school system, so the entire solution and rollout strategy were flawed from the outset. This perspective was supported by an MoE senior executive (Person BD), who stated that, despite the lessons from the 1996 payroll implementation, the MoE repeated the mistake of not engaging with the school sector and enlisting their help with 'creating solutions and identifying problems'.

They went on to argue that this was a cultural issue within the MoE at the time: '[I]t is also a little bit of a mindset ... amongst some people in the ministry ... almost a "stakeholders are to be tolerated" [attitude] rather than a true partnership model.'

A senior teachers' union representative (Person BH) supported the above perspectives, arguing that there was no effective communication or partnership with schools and the project was essentially sold as providing schools with a better system and more autonomy—an argument they said was 'extremely convincing'. The *Education Review* (2013c) gives some indication of how Novopay was sold to schools and why it may have been 'extremely convincing'. The MoE promised a solution that would reduce time spent on payroll management, with increased accuracy and additional easy-to-use features. Person BH stated that there was 'blind confidence' in the MoE's ability to deliver, but the ministry did not know all it needed to and based its planning on 'flaws' that were quickly exposed, leading to a 'nightmare' for schools once the system went live.

An MoE senior project manager (Person P) suggested that this lack of engagement with schools, and with Datacom, meant the MoE was blind to the work schools did for each payroll, the interpretation of various agreements, and the interaction between schools and Datacom. The MoE planners made assumptions that were incorrect as a result. Mayhew et al. (2013) supported this perspective, concluding that the entire requirement-gathering process, and therefore the design to meet those, was 'flawed'.

The second major organisational impact mistake that the MoE made in planning, according to a Datacom executive (Person BA), was to think the worst of Datacom and remove them as quickly as possible as a project dependency. There were two mistakes with this: first, the MoE and Talent2 were heavily reliant on Datacom for knowledge of the existing solution; and second, despite failing to secure the new contract and being in an increasingly difficult relationship with the MoE, Datacom had no intention of walking away. There was evidence of this commitment during and after the go-live, when it was found that 'Datacom collaborated fully with the Ministry in developing the contingency option and continued to do so when post–Go Live issues became evident' (Jack & Wevers 2013: 67).

An MoE senior project manager (Person BC) stated that the MoE had deliberately excluded Datacom from planning and, as a result, had no idea what the rules were, how the system worked, or the challenges—all critical factors to incorporate in planning and forecasting. This was also a finding of Mayhew et al. (2013), who argued that the MoE deliberately excluded Datacom despite its inherent experience in delivering and supporting the current service.

The 'old' Datacom solution was used as the catalyst for the Novopay project: 'it needed to be done as the old system was becoming redundant'. A senior teachers' union representative (Person BH) said schools were told the Datacom solution was at the end of its life and unless schools supported the Novopay project, the payroll would be at risk. This meant the major argument for Novopay was business continuity (Eppel & Allen 2020: 249).

As well as the end-of-life argument, the business case claimed the Datacom solution did not meet all requirements and that Novopay 'would provide greater functionality' (Jack & Wevers 2013: 32). However, an MoE senior executive (Person BF) claimed the flaws in the Datacom solution were inflated to support a change. They argued that while Novopay was being 'sold to ministers as a shiny new payroll system' that would fix everything, the issues with the Datacom solution were 'untidy' but not 'catastrophic'. They were not causing major problems for teachers or schools, they were not creating 'mayhem', and they were not a 'distraction'. The Datacom solution was supportable through to at least 2013 (Jack & Wevers 2013: 51), so the claim about the urgent need to replace Novopay was false (Eppel 2019: 2). Interviewees suggested this resulted in a missed opportunity to explore alternative options.

The guidelines (Synergy International Ltd 2001: 5) acknowledge the potential impact of political factors and the need for the agency/project to identify these at initiation and planning, assess their potential impact, develop mitigation strategies, and factor them into forecasts. For example, Novopay required political support to simplify the collective agreements (Jack & Wevers 2013: 33)—a key requirement if the software package was to be effective. There is little evidence in the available Novopay documentation of the inclusion of potential political factors in the project planning and forecasting. The elite interviewees could offer no direct insight into this and, without access to the business case, it is not possible to assess.

The elite interviewees suggested the business case was written to influence political support. An MoE senior project manager (Person BI) claimed the stated 'urgency' to replace the Datacom solution and the risks of not doing so were a tactic to gain political support for the business case: 'there will be trouble if we do not proceed with the BPO option', rather than identifying the political risks of proceeding. This is supported by a Novopay study by Cranefield and Oliver (2014: 9), who argue that Novopay planning underestimated the BOP option risks to the minister.

It is important to note, however, that the Novopay business case underwent an independent assurance review and was approved and supported. This leads to questions about the value and quality of such assurance. There was a perception that one of the issues the Novopay assurers faced was a reliance on the MoE for information. While the MoE had the organisational knowledge and while the assurers could ask questions, they could only provide assurance on the facts provided. An MoE senior project manager (Person AZ) said this dependency created issues. In assurance meetings with the SSC, the MoE business owner was not always open with details or, as Person AZ stated, the business owner 'was not telling them what is really happening'.

Another MoE senior project manager (Person BC) agreed about the lack of quality evidence provided to assurers, but also argued that part of the problem was that the SSC assurance staff did not have the experience to ask the right questions: 'I do not think I have ever spoken to anyone in SSC who would be really astute at knowing what you were trying to embrace', and to ask the relevant questions.

Of note is that the guidelines (Synergy International Ltd 2001: 26–32) state that monitoring agencies are responsible for assuring all aspects of the business case, including the forecast quality. As the business case and its forecast were approved, it can only be assumed that they passed central assurance. In addition, even though gateway reviews were introduced in New Zealand by the SSC in 2008—in time for use with Novopay—they were not applied to the project at any point (Jack & Wevers 2013: 90).

Novopay complied with the requirements at the time and the project was fully forecast upfront, including the total estimated cost (Synergy International Ltd 2001: 26–32), which then became the project budget. When asked about this practice and its suitability as a funding model, an MoE senior executive (Person BB) who was involved in the preparation of the business case replied: 'Was it the best? It was the way the process worked with Treasury.'

Another MoE senior executive (Person BD) was more direct and argued that the process was 'nonsense', that people knew the Novopay forecast would provide no 'surety', and it was done to satisfy the minister. They argued that this will only change when there is political change: '[P]eople understand the nature of the beast … and that means the politicians have to give up money without serious detail.'

It was argued that this is a cultural issue that must be addressed so that experiences like those with Novopay do not continue. This perspective was supported by another MoE senior executive (Person BF), who argued that there should be a principle of ministers setting parameters but letting agencies plan with confidence within those.

From the vendor's perspective, a Talent2 senior project manager (Person BI) blamed the funding process for many of the later project management issues as the focus was on cost rather than the work required and called the whole process 'stupid'. The 'nonsense' and 'stupidity' were proven: Novopay's original budget was NZ$182.5 million but, at the time of the ministerial inquiry (Jack & Wevers 2013: 76–77), the budget was NZ$206.4 million. This does not include future remediation costs, the establishment of EPL, or the Talent2 financial impacts. Suffice to say, the original forecast was inaccurate, so additional funding was necessary.

It was not possible to explore the financial management capability of the project management team or the resulting impact on forecasting in any detail, largely because there was no awareness among the elite interviewees or in the ministerial inquiry about who was responsible or the processes used. The exception was an MoE senior project manager (Person AZ), who stated that during and after the initiation period, it was the MoE business owner who had financial management responsibilities—the same person who earlier admitted they did not have large project management capability and were learning on the job. The guidelines (Synergy International Ltd 2001: 36) indicate it is a key role of the project board to oversee financial aspects of a project. Interviewees pointed out that the MoE's chief financial officer (CFO) was on the project board. I did ask this person for an interview—mainly to discuss the Novopay forecasting process, funding options, and potential differences in financial management practices for large projects—but they declined, saying it would be 'inappropriate'. I then asked Person AZ about the CFO's involvement at this stage, and they responded that it was 'very hands off … I do not think anyone wanted this to tarnish their reputation'.

Needless to say, the ministerial inquiry was 'surprised that the financial management of this project seems not to have attracted greater attention' (Jack & Wevers 2013: 6).

The final line of questioning of the elite interviewees was to investigate whether any other planning options had been considered as part of the business case preparation, such as breaking the project and its deliverables into smaller components. An MoE senior project manager (Person BC) argued that it was impossible to avoid undertaking Novopay as a large project and the notion that it could have been was 'obviously, crap, actually'.

Other interviewees were more reflective, arguably with the benefit of hindsight. An MoE senior executive (Person BD) mused that it was 'legitimate' to challenge the initial scope and question whether it was 'far too big', and perhaps a better approach would have been to break it into smaller projects. From a stakeholder perspective, a senior teachers' union representative (Person BH) wondered who were the 'drivers' of projects like Novopay—the imputation being it was certainly not the stakeholders, who suffered from these failures. The *Education Review* (2014) argued that a full pilot program or trial would have been worth 'the expense and hassle' and noted that schools had requested this but were told it 'was not feasible'.

The institutional framework does in fact recommend that larger projects be broken into smaller projects, each with its own business case (Synergy International Ltd 2001: 44); despite this, Novopay was assured by central agencies as a large project and approved by the minister. Without access to the business case, it is not possible to ascertain whether other delivery options were considered; the ministerial inquiry's report makes no mention of this, nor were the interviewees specific about this.

I did ask a hypothetical question of an MoE senior executive (Person BF) who experienced firsthand the fallout from Novopay. I asked whether, if Novopay was to be planned today, with the same complexities, it would be planned any differently given all the organisational and political influences. They responded: 'No. Unless things have changed in New Zealand. You would have to have a courageous CEO who could explain it.'

They argued that while it is the minister's mandate to set parameters, the 'courageous CEO' must explain that they do not know everything yet, they will know more as the project progresses, they will keep the minister informed, but the minister must let go and trust a new way of delivery.

In conclusion, first, the Novopay forecast was compiled with the help of external specialist capability and to meet the guidelines in providing a full upfront forecast, although the interviewees believed this was impossible to do with any accuracy or relevance.

Second, a major component of the forecast, the cost of the Talent2 contract, was not negotiated on the work required, which was unknown, or the most suitable contract structure for the project, but on a figure set many months earlier. There was a perception that the MoE was playing hardball and that it believed by doing so it had 'won'. Talent2 interviewees suggested their compliance exposed them commercially; in hindsight, they should have 'walked away' at this stage. The internal optimism and prestige of snaring a major new client kept Talent2 engaged, which was a critical mistake by both parties that all but ensured failure.

Third, while the project claimed to have integrated lessons from the previous payroll system, similar mistakes were made, with more disastrous outcomes.

Fourth, two critical stakeholders, New Zealand schools and Datacom, were all but ignored, which made the gathering of requirements and their inclusion in the forecast all but impossible.

Fifth, the project was not part of a replacement program and was sold on the need to urgently move from the 'old' system, yet that proved to be overstated and was used as leverage to gain political support. As a result, alternative options that could have lowered the risk were lost.

Sixth, assuring forecasts for large complex ICT software projects is as impossible as it is to prepare them. In addition—although the reasons are disputed—Novopay was not subject to a gateway review even though this was available.

Last, Novopay could have been broken into smaller stages to lower the risk, and indeed this was the requirement in the guidelines; why this did not happen is unclear. Interviewees argued for cultural change in the forecasting and funding of these types of projects—a change that would require the minister to 'let go'.

The findings and their conceptual relationship

The elite interviewees indicated that the MoE did not have the required capability or capacity in any of the identified roles or disciplines to undertake Novopay. The MoE at the time was an education policy shop, with little to no organisational priority given to addressing capabilities for large ICT software projects. There was also a belief that actors skilled in their organisational role could transfer those skills to a large ICT project, but interviewees claimed they could not. The perception was that the MoE and Novopay were set up to fail from the outset. In this regard, the ministerial inquiry highlighted an important lesson learned: 'Do not start projects until the required capabilities are in place or identified' (Jack & Wevers 2013: 13).

Second, the guidelines (Synergy International Ltd 2001: 23–24) require central monitoring agencies to assess an agency's capability to undertake a large ICT project before commencement. The elite interviewees claimed this did not happen, and no evidence was found to the contrary. Aligned to this was a perception that the central agencies themselves did not have the capability to undertake their key monitoring roles.

Third, MoE interviewees tried to boost capability and capacity by engaging external resources for various tasks throughout the project; however, in a major failing, the senior project management role was filled internally by an actor without experience or the necessary skills. These efforts were also impacted by financial constraints.

Last, the capability of the minister was raised as an issue. It was argued that while the minister may be capable in their day job, they did not have the project management experience and capability required to make or challenge decisions, or to understand the impact of their decisions.

For financial management, there was a documented requirement for the preparation of a full upfront forecast for the entire project. This was perceived as 'nonsense' that immediately put the project at risk. It was impossible to account for every organisational, political, and technical factor over such an extended time frame. This requirement impacted on not only the MoE but also Talent2 as the complexities and cost and time implications began to be realised.

The replacement of the Datacom payroll solution with Novopay was not part of an asset or portfolio management process. Instead, it was sold as an urgently needed replacement for an end-of-life system. Interviewees claimed the ministry overstated the need for this and, as a result, possible alternative approaches were not considered. This risk to the payroll was also used to gain political support for the Novopay option.

The perception was that the initial contract negotiation with Talent2 was a key factor in the project's failure. The negotiation occurred many months after the Novopay forecast, which included an estimate for the contract cost, was approved. The contract was therefore negotiated not on what needed to be done and a fair cost for this, but on a preset budgetary limitation. Instead of walking away, Talent2 agreed to this, apparently because it wanted to get a foot in a lucrative market and because of optimism that it could deliver within these constraints.

There were three critical stakeholders to manage in Novopay, the first of which was the vendor, Talent2. Interviewees believed the ministry managed this poorly, adopting a take-no-prisoners, combative, and cost-focused approach. Talent2 accepted this to ensure their role on the project—to their later detriment. The second stakeholder was the schools—a relationship that was also poorly managed, with claims the MoE told schools what would happen rather than engaging them in the process. Schools, for their part, trusted the MoE, but that trust was betrayed once the solution went live and its poor quality and the impacts on school staff were realised. It was claimed that the third stakeholder, Datacom, had extensive knowledge of the peculiarities of the schools' payroll and it remained the supporting vendor for the existing solution and as a possible contingency option. However, the MoE excluded Datacom from key areas such as forecasting and requirements-gathering.

Interviewees believed PRINCE2 was used for Novopay to achieve compliance with a jurisdictional guideline rather than because it was of any substantial benefit to the project. Any claimed improvement in project management capability as a result was false.

The Novopay sponsor was held accountable and resigned from the public sector, with a general perception that this was 'deserved'. However, there was also a view that punishment was not the only course of action available and did nothing either to retain learned capability or to increase the likelihood of others willingly undertaking the sponsor role in the future. There was a challenge to the official view that the relevant ministers were free of accountability. It was claimed they did have a direct influence on decision-making, and therefore accountability, but this was ignored in official records.

Despite the then current guidelines (Synergy International Ltd 2001) and Novopay planning documents claiming to have incorporated lessons from past projects, such as INCIS, many of the same mistakes were made. To highlight this, the findings from *Dangerous Enthusiasms* (Gauld & Goldfinch 2006: 132–36)[9] are compared with the Novopay experience (Table 6.3).

Table 6.3 Comparison of lessons from *Dangerous Enthusiasms* with Novopay

Dangerous Enthusiasms (Gauld & Goldfinch 2006: 132–36)	Novopay, 2008–12
Things to do if you want to increase the likelihood of failure:	The Novopay response:
Make the project as big as possible.	It was huge.
Attempt organisational change and link this to the project, then continually change specifications throughout.	Organisational change was a key part of the project but was largely abandoned, resulting in extensive unplanned customisations.
Assume the contract will solve any problems and instead of breaking it into manageable components, award one for the whole project.	Talent2 had one contract — a bad one — and it became a major problem for both it and the MoE.

---

9   Gauld and Goldfinch's book investigated large New Zealand Government ICT projects and their findings included analysis of INCIS and other projects.

Dangerous Enthusiasms (Gauld & Goldfinch 2006: 132–36)	Novopay, 2008–12
Be pessimistic, guiding principles:	The Novopay response:
Be modest about what can be achieved.	There was no modesty in what Novopay planned to achieve.
Believe solutions will work only when they can be shown to work.	Proof of concepts was not part of the plan and proposed pilots were abandoned. The proof of concept happened at the go-live stage, with a big-bang approach, and disaster followed.
Expect to encounter the problems of past projects; they will happen.	They did.
Excluding frontline staff is a high-risk strategy and can undermine the solution even if it works.	The engagement with schools was poor and, as a result, the solution did not meet requirements, with the schools in active and public revolt.

Source: Compiled by author.

When the Novopay findings are compared with those from the earlier chapters on sponsors, project management, and forecasting, the results are revealing from a historical institutionalism (HI) perspective (see Appendix 5). The Novopay findings relate to actions in 2008–12, whereas the findings in previous chapters are from 2018–20. The comparison indicates that the institutional governance issues that plagued Novopay still exist a decade later, and indeed are closely aligned. Under HI principles, we would expect things to change in the intervening 14 years, that lessons would have been learned, and the institutional framework adapted accordingly, but no change is the common outcome.

There are two variances to note. The 2018–20 findings indicate that sponsors are rarely held to account for project failings, but the Novopay sponsor *was* held accountable. Second, in 2018–20, there was a strong belief that it is always possible when planning and forecasting to break down large complex projects and reduce their complexity and risk. Novopay did not do that.

The elite interviewees indicated a lack of leadership within the MoE for Novopay. A deputy secretary was appointed as sponsor but failed to undertake the full responsibilities of the role. The interviews did not identify the MoE CEO/secretary as having a leadership role for Novopay.

The interviewees' perceptions, supported by the ministerial inquiry (Jack & Wevers 2013: 81), were that the MoE leadership team tried to distance themselves from a project leadership role, with negative results.

There was also a leadership failure among the central agencies in their monitoring role for the Novopay project, as outlined in the institutional framework at the time, the *Guidelines for Managing and Monitoring Major IT Projects* (Synergy International Ltd 2001). For example, the elite interviewees claimed that the sponsor was reliant on reading documents to understand the role, whereas the guidelines (Synergy International Ltd: 38) state that it is a central agency responsibility to ensure the sponsor has clarity about the role. There was a perception that the MoE was left to deal with these issues independently. A decision was made to not use gateway reviews even when the problems with Novopay were known.

Ministers were seen to be taking a 'hands-off' approach, wanting to not be tainted. It was also claimed that there were direct and negative influences from politicians on project decision-making.

There was no entrepreneurship identified in the elite interviews and none reported in the ministerial inquiry. The project was troubled from the outset, yet no example of trying to do something differently was identified. Albeit with hindsight, elite interviewees believed the scope and approach should have been questioned and alternatives investigated as Novopay, as planned, was 'just too big'. It is interesting to note that the institutional framework (Synergy International Ltd 2001: 44) recommends breaking large projects into smaller subprojects.

There was an idea posited that the key go-live decision should have been reviewed and approved by a truly independent body to remove it from all organisational and political influences.

The elite interviews and documentation such as the ministerial inquiry report failed to identify positive examples of effective agency. The MoE business owner on Novopay wielded undue influence but did not have the capability in large ICT projects to use this power effectively and, it was claimed, they had this agency only because the sponsor delegated and avoided their own responsibility. The senior project managers were remote from the sponsor and claimed they had little agency. Central agencies should have played a greater role in monitoring the project as per the guidelines but failed to do so. The one example of agency cited by interviewees was the minister, who directly and negatively influenced decision-making at the go-live stage, with a mentality to push the implementation of the system as quickly as possible taking precedence over best practice.

Finally, while risk management was not one of the theoretical concepts used in the analysis, given the poor Novopay outcomes, it is worth mentioning here. This case study highlights the many risks within the project that ultimately impacted on the delivery of the planned benefits. Research by Zwikael and Smyrk (2015) analysed the role of governance in the delivery of these benefits based on principal–agent theory and a control–trust–risk approach. They conclude that in high-risk projects the most effective approach is for the project owner to trust the project manager and governance groups to highlight and address risk, rather than taking a top-down control-based approach. The issue with Novopay was that neither the project manager nor the governance groups demonstrated the capability to manage and mitigate the risks; in Novopay, trust was misplaced.

Conclusion

The elite interviewees highlighted a failure in the institutional governance for Novopay; it was ineffective and contributed directly to the poor outcomes. The MoE should never have been approved to either commence or continue with the project as planned, yet it was. This was not an MoE failing, but an institutional failure.

The elite interviewees also highlighted two distinct variances from the findings of the ministerial inquiry. First, the critical go-live decision-making process was directly influenced by political pressure, while the inquiry absolved ministers of any influence. Second, guidelines within the institutional framework were not enforced by the appropriate central agencies, while the inquiry arguably ignored this perspective and central agency responsibility.

7

EPDP: Doing things differently

[S]ome people live in the past and we need to move on from that. There is history and there are things that went wrong, but having a fresh face sometimes is a lot better because they do not have the wounds of the past. Looking forward perhaps, rather than looking back. (Person BW, Senior project officer)

Introduction

The outcome of this second case study is the opposite of the Novopay case study. Whereas Novopay was widely labelled a failure and an embarrassment for the government, the Education Payroll Development Program (EPDP) was generally claimed to be an outstanding success and an exemplar in New Zealand public administration. This is interesting as the EPDP was similar to Novopay in aiming to provide a payroll service to the New Zealand Ministry of Education (MoE), so therefore had the same stakeholders and challenges and operated within the same institutional governance framework, yet the EPDP succeeded where Novopay did not; what explains this?

In the decade after Novopay, the New Zealand Government's institutional framework for ICT projects underwent changes, some of which were the result of Novopay learnings; however, the institutional framework itself was not adapted effectively and imposed similar top-down constraints on the EPDP, adding complexities to an already complex project. The institutional focus remained on imposing controls.

However, the EPDP leadership did learn from and proactively addressed in their planning the mistakes made in Novopay, such as poor stakeholder management and the extreme risk in delivering a big-bang payroll implementation. The EPDP team was at pains to ensure strategies were in place to address these learnings, and they did so successfully. They also addressed the issue of the MoE having neither the skills nor the staff to undertake a large payroll project—something that was fatal to Novopay. Major work on the EPDP did not begin until those skills and team were in place. They also decided to implement an agile delivery approach to progressively deliver components and build expertise, relationships, and learning as they progressed. They even made uptake an opt-in model and, as evidence of success, the users liked what they saw and opted in.

Nonetheless, it was concluded that these initiatives were not the result of changes in the institutional framework, but were due to the capability and entrepreneurship of the EPDP sponsor, who evaluated the framework and decided, where possible, to step outside the guidelines to avoid being forced down the same path as Novopay. The overriding theme from the interviews was that the EPDP benefited by chance from having a sponsor as capable and entrepreneurial as Arlene White. Without White at the helm, the result may have been quite different. It was stated that there was no appetite within the New Zealand Government for a repeat of Novopay and White and her dedicated, collaborative, and capable team successfully avoided this. They did so by using a different approach and learning from the past; the contrast with Novopay is stark. Doing things differently required strong leadership and a leader willing to take up the fight institutionally. The approach taken also highlights the flaws in the institutional framework and the need to adapt accordingly because White cannot oversee every large ICT software project.

In this chapter, a brief history of the EPDP is provided, followed by sections in which the perspectives of all the part two EPDP elite interviewees (see 'The puzzle' section, Chapter 1: Table 1.1) are analysed, supported by interview vignettes. These findings are summarised by category, followed by a short conclusion.

The interview data were compared with the following institutional framework documents in place for the EPDP: *Better Business Cases: Guide to Developing the Programme Business Case*[1] (The Treasury 2015),

1   'This guidance document is intended to assist investors, senior responsible owners, workshop facilitators and business case developers to prepare Programme Business Cases' (The Treasury 2015: 2).

Better Business Cases[2] (*BBC*) (The Treasury 2019), the *Investment Review Report for Education Payroll Limited, Operational & Benefits Realisation Review*[3] (The Treasury 2020), the *Schools Payroll Detailed Business Case* (EPL 2016), the *Programme Initiation Document for Education Payroll Development Programme Implementation Phase* (*PID*) (EPL 2017), *Expanded Guide to the Leadership Success Profile*[4] (SSC 2016), and *Assuring Digital Government Outcomes: All-of-Government Portfolio, Programme and Project Assurance Framework*[5] (New Zealand Government 2018).

Project history

As detailed in the Novopay case study (Chapter 6), one of the outcomes of that project was that the vendor, Talent2, removed itself from any further involvement in supporting the payroll. To fill this void, in 2014 (EPL 2020a), a separate crown entity called the Education Payroll Limited (EPL) was formed. With this change, the MoE purchased payroll services from the EPL (2016: 8) instead of the previous contractual arrangement with Talent2.

The school payroll is described as non-standard, for which employer responsibilities are only partially devolved to schools. Hence, the EPL provides additional services, including 'compliance monitoring and enforcement, salary assessment, overpayment debt recovery, school payroll support and sector communications, payroll data and reporting, and management of banking staffing and staffing funding for schools' (EPL 2016: 8). This is detailed diagrammatically in Figure 7.1.

---

2   According to the New Zealand Treasury: 'The objective of Better Business Cases is to provide objective analysis and consistent information to decision-makers, to enable them to make smart investment decisions for public value' (available from: www.treasury.govt.nz/information-and-services/state-sector-leadership/investment-management/better-business-cases-bbc).

3   The New Zealand Treasury says: 'Review processes help to ensure that investment propositions are sound, offer value to New Zealand and are set up for success … These reviews help us to assess the performance of investments against expectations and to encourage stated benefits to be realised and assets to be operated near optimal levels of performance' (available from: www.treasury.govt.nz/information-and-services/state-sector-leadership/investment-management/review-investment-reviews).

4   Describes the 'levels of capability which are required in different roles across the New Zealand public sector' (SSC 2016: 3).

5   'This document describes an All-of-Government business capability model for defining and assessing the capabilities and maturity of government agencies or government entities' (New Zealand Government 2018: 2).

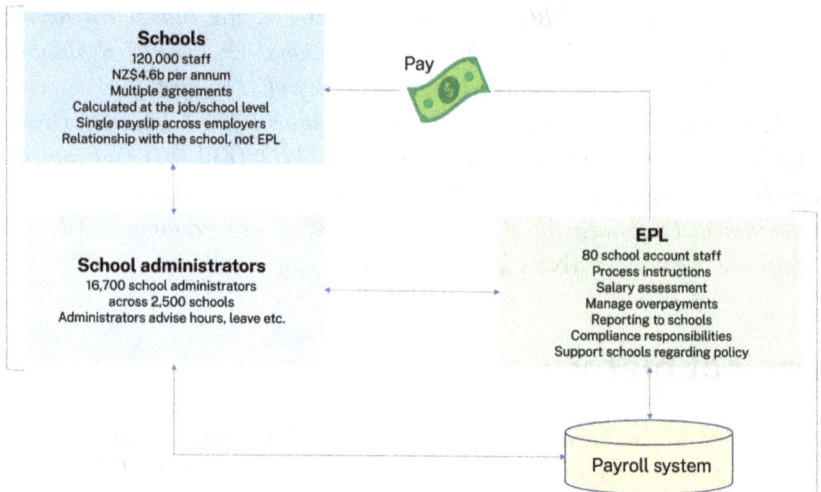

Figure 7.1 The school payroll and the EPL
Source: Created by author. Adapted from EPL (2016: 8).

After the 2012 Novopay go-live, the underlying 'standard' commercial off-the-shelf (COTS) payroll system was in fact 60 per cent customised (EPL 2016: 8). This, together with the many outstanding system issues, resulted in the EPL spending more than NZ$40 million on continual and significant improvements (EPL 2016: 8). Despite this, among other major issues, the core payroll infrastructure was not sustainable and the critical online component was proving impossible to maintain and enhance and would be unsupportable from December 2019 (EPL 2016: 9).

In late 2015, Cabinet requested the EPL advise how it would move the school payroll to a 'steady state including achieving cost efficiencies and long-term sustainability' (EPL 2016: 20). In February 2016, planning began, and a detailed business case (DBC) was finalised in October 2016 (EPL 2016: 22–25). The preferred option was to provide a new digital online interface for interaction between schools and the EPL, effectively replacing the Novopay online component.[6]

This highlights a differing scope from Novopay, which was to implement a new payroll support service and a new payroll system. The EPDP's scope, following a review of options, was to keep the core payroll system implemented by Novopay but replace the Novopay online service—

---

6   The underlying Alesco (Oracle) database was to remain; the focus was on providing a new online interface to this solution.

the major source of concern (EPL 2016, 2017). The complexity of this work should not be misunderstood for, as the business case (EPL 2016) and project initiation document (EPL 2017) argued, dismantling Novopay, developing a replacement online service, and managing all the environmental factors were complex, high risk, and would be done under intense scrutiny.

The program of work was estimated to cost NZ$64 million over 10 years. The DBC highlighted three key considerations in both the planning and the future management of the project: first, a series of packages would drive the program of work (EPL 2016: 123); second, there would be a heavy emphasis on implementing effective change management processes (pp. 149–57); and third, there was no appetite at any level for a repeat of the Novopay outcomes (pp. 15, 92–96, 157).

After approval of the EPDP, the EPL concentrated on preparation to hit the ground running (EPL 2017: 5), with project implementation due to be finalised by December 2019. The program opted for a scaled agile framework (SAFe)[7] delivery methodology (EPL 2017: 15) after successfully arguing that it would benefit from accelerated, progressive, and staged delivery of products and benefits, improved quality of practices, reduced risk, and greater flexibility to accommodate changing priorities and requirements.

As of September 2020, the program deliverables had not been finalised as per the DBC forecasts; however, that does not necessarily equate to the program being 'unsuccessful'. All the available documentation and the lack of negative media publicity indicate the program performed extremely well. An independent investment review report by the New Zealand Treasury in July 2020 stated: 'The Review Team finds that the EdPay programme should be commended as it has effectively delivered capability to the Education Sector, in-line with the Business Case … [A]s a result, the Review Team sees that EdPay has delivered the primary intent of the Business Case' (The Treasury 2020: 3).

---

7   According to the Scaled Agile website: 'SAFe is designed to help businesses continuously and more efficiently deliver value on a regular and predictable schedule. It provides a knowledge base of proven, integrated principles and practices to support enterprise agility' (available from: www.scaledagile.com/enterprise-solutions/what-is-safe/).

This is a quite different reading to that in the Novopay ministerial inquiry report (Jack & Wevers 2013), which found nothing to praise. The investment review report also found that the use of the agile delivery method was beneficial and the EPL had successfully enabled mature inhouse agile capacity and capability to finalise the project and provide future support (The Treasury 2020: 9, 10).

It is pertinent at this point to outline the differences and similarities between the Novopay and EPDP projects. The EPDP was not implementing a new core technology-based payroll solution; the core solution implemented by Novopay remained. However, as will become evident in later sections of this chapter, the EPDP was complex and faced many of the same challenges.

While the EPDP was not implementing a new core payroll solution, due to the failure of Novopay to deliver an effective online solution, the EPDP had to develop a solution removing sections of functionality from the core payroll—something that was later described as a 'complex mess' by the EPDP project sponsor. In addition, due to the failure of Novopay to deliver the BPO and the resulting move to an internal service delivery model, the EPDP had to revisit the core service delivery design and address the previous ineffective organisational change management.

The project had procurement, vendor, and stakeholder management challenges, and needed to develop inhouse capability and capacity to undertake the project and provide ongoing support. The project also had to win back the trust and support of the ministry, school staff, and indeed the New Zealand public—all while under the pressure to not become another government ICT failure. Finally, this had to be undertaken while continuing to resolve the outstanding Novopay remediation tasks.

Hence, while there are differences in some deliverables, both were complex projects. They also had the same vision (to pay staff correctly, have the core and online payroll technology in place, and implement an effective support model), were within the same organisation, and operated under the same institutional framework. Therefore, the comparison is not only relevant, but also highly interesting as it provides a means to analyse the starkly different outcomes of each project.

Table 7.1 outlines the milestones in the EPDP timeline.

Table 7.1 EPDP timeline

Date	Milestone
2014	EPL established.
Late 2015	Cabinet requests EPL move the school payroll to a 'steady state'.
Feb. 2016	Indicative business case prepared, after which Cabinet requests detailed business case (DBC).
Oct. 2016	DBC prepared; preferred option to provide new digital online interface (to replace Novopay online).
Late 2016	DBC approved.
Late 2016 – 2017	EPL concentrates on preparation.
Oct. 2017	EPDP Program Initiation Document (PID) approved; approach changed to agile.
Nov. 2017	Delivery of products begins.
Dec. 2019	Original planned completion date.
Sept. 2020	60 per cent of functionality delivered.

Source: Compiled by author.

Sponsor role analysis

At the start of the EPDP and with the approval of the PID in October 2017, the EPL chief executive was Stephen Crombie, with the then EPL chief operating officer (COO) Duncan Boenic appointed as the EPDP sponsor. The DBC and the PID were prepared and approved during their tenure. In February 2018, Arlene White was appointed as the EPL chief executive. Shortly after White's arrival, Boenic also left the EPL and White assumed the sponsor role, effectively becoming responsible and accountable for the EPDP outcomes from the beginning of development. White also inherited the legacy of the DBC and PID documents and approvals.

White was asked directly about her capability to undertake the sponsor role, including experience: 'I have done large projects for most of my career, working with medium to large-scale projects, not just IT, including time as the Deputy Commissioner of Inland Revenue … [and have been] sponsor and business owner and just about every other role in major business projects.'

There were no negative comments from any interviewee about White's capability as a sponsor; indeed, all were complimentary, with comments such as:

> [She was] good and effective … and competent. (Person BS, Senior audit/assurance)

> I feel she is across what we are doing. (Person BU, Senior project officer)

> There is a fair amount of letting go and empowering the team, so Arlene was pretty good at that anyway, so that came quite naturally to her. (Jeffrey Brandt, EPDP program director)

> She was involved and eager, so, yes, it worked. (Person BT, Senior audit/assurance)

In addition, there has been external acknowledgement with a Treasury review in July 2020 commending the project on its successes, acknowledging the leadership of the project, and recommending that White as the sponsor 'share these good practices' (The Treasury 2020: 15) with other New Zealand Government agencies.

There were also some perspectives on the difference in approach between White and the previous sponsor, with a view that White brought a different focus and skillset to the role. It was argued that the previous sponsor, due to their involvement in the Novopay project for many years, had 'a bit of a mind in the past' whereas White 'was more focused on the future'. This was an advantage for the EPDP, because

> some people live in the past and we need to move on from that. There is history and there are things that went wrong, but having a fresh face sometimes is a lot better because they do not have the wounds of the past. Looking forward perhaps, rather than looking back. (Person BW, Senior project officer)

The PID recommended an agile delivery method for the EPDP (EPL 2017: 15). Earlier chapters have highlighted agile as an emerging capability requirement for sponsors. EPDP program director Jeffrey Brandt was asked how agile delivery impacted on the sponsor's capability. He argued that, in some ways, agile can be more difficult for sponsors than traditional delivery methods as there is a need to constantly revisit plans and be 'far more nimble', resulting in more decision points and regular reprioritisation. Nonetheless—perhaps as testament to her attitude and style—when White was asked about this, she said it was an easy adjustment as it enabled greater visibility and rapid adaptation. She posited:

[Y]ou always need to have a process to pivot, or to proceed, or punt. I mean, if it is a dog, you punt it, and I think that is the agile mantra. Always be ready to pivot and continue to evaluate as you go, so for me it was really easy to fit within agile. Really easy for me to lead Grant, absolutely [easier than a traditional waterfall approach] without a doubt, constantly looking at what is being built and delivered ... and what the challenges are ... and putting decision-making at the right level in the organisation.

Brandt identified a benefit of agile to sponsors and the project, arguing that the approach can make projects more interesting to sponsors and therefore drive greater engagement and ownership. They see things happening quicker, which creates 'curiosity' due to the constant delivery cycles. White fully supported this perspective by stating that, with agile delivery, 'I was able to get excited about the product, about the customer, about what I do in my day job as [chief executive], and that kept my interest, and that is the difference in this project'.

Last, White confirmed that no assessment of her capability to undertake the sponsor role was undertaken as part of the institutional framework. Interviewees' perspectives indicate she was capable and undertook the role well, which arguably reinforces findings in earlier chapters that having an experienced and capable sponsor is down to luck and not initiative within the institutional framework.

White was asked whether she fully understood her role, responsibilities, and accountability as the sponsor. She said: 'Yes, absolutely ... I need to contribute to the outcomes ... [I]t is my responsibility to help wherever I can and to put in my expertise wherever I can.'

White also stated that the Better Business Cases (The Treasury 2019) guidelines included the sponsor role and responsibilities and this 'was a fine process'. Person BS (Senior audit/assurance) indicated that a responsibility assignment matrix (RACI)[8] chart had been completed for the project, which made it clear to all that the sponsor 'was pretty much responsible and accountable for the delivery of the whole program'.

---

8   RACI 'describes the participation by various roles in completing tasks or deliverables for a project or business process. RACI is an acronym derived from the four key responsibilities most typically used: responsible, accountable, consulted, and informed' ('Responsibility Assignment Matrix', *Wikipedia*, available from: en.wikipedia.org/wiki/Responsibility_assignment_matrix#cite_note-2).

The other elite interviewees were also clear about who the sponsor was and there was a common perspective that White understood her role and accepted its responsibilities and accountability. Brandt argued that White understanding the role and actively taking on the responsibilities were crucial to overcoming any resistance the project encountered.

The elite interviewees were also positive about the management style White employed in her sponsor role. One of the key relationships identified in earlier chapters is that between the sponsor and the program director, which in Novopay did not exist. When asked how she structured and managed this relationship, White stated that Brandt as the EPDP program director was made part of the EPL senior leadership team, so that 'he would come into our day-to-day business decisions and understand what we were trying to achieve as a business, and then take that back into the program and vice versa. Then he kept the SLT [senior leadership team] informed of what was going on'.

Brandt in turn stated that he had a 'very good' working relationship with White and 'continues to do so', and that this was built on a culture of openness and trust. He said White expected transparency from him, particularly when any issue arose, as 'she was a no-surprises kind of person'. Brandt also indicated that White was clear that their relationship was important to the success of the project and, while she was ultimately accountable, Brandt in his role was responsible for the successful delivery of the products.

All other elite interviewees stated that they had direct access at any time to White and she was always accessible to team members; she would take the initiative to talk with them to improve her understanding of the project. Person BT (Senior audit/assurance) stated:

> For Arlene to get to her desk, she walks past mine, and so very often in the morning—I mean I was in fairly early—she would walk past and say, 'Okay, anything I need to know?' We then have an informal discussion right there and then. We have a good relationship that if I do have a concern, I can get up and go speak to her. I must not come to her with a rumour. I must come with fact.

Person BU (Senior project officer) said White was 'always present' at the 'agile rituals' and therefore always had a current and good overview of the project and its progress and issues. Person BV (Senior project officer), while not a direct report to White, maintained they had a 'very close' and 'genuine' relationship due to their key role in the project, and White would often stop by for an update. Person BW (Senior project officer), who led a key project team, provided a similar story, saying that White would meet with them weekly for an update and it was clear there was never an issue with making contact outside these meetings. Brandt argued that while White encouraged and enabled a close relationship with him and others, it was not micromanagement. He said White expected and encouraged 'good productive working relationships' across the program and the senior leadership team.

White undertook the sponsor role on top of her substantive chief executive responsibilities. When asked why she took on the role, White stated that her agency as chief executive was an important factor. Taking on the role ensured the program was given the appropriate organisational priority and focus within and outside the organisation. In addition, White believed a critical program success factor was customer focus, which would be reinforced by her taking on the role. The other factors White cited were the dark cloud of Novopay and her personal accountability for the project outcomes. White stated:

> I was very interested in making sure that this program was a success and, as the [chief executive], I was told that I was accountable. So, yeah, being the SRO [senior responsible officer] was a role I took on after our COO left, but I was always the one who was going to be delivering the program to the public sector, and I think that is important. I know a lot of [chief executives] do not step into that SRO role, but I think that is at their peril, to be very honest.

Brandt agreed that White taking on the sponsor role demonstrated senior leadership support for the program. He said that White taking charge had a 'tremendous impact on stakeholders outside the organisation' as White became the public face of the program. Brandt argued that as the EPL chief executive, White was responsible for the relationship with the MoE and the delivery of the payroll service, therefore taking on the EPDP sponsor role was a demonstrable acceptance of this accountability.

There were several interviewees who, while acknowledging White's success in the role, argued that it was not appropriate to have the chief executive as the sponsor, with Person BS (Senior audit/assurance) saying they were not a fan of this approach. The common reason given was the lack of separation between the program and the chief executive or, as Person BT (Senior audit/assurance) posited: 'Who is she criticising—herself?'

Brandt argued that there were three reasons having the chief executive as sponsor worked for the EPDP. First, the 'EPL is a single line of business' and not an organisation with many business streams. Its business was to provide an efficient school payroll service, with White accountable for this. Second, the project would be implementing major organisational change, so White undertaking the role displayed ownership of the change. This was supported by Person BT, who agreed that White making project decisions gave them power and impetus. Third—and with his program director hat on—Brandt argued that no matter how skilled a program director was, they would never have the 'full visibility of stakeholder sensitivities that a chief executive would have'.

There were other arguments for the success of the chief executive as sponsor, including the small size of the EPL and its 'flat structure' (Person BU, Senior project officer). Person BV (Senior project officer) added that it enabled senior project staff to communicate directly with White and gave them confidence that details were reported openly and factually: 'Having a direct line to the SRO and the [chief executive] at that stage means that I know there are no filters that can be applied to my story. So, I can tell my story straight and I know things cannot get lost in translation.'

On that theme, Person BW (Senior project officer) argued that this direct line to the chief executive and therefore to decision-making was a major advantage over the earlier model of the COO as the sponsor reporting to the chief executive:

> [The previous model] could get a little confusing between who was the ultimate decision-maker ... [W]as the COO just taking decisions and then going to the CE [chief executive] to ask for permission ... I did wonder whether there was someone who was fundamentally in the role, but still had to go and answer questions to a higher-up, which of course does not happen with Arlene as the SRO.

White was asked about her ability to undertake both roles simultaneously. She argued that this was made possible by the project's structure, the capability of key project staff, and the engagement of Deloitte specialists, particularly Brandt.

White confirmed that she had not been offered any training by central agencies as part of the institutional framework, although she also said that due to her experience, 'she did not seek it'.

For support, White singled out two major contributors to the successful model: the engagement of Deloitte 'was extremely useful' and the gateway reviews 'were instrumental in helping' as they had a good mix of experts who provided effective feedback. There also was a series of regular total quality assurances and independent quality assurances throughout. White said central agencies such as the SSC 'did not get involved too much' in sponsor-support roles.

The EPL and the EPDP had internal assurance roles, which Person BT (Senior audit/assurance) claimed were to provide advice to the chief executive. Person BT supplied an example of the team providing real benefit to White at an important time, when she was being challenged about project benefits in the DBC, particularly the claim that staff numbers would be reduced, which had not happened. Person BT said the team was proactive and provided advice to White that while staff numbers had not reduced, there were other substantial tangible and intangible benefits, such as reduced overtime, more time to address outstanding historical issues, plus a rapidly increasing school satisfaction rate. They claimed White was delighted with the data and used this to present to central agencies the demonstrable benefits being obtained. In another example of internal assurance supporting White in her decision-making, Person BS (Senior audit/assurance) said they had raised concerns about a particular release to White, who then deferred the release until these concerns were resolved.

Interestingly, particularly given the problems with Novopay and the subsequent political fallout, White said there was little ministerial contact during the EPDP project other than preparing 'two-monthly briefing notes to the minister'. White (Pers. comm., 1 February 2021) posited that the 'minister was most concerned with the end user impact given the level of anxiety that Novopay created amongst teachers'.

In conclusion, from the perspectives of the elite interviewees and external reports, Arlene White was a capable and motivated sponsor. However, this was the result not of a formal process within the institutional framework, such as training, but of the fact that White came to the chief executive role with vast operational experience in large projects. White was also quick to adapt to and appreciate the benefits of agile delivery, which she argued created 'interest' in the sponsor role.

White understood the sponsor role well and accepted the responsibilities and accountabilities that came with it; her experience was instrumental to this awareness. White supplied the platform that enabled a successful program;

she formed open, trusted, and continuing relationships with the program team and made a direct acknowledgement of the program director's role by including him in the EPL senior leadership team.

White personally decided to take on the sponsor role, full-time, on top of her substantive role as chief executive. While some interviewees argued that this was not an appropriate model, all agreed it worked. White argued that it was important for her to be in the role 'as, given the lack of any appetite for a repeat of Novopay' and the fact that she would be held accountable, she wanted to be leading from the front. This supplied the priority and visibility of the program both internally and externally.

Project management role/discipline analysis

The PID (EPL 2017: 15) proposed and received approval for the move to an agile delivery using the SAFe[9] method. Agile and SAFe were new to the EPL, so the discussion with the elite interviewees focused on how this capability was obtained. There was a commonly held view that the EPL did not initially have the internal capability or capacity to provide the project management roles and disciplines required for the EPDP, particularly given the use of the new delivery methods. White said the EPL's initial focus was to gain that capability and capacity.

As an example of this, White stated that the EPL did not have the capability internally to fill the program director role, so a skilled resource was sourced externally: Brandt, a Deloitte employee with extensive large ICT program experience. White said the move to agile meant the EPL was reliant on externally sourced skilled project management resources. The team was a mixture of staff from Deloitte and other external firms and individual contractors, complemented by internal staff. Brandt said the focus was to

---

9   According to the Atlassian Agile Coach website: 'The Scaled Agile Framework® (SAFe®) is a set of organizational and workflow patterns for implementing agile practices at enterprise scale. The framework is a body of knowledge that includes structured guidance on roles and responsibilities, how to plan and manage the work, and values to uphold. SAFe promotes alignment, collaboration, and delivery across large numbers of agile teams. It was formed around three primary bodies of knowledge: agile software development, lean product development, and systems thinking' (available from: www.atlassian.com/agile/agile-at-scale/what-is-safe).

'invest heavily at the outset on our service design, or change management, our agile developers, API [application programming interface]—all of those capabilities'.

There were also two important capability strategies implemented by the EPL that the elite interviewees believed paid dividends—views supported by findings in the investment review report (The Treasury 2020: 10). First, there was a concerted effort to gain capability early before undertaking major development work, so as to 'hit the ground running'. White said this was deliberate and 'was key to any agile project, or any waterfall [project], too, [and was] the right thing to do'.

Second was an acknowledgement that although external sourcing of capability was necessary for the start of the project, this was not sustainable or suitable for the long-term support of the solution. There was therefore a deliberate strategy of skills transition to internal capability and capacity. The investment review report (The Treasury 2020: 10) found that the EPL made a 'concerted effort to retain key staff as permanent employees rather than contractors, improving continuity, retaining key IP [intellectual property], and reducing costs'. It said this capability delivery was 'of high quality and implemented successfully'. White argued that this strategy was key, particularly given the uniqueness and complexity of the school payroll solution; reliance on external contract staff would have exposed the EPL and the payroll solution to added risk and greater expense.

It is also worth noting that the EPL engaged a management accountant specifically to manage the EPDP financials—someone whom Brandt described as 'extraordinarily good' and who eventually gained 'kudos from our external auditor, Ernst & Young', resulting in the program being sponsored by the New Zealand Treasury to present a series of talks on how the project finances were managed so effectively.

For White, the priority given to obtaining and retaining the required mix of project management resources across the various roles and disciplines was paramount, not just to steer the project through to completion but also to ensure the skills remained internally to support and maintain the solution post completion. White said the costs to achieve this came from and were managed within the EPL, without external influence. It was up to White as the chief executive to set it as a critical priority. An early example of this was the engagement of Deloitte to manage the delivery of the program and the skills transfer to internal staff—something that White said was an 'expensive option' but one that was validated via program successes.

Elite interviewees supplied evidence of this executive priority, with a common response that while cost was always a consideration in recruitment, this did not limit the ability to engage the 'best' resource. That is, there was no pressure to find cheaper, less-capable resources due to an imposed cost limitation. The focus was on obtaining the capability required to best enable the program to deliver successfully. Person BU (Senior project officer) said recruitment 'decisions should be based on capability required rather than the money available … I had approval, so I have been very lucky.'

Another team manager, Person BW (Senior project officer), confirmed this, saying they were always aware of 'excess' costs, but 'the great thing about it is that if there was expertise that was required to do impact work then we did get that expertise to enable us to move forward. So, it was not like money being a showstopper'.

White argued that her background in operational roles aided understanding of and commitment to improving the EPL project management discipline across the organisation, as it was critical for the delivery of the EPDP and the ongoing support of payroll services. However, White believes this is uncommon across both the Australian and the New Zealand public sectors, as their priority is government political or policy work. White argued that these agencies 'serve the minister and policies. Do they understand the operational stuff? No. For the most part, government agencies in New Zealand, Australia, and Canada are policy departments, not operational, so it does not resonate in the political sphere until it does not work!'

As detailed earlier, the SAFe methodology was set up independently by the program. There was overwhelming support for the use of this methodology, with agreement that its benefits outweighed any disadvantages and claims that it helped provide the capability to both deliver and support the payroll solution. The agility of the methodology was commonly perceived as an advantage over a more traditional waterfall method. Tasks could be delivered in priority order, with results seen and evaluated quicker, mistakes identified earlier, and damage from those mistakes limited and more easily corrected. Person BV (Senior project officer) perhaps best sums this up:

> [I]t is putting the most valuable things at the front of what we are doing. So, the ability to pivot is very difficult in a waterfall project. You have spent six months developing something and then someone tells you it is wrong … [With agile,] you spend two weeks developing something and [if] we find out it is the wrong thing, we can pivot very quickly.

One of the goals of the EPDP was incremental change, and Person BU (Senior project officer) argued that agile supported this through the progressive and iterative design, development, and implementation of solutions. Person BU also explained why they liked agile methodology: '[I]t makes my life go really fast ... I like the cadence of it, and I like the planning, I like chunking work down. I think it is really manageable; there are no surprises. I like the iterative nature [of it].'

The advantage of iterative change was also expressed by Person BV (Senior project officer), who posited:

> [F]or us, agile is getting it out, using it beta ... getting it into the hands of the users ... and then the ability to roll features on and on, which the user then goes, 'Gee, it just gets better and better and better.' I think that has really been the big win for this program ... [W]e had a whole lot of people saying, 'Give us more, give us more, change this bit.' That is what agile has done, rather than saying, 'We beavered away for five years and we have built something and here you go, what do you think?' And everyone goes, 'That's not what I thought it would be.'

The methodology also created an effective team environment, in which all members were valued and part of the process. Person BW (Senior project officer), who was involved in testing, stated that in the past there was a view that 'we do not need testers yet, let them come later, and do not let them talk to the developers'—something that led to a sense of being undervalued. Person BW said:

> Now agile brings everyone on a [level] playing field, and the other thing I like about it is we pass and fail together. The team passes and fails ... [I]t is not 'Oh, you failed as you missed it as a tester' or ... 'the developer made a mistake here'. It is now, 'As a team, we succeed, and we fail.'

The testing area was not the only example of agile methodology improving collaboration between the various teams and functions. Representatives from the audit/assurance area argued that it provided the basis to change from a traditional 'review after the work was completed' to being able to provide real-time feedback. It also enabled those in the audit/assurance role to become part of the team, as valued collaborators, rather than being viewed 'with suspicion' as outsiders. Person BS (Senior audit/assurance) stated: 'If we were to look at the traditional approach for auditing, we would come in months and months after it started and by then the learnings would be useless. I do not think the project would have been as successful if these approaches were not used.'

Agile methodology encouraged and enabled a cross-functional team, in which varied expertise was valued and valuable.

There was a commonly held perception that agile methodology, for those new to it, required some adaptation and a change in mindset from the tasks and processes in a more traditional waterfall method. Person BU (Senior project officer) said they were used to preparing reams of documentation to pass the 'weight test', but with agile, documentation was lean, which took a bit of 'getting used to' and almost a need to 'let go'. However, they adapted and embraced the change: 'It really helped for team efficiencies: "Why do we have to do a 50-page spreadsheet around this change?" … [when instead] what is the outcome we need?'

The consistent view was that agile methodology and its related iterative component-based delivery aided and improved learning. Instead of a 'lessons learned' report completed after everything was finished and then filed away, there was a cycle of continuous learning, with those learnings applied progressively throughout the project. The following quote from Person BW sums up these perspectives:

> [W]e have just learned as we have gone, what worked for us what did not … [W]e look at the program increment and say, 'What did we do well? What did we not do so well? What can we do better next time?' All those sorts of things … [S]o at a team level, we are asking that every two weeks.

There were external acknowledgements of the EPL's success in using agile in the EPDP. Brandt stated that Red Hat, a major global software company, had nominated the program for a global innovation award in recognition of 'the way we have deployed open shift to develop our customer-facing product' (Red Hat Software 2020). Anna Brodie, the EPL CIO, was recently named in the top 50 CIOs in New Zealand across all sectors— in part, as recognition for her role in the EPDP (CIO 2022).

The PID (EPL 2017: 32–36) detailed a program management structure with roles and responsibilities. As indicated earlier, the team was a mix of staff from Deloitte and other firms, external contractors, and internal staff, to provide the required capability and capacity and particularly to address agile capability requirements.

External staff were selected for their agile experience, with internal staff then upskilled in the methodology. The EPL employed a mixture of training approaches to bring internal resources up to the agile standard. Some staff attended formal external or internal training courses, some picked it up through involvement in the process, but seemingly the major process was skills transfer from external specialised staff, who trained the internal staff on the job. There was a common perspective among interviewees that this coaching by skilled external resources was effective, and even preferred. Person BU (Senior project officer) stated: '[T]hey got people to come into the office and work with you and go through everything ... which I prefer. I thought that was really successful.'

Brandt described this as like a 'master and apprentice' model, for which the EPL sourced external experts who were 'going to do the work and then coach and develop the team throughout the process so that ... there is a lasting capability'.

This model is diagrammatically displayed in Figure 7.2.

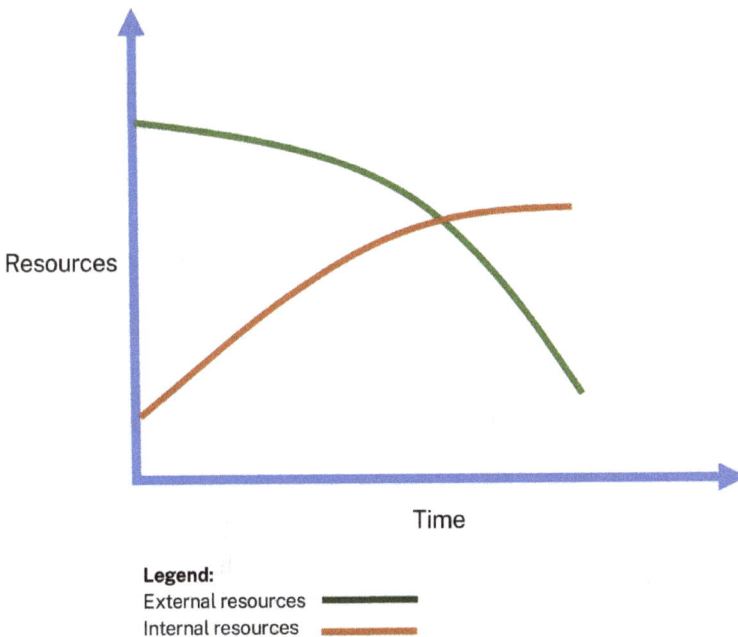

Figure 7.2 The changing EPL/EPDP resource model
Source: Created by author.

Person BV (Senior project officer), one of the agile experts who joined the team, stated that initially the skills transfer 'was difficult at times' and that there was some early resistance. They posited that this was likely a reaction to change and, with time, it improved, aided by the team work ethic of agile. Person U (Senior project officer), a permanent internal resource, said the transition did not always work to plan as it left the team rather 'green' when the external experts departed; however, the transition meant there were 'sustainable processes and practices in place'. Person BV argued that the transition was largely successful and the intellectual property knowledge was transferred and 'is secure'. They added: '[W]e have really good systems in place as far as how we build and how we document and how we transfer knowledge between people. So, if you join the team, you can hit the ground running pretty quickly.'

White said she had been challenged about this approach and asked why she needed inhouse capability. Her response was that because the core solution was so heavily customised support could not be provided at a base cost and there was a risk to the organisation and the payroll service. White argued: '[W]e cannot afford to keep on bringing people in to do this ... [I]t takes at least a good six to eight months to even understand the solution.'

Stakeholder engagement was front and centre of all program activities. White argued that after the Novopay issues, schools lacked trust in the EPL; winning back that trust was important. White claimed that it took about two years from the establishment of the EPL to do so and this was achieved by engaging with the various sector leaders, including unions, and developing reference groups. White argued that there is now a 'very tight' and 'very good relationship'. Given the effort to build this trust, effective school stakeholder management in the EPDP was critical.

Brandt argued that the EPDP had a 'compelling case for change' given the Novopay legacy, so people had to be engaged thoroughly in this change and remain committed to it if the program was to be successful. Brandt argued that this was his priority as program director: 'Most people think that the program director is there to manage scope, cost, and time. I fundamentally disagree. Those are things you need to control, but what we are to manage is energy and stakeholder engagement. That is everything.'

Brandt said there was a 'humility' in the program initially—a recognition that they did not know their customer well enough. To address this, approximately 10 per cent of the program team were dedicated to customer engagement activities. Brandt stated that 'customer insight drove everything

... [W]e put everything into sensing our customers and were not willing to make any assumptions as to what they wanted. That, to me, is the most important thing.'

An example of this engagement was the 'beta group' approach. A group of 200 school users—roughly 10 per cent of the total—received early prototypes of the functionality, reviewed it, and provided comments. The program team then acted on those and amended the solution accordingly. The result was the stakeholders could see their feedback in action. Person BU (Senior project officer) described the process as the team asking, 'Does this work? Does the flow make sense? Is the language meaningful to you?'

Person BW (Senior project officer) added: 'They get to see things first. They will tell us they will not get upset if something [initially] is not quite right ... [The schools are] helping us to be successful.'

Brandt argued that this approach meant the school users effectively became 'advocates' for change and that, because of the customer-focused approach, there is now a trusting and collaborative relationship between the schools and the EPL.

Person BU (Senior project officer) stated that the schools were engaged from 'end to end', citing strategies such as road-trips around the country to conduct face-to-face interviews, telephone interviews, and the formation of user groups. The project was also accepted into school forums such as the school managers' associations, for whom demonstrations and updates were provided and questions answered. Person BU claimed the intent was to 'make it really easy for schools to provide feedback'. As a result, the schools felt they had been listened to and provided 'really good feedback' about the approach employed.

This enabled the program team to adapt plans as they went. Person BV (Senior project officer) cited an example of an initial plan to provide schools with a variety of 'learning' tools such as videos and online training courses, but the schools' feedback indicated this would be overkill; they just wanted a solution that was simple to use. Person BW stated:

> They just wanted the product to work, and they just wanted it to ... be like a flight booking system. It should be like booking a car or doing internet banking. I do not need to watch a video 10 times and get a certificate. I just go in and make a payment. So, we changed that, we took money from those buckets and put it back into the product itself to help with the design.

The program established a communications team whose objective was to ensure 'everything is understood by all levels of schools—the professional administrators down to the 80-year-old granny who comes in one hour a day' (Person BT, Senior audit/assurance).

Open and honest communication were a key mantra in this approach, with Person BU (Senior project officer) stating that they did not 'hide' anything, while Person BV agreed there were 'no secrets'. The communication was framed around the idea that 'things are not perfect' but here is your opportunity to participate in making things better.

Person BU said the schools wanted an account management model as they preferred a consistent and familiar person to talk to—one to whom they 'did not have to explain things over and over again' and with whom they could build a relationship. To this end, the design of the school service model was changed to provide a more customer-focused and personalised service. White explained the model:

> [E]ach [EPL] advisor has a group of schools that they are responsible for and, wherever possible, we maintain that relationship with them in the schools. We have about 70 advisors that look after the 2,600 schools and that is really important. The relationship is huge. They trust their advisor … intimately.

Several interviewees stressed that internal stakeholder management was a key strategy and another factor in project success. The culture of open and honest communication was shared between the program team and EPL management. In the sponsor section of this chapter, there was evidence of direct access by team members to the chief executive/sponsor. Person BW (Senior project officer) stated that they liaised regularly with another member of the EPL senior leadership team: 'We are in constant communication, just around resources and how things are working and the like.'

An outcome of the success of the project in both its deliverables and its engagement with schools is the change in school satisfaction rates recorded by the EPL. White stated that at the start of the program, the 2016 satisfaction rate was at 51 per cent. In the EPL's 2020 annual report, the customer satisfaction rating was at 80 per cent approval, with 17 per cent neutral, and only 3 per cent dissatisfied—an impressive turnaround (EPL 2020b: 13). White argues that EPL is now to some extent a victim of its own success, as it has raised the expectations of schools, so with each release, 'we better have the very best it can be, but that is okay. We expected that to happen'.

All the elite interviewees were proud of what the project had achieved and believed the team and organisation had done well. Some perspectives include the following:

> We have a great product out in schools that schools are using. We have a great adoption rate and we are already seeing great benefits coming through. So, yeah, I think it is going well. (Person BU, Senior project officer)

> [W]e have delivered some really, really awesome stuff from the get-go. (Person BW, Senior project officer)

> [W]e have managed to get a product built ... and used by schools and we have not been in the paper. We have very, very happy customers ... I would say that would be the most successful piece of this ... [the] happy customers. (Person BV, Senior project officer)

The elite interviewees were asked about their greatest learnings from the program, the first of which were the benefits obtained by undertaking the project using the agile methodology. Brandt said his greatest learning was

> a kind of renewed appreciation of how hard these things really are, and ... I was not an 'agile-ist' beforehand, but believe me, I am one now: small iterations, each one delivering value, and allowing the compounding effect of continuous improvement to let it work its magic.

The second was the benefit to be obtained from having a customer focus and therefore a resulting need to engage with stakeholders with open, honest, and trusted communication as a central part of the project management approach. This applied to external stakeholders such as the schools and to internal stakeholders such as the project teams. For White, the criticality of this customer focus was her key learning, and it meant the project did not get 'pushback' from the schools and helped the program deliver 'so much with so little'. Person BU (Senior project officer) agreed with this perspective and stated that 'communication was the key' as it ensured that 'the right people were talking and that the decisions being made were very visible'.

The third lesson was that, despite the benefits of using agile, a program of the complexity and size of the EPDP is still a 'hard' process.

In conclusion, at project initiation, there was recognition that the EPL, particularly given the agile delivery approach, did not have the required project management capability or capacity to undertake the EPDP. There was therefore an initial organisational priority to source externally the variety of skills required, including a very experienced and capable program director. The EPL implemented successful strategies to upskill internal staff and to progressively transfer the capability and capacity internally; this was made a priority by the EPL chief executive.

The SAFe methodology was successfully applied to deliver via agile, which the elite interviewees praised and credited for much of the program's success. Among its advantages were that it enabled progressive delivery and a cycle of continuous real-time learning. The program was also imbued from the outset with an emphasis on stakeholder engagement and a customer-focus dogma, which resulted in substantial improvements in the MoE's relationships with schools.

While no interviewee claimed the program was perfect, all agreed that the agile delivery and project management approach were successful, and this success was recognised externally. Despite this, there was the realisation that large projects remain difficult beasts.

Forecasting role/discipline analysis

As highlighted earlier, the DBC (EPL 2016) was the original document that argued the case for change and became the basis for the approval of the EPDP. The forecast in the DBC set the EPDP benchmark of cost, time, and scope. The document proposed a waterfall delivery method. With the later preparation of the PID (EPL 2017), the approach was changed to agile delivery. The EPL senior leadership team managed the preparation of both documents and they were inherited by the new EPL chief executive, Arlene White, in early 2018.

It is not possible to analyse how the forecasts in these documents were prepared as the elite interviewees were not involved. In addition, in early 2018, after White began and her EPDP project management team took shape, the plans in the PID were revisited and a new plan was undertaken that superseded both the DBC and the PID. The focus of this section is how this forecasting process for all deliverables was undertaken, as it aligns with the SAFe methodology and program approach implemented.

It is important to note that according to the institutional framework, the EPDP was approved based on the full upfront forecasts in the DBC. The estimated cost became the budget, even though the program went through later replanning and a change in delivery approach. Therefore, the impact of this initial forecast, given the later changes, is also discussed in this section.

White was asked about inheriting the DBC forecast and approvals. She said this created 'challenges', such as with the schedule, which she immediately determined was unrealistic. For example, when White assumed the sponsor role, the vendor had not yet been chosen, and White argued that this time 'could not be made up' and had flow-on impacts on other tasks. White argued that the DBC's forecasts had made a 'lot of assumptions' about the use of the core payroll solution, such as the complexity of interfacing with it. The reality was the project and its tasks were much more complicated. White described the core solution as a 'complex mess' due to the extent of customisation from Novopay and argued that only with time and knowledge gained would the forecasts have any relevance.

Due to the inherited DBC forecasts—and even with the acknowledged success of the EPDP—the project was behind schedule and over budget, with some original goals not achieved. White was asked about this and what impact it had on perceptions of the program's outcomes. She argued that success in this case was not a measure against the original DBC forecast, but rather factors such as avoiding negative publicity, delivering the primary benefits, improved customer satisfaction, and 'reducing risk' to the schools, the EPL, and the government. White said a distinctly successful outcome for the program has been that 'our costs to maintain and even replace will be lower inhouse than it would be if we had outsourced'.

Brandt was asked for his perspectives on assessing EPDP outcomes based on the DBC forecast. He said that 'there are a few people that would say it is a failure for those reasons'; however, they tried to change the definition of success 'to school support for EPL'.

Brandt argued that the success in providing this improved and efficient support to schools was the true measure, although it took some time for groups such as the governance board to understand and embrace this rather than traditional cost and time measures. Brandt claimed that initially these groups thought 'there was something fishy going on', but their later acceptance of this measure was 'magical' and was a credit to White's leadership, taking responsibility head-on.

Most other interviewees were not aware of this impact and relationship to the DBC; however, Person BT (Senior audit/assurance), who had experience in other large New Zealand Government projects, had a firm view on the DBC and its usefulness and eventual relevance to outcomes:

> I have come to the conclusion that the worst thing in any project is a business case. I think, in hindsight, it is possibly the biggest waste of time … [E]ither look at it as a bunch of lies or you have no idea what you are doing. I think my review of projects has confirmed it. How do you deliver a business case when you realise that once you lift the rock you knew nothing, you had it all wrong … [T]he [DBC] was a crock of shit.

Person BT argued that factors such as estimated time frames in the DBC had placed unrealistic expectations on the EPDP. This was a similar view to that of Person BS (Senior audit/assurance), who said it was unrealistic to expect the program to adhere to the DBC forecasts. They said that to fit within the EPDP's agile approach, there should have been periodic re-estimations, but they claimed this was not how Treasury worked.

Discussions with Brandt about the DBC forecasts and the impact on later EPDP planning led to a question about whether the DBC was even useful given the program's long time frame. Brandt responded: 'Amen, brother.'

However, Brandt did say that he believes there is a place for business cases, as they propose the vision, the reason for the project, and the potential business benefits to be gained. The primary issue is with the estimates, such as for time and cost. Brandt argued that business cases must clearly acknowledge that 'this is as good as we have it right now' but it could prove to be 'wrong' as the project progresses. This was the case with the EPDP's DBC: the vision remained, but the forecast time and cost lacked validity for what was required, the risks, and the change in delivery approach. In summary, Brandt stated that the forecast cost in the DBC was 'not nearly enough' to cater for what had to be done.

However, the DBC was praised for detailing the core issues and the need to address Novopay's shortcomings, particularly the central aim to replace the online solution. Criticism concerned the folly of trying to forecast in full upfront for this change, not the argument for change.

Brandt joined the program after the PID was completed and, after five months in the position, he 'threw it out because I fundamentally disagreed with it' as it did not fit within the agile philosophy or the EPL's desire to progressively deliver benefits and ensure a customer focus. When asked to explain this, he stated:

[T]he fundamental problem with it was it broke the program into these things that they called workstreams … [S]o, it had all these little bits, like a standard waterfall project … [T]he *PID*, [despite proposing agile delivery, was in fact] a waterfall PID … I took it apart and I said, this is never going to work. We are losing sight of benefits of essentially a value and effort for each one of the 'investments'. So, we overturned it in this thing that we call the replan.

White said that as an outcome of the replanning, the program was broken into 21 'investments' or components that were to be delivered progressively to schools in a prioritised order.

White and her team presented the replan to the EPDP governance board and it was approved. However, even after this, the DBC forecasts, such as for the budget, remained the program's centrally approved boundaries even though they were essentially two different programs.

As the person with responsibility for the replanning, Brandt was asked how this was undertaken. He said the process analysed the DBC and the various assumptions within it. He then listed 'all of the things that have changed since' and that formed the basis for the 'rethink and restructure' of the program. Brandt said the DBC highlighted what was 'valuable' and, as part of the replanning process, that value was 'double-checked'. He identified this as an extremely important process:

[W]e could assess every initiative that we wanted to undertake against that set and move through it, and it also gave us the flexibility at that point in time to say, 'Well, we are not going to chase the scope that was in the business case because we have a new idea that has a better NPV [net present value] than anything else that we have'.

This led to the development of the 21 investments for which individual forecasts were then made. Person BV and Person BW (Senior project officers) described the initial forecast as 'T-shirt sizing'[10] based on known facts and assumptions at that stage, and the results of a workshop to discuss the product. There was a clear perception that this was a 'starting point' to

10   According to the Red Agile website: 'T-Shirt sizing is a technique used for relative estimation and high-level sizing of items. You use this technique of relative estimation as opposed to absolute estimation when you just need a rough estimate or comparison of items. Speed is valued over accuracy which stops people from overthinking and overanalyzing, as you just want people to use their instincts and gut feeling. Information may not be available at this point anyway for detailed estimates. It is therefore used early on in agile projects or when there are a lot of items to estimate in a relatively short time' (available from: www.redagile.com/post/tshirt-sizing).

be refined with the delivery of each component and with the benefit of the learnings of that process. Person BV described it as starting with the smaller things and building up to the more complex, with the acquired knowledge: 'We will start here. We think these things are okay and, as we move on, we get more certainty to how much these bigger things will cost.'

Person BS (Senior audit/assurance) said that with the forecasting iterations, 'competence improved in each progressive phase from learning [from] the previous phases'.

This process and the relevance of its forecasts were possible because of the culture of agile, in which a team's resources are 'stable' and therefore forecastable, and can be applied to the estimated effort. This concept of 'stable teams' and its relevance to forecasting were explained further by Brandt:

> For example, each product owner has a team or a set of teams, and that capacity is by and large fixed. So, the amount that a team costs per quarter is almost identical quarter after quarter. So then if the money is constant and the burn is constant and the delivery teams and the resourcing are constant, all we need to do is say what is going to deliver the highest possible value this quarter and allocate to teams ... [I]t is a very simple concept.

Another team lead, Person BV (Senior project officer), supported this 'capacity' mode within agile, saying that 'rather than "here is our budget"', it was more about 'understanding what we can deliver' with the team's capability and capacity and, from this, they could 'get an idea of exactly' how much the team could deliver in the time frame. The concept was supported by other elite interviewees such as Person U (Senior project officer), who, as a team lead, stated: 'I like the fact that we can size or work accurately, so I know exactly what we are committing to ... [I]t is very easy and visible to monitor.'

Brandt said that under the replan, the EPDP was thought of 'in terms of program increments' over 12 weeks. He believed the program could never forecast beyond a three-month period, at which point recent learnings were considered and changes in approach made. Brandt claimed this included the ability to factor the key customer feedback into the next sequence of planning, which he described as 'critical information'. Did the schools like it? What was the impact on them? Brandt said that with this information at each iterative planning stage, he 'could feel confident to have a conversation with Arlene [White] and our boards ... so that is quite a different model' to the traditional waterfall planning approach.

Brandt believed the iterative process of forecasting in agile was better for dealing with the complexities and unknowns of the organisational and environmental issues and for adapting the EPDP plans. An example of this for Person BW (Senior project officer) was the schools' change culture. Ideas such as including 'Smartform PDFs' to streamline processing met resistance, so a timely rethink of the approach was possible. Another organisational realisation was that the solution had to cater for every size of school and payroll processing resource. Bigger schools had dedicated full-time payroll staff, while others had 'a person who comes in one hour every fortnight'. Person BW argued that all these factors were identified progressively with each deliverable, and then factored into future planning.

Elite interviewees indicated that a 'time and materials' contract was the norm for individual contractors or a vendor/company. The typical arrangement for the EPDP was that a statement of work for a deliverable would determine the resources required, such as for testing. The relevant vendor would then be asked to provide those resources and there would be a fee-for-service arrangement with that organisation. Person BW (Senior project officer) said this could cause issues with the retention of a skilled resource as the project moved from one deliverable to the next, but with planning and the use of a non-chargeable vendor delivery lead, these issues were mitigated. Person BW argued that an alternative approach based on payment for a documented outcome would have led to a need for extensive negotiation and documentation, and perhaps inevitably disagreements over the outcome. They argued that the time and material approach, with its flexibility for moving resources in and out as required, was more suitable to agile development and moved the focus to delivering a quality outcome, rather than a contractually limited one.

It is important to note that no elite interviewee was critical of Novopay; rather, there was recognition that the MoE and the project had a difficult task in a different environment. The following statement by Brandt sums up these perspectives: the Novopay 'predecessors on this, they have all my respect. They have done something incredibly difficult in an incredibly difficult set of circumstances. Our world is different'.

White acknowledged the differing scopes of Novopay and the EPDP, saying the former had to implement the core payroll solution, whereas the EPDP's objective was to change the online interface to the core solution. She said this was a 'different level of risk than what Novopay had. They had the whole thing, core plus user interface. We just had the user interface, but connecting to the core is still no easy task, believe me.'

That said, all the elite interviewees were familiar with Novopay's failings, which hung like a dark cloud over the project. White stated that while there was no central agency mandate to ensure the Novopay lessons were being addressed, she made an independent decision that they must be factored into the EPDP's planning and approach, saying it was critical to not 'make the same mistakes again; there is no excuse for not listening to the lessons learned from the ministerial inquiry'.

Brandt said the ministerial inquiry report was 'like the founding document' for the program planning as it helped define and explain the EPDP approach. When quizzed about whether central agencies had checked if the Novopay lessons had been incorporated in planning, Brandt said he had visits from central agencies early on asking how the Novopay lessons were being addressed, but after the initial interest, they 'kind of went away'. Within the EPL, however, Person BS (senior audit/assurance) stated that their team was 'always aware' of the Novopay risks and this 'helped us to be a lot more vigilant'.

Brandt argued that the spectre of Novopay was beneficial in leveraging and gaining support for the argument that 'things needed to be done differently'. The Novopay lessons were in effect a 'very powerful' tool in enabling a change in approach. White and others indicated that at the outset of the program, Murray Jack, a co-author of the Novopay ministerial inquiry report, was chair of the EPL Board and provided regular input, as well as discussing key Novopay issues with the organisation and program staff (Person BT, Senior audit/assurance).

The ministerial inquiry (Jack & Wevers 2013: 30, 38, 49) was critical of the decision to make a single 'big-bang' release of Novopay to all schools, which proved disastrous. Person BU (Senior project officer) argued that the ability within agile for incremental releases was effective in addressing this issue, saying the 'agile framework is very beneficial for' the staged delivery approach 'because schools told us over and over again, "Post Novopay, we do not want big-bang change. We do not want to arrive at our desks and everything has changed overnight. We like incremental"'.

This staged-release strategy was also raised by Person BV (Senior project officer), who said there was 'reputational risk' at stake: '[T]he PTSD hangover from that project [Novopay] inside the organisation is something that we even deal with today. So, we are still incredibly cautious with our releases.'

White explained how the initial plan was to 'push' a deliverable to about 200 schools and build up progressively. As feedback from the schools started to come into the program, it was determined that a 'pull' model would be better for us and for the schools'. This meant that schools could choose when to use the deliverable—to 'pull' it down for use when they were ready rather than having the solution forced on to them. White stated: '[O]nce they have seen it, they pull it, then they tell their friends and other schools.'

As White posited, while this empowered schools to choose when to use the deliverable, it was also a 'scary' approach for the program; what if no one decided to pull anything? White stated: '[I]t was scary, not because I had no control over it, but it is that point of the customer wanting the product.'

To further differentiate the EPDP from the Novopay approach, White said while this 'pull' option was in place the old system would continue to run parallel until '100 per cent of the schools are comfortable with the new product'.

I asked Brandt a hypothetical question, as I was curious about his perspective on whether the Novopay learnings would be similarly addressed in other New Zealand Government projects, or whether the EPDP approach was due to the leadership of Arlene White. Brandt posited that without White in the sponsor role, 'things would probably have been different': 'We had all the difficult stakeholders, we had all the big challenges, we had big change, and there is no noise, only goodness. That is very unusual. We are very fortunate.'

Without naming any other New Zealand Government projects for reasons of confidentiality, Brandt said there is evidence that since the Novopay ministerial inquiry similar mistakes have been made and projects have failed for 'all of the same reasons'. Person BT (Senior audit/assurance), while also not naming names, said they had witnessed evidence of projects post Novopay 'forgetting' these written lessons and, as a result, 'the same issues rise again'.[11]

---

11   The New Zealand Customs Service Joint Border Management System (JBMS) from 2013–17 is one example, with an externally sourced independent review finding issues encountered in Novopay such as governance, assurance, contract management, open and trusted communication, and engagement all listed as problems in the JBMS (Deloitte 2017).

In conclusion, Brandt stated that because the EPDP was so aware of Novopay's failings and because it changed its approach in response, the program was 'fundamentally different' in structure and approach to Novopay and therefore 'had every reason to succeed'.

According to White, because of Novopay, 60 per cent of the core solution had been customised. Brandt argued that the unique and changing requirements of the New Zealand education payroll became part of the core solution, morphing it into something it was never meant to be. This added support and cost risk to the payroll service. For these reasons, Brandt stated that the EPDP, with the use of agile, removed some of those organisationally unique requirements from the core payroll solution. Brandt described it thus:

> [T]here are a whole bunch of requirements for the education sector that are absolutely unique, and what we are doing now is we are building those requirements outside of the core payroll system. Essentially, we are taking capability that was in the core payroll and we are moving it outside … So, you can imagine each one of those components, we are building best in class for each one in an agile manner. So, there is the attestations engine, the thing that delivers the incremental pay for teachers. There is something that we call the service accumulator, so that is the thing that tallies up how much service a teacher has based on the rules. That is its own engine. In New Zealand, we have unique and special tax laws. Those laws we have built in a special engine. So, we are building all of those outside [the core payroll] … and we can do those things incrementally.

To greatly simplify this intent, the core payroll solution obtains data via an interface to pay each person for their work. The core solution processes this and keeps the appropriate payroll records. External to this, bespoke solutions manage the unique organisational and environmental complexities. Each of these can be treated as a component and delivered progressively via an agile method. As these unique rules change over time, they can be managed within the specific component, external to the core payroll. White said this was not exactly the plan at the outset, but the program adapted its approach as it was essential to continue to use the Novopay core solution and 'utilise the asset', rather than incur the expense of total replacement.

In discussions about Novopay's approach and planning, which was to customise the core solution, it was claimed that Talent2's solution was sound in all its core functions; the problems and complexities arose when the multitude of customisations began, meaning it was no longer a COTS solution. With hindsight—and evidence of learning and adapting—the argument was that Novopay could and should have been planned as a mixture of waterfall, for delivery of the core solution, and agile, for the delivery of the organisational requirements, or as Brandt argued, 'a mixture of COTS and inhouse development'.

White argued that the governance bodies had difficulty understanding agile: '[P]eople are not good at governing in agile. They want project plans and critical paths, and what happens when target dates are missed, and that is not what you do in agile, so it is really hard to get people to understand.'

This was supported by Brandt, who argued that part of the challenge of adopting agile is the required change in governance and the move away from 'this whole adherence to scope, time, and cost'.

White added that while 'we still get nagged for all the checkpoints of a waterfall approach', the governance group has become more 'keenly aware' of the approach and how it is to be delivered, and in general they 'have been great'. This was assisted by the inclusion of external members of the boards who 'actually understand what we are trying to do'. Person BT (Senior audit/assurance) believed that one of the major governance challenges White faced was explaining how project finances worked in agile, which has a focus on deliverables, as distinct from a traditional waterfall approach, which focuses on fiscal year expenditure. Person BS (Senior audit/assurance) agreed that there was a learning curve for the governance groups, but also claimed that they had progressively adapted.

White was asked about the role of central agencies fulfilling their institutional assurance responsibilities, and her views were mixed. She described Treasury's engagement as excellent: 'I give kudos to them.' The office of the Government Chief Digital Officer (GCDO) was also 'very good' (White, Pers. comm., 1 February 2021). She believes this was because of the successes of the EPDP and the fact they were doing things differently—something she argued that Treasury 'would like to see more of'. White said Treasury came to trust the program and started sponsoring agile workshops across New Zealand. When asked whether she believed this would lead to a change in the institutional framework, White posited that while Treasury was supportive, adaptation remains a work in progress. The Treasury and the GCDO aside, White said the EPDP approach did not neatly slot into the standard New Zealand Government approach and, at times, dealings with other central agencies had been less effective.

When asked about central agency involvement in their areas, other elite interviewees indicated they had no or only scattered involvement at initiation. Brandt said the program worked with the GCDO, which he claimed had responsibility 'for the assurance of technology programs' and developed an overall self-assurance framework for the program—one that fitted the agile methodology. According to Brandt, the GCDO said: 'If that would work, that would be amazing.'

The final argument from Brandt was that it did work and it made 'the difference' with the program. Unlike Novopay, the EPDP utilised gateway reviews, which Brandt argued benefited from having respected and 'high-powered' actors on the review panels. According to Brandt, the reviews 'consistently reported extremely favourably about what we were doing and called this out as exemplars on a number of fronts'.

The elite interviewees from various teams all agreed that agile methodology enabled beneficial change in internal assurance at each iteration because the assurance of deliverables was in real time, with the benefits applied before planned release, and there was a cycle of continuous learning. Persons BU and BV (Senior project officers) provided a simplified example of the process used: dummy screen designs were agreed to, followed by a beta model development and, following reviews and testing by relevant stakeholders, progression to a 'clickable prototype' for more intensive assurance and school involvement. The EPL and the EPDP benefited from each team having an 'open door' policy that enabled people to attend any team meeting they wished, to inform, learn, or provide feedback (Person BV, Senior project officer).

There was oversight and assurance via an internal audit team, which developed their approach 'based on those of the overarching assurance plan' (Persons BS & BT, Senior audit/assurance). The role and approach of the internal audit team are worthy of special mention, as they ultimately led to the EPL internal audit team winning the Institute of Internal Auditors New Zealand 2019 Award for Team Excellence in Internal Auditing (EPL 2020d)—no mean feat and great recognition of public sector innovation. In short, the team adapted its processes to fit the agile methodology, and did so independently, not as the result of an institutional initiative, and not vetted by a central agency (Person BS). Person BT argued that the willingness to adapt and try something new within the EPL was a key factor in success. They said that in a previous role when they had argued for a similar change in process, it 'was not well accepted', yet in the EPL it was 'embraced' by senior management. Person BT argued that much of the audit world remained caught up in the

> old audit approach: bayonet the wounded, and providing assurance after the fact, and writing long reports. When I was there [in their previous role], an audit would take me a whole quarter because it was so big, and then we would take another two months to get the report out. What is the point?

The audit change that was implemented, complementing the agile methodology, was to 'shift left', which was explained as a process of moving the audit/assurance to earlier in the development process, doing it before the project is finished and when value is added, and to resolve issues before they become bigger. Person BT argued that this change was accepted easily in the EPL and EPDP due to its close fit with agile processes; it added value early. Person BS said this 'transformed' the way the audit team worked.

Person BS argued that the internal perspectives about the auditors had changed and they were seen as valuable members of the team, 'trusted advisors' who provided timely advice not only to program teams but also to the chief executive/sponsor. It was claimed that the audit team had open invitations to all EPDP team meetings, where questions were welcome. In fact, audit interviewees claimed they had 'become part of the team'. In this role, they provided a valuable bridge between the technical roles and the customer to ensure solutions were customer-focused. Person BS explained the process:

> [W]e contribute at the time of the meetings and say this is what we want you to do. Make sure you incorporate all of this into your thinking. Any risks you have I want to know. Have you thought about dependencies and things like that, and make sure everyone walks along at the same pace? It has been quite successful.

Person BT said a side benefit of the change in audit approach was an increase in job satisfaction because of the direct evidence of the value their role brought to the program: 'From an auditor's point of view, all four of us now are much happier in our roles because we are affecting change, and we have an input.'

The use of agile was the catalyst for a realisation of new ways to assure and audit projects, providing benefits over past methods. Person BS is now 'trying to sell it to anyone who wants to listen'.

On this point, Person BT stated that the team had 'entertained nine different audit teams from different organisations. We have presented to Treasury, we have presented to the Institute of Internal Auditors, and to the Agile Assurance Forum'.

I asked Person BT whether these forums had initiated any institutional change. They said there had been no central jurisdictional change, but argued that it was up to the agency's leadership to accept change. When asked why there was resistance to change, they said:

> I think a lot of them are dyed-in-the-wool, old professional auditors, and a lot of them are too afraid to make the change, or the governance structure does not want that … It [the EPDP] was a fairly well-run project in the first place, and our senior leadership was quite comfortable with us going in a new direction. We were lucky in that respect.

The consideration of organisational factors in forecasts, at the EPDP replanning stage, has been covered in earlier sections of this chapter. There was evidence that schools were placed front and centre of planning with a customer focus central to the program ethos. Agile delivery, and iterative, cyclical planning and deployments assisted in identifying and addressing these and other factors in a timely manner.

White was asked about the suitability of the current institutional financial management practices for projects like the EPDP. She said the EPL, as a scheduled 4A[12] company, does not receive appropriation through government, but is instead funded by an annual 'service fee' from the MoE. White said, with the approval of the DBC, the approved funding model was an increase in the annual service fee of NZ$3 million over the 10 years of the program plus a NZ$14 million loan that is drawn on as needed but is to be repaid once 'benefits start to realise'. White said this model differed from the normal practice of funding a business case and meant she had to deliver

---

12 According to the New Zealand Treasury: 'Schedule 4A companies are established when the objectives sought (which could be a mixture of social and commercial objectives) might be best supported by joint ownership. The Crown may not own all shares at the start or it may wish to reduce its shareholding in future. An example is City Rail Link Ltd in which the Crown and Auckland Council each have a 50% shareholding. Companies listed in Schedule 4A of the *Public Finance Act 1989* are subject to the *Companies Act 1993* and relevant provisions of the *Crown Entities Act 2004*' (available from: www.treasury.govt.nz/information-and-services/company-and-entity-performance-advice/portfolio-companies-and-entities/types-companies-and-entities#:~:text=Entities%20Act%202004.-,Public%20 Finance%20Act%201989%20Schedule%204A%20companies,reduce%20its%20shareholding%20in %20future).

both core payroll delivery services and the EPDP from the annual service fee. White inherited this funding model and said she 'never understood why financing had to come through as a loan', and that this has had continuing implications for the program: 'Is this the way I would have preferred this? Absolutely not. [I]t made things extremely tight for us in the program … [I]t was a nightmare.'

Person BT claimed that the financial requirements established in the DBC, based on the traditional fiscal year spending, were a mismatch for the EPDP, which was operating in an agile world, where the focus was on delivery. They argued that this created a problem for the program's financial manager and for White in explaining this to central agencies and governance bodies. White said the EPDP had to navigate all the checkpoints required, such as Treasury and gateway reviews, and at each step had to explain to each party the financial management practices of agile and the differences from traditional methods:

> They were not convinced that the way we were reporting was going to make them happy, but once we had several independent quality assessments, we had gateway reviews, and people saw we were delivering and the customer satisfaction scores were going steadily up, and all the way we had developed a program plan, they became quite used to the process.

White highlighted a difference in the financial management between a traditional waterfall delivery and agile: in a waterfall project, the budget is for the whole project and money can be 'shuffled' between tasks, whereas in agile, a budget is allocated to each deliverable. To amend this required governance approval, based on solid arguments; however, White said this was an advantage of agile as it made the program 'more focused' on budget allocation and management at a macrolevel.

A point of difference between the EPDP and Novopay, and indeed the part one findings, is the stated intention to treat the EPDP product as an asset. White stated that the EPDP products will be depreciated over 12 years, while Brandt said it was not the intention of the program to build it, hand it over, and 'let it rust away'. He said the program had been structured to deliver several products and a key objective was to establish a financial and team structure to ensure ongoing maintenance.

The elite interviewees were asked whether, based on their experience with the EPDP, they thought component-based delivery such as agile could be applied to all or most large ICT software projects. The consistent response was yes, such as that from Person BW (Senior project officer), who stated that 'particularly from a development side … I do not think that there is any project that could not be done' with agile.

Others, such as Person BS (Senior audit/assurance), argued that people must think differently and look at alternatives. In future, Person BS said, if a waterfall approach was the only option recommended, they would 'question the value of it because with the waterfall format you could still possibly do it in an agile way. It is easy enough to adapt'.

Person BW related a story from the replanning stage about asking an external agile consultant brought in to assist how it was going to be possible to do the work using agile. The consultant, who had been at a large organisation that had '80,000 developers or something ridiculous, [and] worked with some really big companies', told Person BW that he had 'never seen a piece of work … that you cannot break down'.

Others suggested that some projects, or parts of projects, may require a mixture of agile with more traditional methods. Reflecting on a previous major transformation project, White mused that while she could not imagine doing some parts of it in agile, there were other parts that could have been done that way.

In conclusion, the EPDP fundamentally changed the delivery approach initially outlined in the DBC, yet the EPDP was and is still being approved on forecasts made in the DBC, including the funding model. This has created ongoing problems for the EPL and EPDP management in terms of governance, financial management, assurance, and assessment of outcomes. Some interviewees believed that DBCs generally are a waste of time and irrelevant if used as a tool to forecast and gain approval. They were deemed useful for outlining the vision and scope, but not for forecasting when there are so many unknowns.

With the replanning, the program was broken into 21 prioritised 'investments'. While an initial 'T-shirt estimate' was made of the work, the true forecasting followed the agile ethos of iterative development, learning, adapting, applying, and reforecasting for the next investment. This improved the relevance of forecasts at each cycle and was aided by the agile 'stable team' approach, which provided a consistent cost and effort baseline.

Other factors considered in the forecast were the simplification of contracts with vendors and the inclusion of Novopay lessons learnt, particularly the requirements for school engagement and progressive deployments. The process was also aided by strong assurance, mainly internally applied and consistent with the agile mantra of review and learning at each stage. The EPL's internal assurance approach was nationally recognised. There was a perception that the implementation and ongoing support and defence of the EPDP's agile approach were due to the agency and capability of Arlene White.

Finally, there was a common perception that agile can be applied to all large ICT software projects, in full or for certain components.

The findings and their conceptual relationship

There was early recognition that the EPL did not have the internal capability or capacity to undertake the EPDP, particularly given the decision to use agile delivery. Organisational priority was given to establishing both as a precursor to major program tasks. Initially, skills were primarily sourced externally, but through a deliberate strategy, skills were progressively transferred to internal staff, boosting their capability and capacity, with the program now largely internally resourced.

Both critical program roles benefited from having a capable resource from the outset. Arlene White, the EPL chief executive, as the sponsor, had extensive operational experience in many aspects of a large ICT project. White was aware of the responsibilities and accountabilities of the sponsor role and willingly and successfully took them on. This was down to chance, not an outcome of the institutional framework to improve sponsor capability. Second, the program director's role was filled by a vastly experienced external resource who worked hand-in-glove with White and was made part of the EPL senior leadership team.

The EPDP's full upfront forecast and the funding model were approved as part of the DBC, as required by the institutional framework. The approach changed substantially afterwards, including from waterfall to an agile delivery method with a quite different financial management approach, yet the centrally approved forecast remained from the DBC, which created ongoing challenges for the EPL.

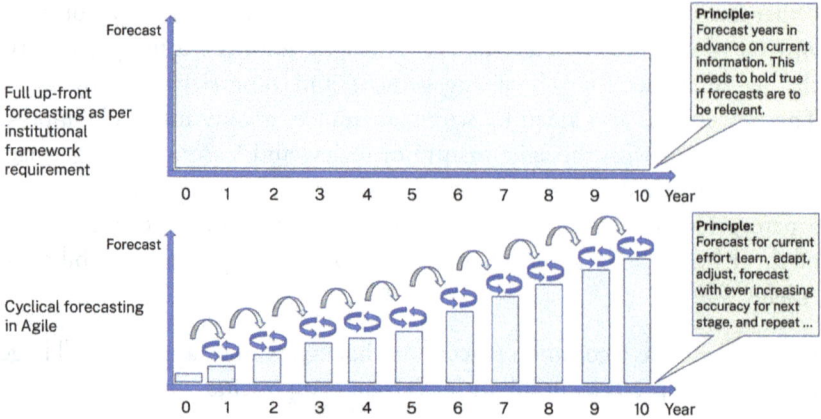

Figure 7.3 Simplified variances in forecasting approaches
Source: Created by author.

The dynamic between the requirement for a full upfront forecast and the progressive forecasting of agile is displayed in Figure 7.3. The DBC's full upfront forecast is an estimate of what lies many years in the future largely made before any major development. Agile's mantra is to do a small bit to learn how long it takes, what resources are required, what the cost is, and what needs to change, before using this information to forecast for the next stage, the argument being that the accuracy and relevance of the forecast will increase as the program progresses. This method of component-based funding, with review and forecasting for the next component, adds a level of financial management and governance that does not exist in the more traditional waterfall method.

The EPDP opted for simple contracts. To fit with the agile mantra, vendors were engaged to supply services for an 'investment' based on the time and materials to deliver that product. This was reviewed for the next 'investment', the appropriate skills were agreed with the vendor, and the work began. This approach was perceived as a 'win-win' for both the EPL and the vendors.

Schools were the primary stakeholders and were front and centre of all planning and project activities. This was driven from the top down and the elite interviewees indicated this customer focus was incorporated in all aspects of the program. Substantially improved school customer satisfaction ratings indicate the success of the program's stakeholder management.

Internal stakeholder management was also a priority, with a culture of open and honest communication between all levels of the program and the EPL.

The EPDP utilised the SAFe methodology and, from the perspective of the elite interviewees, this was effective in enabling the delivery of products. Gateway reviews were utilised, with EPL management considering these useful.

EPL chief executive Arlene White was clear that accountability for the delivery of the program rested with her, and this was cited as one of the reasons she took on the EPDP sponsor role.

The EPDP incorporated past learnings, particularly from Novopay, into both written plans and the culture of the program, such as the heavy customer focus and staged voluntary deployments to schools. The agile methodology enabled real-time continuous learning—a feature that greatly assisted with progressive delivery. There was awareness among all interviewees that the major mistakes of Novopay were not to be repeated.

Like the comparison used in the Novopay chapter, findings from *Dangerous Enthusiasms*[13] (Gauld & Goldfinch 2006: 132–36) are compared with those from the EPDP (see Table 7.2). Gauld and Goldfinch would be pleased to note that their findings and the successful EPDP are aligned.

Table 7.2 Comparison of lessons from *Dangerous Enthusiasms* with EPDP

Dangerous Enthusiasms (Gauld & Goldfinch 2006: 132–36)	EPDP, 2016–20
Things to do if you want to increase the likelihood of failure:	The EPDP response:
Make the project as big as possible.	The project was broken into 21 small, progressively delivered projects or 'investments'.
Attempt organisational change and link this to the project, then continually change specifications throughout.	A customer focus on schools was central to change management. Extensive engagement in design, review, and testing, plus a progressive voluntary rollout, were utilised successfully. A proposed change in schools' industrial awards was removed as a dependency of the project.
Assume the contract will solve all problems and instead of breaking it into manageable components award one for the whole project.	Simple 'win-win' contracts based on the time and materials for each deliverable were utilised successfully.

13　This book researched previous large New Zealand Government ICT projects and analysis of INCIS and other projects were included in its findings.

Dangerous Enthusiasms (Gauld & Goldfinch 2006: 132–36)	EPDP, 2016–20
Be pessimistic, guiding principles:	**The EPDP response:**
Be modest about what can be achieved.	With the use of agile, achievement was based on the delivery of each of the 21 'investments'. Each was modest as an individual challenge, but collectively became a substantial achievement.
Believe solutions will work only when they can be shown to work.	Each product went through a careful process of design, prototype, review, test, review, and release. Schools' decision to use the product was voluntary and dependent on the quality of the product.
Expect to encounter the problems of previous projects; they will happen.	They did, however, the use of agile mitigated these and provided the ability to adapt to challenges.
Excluding frontline staff is a high-risk strategy and can undermine the solution even if it works.	Frontline staff within schools and the EPL service centre were central to the program ethic. They were considered part of the 'team' and vital to the design and review of all products.

Source: Compiled by author.

When the EPDP findings are compared with those from the Novopay chapter (see Appendix 6), the differences could not be starker. The EPDP approached things differently and addressed many of the Novopay issues.

From the perspectives of the elite interviewees, the EPDP benefited from strong, capable, effective, and supportive internal leadership. The program was given organisational priority by the chief executive, who championed and supported the program throughout. The role of central agency leadership, however, was variable—at times supportive and at other times minimal.

The EPDP did things differently not only from Novopay, but also from norms within the New Zealand institutional framework. While the move to agile delivery was proposed and approved under an earlier EPL management team, the concept was embraced and fully supported by the new chief executive, Arlene White. Agile delivery encouraged entrepreneurship through its cycle of continuous revision and adjustment.

The EPL internal audit team displayed entrepreneurship by implementing a revised assurance approach that was judged effective by the elite interviewees and recognised nationally for its innovation and effectiveness. The EPL CIO was also nationally recognised for her initiative in the program, and the EPL/EPDP was nominated for an international technology award.

The program is considered a success internally and externally.

The EPL chief executive supported and defended the use of the agile delivery method for the EPDP. The elite interviewees believed that without this support from the very top of the organisation, the EPDP outcomes would have been quite different.

Conclusion

No interviewee argued that the EPDP was perfect because of the use of the agile methodology, as there are always challenges with such large projects. Their argument was that, despite these issues, the program succeeded because of the benefits of agile, including being able to quickly adapt to organisational challenges as they arose. There was common agreement that agile could be used either in full or in part for any large ICT software project; the issue is that the financial management, budgeting, and assurance of agile projects remain at odds with the requirements of institutional frameworks.

The overriding theme from the interviews is that, despite the overwhelming support for agile and the role it played in the program's success, the EPL and the EPDP benefited by chance from having a chief executive and sponsor as capable and entrepreneurial as Arlene White. Without White at the helm, the outcome could have been quite different.

The findings of this case study are not advocacy for agile. Agile was the approach employed in the EPDP and the analysis highlights that it was effective and fitted this project well. The earlier project management chapters found that agile is not always a suitable approach—something admitted by even its staunchest advocates. Would agile have been suitable for Novopay? That is open to debate; however, if the findings advocate anything, it is to break down complexity, and that is something Novopay did not do.

8

Change the nature of what is to be governed

No institution can possibly survive if it needs geniuses or supermen to manage it. It must be organized in such a way as to be able to get along under a leadership composed of average human beings. (Drucker 2008: 26)

The narrative

The narrative to emerge from the stories of the elite interviewees is one of institutional inertia leading to a failure in governance leadership. It is a narrative of organisational forgetting, ignored complexity, and a spattering of entrepreneurship by actors with agency. It is a narrative of possibility that effective governance change can happen if, instead of imposing bureaucracy, leadership in governance is collaborative and flexible with a focus on delivery. Finally, it is also a narrative of hypocrisy: imposing governance controls, yet in some instances ignoring them.

The governance enacted by institutional frameworks has failed to adapt to lessons from the past; it is almost as though they are forgotten until they happen again. While there is evidence of some change, and some attempts to change, this has been slow and has not addressed the critical governance issues. This is an interesting dynamic, as all interviewees highlighted the governance weaknesses and stressed the need for change, yet it has apparently not been an executive priority to do so. More to the point, there is no evidence that governance leaders are collaborating with these actors to identify the issues and ideas for change; these actors have much to give.

The complexity of large ICT software projects is a major factor in current governance. These projects were identified in the literature and by the elite interviewees as being difficult, volatile, and arguably uncontrollable against original forecasts over extended periods. Therefore, governance must focus on reducing complexity, not adding to it. If not inert, leadership in governance is at best indifferent to this issue. There is a high likelihood that the same mistakes will be repeated and poor outcomes for large ICT software projects will continue across the Australian and New Zealand public sectors.

This narrative was highlighted in each of the three roles/disciplines analysed in this book. The sponsor is a critical project leadership role, yet it remains misunderstood, not prioritised, with little to no training provided, and the skills exist only by chance. The project management discipline is also misunderstood, with an executive focus on project management skills rather than an acknowledgement of it as an organisational discipline of which a project manager is just one aspect. Finally, there is executive failure to understand the folly of the current guidelines for the approval and funding of large projects, and to treat ICT solutions as assets and manage them accordingly.

While the intent of governance via institutional frameworks is to provide control and consistency, they in fact limit the adaptation and entrepreneurship necessary to address complexity and force projects down a path that increases the likelihood of poor outcomes. The frameworks are about bureaucratic control rather than supporting and enabling effective outcomes. Paul Barratt, former secretary of the Australian departments of Primary Industries and Energy and Defence and former executive director of the Business Council of Australia, when asked about the intent of institutional frameworks, stated:

> [T]hey are designed to reduce risk but they do not enhance innovation and creativity ... [T]hey are almost the last common denominator [and are designed to] prevent the worst abuses, or the worst of incompetency, so you have to do A, B, C, but a person with their head screwed on right will operate within those boundaries but ignore them.

There is a dichotomy between the formal rules of the institutional framework that actors must follow and that limit 'bad behaviour' and the entrepreneurship of an actor with agency to apply a more pragmatic approach to avoid further disasters. There is evidence that entrepreneurs have stepped outside some aspects of the framework to improve outcomes yet remain limited by others. The problem is such entrepreneurs are rare, and most actors are left to follow the formal rules. There is also a hypocritical aspect to the application of the formal institutional framework guidelines. Projects are approved jurisdictionally and governmentally to begin following these rules, yet the agency with responsibility for the project does not have the capability to deliver, setting the project up for failure from the outset.

To address, or perhaps avoid, the collective governance issues, this book posits that it is time to acknowledge that large ICT software projects are complex beasts and the complexity, capability requirements, and risk must be reduced by doing things differently. Projects must be planned differently, funded differently, and governed differently or else more of the same can be expected. These issues are currently being left up to actors with the entrepreneurship, initiative, and agency to address them, rather than executive leadership attending to governance. It is time for those with responsibility for leadership in governance to ask, listen, act, and let go of some control.

The case studies: A comparison

Novopay was approved in 2008 and followed the institutional framework guidelines for planning and approval. It was not a rogue project operating in secret. The institutional framework and the Novopay planning documents indicate that lessons from previous failed projects had been incorporated into its management; however, the mistakes were repeated—and arguably magnified—with some particularly important institutional governance issues highlighted. The Novopay project operated within the institutional framework throughout and was approved to start, continue, and go live by project governance, central agencies, and government. The project was approved to begin even though there was an acknowledgement that the Ministry of Education (MoE) did not have the capability to undertake such a complex project, and it was approved as a large single project even though the guidelines recommended complex projects should be broken into smaller components. The MoE was then largely left to manage independently without the capability to do so, which was a failure of institutional governance, not a personal failing of the sponsor or the MoE. It is a tragic tale, with disastrous outcomes for all stakeholders.

The EPDP had a direct relationship with Novopay as it was to replace critical ineffective components of the Novopay solution. Because the EPDP would encounter many of the same challenges as Novopay, the EPDP made the Novopay lessons learnt central to planning and management. The EPDP has been successful and addressed the risk of repeating the problems with Novopay, which is due to three major factors. First, the program benefited, by chance, from having an extremely capable project sponsor who took on the role, all its responsibilities, and accountability with entrepreneurial gusto and skill; what a difference that made to the Novopay model. Second, capability and capacity to undertake the project were assessed and acknowledged upfront, and anything lacking was acquired before beginning key tasks. Finally, the project was broken into components to reduce complexity and aid learning and was delivered via agile methodology. This approach was not necessarily supported by the institutional framework and the sponsor used her agency as the chief executive to work around this. The EPDP findings indicate that, despite the successful use of agile, change in the institutional framework has been slow.

The Novopay and the EPDP case studies highlight the hypocritical nature of the governance. It was widely acknowledged that the MoE did not have the capability to undertake the project, yet it was asked to do so. Novopay, which followed the institutional framework and maintained government support throughout, has now been widely cited as a catastrophic failure, costing the careers of senior bureaucrats. The EPDP is a project that has, where possible, avoided or worked around the standard guidelines because they would not have allowed it to achieve the desired outcomes. This project is classified as a success and is being held up as an exemplar in New Zealand. Which governance path should future projects follow—the one to avoid 'bad behaviour' or the one to focus on successful outcomes?

This book is not researching how large government ICT software projects are classified as a 'success' or a 'failure' or something in between. That would require a different methodology to the one applied here, and indeed is a different research question. However, the nature of the two cases and the perceptions of their outcomes provide an opportunity to analyse why one is seen as a failure and the other as a success. Allan McConnell (2010a, 2010b; Howlett 2012) proposes a spectrum of success as a suitable means of undertaking such an assessment. Assessment based on traditional program outcomes—for example, technical goals, cost, and time—is not suitable, so two additional measures have been introduced. The first is the outcome as policy—whether due to institutional policies or processes, there is a failure to move from idea to reality. The institutional frameworks in our case studies reflect this, as they directly influenced how the projects were approved and managed. The second is the political implications. For each, McConnell proposes a spectrum roughly equal to moving between virtual universal support for the outcomes and an all but total lack of support: success to failure or parts in between. It is important to note—and aligned with comments in the introductory section of this book—that the concept of universal agreement is utopian.

The two cases are analysed against McConnell's spectrum (adapted from McConnell 2010a: 352–56). For the policy factor in Novopay, Table 8.1 indicates that while there was compliance success in following the governance framework, this was at best conflicted as it contributed to the eventual poor outcomes, and there was a subsequent push for change. As a program, support for Novopay's outcomes was and remains virtually non-existent, as evidenced by the findings of the ministerial inquiry (Jack & Weevers 2013). Novopay was also politically damaging. Based on this analysis, it is not difficult to understand why Novopay has been classified as a failure—almost universally so.

Table 8.1 Novopay assessment against McConnell's spectrum

Spectrum	Policy	Program	Politics
Success			
Resilient success			
Conflicted success	• Governance framework was followed, but with signs of disagreement. • Long-term legitimacy was tainted.		
Precarious success	• Out of touch with viable alternatives.		
Failure	• Support for the governance framework was virtually non-existent.	• Implementation was not executed in line with objectives and did not achieve desired outcomes. • Damaging to a particular target group (i.e. schools). • Program support is virtually non-existent.	• Damaging to the reputation of the government and leaders, with no redeeming political benefit.

Source: Compiled by author.

Table 8.2 EPDP assessment against McConnell's spectrum

Spectrum	Policy	Program	Politics
Success		• Implementation in line with objectives, has been almost universally perceived as successful, and cited as an exemplar in New Zealand government. • Schools have greatly benefited and there are now strong relations and renewed trust between them and the ministry.	• Political reputations have not been damaged. • Opposition to the government for the initiative is virtually non-existent.
Resilient success		• Outcomes broadly achieved despite some shortfalls (e.g. time, cost).	
Conflicted success	• Governance framework was followed, but with signs of disagreement. • Long-term legitimacy was tainted.		
Precarious success	• Out of touch with viable alternatives.		
Failure	• Support for the governance framework was virtually non-existent.		

Source: Compiled by author.

For the policy factor in the EPDP, Table 8.2 indicates much the same findings as for Novopay: the governance framework was followed where mandatory but was ineffective in meeting the requirements of the project and did not support innovation. There was a desire for governance change as a result. The EPDP has found and continues to find wide support from all stakeholders in meeting program deliverables and has been cited as an exemplar in New Zealand government. Given this success, there has been virtually no negative political impact. As identified earlier, the EPDP has not delivered to time or budget, yet its 'success' remains resilient. In this case, effectively delivering a product and meeting stakeholder and political expectations arguably override this factor. The EPDP program and its political successes were only possible due to the ability and determination of the project sponsor to do things differently and step away from policy shortcomings.

Comparing the part one (Chapters 3–5) findings with the case study findings

The conceptual findings from the Novopay and EPDP case studies (part two) are very closely aligned with those from part one (Chapters 3–5), where the same issues were highlighted. To break this down further, Table 8.3 compares the theoretical concept findings from parts one and two (also see Appendices 5 and 6). The correlation between the part one and Novopay findings is eerie; sadly, the Novopay issues remain a decade later. The EPDP findings highlight the fact that the part one and Novopay issues were known to exist, but things were done differently to address these. To avoid the governance shortcomings, the EPDP stepped outside the institutional framework; the project adapted, but the governance framework did not.

Therein lies a key finding when comparing parts one and two. The research spans 2008 to 2020 and the findings indicate that, within that period, little has changed and there is no evidence of widespread governance adaptation of the institutional frameworks. The findings in Table 8.3 are not listed in order of priority. Without leadership to recognise the need for, and to drive and prioritise, change across sectors, none of the concepts is likely to be addressed.

These findings fit within and support the overall narrative that the institutional frameworks are insufficient to provide effective governance for large ICT software projects in the Australian and New Zealand public sectors. Effective governance has been provided through adaptation due to individual agency. Therefore, despite experiences, much learning, and an even greater desire for change from the elite interviewees, poor outcomes will continue because change is simply not happening.

Table 8.3 Comparison of theoretical concept findings

Theoretical concept	Part one, general (2018–20)	Novopay case study (2008–12)	EPDP case study (2017–20)
Capability and capacity-building	Capability and capacity do not exist and there is no organisational priority to address the issue. Where they do exist, this is a result of chance or luck rather than institutional framework outcomes.	The MoE did not have the capability to undertake Novopay and failed to address this. It was left to act independently. The sponsor lacked capability and experience.	There was early recognition that both capability and capacity were lacking, so the leadership focus was to implement capability upgrades and maintenance strategies before beginning key tasks. The sponsor had vast experience in large ICT software projects, which was a product of chance, rather than a designed outcome.
Financial management	The requirement to forecast in full upfront at the initiation stage is impossible, produces irrelevant figures, and is a major issue with these projects.	Required a full upfront forecast, which proved to be wildly inaccurate.	The program had to prepare a full upfront forecast, which remains a benchmark. This was inaccurate and eventually became irrelevant as the project moved to an agile delivery method.
Organisational learning	Learning is not happening. There is a reliance on written reports after the event and a culture of 'learned helplessness' and forgetting. Real-time continuous learning is preferred.	Despite many past learnings being available, Novopay learnt nothing and repeated and exaggerated previous errors.	The project effectively addressed key Novopay learnings and has not repeated the same mistakes. This was largely enabled by the agile methodology with a cycle of continuous learning and breaking down risk and capability demands. It also enabled staged delivery.
Stakeholder management	This capability is missing. Vendor management is particularly poor.	Stakeholder management was poor. Schools were not engaged effectively, and the relationship with the vendor became toxic.	Stakeholder management was a key focus of the program. Schools were actively and successfully engaged from the outset. Vendor management was effective.

Theoretical concept	Part one, general (2018–20)	Novopay case study (2008–12)	EPDP case study (2017–20)
Contract management	Capability does not exist and there is a focus on entering long-term contracts based on upfront estimates, for which accuracy is impossible and which set the relationship up for failure.	The long-term contract with Talent2 was based on a predetermined forecast, not on the work to be undertaken, which was largely unknown.	Vendor management was effective due to the use of multiple vendors for specific tasks, with a focus on the capability and capacity to undertake each component, based on time and materials, which was seen as a 'win-win' for all.
Accountability	Misunderstood, avoided, and applied inconsistently. Seen as all risk and no reward.	The sponsor misunderstood their accountability and avoided key responsibilities; however, they were held accountable and resigned from their MoE role as a result.	The sponsor, who was also the chief executive, fully understood her accountability, actively participated in the program, and led from the front.
Methodologies	Methodologies exist but are applied inconsistently and are largely ineffective in improving outcomes.	PRINCE2 was used but was seen as 'ticking a box' to comply with an institutional requirement. It did not improve project outcomes. Gateway reviews were not used.	The program used an agile delivery methodology, which was highly effective and enabled the program to meet many of its objectives. Gateway reviews were also used and were helpful.
Leadership	There are two key areas of leadership failure: government and jurisdictional executive leadership to adapt institutional frameworks, and senior project leadership, particularly from the sponsor role.	The sponsor failed to provide the leadership required and distanced herself from the project; however, there was also a failure of governance from government and central agencies, who endorsed the project throughout, including the go-live decision.	The sponsor, who was also the chief executive, provided highly effective leadership and was a major contributor to the program's success. The government and central agencies had little leadership input and largely left the program to its own devices.

Theoretical concept	Part one, general (2018–20)	Novopay case study (2008–12)	EPDP case study (2017–20)
Entrepreneurship	Stop doing large projects. The preferred approach is to break large projects into smaller components to reduce complexity, risk, and capability demands.	Novopay was undertaken as a single large complex project and implemented with a 'big bang'.	The program was broken into smaller components and delivered incrementally via an agile methodology.
Agency	Some institutional frameworks support doing things differently; however, there is a reliance on the agency of the project executive for this, which is seen as positive. Political agency is a negative as it can usurp institutional guidelines.	Agency was not used effectively, with the sponsor avoiding responsibility. Political influence negatively impacted on the go-live decision.	The use of agile in the EPDP was not an institutional framework guideline but was pursued and supported due to the initiative and agency of the sponsor/chief executive. Political influence was not a factor, arguably due to the ongoing success of the program and therefore a contented minister.

Source: Compiled by author.

Theoretical implications

Institutionalism is the study of institutions as 'humanly devised constraints that shape human interaction' (North 1990: 3). These constraints shape required behaviour, with actors adhering because it is in their interest to do so (Ferris & Tang 1993: 7). These constraints in turn provide 'stability and meaning to behaviour' through the 'routinisation' of tasks (Timney 1996: 101). This system of formal and informal rules, guidelines, and procedures that guide the behaviour of actors is classified as an institutional framework (North 1990: 6). All jurisdictions within the Australian and New Zealand public sectors have institutional frameworks for the operation of large ICT software projects, guiding how they are initiated, approved, and funded, what methodologies are used, resources, assurance mechanisms, and so on. This provides project governance with an emphasis on 'consistent and coordinated' practices (Peters 2011: 78).

Analysis of the elite interview data indicates that governance via the institutional frameworks within the Australian and New Zealand public sectors is generally adhered to—for example, the preparation of business cases in a prescribed format and timing to gain approval. However, as identified in the narrative, this adherence forces agencies and projects down a path that increases the likelihood of poor outcomes. Therefore, compliance may be achieving consistency, but it could be consistent ineffectiveness.

That leads to the issue of adaptation, which is an important part of institutional theory. Institutions and their governance are not static; they innovate and adapt to evolving circumstances and environmental issues (Peters 2011: 84). This book argues that, despite overwhelming evidence supporting change, institutional frameworks have not adapted. Adaptation is slow or non-existent and there is effectively an institutional inertia when it comes to addressing the issue. Inertia can be thought of as the 'stickiness' of institutions (Pierson 2004: 8); they can be hard to budge. Alternatively, this stickiness can be thought of as the embeddedness of structures and practices (Starik & Rands 1995; Dacin et al. 1999), which can make change a formidable task. The data in this book indicate the structural constraints embedded in the institutional frameworks are a major factor in this inertia. To analyse and explain this inertia through an institutionalist lens, the findings can be interpreted against several factors.

First, the cost to implement all the issues highlighted—new structures and skills, changed executive expectations, asset management, and portfolio funding, to name a few—would be extensive. The interview data show this cost is a factor in the failure to actively address the change required. Politicians and the executive baulk at this as they see little benefit for themselves and fail to understand the true cost of failure from not acting. As one example, a former government education minister explained that a choice between spending money on ICT software maintenance or on improving school facilities was politically challenging—or, in the immortal words of Sir Humphrey Appleby, 'a most courageous decision, minister'. The problem of course, as has been identified in this book, is that not maintaining a school payroll solution can lead to major organisational, political, and public fallout. It has been argued that change will only happen when the costs are low, the current framework is identified and accepted as being poor, and all parties accept that change is necessary (Espín-Sánchez 2014). Given the misalignment of those factors for large ICT software project governance, adaptation of the various institutional frameworks can be expected to remain inert.

Second, path dependence is interesting from a historical institutionalism perspective, as events over time seem to have had little impact on improving outcomes. That is not to say that institutional frameworks have not evolved because of endogenous and exogenous factors. They have—for example, with the introduction of gateway reviews. However, these changes have so far failed to address the core issues with large ICT software projects. Mahoney (2000: 511) argues that this is a factor in institutional inertia as historically driven change once set in motion tends to continue to track that change and become embedded to the exclusion of other possibilities. This is supported by Pierson (2000b: 75), who states that once a path has been set and other options discarded, an institutional commitment has been made and change becomes difficult. An example is the requirement for a detailed business case at project initiation—which can only be a guess about what will happen in the future—on which the project is approved and funds allocated. The overwhelming perspective from the data in this book is that this alone contributes significantly to continuing poor outcomes, although there is resistance to 'letting go' from central agencies and politicians for fear of losing control. So, while some forces may be pushing for change, public sector bureaucrats remain resistant to that change and innovation (Gains & John 2010).

The third factor is the role of agency, how it is applied, and by whom. The problem identified in this book is that institutional frameworks can subjugate agency or, as Schmidt (2008: 314) states, there is a subordination of agency to structure. However, while subjugated institutionally, actors with agency are exerting influence over individual large ICT projects. If agency is thought of as 'the capacity of individuals to act independently and to make their own free choices' (Barker 2005: 448) or to 'manipulate institutions' (Abdelnour et al. 2017: 1781), the use of agency is largely positive. Actors used their agency and entrepreneurial skills effectively to circumvent perceived shortcomings in the institutional framework. This was a consequence of a struggle between institutionalised practices and the goals of the actor (DiMaggio 1988; Fligstein 1997; Beckert 1999; Lawrence 1999; Lockett et al. 2012: 357)—in this case, to improve the likelihood of good project outcomes. The problem is these actions and ideas are not leading to demonstrable institutional change; they are independent initiatives, with localised learning, while the institutions remain inert. Bell (2011: 886) argues that the answer is to bring agency back into the equation for a more 'discursive institutionalism'—a process in which ideas and interactive discourse are communicated and feed into institutional change

(Schmidt 2011: 684). This is not happening. For example, the EPDP has been lauded nationally for changing internal audit practices, nominated internationally for its use of agile methodology, and cited by New Zealand central agencies as an exemplar. However, this has not yet led to any change to the institutional framework—in fact, the internal auditors seem to be viewed suspiciously by their peers. This is like the findings from the ATO mini case study (see Boxes 5.1 and 7.6): while the commissioner used his agency to drive entrepreneurial change to great effect, there is no evidence that this has resulted in wider endogenous change in the Australian Public Service. If the use of agency is viewed as a reaction to the ineffectiveness of the governance framework, a failure to learn from these successes and adapt governance accordingly reflects a weakness in governance.

Fourth, a failure of leadership has contributed to governance inertia. The failure is twofold—the second a consequence of the first: executive leadership has failed to adapt and transform governance for these projects, and the project sponsor has failed to provide leadership.

Executive leadership in government has focused on control and the application of rules, guidelines, constraints, and the like. This approach is a poor fit with modern governance principles, the primary aims of which, according to Denhardt and Denhardt (2011: 422), include fostering collaboration and building adaptive capacity and resilience. Whereas traditionally adaptation was considered the result of transformational leadership (Van Wart 2003; Denhardt & Denhardt 2011: 424), modern governance requires leadership that enables actors to fulfil their needs (Burns 1978: 19; Dugan 2012: 8). For example, while funding guidelines may support Treasury's self-interest, they are ignoring the substantial negative impacts this has on a project, with the two at odds with each other. Collaboration addresses this dilemma when decision-makers recognise the legitimate interests of stakeholders by supporting collaborative outcomes and letting go where necessary (Thomson & Perry 2006). This is a style of governance leadership that I could not identify in any document or evidence from the elite interviewees; there was no widespread engagement with the public sector stakeholders on governance concerns and no adaptation of the governance framework. Governance remains largely hierarchically controlled.

The second aim of leadership is to build adaptive capacity and resilience into governance. When everything seems to be out of control, such as in large ICT projects, the natural leadership reaction is to apply more control via governance (Sutcliffe & Vogus 2003), which can further reduce organisational management capacity and resilience (Denhardt & Denhardt 2009). This does not result in adaptation that will transform; its intent is applying more control—a move from inertia to strangulation. The findings in this research support the idea that institutional frameworks are more about what must and must not be done than about what can and should be done. Duit and Galaz (2008: 326) argue that this rigid application of control is an inappropriate governance model when unpredictability exists, as it does in these projects. They argue for a more flexible governance model that is adaptive to changing circumstances. Perhaps it is time for leadership to collaborate, listen, and act on these perspectives.

The leadership failure in the critical role of project sponsor can be causally related to the failure of governance to adapt for these large ICT projects. Actors are appointed to the role without the necessary skills or experience and there is no effective strategy to address this. There is evidence of some jurisdictional movement in this area, but it is insufficient.

The fifth factor is the matter of organisational learning, which is when 'the experiential lessons of history are captured in a way that makes the lessons, but not the history, accessible to organisations and organisational members who have not experienced that history' (Levitt & March 1988: 320). This learning is then reflected in the cumulative adaptation of the 'formal rules and structures, policy documents, manuals, [and] standard operating procedures' (Dekker & Hansen 2004: 217)—that is, the adaptation of governance via the institutional framework. There has been a failure to apply these learnings, contributing to governance inertia and the lack of adaptation in the institutional frameworks. This is a case of institutional amnesia—the 'ways in which government agents and organisations ... no longer remember or record policy-relevant lessons from the past' (Stark & Head 2019: 1526). Pollitt (2000: 6) adds to this definition by arguing that institutional amnesia is the ability and willingness of public sector institutions to access and use relevant experiences. Stark (2019: 150–56) argues that this amnesia occurs when, among other things, there is organisational churn. As has been noted in previous chapters, large ICT software projects are typically the responsibility of an individual agency, hence learnings have been siloed; exacerbating this is the fact that teams can be transitional, so learnings and storytelling walk out the door when individuals leave. Regular organisational restructuring and change of policy or government compound this issue.

The inability of an organisation to institutionalise change limits its capacity to adapt. The complexity of the institutional frameworks for large ICT software projects, and their embeddedness, limits the ability of an organisation to be an adaptive change agent, as change then requires 'intense and long-term political bargaining, such as planning regimes' (Stark 2019: 152). The passage of time can have two impacts: a 'drift' in which risk perceptions fade, and the organisational churn factor, which means there is an absence of historical storytelling to relive the lessons from past projects. This has a relationship with learning-curve theory, which posits that organisational and individual learnings are forgotten when activities slow or cease for a period (Globerson & Levin 1987; Cappelli 2000). There is danger in an organisation forgetting key lessons from the past (Rigg 2016; Pedler & Hsu 2014; Biesenthal et al. 2018: 44). This is relevant to large ICT software projects as they can be generational, with stories lost or fading between each.

An example of this is the Novopay case study. Project documentation stated that it had applied learnings from past projects, including the previous payroll implementation many years earlier; however, the mistakes were amplified. This organisational and individual forgetting was arguably because a new project team was in place, with no individual learning or history to bring forward; they were learning from scratch. Novopay was the responsibility of a single agency, but there was no evidence of effective cross or interjurisdictional learnings. This supports a finding by Swan et al. (2010: 327), who argue that organisations fail to learn from past projects when the learning is localised rather than organisation wide. This aligns with the perceptions of the elite interviewees who said it was unrealistic to expect an agency to have the knowledge, experience, and skills to undertake large ICT projects when they are generational; people move on and technology and software change. Therefore, when planning large projects, Kleiner et al. (2012) argue, the agency should first understand it has forgotten how to undertake them or is not privy to localised learnings. Institutional frameworks are adapted by adding 'lessons learned', but these are likely to have been forgotten and inertia remains, as was the case with Novopay.

McConnell (2010a, 2010b) argues that the spectrum for measuring policy success requires assessment against three areas: policy, program, and political. A comparison of the two case studies identified similar problems with the policy area, as strict adherence to or reliance on the institutional governance framework and the policies therein would contribute to poor outcomes. Novopay followed the prescribed path, with disastrous outcomes.

The EPDP did not adhere strictly to the framework thanks to the agency, skill, and entrepreneurship of the sponsor, and achieved program and political success. Howlett (2012) argues that policy is the most difficult area in which to address shortcomings due to leadership and organisational capability and capacity issues. Limitations must be detected, altered, and given organisational priority. Hence, as with other theoretical findings, the road to policy success is challenging.

In conclusion, the findings indicate that the institutional frameworks are intended to create the 'conditions for ordered rule and collective action' (Stoker 1998: 17). However, if the effectiveness of this governance is to be measured as performance against desired outcomes (Baekkeskov 2007: 258) then governance has been ineffective or, at best, insufficient in key areas. Part of the problem is that the multilevel nature of the governance opens effectiveness to dispute (Baekkeskov 2007; McConnell 2015). An example would be the financial guidelines for these large projects, which were widely criticised by the elite interviewees yet supported politically and by the executive because they were seen to provide surety over costs.

The findings indicate that governance is largely 'impositional' (Richardson 2012): imposed from above, with a focus on control, and little evidence of adaptation through collaboration, participation, or responsiveness to the experiences of those impacted (Heclo 1978; Katsamunska 2016). This introduces a dilemma for project leadership: should they follow an imposed governance model that could lead to loss of control of project outcomes for which they will be held accountable, or should they put self-interest first and step away from aspects of governance to improve the likelihood of good outcomes? The research indicates self-interest in the project occurs when there is both capability and agency, hence agency is used to provide a balance between compliance and flexibility. The interesting aspect of this finding is that it is no secret when this happens: central agencies are aware of this 'stepping away' and there is evidence of tacit support and trust, with the EPDP case study a prime example. This is perhaps an acceptance that institutional governance adaptation is slow, so localised adaptation is tolerated.

With a new institutionalism focus on understanding the relationship between institutions, behaviour, and outcomes (Diermeier & Krehbiel 2003; Scott 2005; Parsons 2007), the findings indicate institutional inertia, which is leading to tensions between the institution and the behaviour of individuals. This inertia is due to several factors. First, while the elite interviewees believed the institutions were ineffective, they largely followed them, almost through fear—a key tenet of rational choice institutionalism (Schmidt 2010). As a result, change is static. Second, actors can be influenced by the social legitimacy of the institution, which is a key tenet of sociological institutionalism (Thelen 2004; Parsons 2007; Kenny 2007). They act not from fear of the consequences for not doing so, but because they believe it is appropriate to do so (Schmidt 2010). A potential future example would be widespread use of agile delivery methods as it (presumably) gains legitimacy. Gaining legitimacy, however, takes time (Bevir 2010). Third, there is evidence of historical institutional change such as the introduction of PRINCE2, gateway reviews, and revisions to financial rules, but these have not addressed the key governance issues identified by the elite interviewees. Institutions have become sticky, with embedded rules that tend to exclude alternatives (Starik & Rands 1995; Dacin et al. 1999; Pierson 2004).

Finally, ideas are a dynamic and endogenous means of change. Discursive institutionalism argues that ideas are weapons for institutional change, and can both identify problems and provide solutions (Blyth 2001). The problem is, our findings indicate that while the ideas exist, change is not happening because the discursive interaction is absent. This lack of change in institutions to address key issues causes tension and actors with capability and agency circumvent this by stepping away from the institutional framework and doing things differently to improve the likelihood of good project outcomes.

However, the dilemma of a reliance on matching capability and agency to address shortcomings in governance and its frameworks is that, as this book has found, capability can be a matter of chance or luck. Therefore, actors and projects will continue to rely on existing institutional governance arrangements.

Public policy implications

The elite interviewees provided no disagreement about the necessity of an effective governance framework for large ICT software projects; the argument was that existing frameworks are ineffective or inconsistent in achieving the desired outcomes, are failing to adapt, and there is institutional inertia. The frameworks have become 'sticky' and are a constraint on change so that this inertia has public policy implications (see Table 8.4).

Table 8.4 Policy implications of institutional inertia

Institutional inertia factor	Type of inertia	Implications for behaviour and project outcomes	Implications for policy
Cost	Cost is a barrier to change as the benefit of the expenditure is not recognised institutionally or politically, nor is the cost of failure understood.	Projects will continue to struggle within the constraints.	The funding of all components related to a large ICT project (structure, skills, training, maintenance, etc.) must meet requirements.
Path	There is ongoing commitment to historically implemented policy.	Forced to follow the same path that has previously led to poor outcomes.	Removing ongoing commitment to past changes.
Agency and entrepreneurship	Governance is imposing structure on agency; agency becomes reliant on entrepreneurship.	Due to a perceived lack of capability, actors with agency are following the framework. Those with agency and capability are being entrepreneurial and doing things their own way.	Removing structure from agency when actors do not have capability can lead to problems. The imposition of complex controls leads to agency being applied to circumvent these controls to improve outcomes.
Leadership (in governance)	Failure in governance leadership to address major issues. Failure to collaborate; controls imposed from above with disregard to discourse/ideas from jurisdictional actors. The typical response to crisis is to add more control.	Imposing controls from above. Lack of capability and capacity to undertake large ICT software projects.	Governance requires a collaborative approach, not a hierarchically imposed one that ignores the needs of those impacted.
Organisational learning	There is a culture of forgetting, not learning, arguably because of the extended period between each large project and the siloed approach to undertaking them.	Mistakes are repeated. This is exacerbated by the fact that large ICT projects are typically the responsibility of an agency, and there is little collaboration or sharing between agencies.	If you proceed with large ICT software projects, acknowledge there is much that you cannot know upfront. The alternative is to not do large projects.

Source: Adapted from Munck af Rosenschöld et al. (2014: 645).

Commitment to major policy and cultural change is required over an extended time frame to address inertia. This can be overwhelming because, as stated in the interviews, such change is likely to be just one of many policy issues within a jurisdiction at any given time. Therefore, it is a matter of leaders not just recognising and prioritising the need for change, but also prioritising this ahead of or along with other policy agendas and over an extended period. Given the lack of change historically and a stable political environment to support it, it is not unreasonable to expect that these issues will not be addressed in a timely manner, if at all.

Therefore, the major policy implication to be drawn is that what is required is not more governance, but less complexity. This is not an argument against governance; rather, the focus should be on increasing the effectiveness of governance to improve outcomes, not adding further project controls. This was a finding of a Gartner report (Moore 2015) that posited that, despite 50 years of failures and lessons learnt, the same things keep happening, and the common organisational response is more governance control, which has never worked. Moore argues that the crux of the problem is a 'refusal to address complexity' and the solution is less bureaucracy in governance and a renewed emphasis on ensuring a project can achieve its outcomes. In summary, if there is a problem in the capacity of governance (inertia), the nature of the problem must be changed (reduce complexity).

Several key policy implications to address complexity have been identified. First, it is lunacy to expect the public sector to have the capability and capacity across the range of roles and disciplines required to undertake these extraordinarily complex large ICT software projects. However, the public sector does have capability for smaller, less complex projects, which it has proven it can successfully deliver. Drucker (2008: 26) supports this perspective by arguing: 'No institution can possibly survive if it needs geniuses or supermen to manage it. It must be organized in such a way as to be able to get along under a leadership composed of average human beings.'

The argument from the elite interviewees is that policy should be concentrated on the development of project management roles and disciplines across organisations to support smaller projects. There is rarely a need for 'superheroes', but when they are required for a large project, you bring in from outside those with the experience and currency of skills. Single long-term projects should not be approved; solutions should be delivered progressively via a series of smaller component-based projects. Continuation of a project is dependent on the successful delivery of each component and evidence of benefit delivery to support the next component. There is evidence across jurisdictions of increasing delivery through component-based methods such as agile, as well as some resistance, but the argument here is that this approach should be not just applied to smaller projects, but also used to break down the complexity of large projects.

The second policy implication—linked to the first—is the issue of how large ICT software projects are forecast and funded. An alternative to full upfront forecasts and funding is progressive funding based on learnings and outcomes from each stage. This is different to some current policy, such as in Victoria, where a project must submit an upfront forecast, on which approval is based, but the funding is allocated in stages based on previous outcomes. This is the equivalent of saying: 'Though I have clear scope and defensible benefits for the project, I do not know how much it will cost; I need so much to begin and, as I progress, the total cost and time will become clearer. I expect to be supported only if I have succeeded and the project is deemed worthy of continuation.' Forecasting in full is driven by political need; however, if the ethical requirement is to forecast with accuracy, change is required (Wachs 1990). This represents a major cultural change in project governance.

Third, regardless of any move to component-based delivery, the sponsor role remains critical. It was unanimous among interviewees that the public sector does not have this capability and leadership has failed to address this gap, principally because of the effort and cost required to establish a detailed program for sponsors within a jurisdiction. For example, in Tasmania, it was stated that such a move could not be justified. This is arguably the situation across the Australian and New Zealand public sectors. The economies of scale are not there within individual jurisdictions to establish something akin to the Major Projects Leadership Academy (MPLA), which is sponsored by the United Kingdom's Infrastructure and Projects Authority and delivered in partnership with the Säid Business School at the University of Oxford. While the MPLA is not targeted specifically at ICT projects, it focuses on the leadership skills needed to 'transform the implementation of government policy through world-class delivery of major projects' with a focus on 'securing transformational outcomes'. The course is intensive and extensive, recognises the criticality of effective leadership in large projects, and is a prerequisite for undertaking specific roles in a large project. It has been argued that:

The launch of the MPLA makes the UK Government the first in the world to introduce mandatory leadership development across its entire major project portfolio, supporting and equipping its project leaders at the most senior levels in Government with the right skills and capabilities to deliver major projects effectively. (Deloitte 2016)

There is potential for a similar school to be established for Australian and New Zealand public sector use. The Victorian Government, to its credit, in 2019 established the Victorian Major Projects Leadership Academy in cooperation with the Säid Business School and based on the UK model, providing a 12-month tertiary-level course. It has since been rebranded as the Australian Major Projects Leadership Academy (AMPLA)[1] and is open to participants from across Australia. However—and arguably confirming the perception that ICT project skills are treated as playing 'second fiddle' to other infrastructure project skills—Person BN (Senior assurance officer, Pers. comm., 18 September 2018) confirmed that the course is not open to ICT project staff. Therefore, a policy gap remains in how to address the capability of senior leadership roles in large ICT projects. This is an opportunity for other jurisdictions to work with the AMPLA stakeholders to expand this course to include ICT project leaders. There is also potential for an institution such as the Australia and New Zealand School of Government (ANZSOG) to take leadership on this issue, like that for the Executive Master of Public Administration initiative in partnership with jurisdictions and universities across Australia and New Zealand. A key part of such a policy would be a requirement that senior executives have this training as part of their organisational skillset and as a prerequisite for appointment to a project leadership role.

Last, almost as an acknowledgement that major policy change may take time, meet with organisational resistance, or not happen, it is possible to achieve a 'quick win' via the implementation of a checkpoint at project initiation. While institutional frameworks may mention the need for capability to undertake a project, there is little evidence of assessments being made at initiation or of this being part of the approval to proceed, with Novopay a classic example of an extremely difficult and complex project approved without the required capability, and therefore set up to fail from the outset. The logical time to assess a large project and the ability of the

---

1   See: www.opv.vic.gov.au/System-wide-improvements/Australian-Major-Projects-Leadership-Academy.

agency to deliver as planned is the project initiation stage. The notion is simple: if you do not have the capability to deliver as planned, rethink the approach before commencing.

While elite interviewees acknowledged the need for a gateway review at the project initiation or business case preparation stage, they believe this is done mainly to provide assurance of the information in the proposal. There is a reliance on the agency to provide this information—with its inherent enthusiasm, optimism, and self-interest—rather than being a truly independent assessment of the ability to deliver. This is supported by the fact that, since the implementation of gateway reviews, poor outcomes have continued, largely due to the inability of agencies to deliver as planned.

It has been highlighted throughout this book that projects operate in a political environment and, regardless of policy, invalid decisions can be made.

Practical implications

The practical steps outlined below align with the identified policy implications, resulting in a five-step process for project approval and funding. The intent is to stop poorly conceived large ICT projects at the initiation stage, and it is a process to match the approach with capability. It is also a practical solution to the policy implications set out earlier in this chapter—namely, that because governance change through policy change is in a state of inertia, the problem must be changed by reducing the complexity of projects at initiation.

1. Assessments of the organisational capability to undertake the project must be made at the initiation stage. If the capability does not fit the plan, the project is not approved. There should be no avoidance or transfer of accountability for jurisdictional approval of a project that an agency is incapable of delivering.
2. No project is approved to begin unless it is broken into component-based projects or, at worst, a mixture of traditional waterfall and component-based sections, together with a capability and capacity plan to deliver.
3. Product delivery must be iterative and progressive—not a big-bang approach. Learning must be applied from each stage to the next.
4. The sponsor must be experienced, skilled, and assigned with an appropriate resource and support model.

5. A full upfront forecast should not be required for the project, nor should the project be funded based on an upfront forecast. While a goal for project scope and deliverables is required—as all parties need to know what the objectives and benefits will be—there should be acknowledgement that final costs will only be known and become relevant as the project progresses. There should be a process of providing seed money, delivering, replanning, and providing more money based on results. The total cost is not yet known, it will evolve—a paradigm shift in the way these projects are financed.

During the review of the final draft of this book, I came across a timely article in *iTnews* (Hendry 2021) that is pertinent to the above practical implications (Box 8.1).

Box 8.1 Change afoot in New South Wales

The heading of an article in *iTnews* was 'NSW Govt IT Cost Overruns Fall by 90 Percent in Four Years' (Hendry 2021). The article claimed that an initiative by a NSW Government agency to introduce a new assurance framework for large ICT projects had successfully reduced the risk, failure rate, and cost overruns of these projects. Under the auspices of the Digital Restart Fund, any project forecast to cost more than A$5 million must undergo extensive review before it can proceed. The initiative was also successful in reducing the average cost and size of these projects.

Via the Digital Restart Fund (Digital.NSW 2022c), the NSW Government allocated A$1.6 billion over three years to invest in ICT projects, administered by the Department of Customer Service. Projects that are eligible for funding include customer journeys and life events, state digital assets, legacy systems, and capability-building. The fund develops a 'pipeline', or portfolio, of eligible projects from across the jurisdiction and investment is prioritised against specific criteria. Successful projects are allocated a budget from the fund but must comply with monitoring guidelines.

The fund provides up to A$5 million as 'seed money', which the project can use in discovery, alpha, or beta phases or to build prototypes. Projects of more than A$5 million must prepare a more detailed business case and assessment; however, a key part of this is a plan to break the project into iterative component-based deliverables. For these projects, while a full upfront forecast is required, funding is provided in tranches. Continued funding is dependent on the outcomes of each stage (this has similarities with the Victorian model) and as a guide funding is set at A$20 million per tranche.

Key to the provision of funding, and approval for the project to begin, is the project passing an initial assessment that includes factors such as strategic alignment and desirability. Also included is an upfront assessment 'to ensure the project can be delivered with reasonable effort given existing capabilities'— that is, if you cannot deliver as planned with existing internal or purchased capabilities then the project will not be funded.

I contacted Mark Howard, Executive Director of ICT/Digital Investment and Assurance at the Department of Customer Services, to discuss this initiative. He confirmed that the aim is to reduce the risk in large projects by reducing their complexity, which means component-based delivery methods, reduced time frames, progressive and restricted funding based on demonstrable outcomes, and reduced capability demands. Howard said the seed funding is an acknowledgement that these large projects have many unknowns and allows the project to 'test the water' before committing to a path or major investment.

Howard said the unit has paused approval on planned projects until complexity and capability concerns are addressed. He also confirmed that the unit has stopped large projects that, although initially funded, had failed to deliver as planned. A major factor is the time frame, with Howard saying it is highly unlikely that any project beyond a two-year time frame will be approved, unless there is progressive delivery of benefits/outcomes. The framework that governs this fund was developed after consultation with jurisdictional project stakeholders and was collaboratively developed, not imposed from above.

The intent of this framework is closely aligned with the practical implications identified from the findings in this book—that is, it is better to stop a project at initiation and look for a less complex path if the capability is not there to deliver as planned. There is arguably much to learn from this initiative. It is, however, interesting to note that for large projects of more than A$5 million, a full upfront forecast is still required. It seems that change is one step too far.

Conclusion

It is important to reiterate that there were no major divergences between the perspectives of the Australian and New Zealand elite interviewees. This consistency provides added relevance and emphasis to the findings for all Australian and New Zealand public sector agencies.

In answer to research question one, the overwhelming perspective of the elite interviewees was that the governance of large ICT software projects within the Australian and New Zealand public sectors has not been effective in achieving the desired outcomes.

In answer to research question two, governance has not been adapting as required; it is static, with historically embedded practices. Governance is being imposed from the top down rather than evolving through collaboration with actors with the necessary knowledge, experience, and ideas. Governance is focused on control, adding to the complexity of projects for which less complexity and more flexibility are required.

The key theoretical conclusion is that major and timely reform of the governance for large government ICT software projects across the Australian and New Zealand public sectors is unachievable because of inertia and the lack of leadership commitment to and prioritisation of adaptation. A practical solution to avert future large-scale disasters is avoiding large complex projects that require superhuman efforts and capabilities. Instead, large projects should be broken into components that align with capabilities.

This effectively is an acknowledgement that, if there is difficultly in changing the capacity to govern, the nature of what is to be governed must be changed.

Potential for further research

While this book aims to address an identified gap in the literature and answer two research questions, many other issues were identified in the process of this research and have been documented. It is not feasible or appropriate to expand on all of these in this book, however, many present possibilities for further research, several of which are listed below.

First, the possibility of political issues overriding institutional governance guidelines was highlighted. The 'Robodebt'[2] project was an Australian Government policy initiative to be managed via an ICT solution. It became a disaster of monumental proportions that resulted in a class action against the government that was eventually settled at a cost of A$1.2 billion (Whiteford 2020). Robodebt remains a highly political national issue. Following a qualitative interpretative approach as employed in this book, it would be valuable and interesting to gain the perspectives of the public servants and other stakeholders involved in the development and

---

2   This is a 'label commonly applied to the initiative starting in 2016 designed to increase recoveries by government of "overpayments" made to social security recipients, retrospectively dating back to 2010' (Whiteford 2020).

implementation of Robodebt. This would provide an understanding of the impact of politics on effective governance of the project and on accountability for outcomes. This would be timely given the commencement of the Royal Commission into the Robodebt Scheme.

Second, while there remains an 'official' assessment of project outcomes against original forecasts of time, cost, and scope, it appears this is flexible in its application. This was highlighted by the EPDP project, which has been classified as a success despite being over time and budget. The EPDP has been highly effective in delivering quality outcomes and continues to gain strong government support, while other projects highlighted in this book are considered failures for running over time and budget. Who makes these calls and to whom is it important? What is a successful project and what is a failed project in the Australian and New Zealand public sectors? Is it even possible to provide a consistent assessment? There is much literature on this issue, but a concentration on large ICT software projects in the Australian and New Zealand public sectors would provide a new perspective and potentially inform public policy.

Third is the failure to treat ICT solutions as assets. Why is this? What are the barriers? What change is required? Are there international comparisons of where this occurs?

Fourth is the political influence on decision-making and the resulting accountability. The Novopay case highlighted a perception of political interference in the go-live decision, with actors influenced by a 'need' to get the solution in and 'fix' it later—a disastrous decision. This raises issues such as the capability of the minister, who is unlikely to have experience in such projects, so on what basis are decisions made? Do ministers understand the implications? What can public servants do? This was something former APS departmental secretary Paul Barratt described as ministers exhibiting the 'Dunning–Kruger' effect: they have little experience in an area and overestimate their knowledge and ability based on their position.

Fifth is the matter of institutional amnesia—not just a failure to learn, but also forgetting the lessons learnt, and the resulting ineffective governance adaptation. The theoretical implications section identified factors behind this amnesia, such as organisational churn, the fading of risk and memory between projects, and the embeddedness of institutional frameworks. Stark and Head (2019: 1528–29) argue that the idea of solving all the issues of institutional amnesia is 'utopian and partly misplaced'. Instead, they argue that a more reasonable approach is to tackle 'specific deficiencies rather than seek general cures'. For large government ICT software projects, what are these specific deficiencies and how can they be addressed?

Finally, although they were not originally intended as such, the chapters on the role of sponsors, project management, and forecasting can be read as standalone stories, providing rich detail on each of these areas. There are options within each for further research, such as into accountability, which is seen to be variable and situational.

Appendix 1: The concepts and their relevance

Concept	Description	Why is this of interest to this book?
Capability and capacity-building	'[A]ctivities that strengthen the knowledge, abilities, skills and behaviour of individuals, and improve institutional structures and processes, so that the organization can efficiently meet its goals in a sustainable way' (Ku & Yuen-Tseng 2011: 469).	Policies such as capability frameworks address strategies to build both capability and capacity for large ICT software projects. Has this been addressed institutionally?
Financial management	'[T]he allocation of financial resources to support specific government activities and public purposes/ tasks; as well as an expression both of current policy preferences of government and of past policy commitments. It is thus not simply an accounting process. Its importance lies in three major aspects: resource allocation; the satisfaction of social and political demands; and the securing of political and social support' (Cheung 2011: 270).	Strict financial guidelines for the funding of large ICT projects exist in all jurisdictions. These directly influence how projects are forecast, funded, and approved. Do these guidelines assist in achieving good outcomes? How suitable are they for large ICT software projects?
Organisational learning	'Organizational learning is the process by which an organization gains new knowledge about and responds to its environment, goals, and processes … Learning happens when an organization discovers that its actions have led to an intended outcome or when the organization identifies and corrects a mismatch between intended and actual outcomes. In both conceptions, individuals perform the actions that lead to learning, but it is the organization that develops roles, a culture and structure, routines, and values to direct its members' decision making' (Smith 2007).	Large ICT projects have been happening for many decades and from each there are lessons for future projects. The institutional frameworks detail how these lessons are to be captured and applied. How are they captured and applied institutionally to develop learning and aid adaptation for future projects?

Concept	Description	Why is this of interest to this book?
Stakeholder management	'A stakeholder can be defined as any individual, social group, or actor who possesses a stake (e.g., interest, legal obligation, moral right) in the decisions or outcomes of an organization (typically firms, corporations, or governments). Thus, stakeholders are characterized by either being affected by or affecting the achievement of an organization's objectives. The stakeholder approach is based on the assumption that governance is more advantageous when it is guided by a principle of inclusiveness' (Manuel-Navarrete & Modvar 2007: 918).	Stakeholder management is key to any large ICT project, which typically has many internal and external stakeholders. The institutional frameworks highlight this. How capably has stakeholder management been undertaken in these large ICT software projects?
Contract management	'[This is] taken to mean government "contracting out" or "outsourcing" with a for-profit firm, a non-profit organization, or another government to produce or deliver a service. Although the job of delivering services is contracted out, the services remain public, funded mainly by taxation, and decisions regarding their quantity, quality, distribution, and other characteristics are left to public decision makers ... [C]entral to this definition is the notion of public control, funding, and decision-making. The government is the principal, and the contractor is simply the agent' (Cohen & Eimicke 2011: 237–38).	The engagement of one or more vendors is typical in a large ICT project. The institutional frameworks detail how contracts are to be managed. An important part of the literature is the idea that while services may be contracted out, responsibility remains with the public sector organisation or responsible officer. How capably has contract management been undertaken?
Accountability	Someone has been put in a position of responsibility in the interests of someone else and is required to give an account of how they discharged their duties, and there is either reward or punishment in relation to the outcome (Castiglione 2007: 44).	The responsibilities and accountabilities for delivery of large ICT projects are included in institutional frameworks. How aware of these factors are the stakeholders in these projects?
Methodologies	Project management methodologies 'were developed to support project managers in achieving more predictable project success rates' by providing a standardised or customised series of methods/processes to follow throughout the project (Joslin & Müller 2015: 1377–78).	All jurisdictional institutional frameworks refer to the use of methodologies in large projects (e.g. PRINCE2). They aim to be a key factor in enabling project success, but do they achieve this?

Concept	Description	Why is this of interest to this book?
Leadership	'While the traditional aims of leadership can be conceived of as control, production, and organizational goal attainment, we argue that the primary aims of leadership in governance are: (1) fostering collaboration, (2) building resilience and adaptive capacity, (3) resolving ethical concerns through dialogue, and (4) engaging citizens. These imperatives are not mutually exclusive, but rather mutually reinforcing interrelated ideas that outline the shape of leadership in contemporary governance' (Denhardt & Denhardt 2011: 422).	For large ICT software projects, leadership can be applied to two aspects: first, executive leadership to address factors enabling better outcomes, such as prioritising capability development; and second, leadership of the project itself. How has this leadership been applied?
Entrepreneurship	'The entrepreneurial function implies the discovery, assessment, and exploitation of opportunities, in other words, new products, services or production processes; new strategies and organizational forms ... Entrepreneurial opportunities exist because different agents have differing ideas on the relative value of resources or when resources are turned from inputs into outputs' (Cuervo et al. 2007: 2).	Is there evidence in the public sector of entrepreneurship to look at opportunities to do things differently to improve the likelihood of success in large ICT projects? Has this been possible through factors such as 'agency' or does the structure constrain this?
Agency	Outcomes 'cannot be explained solely by reference to structure ... [T]hey are the result of actions of strategically calculating subjects ... so agents matter. It is agents who interpret and negotiate constraints or opportunities. However, these agents are located within a structured context ... [T]hose contexts clearly affect the actor's resources. Most significantly, the agents do not control either aspect of that structured context. At the same time, they do interpret that context and it is mediated through that interpretation that the structural context affects the strategic calculations of actors' (Marsh & Smith 2000: 5–7).	Do actors in these large ICT projects follow structure (e.g. the institutional framework, hierarchy) or do they make different choices (defined by factors such as role and position, and hence power)?

Appendix 2: Part one interviewee data

No.	Identifier/name	Jurisdiction	Role	Date interviewed
1	Person A	APS	CIO	25 May 2018
2	Person B	NSW	Executive	21 May 2018
3	Person C	NSW	Senior IQA/consultant	24 May 2018
4	Person D (Professor Ofer Zwikael)[1]	Private sector	Academic	18 May 2018
5	Person E	NSW	Executive	25 May 2018
6	Person F	APS	Senior project officer	30 May 2018
7	Person G	APS	CIO	30 May 2018
8	Person H	NSW	Assurance	24 May 2018
9	Person I (Adrian Piccoli)[2]	NSW	Politician	31 May 2018
10	Person J	NZ	Senior project officer	12 June 2018
11	Person K	NZ	Executive	12 June 2018
12	Person L	NZ	CIO	13 June 2018
13	Person M	NZ	Senior project officer	14 June 2018
14	Person N	NZ	Senior project officer	19 June 2018
15	Person O	NZ	CIO	19 June 2018
16	Person P	NZ	Senior project officer	20 June 2018
17	Person Q	NZ	Assurance	21 June 2018
18	Person R	NZ	Assurance	22 June 2018
19	Person S	NZ	CIO	28 June 2018

---

1   Director, Research School of Management, The Australian National University, and Associate Editor, *International Journal of Project Management*.
2   NSW Education Minister, 2011–17.

No.	Identifier/name	Jurisdiction	Role	Date interviewed
20	Person T	NZ	Assurance	28 June 2018
21	Person U	NZ	Executive	29 June 2018
22	Person V	Private sector	Academic	4 July 2018
23	Person W	NZ	CIO	5 July 2018
24	Person X	NZ	Executive	6 July 2018
25	Person Y	NZ	Senior project officer	6 July 2018
26	Person Z	NSW	Assurance	25 July 2018
27	Person AA	NSW	Assurance	25 July 2018
28	Person AB	APS	Senior project officer	31 July 2018
29	Person AC (David Boyle)[3]	Private sector	CIO	8 August 2018
30	Person AD	APS	Assurance	13 August 2018
31	Person AE	APS	Assurance	15 August 2018
32	Person AF	Vic.	Assurance	20 August 2018
33	Person AG	Vic.	Assurance	20 August 2018
34	Person AH	Vic.	CIO	20 August 2018
35	Person AI	Vic.	CIO	20 August 2018
36	Person AJ	Private sector	Academic	21 August 2018
37	Person AK	Vic.	CIO	22 August 2018
38	Person AL	Private sector	Senior project officer	23 August 2018
39	Person AM	NT	Executive	10 September 2018
40	Person AN	NT	Executive	10 & 11 September 2018
41	Person AO	NT	Assurance	11 September 2018
42	Person AP	NT	Assurance	11 September 2018
43	Person AQ	NT	Assurance	11 September 2018
44	Person AR	NT	Executive	12 September 2018
45	Person AS	NT	Assurance	12 September 2018
46	Person AT	NT	Assurance	12 September 2018
47	Person AU	NT	Senior project officer	12 September 2018
48	Person AV	NT	Senior project officer	12 September 2018
49	Person AW	NT	Executive (private sector)	10 September 2018

---

3   CIO, National Australia Bank, 2014–17; CIO, Financial Services, Commonwealth Bank of Australia, 2009–11; CIO, Group Services, Commonwealth Bank of Australia, 2006–08.

No.	Identifier/name	Jurisdiction	Role	Date interviewed
50	Person AX	NT	Assurance	12 September 2018
51	Person AY (Michael Carmody)[4]	APS	Executive	19 December 2018
52	Person BL	Tas.	Executive	21 August 2019
53	Person BM	Tas.	Senior project officer	21 August 2019
54	Person BN	Vic.	Assurance	6 October 2020
55	Person BO	Tas.	Assurance	26 March 2019
56	Person BP (Paul Barratt)[5]	APS	Executive	23 June 2020
57	Person BQ	Anonymised[6]	Executive	2018

---

4   Australian Commissioner of Taxation, 1993–2005; CEO, Australian Customs Service, 2006–09; CEO, Australian Customs and Border Force Service, 2009–12.
5   Secretary, Australian Department of Defence, 1998–99; Secretary, Australian Department of Primary Industries and Energy, 1996–98; Executive Director, Business Council of Australia, 1992–96.
6   This interviewee provided sensitive information and has been anonymised to reduce the likelihood of identification.

Appendix 3: Novopay interviewee data

Identifier/name	Jurisdiction	Role	Date interviewed
Person AZ	MoE	Senior project manager	11 July 2019
Person BA	Datacom	Executive	12 July 2019
Person BB	MoE	Senior executive	12 July 2019
Person BC	MoE	Senior project manager	15 July 2019
Person BD	MoE	Senior executive	16 July 2019
Person BE	NZ	Senior ICT executive	18 July 2019
Person BF	MoE	Senior executive	25 July 2019
Person BG	Talent2	Executive	29 July 2019
Person BH	NZ teachers' union	Senior representative	15 August 2019
Person BI	Talent2	Senior project manager	16 August 2019

Appendix 4: EPDP interviewee data

No.	Identifier/name	Jurisdiction	Role	Date interviewed
1	Arlene White	EPL	EPL chief executive & EPDP sponsor	16 August 2019 & 6 October 2020
2	Jeffrey Brandt	Deloitte	EPDP program director	16 August 2019 & 15 August 2020
3	Person BR	EPL	Senior project officer	6 October 2019
4	Person BS	EPL	Senior audit/assurance	6 October 2020
5	Person BT	EPL	Senior audit/assurance	9 October 2020
6	Person BU	EPL	Senior project officer	22 August 2020
7	Person BV	EPL	Senior project officer	14 August 2020
8	Person BW	EPL	Senior project officer	9 October 2020

Appendix 5: Comparison of Novopay findings with part one findings

Novopay findings, 2008–12	Part one findings, 2018–20	Match?
Sponsor capability	**Sponsor capability (Chapter 3)**	
Sponsor not capable.	Capability does not exist.	✓
No assessment of sponsor capability before appointment (even though this was a requirement in the institutional framework).	No capability assessment is undertaken.	✓
Reliance on written documentation for sponsor roles and responsibilities.	Simply reading documents does not provide the level of understanding required.	✓
Sponsor held personally accountable for project failure; punishment was the action.	Sponsors are not held to account.	✗
Selected and appointed due to senior organisational role and line responsibility for the project.	Selected on domain rather than capability.	✓
Sponsor had to undertake role on top of existing substantive role, which was already excessively busy.	Default model is to undertake the role on top of the substantive position.	✓
Sponsor was provided with no training.	While some initiatives to provide training exist, in the main, it does not exist or is unsuitable.	✓
A support model existed but failed to provide quality advice to the sponsor.	Models exist, but their effectiveness is variable.	✓
Project management capability	**Project management capability (Chapter 4)**	
MoE not capable.	Capability does not exist.	✓

Novopay findings, 2008–12	Part one findings, 2018–20	Match?
No assessment of capability before appointment (even though this was a requirement in the institutional framework).	No capability assessment is undertaken.	✓
Not an organisational priority.	Capability is not an organisational priority.	✓
MoE had to act independently to address capability issues.	Largely left to individual agencies to address.	✓
PRINCE2 was used to 'tick a box' but did not aid capability.	Methodologies alone do not uplift capability and are often used as 'lip-service'.	✓
Project team a mixture of internal and external/contract staff.	A blend of internal and external resources is commonly used.	✓
A skilled project/program director was not engaged; the role was undertaken by an internal resource without the capability.	While the project/program director should be sourced externally, agencies are still allocating the role to internal resources without the capability.	✓
Budget constraints restricted the ability to get the A-team, resulting in focus on capacity instead of capability.	Cost concerns can limit engagement of the best resources.	✓
Vendor management capability was particularly poor.	Vendor management capability is typically poor and must be made a prerequisite.	✓
Forecasting capability	**Forecasting capability (Chapter 5)**	
Capability did not exist internally; it was sourced externally but poorly undertaken.	Capability does not exist.	✓
Upfront forecast for whole project required.	Upfront forecast for entire project is common.	✓
Upfront forecast seen as a major contributor to Novopay problems.	Upfront forecast a major contributor to past and ongoing poor outcomes.	✓
Novopay planners did not know what was involved yet prepared a forecast anyway.	It is an incorrect assumption that you can plan now for future complex unknowns.	✓
No standard forecasting method; used workshops run by a consultant.	Jurisdictional standards/methods for forecasting do not exist.	✓
The forecasting (full upfront) described as 'nonsense' and 'impossible'.	Forecasting accurately for long-term plans is impossible.	✓
The assurance process was poor and ineffective.	Assurance capability is seen as poor.	✓
Central agency capability to provide assurance and advice was poor.	Central agency role varies as does capability.	✓

Novopay findings, 2008–12	Part one findings, 2018–20	Match?
Customisation was not factored into planning/forecasting, hence impacts excluded.	Customisation costs regularly excluded.	✓
Planned organisational change did not happen; the solution was instead customised.	Organisations do not change processes to fit the solution as it is easier to change the solution than to change the organisation.	✓
Contract management was poor and led to major project issues.	Contract management capability is a problem.	✓
MoE took a commercial and aggressive stance with the vendor, rather than a collaborative partnership from which both would win.	Culture of mistrust of the vendor leads to poor outcomes; focus is not on mutual benefit, but it should be.	✓
Talent2 contract was long term and there were many unknowns when it was negotiated.	Long-term contracts have the same problems as long-term plans: you cannot plan for the unknown.	✓
Lessons learned were included in planning; however, the mistakes were largely repeated.	Same issues reappear in future projects. A failure to learn?	✓
There was no evidence of seeking an 'outside view' as part of planning/forecasting.	No standard method for or requirement to include an outside view.	✓
There was a failure to include, or an underestimation of, organisational factors in forecasting.	Including organisational factors in forecasts is uncommon.	✓
Financial management capability for large ICT project was missing.	Project financial management capability is missing.	✓
Project promoted as an urgently needed replacement rather than as part of a long-term asset management or portfolio of works program.	Public sector does not do ICT asset management as a formal process.	✓
Novopay was planned only as a large ICT project; no alternatives seem to have been considered.	There is no need to do large projects as there are always alternatives in planning.	✗

Appendix 6: Comparison of Novopay findings with EPDP findings

Novopay findings, 2008–12	EPDP findings, 2016–20	Match?
Sponsor	**Sponsor**	
Sponsor not capable.	Sponsor was capable with extensive operational experience in large ICT software projects; however, this was due to chance rather than a result of an institutional framework initiative.	✗
No assessment of sponsor capability before appointment.	No assessment of sponsor capability before appointment.	✓
Reliant on written documentation of sponsor roles and responsibilities.	Reliant on written documentation of sponsor roles and responsibilities; however, due to personal experience, the sponsor was aware of the roles and responsibilities.	✓
Sponsor was held personally accountable for the project failure; punishment was the action.	The sponsor was aware and accepting of their accountability for program outcomes.	✓
Selected and appointed due to senior organisational role and line responsibility for the project.	The chief executive undertook the sponsor role due to their accountability for outcomes and experience in the role.	✗
Sponsor had to undertake role on top of existing substantive role, which was already excessively busy.	Sponsor undertook role on top of existing substantive role: however, this was manageable due to implementation of support structure.	✓
Sponsor was not provided with training.	Sponsor was not provided with or offered training; however, it was not sought because of the sponsor's own experience.	✓

Novopay findings, 2008–12	EPDP findings, 2016–20	Match?
A support model existed but failed to provide quality advice to the sponsor.	The sponsor implemented a successful, largely internal and independently organised support structure. Central agency assurance and support were variable in quality and effectiveness.	✗
Project management capability	**Project management capability**	
MoE not capable.	The EPL identified that both capability and capacity to undertake the EPDP were missing, and embarked on a strategy to successfully address this.	✗
No assessment of capability before appointment (even though this was a requirement in the institutional framework).	See above; however, this was an EPL initiative not part of a formal institutional assessment.	✗
Not an organisational priority.	The EPL chief executive made it an organisational priority to address capability and capacity issues.	✗
MoE had to act independently to address capability issues.	EPL had to act independently to address capability issues.	✓
PRINCE2 was used to 'tick a box' but did not aid capability.	The training in and use of SAFe methodology was an important tool in the successful implementation of the agile delivery of the project.	✗
Project team a mixture of internal and external/contract staff.	Project team a mixture of internal and external/contract staff.	✓
A skilled project/program director was not engaged; the role was undertaken by an internal resource without the capability.	Sourcing a highly skilled and experienced external resource to fill the program director role was prioritised.	✗
Budget constraints prevented hiring of the A-team, resulting in focus on capacity instead of capability.	Sourcing the best resource was prioritised and not influenced by cost limits.	✗
Vendor management capability was particularly poor.	Vendor management was simplified and aligned to each product, worked well, and was focused on a 'win-win' arrangement.	✗
Forecasting	**Forecasting**	
Capability did not exist internally so was sourced externally but poorly undertaken.	The original forecast in the DBC was inaccurate.	✓
Upfront forecast for full project required.	Upfront forecast for full project required, which negatively impacted project throughout.	✓

Novopay findings, 2008-12	EPDP findings, 2016-20	Match?
Upfront forecast a major contributor to Novopay problems.	Assessing EPDP outcomes against the DBC forecast, which bore no relationship to the agile approach implemented, has caused ongoing issues.	✓
Novopay planners did not know what was involved yet prepared a forecast anyway.	The EPDP DBC planners made incorrect assumptions about future tasks; however, if considered as forecasting progressively in the agile delivery method, it was relevant and improved at every cycle.	✗
No standard forecasting method; used 'workshops' run by a consultant.	The DBC methods are unclear; however, for agile delivery, the iterative review, and reforecasting cycles were effective and part of the methodology.	✗
The forecasting (full upfront) described as 'nonsense' and 'impossible'.	The requirement to forecast in full upfront and base approval on this was perceived to be a waste of time.	✓
The assurance process was poor and ineffective.	The assurance process was effective, but this was largely due to independent and internally applied processes.	✗
Central agency capability to provide assurance and advice was poor.	Central agency capability to provide assurance and advice was variable.	✓
Customisation not factored into planning or forecast, so impacts excluded.	The impacts of the Novopay customisations were well known and strategies were implemented to remove some of these complexities for future support.	✗
Planned organisational change did not happen; the solution was instead customised.	Organisational change, via schools' and EPL service centre's adoption of the new products, was central to EPDP planning. It has been successful.	✗
Contract management was poor and led to major project issues.	Contract management was effective, aided by the simplification of the contractual arrangement.	✗
MoE took a commercial and aggressive stance with the vendor, rather than a collaborative partnership from which both would win.	The vendors were seen as an integral part of the EPDP team and treated as such.	✗

Novopay findings, 2008–12	EPDP findings, 2016–20	Match?
Talent2 contract was long term and there were many unknowns when it was negotiated.	Contracts were largely based on the time and materials for the provision of services for each deliverable, which was no longer than 12 weeks in duration.	✗
Lessons learned were included in planning, however, the mistakes were largely repeated.	Past lessons, particularly from Novopay, were included in planning documents and in program culture. Key mistakes were not repeated. The iterative real-time learning aspect of agile was key.	✗
There was no evidence of seeking an 'outside view' as part of planning or forecasting.	The external experience in agile brought into the program, combined with the progressive planning and forecasting of the deliverables, provided an outside perspective and internal learning from each stage.	✗
There was a failure to consider, or an underestimation of, organisational factors as part of forecasting.	While organisational aspects were considered in planning, agile assisted by progressively identifying and addressing these for each deliverable.	✗
Financial management capability for a large ICT project was missing.	The use of a specialised financial manager meant the project finances were managed well. The issue was not within the project but with trying to explain agile financial management to central agencies and gaining acceptance of this.	✗
Project promoted as an urgently needed replacement rather than as part of a long-term asset management or portfolio of works program.	EPL intend to treat the EPDP suite of products as assets and manage appropriately.	✗
Novopay was planned only as a large ICT project; no alternatives seem to have been considered.	The EPDP was undertaken as a series of 21 small progressive projects.	✗

Bibliography

Abdelnour, S., Hasselbladh, H., & Kallinikos, J. 2017, 'Agency and Institutions in Organization Studies', *Organization Studies*, vol. 38, no. 12, pp. 1775–1792, doi.org/10.1177/0170840617708007.

Abend, G. 2008, 'The Meaning of "Theory"', *Sociological Theory*, vol. 26, no. 2, pp. 173–199.

Abrahamsson, P., Conboy, K., & Xiaofeng, W. 2009, '"Lots Done, More to Do": The Current State of Agile Systems Development Research', *European Journal of Information Systems*, vol. 18, no. 4, pp. 281–284, doi.org/10.1057/ejis.2009.27.

Al-Ahmad, W., Al-Fagih, K., Khanfar, K., Alsamara, K., Abuleil, S., & Abu-Salem, H. 2009, 'A Taxonomy of an IT Project Failure: Root Causes', *International Management Review*, vol. 5. no. 1, pp. 93–106.

Aleinikova, O., Kravchenko, S., Hurochkina, V., Zvonar, V., Brechko, O., & Buryk, Z. 2020, 'Project Management Technologies in Public Administration', *Journal of Management Information and Decision Sciences*, vol. 23, no. 5, pp. 564–576.

Alie, S.S. 2015, 'Project Governance: #1 Critical Success Factor', Paper presented at PMI Global Congress 2015–North America, Orlando, Fl, 10 October, Project Management Institute, Newtown Square, PA, available from: www.pmi.org/learning/library/project-governance-critical-success-9945.

Altuwaijri, M.M., & Khorsheed, M.S. 2012, 'InnoDiff: A Project-Based Model for Successful IT Innovation Diffusion', *International Journal of Project Management*, vol. 30, no. 1, pp. 37–47, doi.org/10.1016/j.ijproman.2011.04.007.

Andersen, B., Samset, K., & Welde, M. 2016, 'Low Estimates—High Stakes: Underestimation of Costs at the Front-End of Projects', *International Journal of Managing Projects in Business*, vol. 9, no. 1, pp. 171–173, doi.org/10.1108/ijmpb-01-2015-0008.

Andrews, D. 2018, 'Building Skills, Leadership and Infrastructure Victoria Needs', Media release, 4 September, Premier of Victoria, Melbourne, available from: www.premier.vic.gov.au/building-skills-leadership-and-infrastructure-victoria-needs/.

APNZ 2013a, 'Novopay Signed Off by Minsters Despite Flaws', *NZ Herald*, [Auckland], 1 February, available from: www.nzherald.co.nz/nz/news/article. cfm?c_id=1&objectid=10862867.

APNZ 2013b, 'PPTA Files Class Action Over Novopay Debacle', *NZ Herald*, [Auckland], 13 June, available from: www.nzherald.co.nz/nz/news/article.cfm? c_id=1&objectid=10890389.

Aronson, J. 1995, 'A Pragmatic View of Thematic Analysis', *The Qualitative Report*, vol. 2, no. 1, pp. 1–3.

Association for Project Management (APM) 2018, *Building Sponsors: Future Project Leadership*, APM, Princes Risborough, UK, available from: www.apm.org.uk/ media/15103/a-guide-to-project-sponsorship.pdf.

Association for Project Management (APM) 2019a, *What is Project Management?*, APM, Princes Risborough, UK, available from: www.apm.org.uk/resources/ what-is-project-management/.

Association for Project Management (APM) 2019b, *What is Project Sponsorship?*, APM, Princes Risborough, UK, available from: www.apm.org.uk/body-of-knowledge/context/governance/sponsorship/.

Aucoin, B.M. 2007, *Right-Brain Project Management: A Complementary Approach*, Management Concepts Inc., Vienna.

Audit Office of New South Wales 2014, *Auditor-General's Report—Performance Audit: The Learning Management and Business Reform Program—Department of Education and Communities*, Audit Office of New South Wales, Sydney, available from: www.audit.nsw.gov.au/sites/default/files/pdf-downloads/2014_ Dec_Report_The_Learning_Management_and_Business_Reform_Program.pdf.

Auditor-General of Queensland 2010, *Report to Parliament No. 7 for 2010: Information Systems Governance and Control, including the Queensland Health Implementation of Continuity Project*, Financial and Compliance Audits, Queensland Government, Brisbane, available from: www.parliament.qld.gov.au/ Documents/TableOffice/TabledPapers/2010/5310T2470.pdf.

Australia and New Zealand School of Government (ANZSOG) 2018, 'What We Do', [Online], ANZSOG, Canberra, available from: anzsog.edu.au/about-us/ what-we-do/.

Australian Institute of Project Management (AIPM) 2020, 'Project Manager Job Description: What Skills Do You Need?', *Blog: Technical Skills*, 24 November, AIPM, Sydney, available from: www.aipm.com.au/blog/project-manager-job-description-what-skills-do-yo#:~:text=THE%20ROLE%20OF%20A%20 PROJECT,the%20%22project%20life%20cycle%22.

Australian Institute of Project Management (AIPM) 2021, 'The Definitive Guide to Project Forecasting', *Blog: Technical Skills*, 24 August, AIPM, Sydney, available from: www.aipm.com.au/blog/the-definitive-guide-to-project-forecasting.

Australian Institute of Project Management (AIPM) & KPMG 2018, *The State of Play in Project Management: AIPM and KPMG Australian Project Management Survey 2018*, 9 November, AIPM, Sydney, available from: info.aipm.com.au/hubfs/Reports%20and%20major%20content%20assets/The%20state%20of%20play%20in%20project%20management%20AIPM%20KPMG%20report.pdf.

Australian Institute of Project Management (AIPM) & KPMG 2022, *The State of Project Management in Australia 2022: Leading Projects through Volatility*, AIPM, Sydney, available from: info.aipm.com.au/hubfs/Reports%20and%20major%20content%20assets/The%20State%20of%20PM%202022%20Report%20FINAL.pdf.

Australian Public Service Commission (APSC) 2010, *Whole-of-Government ICT Strategic Workforce Plan 2010–2013*, [Online], APSC, Canberra, available from: ict-industry-reports.com.au/wp-content/uploads/sites/4/2013/09/2010-Australia-Whole-of-Government-ICT-strategic-workforce-plan-2010-2013-AGIMO-April-2010.pdf.

Baccarini, D. 1996, 'The Concept of Project Complexity: A Review', *International Journal of Project Management*, vol. 14, no. 4, pp. 201–204, doi.org/10.1016/0263-7863(95)00093-3.

Baekkeskov, E. 2007, 'Effectiveness', in M. Bevir (ed.), *Encyclopedia of Governance*, SAGE Publications, Thousand Oaks, CA, pp. 258–259.

Bakhshi, J., Ireland, V., & Gorod, A. 2016, 'Clarifying the Project Complexity Construct: Past, Present and Future', *International Journal of Project Management*, vol. 34, no. 7, pp. 1199–1213, doi.org/10.1016/j.ijproman.2016.06.002.

Baldry, D. 1998, 'The Evaluation of Risk Management in Public Sector Capital Projects', *International Journal of Project Management*, vol. 16, no. 1, pp. 35–41, doi.org/10.1016/s0263-7863(97)00015-x.

Bannerman, S. & Haggart, B. 2015, 'Historical Institutionalism in Communication Studies', *Communication Theory*, vol. 25, no. 1, pp. 1–22, doi.org/10.1111/comt.12051.

Barback, J. 2014, 'Let Novopay Be a Lesson', *Education Review*, August, accessed from: archive.educationreview.co.nz/magazine/august-2014/eds-letter [page discontinued].

Barker, C. 2005, *Cultural Studies: Theory and Practice*, SAGE Publications, London.

Batselier, J. & Vanhoucke, M. 2017, 'Improving Project Forecast Accuracy by Integrating Earned Value Management with Exponential Smoothing and Reference Class Forecasting', *International Journal of Project Management*, vol. 35, no. 1, pp. 28–43, doi.org/10.1016/j.ijproman.2016.10.003.

Battilana, J. 2006, 'Agency and Institutions: The Enabling Role of Individuals' Social Position', *Organization*, vol. 13, no. 5, pp. 653–676, doi.org/10.1177/1350508406067008.

Beck, K., Beedle, M., van Bennekum, A., Cockburn, A., Cunningham, W., Fowler, M., Grenning, J., Highsmith, J., Hunt, A., Jeffries, R., Kern, J., Marick, B., Martin, R.C., Mellor, S., Schwaber, K., Sutherland, J., & Thomas, D. 2001, *Manifesto for Agile Software Development*, [Online], available from: agilemanifesto.org/.

Becker, H.S. 1996, 'The Epistemology of Qualitative Research', in R. Jessor, A. Colby, & R.A. Shweder (eds), *Ethnography and Human Development*, University of Chicago Press, Chicago, IL, pp. 53–72.

Beckert, J. 1999, 'Agency, Entrepreneurs, and Institutional Change: The Role of Strategic Choice and Institutionalized Practices in Organizations', *Organization Studies*, vol. 20, no. 5, pp. 777–799, doi.org/10.1177/0170840699205004.

Beckinsale, M. & Ram, M. 2006, 'Delivering ICT to Ethnic Minority Businesses: An Action-Research Approach', *Environment and Planning C: Politics and Space*, vol. 24, no. 6, pp. 847–867, doi.org/10.1068/c0559.

Béland, D. 2009, 'Ideas, Institutions, and Policy Change', *Journal of European Public Policy*, vol. 16, no. 5, pp. 701–718, doi.org/10.1080/13501760902983382.

Bell, S. 2011, 'Do We Really Need a New "Constructivist Institutionalism" to Explain Institutional Change?', *British Journal of Political Science*, vol. 41, no. 4, pp. 883–906, doi.org/10.1017/s0007123411000147.

Belot, H. 2017, 'Federal Government's $10b IT Bill Now Rivalling Newstart Allowance Welfare Spend', *ABC News*, 28 August, available from: www.abc.net.au/news/2017-08-28/federal-governments-$10bn-bill-rivals-newstart-cost/8849562.

Berger, H. & Beynon-Davies, P. 2009, 'The Utility of Rapid Application Development in Large-Scale, Complex Projects', *Information Systems Journal*, vol. 19, no. 6, pp. 549–570, doi.org/10.1111/j.1365-2575.2009.00329.x.

Bertsche, R. 2014, '7 Steps to Stronger Relationships between Project Managers and Sponsors', *PM Network*, vol. 28, no. 9, pp. 50–55.

Besancon, M. 2003, *Good Governance Rankings: The Art of Measurement*, World Peace Foundation, John F. Kennedy School of Government, Harvard University, Cambridge, MA.

Bevir, M. 2007, 'Governance', in M. Bevir (ed.), *Encyclopedia of Governance*, [2 vols], SAGE Publications, London, doi.org/10.4135/9781412952613.

Bevir, M. 2010, 'Institutionalism', in M. Bevir (ed.), *Encyclopedia of Political Science*, SAGE Publications, Thousand Oaks, CA, pp. 700–702.

Bevir, M. (ed.) 2011, *The SAGE Handbook on Governance*, SAGE Publications, London.

Bevir, M. & Rhodes, R.A.W. 2010, *The State as Cultural Practice*, Oxford University Press, New York, NY.

Bhargav, D., Koskela, L.J., Kagioglou, M., & Bertelsen, S. 2008, 'A Critical Look at Integrating People, Process and Information Systems within the Construction Sector', in *Proceedings of IGLC16: 16th Annual Conference of the International Group for Lean Construction, Manchester, 16–18 July*, University of Salford, Salford, UK, pp. 795–807.

Biesenthal, C., Clegg, S., Mahalingam, A., & Sankaran, S. 2018, 'Applying Institutional Theories to Managing Megaprojects', *International Journal of Project Management*, vol. 36, no. 1, pp. 43–54, doi.org/10.1016/j.ijproman.2017.06.006.

Blatter, J. & Haverland, M. 2014, *Designing Case Studies: Explanatory Approaches in Small-N Research*, Palgrave Macmillan, Basingstoke, UK.

Bleijenbergh, I. 2010, 'Method of Difference', in A.J. Mills, G. Durepos, & E. Wiebe (eds), *Encyclopedia of Case Study Research*, SAGE Publications, Thousand Oaks, CA, pp. 558–559.

Blyth, M.M. 1997, '"Any More Bright Ideas?": The Ideational Turn of Comparative Political Economy', *Comparative Politics*, vol. 29, no. 2, pp. 229–250, doi.org/10.2307/422082.

Blyth, M.M. 2001, 'The Transformation of the Swedish Model: Economic Ideas, Distributional Conflict, and Institutional Change', *World Politics*, vol. 54, no. 1, pp. 1–26, doi.org/10.1353/wp.2001.0020.

Bogner, A., Littig, B., & Menz, W. 2018, 'Generating Qualitative Data with Experts and Elites', in U. Flick (ed.), *The SAGE Handbook of Qualitative Data Collection*, SAGE Publications, London, pp. 652–665, doi.org/10.4135/9781526416070.n41.

Bolin, A.U. 2012, 'Salvaging Value from Project Failure', *Performance Improvement*, vol. 51, no. 5, pp. 12–16, doi.org/10.1002/pfi.21262.

Bolles, D. 2002, *Building Project Management Centers of Excellence*, [e-book], Amacom, New York, NY, available from: www.academia.edu/8178636/BUILDING_ PROJECT_MANAGEMENT_CENTERS_OF_EXCELLENCE_This_Page _Intentionally_Left_Blank_BUILDING_PROJECT_MANAGEMENT_ CENTERS_OF_EXCELLENCE.

Bottomore, T. 1993, *Elites and Society*, 2nd edn, Routledge, London.

Bovens, M. & 't Hart, P. 1996, *Understanding Policy Fiascos*, Transaction Publishers, Piscataway, NJ.

Bowen, G. 2009, 'Document Analysis as a Qualitative Research Method', *Qualitative Research Journal*, vol. 9, no. 2, pp. 27–40.

Braun, V. & Clarke, V. 2012, 'Thematic Analysis', in H. Cooper, P.M. Camic, D.L. Long, A.T. Panter, D. Rindskopf, & K.J. Sher (eds), *APA Handbook of Research Methods in Psychology. Volume 2. Research Designs: Quantitative, Qualitative, Neuropsychological, and Biological*, American Psychological Association, Washington, DC, pp. 57–71, doi.org/10.1037/13620-004.

Bredin, K. 2008, 'People Capability of Project-Based Organisations: A Conceptual Framework', *International Journal of Project Management*, vol. 26, no. 5, pp. 566–576, doi.org/10.1016/j.ijproman.2008.05.002.

Breese, R., Couch, O., & Turner, D. 2020, 'The Project Sponsor Role and Benefits Realisation: More Than "Just Doing the Day Job"', *International Journal of Project Management*, vol. 38, no. 1, pp. 17–26, doi.org/10.1016/j.ijproman. 2019.09.009.

Briggs, L. 2007, 'Program Management and Organisational Change: New Directions for Implementation', in J. Wanna (ed.), *Improving Implementation: Organisational Change and Project Management*, ANU Press, Canberra, pp. 123–132, doi.org/ 10.22459/ii.02.2007.11.

Briner, W., Geddes, M., & Hastings, C. 1990, *Project Leadership*, Van Nostrand Reinhold, New York, NY.

British Computer Society (BCS) 2013, *The BCS Glossary of ICT and Computing Terms*, 13th edn, BCS Learning and Development Limited, Swindon, UK, available from: learning.oreilly.com/library/view/bcs-glossary-of/9781780171500/11_ GlossaryofICT_partA1.xhtml.

Bryde, D. 2008, 'Perceptions of the Impact of Project Sponsorship Practices on Project Success', *International Journal of Project Management*, vol. 26, no. 8, pp. 800–809, doi.org/10.1016/j.ijproman.2007.12.001.

Bryman, A. 2015, *Social Research Methods*, 5th edn, Oxford University Press, Oxford, UK.

Budzier, A. & Flyvbjerg, B. 2011, *Double Whammy: How ICT Projects are Fooled by Randomness and Screwed by Political Intent*, Saïd Business School Working Papers, University of Oxford, Oxford, UK, doi.org/10.2139/ssrn.2238057.

Burns, J.M. 1978, *Leadership*, Harper & Row, New York, NY.

Butcher, J.R. 2014, Compacts between Government and Not-for-profit Sector: A Comparative Case Study of National and Sub-national Cross-sector Policy frameworks, Doctoral thesis, The Australian National University, Canberra.

Buttrick, R. 2019, *The Project Workout: The Ultimate Guide to Directing and Managing Business-Led Projects*, 5th edn, Routledge, London, doi.org/10.4324/9781315194424.

Caliste, A.L.E. 2013, 'The PMO, Maturity and Competitive Advantage', Paper presented at PMI Global Congress 2013—North America, New Orleans, LA, 27–29 October, Project Management Institute, Newtown Square, PA, available from: www.pmi.org/learning/library/project-office-management-competitive-advantage-5843.

Campbell, J. 1998, 'Institutional Analysis and the Role of Ideas in Political Economy', *Theory and Society*, vol. 27, no. 3, pp. 377–409.

Campbell, J., McDonald, C., & Sethibe, T. 2009, 'Public and Private Sector IT Governance: Identifying Contextual Differences', *Australasian Journal of Information Systems*, vol. 16, no. 2, pp. 5–17, doi.org/10.3127/ajis.v16i2.538.

Campbell, J.L. & Pedersen, O.K. 2001, 'Introduction', in J.L. Campbell & O.K. Pederson (eds), *The Rise of Neoliberalism and Institutional Analysis*, Princeton University Press, Princeton, NJ, pp. 1–24, doi.org/10.1017/s1537592703670155.

Campbell, S. 2010, 'Comparative Case Study', in A.J. Mills, G. Durepos, & E. Wiebe (eds), *Encyclopedia of Case Study Research*, Sage Publications, Thousand Oaks, CA, pp. 175–176, doi.org/10.4135/9781412957397.

Cao, L., Mohan, K., Ramesh, B., & Sarkar, S. 2013, 'Adapting Funding Processes for Agile IT Projects: An Empirical Investigation', *European Journal of Information Systems*, vol. 22, no. 2(SI), pp. 191–205, doi.org/10.1057/ejis.2012.9.

Cappelli, P. 2000, *Examining the Incidence of Downsizing and Its Effect on Establishment Performance*, NBER Working Paper No. 7742, June, National Bureau of Economic Research, Cambridge, MA, doi.org/10.3386/w7742.

Caravel Group 2013, *A Review of Project Governance Effectiveness in Australia*, Report for Infrastructure Australia, March, Canberra: Australian Government, available from: www.infrastructureaustralia.gov.au/sites/default/files/2019-06/caravel_group_project_governance_effectiveness_march_2013.pdf.

Cardona, M., Kretschmer, T., & Strobel, T. 2013, 'ICT and Productivity: Conclusions from the Empirical Literature', *Information Economics and Policy*, vol. 25, no. 3, pp. 109–125, doi.org/10.1016/j.infoecopol.2012.12.002.

Cassell, C., Cunliffe, A.L., & Grandy, G. 2018, *The SAGE Handbook of Qualitative Business and Management Research Methods: History and Traditions*, SAGE Publications, London, doi.org/10.4135/9781526430212.

Castiglione, D. 2007, 'Accountability', in M. Bevir (ed.), *Encyclopedia of Governance*, SAGE Publications, London, pp. 44–47.

Castleberry, A. & Nolen, A. 2018, 'Thematic Analysis of Qualitative Research Data: Is It as Easy as It Sounds?', *Currents in Pharmacy Teaching and Learning*, vol. 10, no. 6, pp. 807–815, doi.org/10.1016/j.cptl.2018.03.019.

Change Dynamics 2011, *Assessment and Improvement of Culture in the Novopay Project*, Report for the Ministry of Education, June, Change Dynamics Limited, Wellington.

Chapman, A. 2017, 'What is the Role of a Project Sponsor?', *CEO Magazine*, 3 February, available from: www.theceomagazine.com/business/management-leadership/role-project-sponsor/.

Chenail, R. 2008, 'Institutional Research', in L.M. Given (ed.), *The SAGE Encyclopedia of Qualitative Research Methods*, SAGE Publications, Thousand Oaks, CA, pp. 437–439.

Chesterman, R.N. 2013, *Queensland Health Payroll Systems Commission of Inquiry: Report*, Queensland Department of Justice and Attorney-General, Brisbane, available from: www.healthpayrollinquiry.qld.gov.au/?a=207203.

Cheung, A.B.L. 2011, 'Budgeting and Finance', in M. Bevir (ed.), *The SAGE Handbook of Governance*, SAGE Publications, London, pp. 270–285, doi.org/10.4135/9781446200964.n17.

Cho, W. 2020, *Novopay Case: Case-Based Learning*, School of Government, Victoria University of Wellington, Wellington.

Chua, A.Y.K. 2009, 'Exhuming IT Projects from Their Graves: An Analysis of Eight Failure Cases and Their Risk Factors', *The Journal of Computer Information Systems*, vol. 49, no. 3, pp. 31–39.

CIO 2022, 'CIO50: New Zealand's Most Innovative CIOs', *CIO*, available from: www2.cio.co.nz/cio50/.

Cohen, S. & Eimicke, W. 2011, 'Contracting Out', in M. Bevir (ed.), *The SAGE Handbook of Governance*, SAGE Publications, London, pp. 237–251, doi.org/ 10.4135/9781446200964.n15.

Connolly, B. 2017, 'NT Govt Readies for $259m Health IT Rollout', *CIO*, 23 June, available from: www.cio.com/article/205810/nt-govt-readies-for-259m-health-it-rollout.html.

Cooke-Davies, T., Crawford, L., Patton, J.R., Stevens, C., & Williams, T.M. (eds) 2011, *Aspects of Complexity: Managing Projects in a Complex World*, Project Management Institute, Newtown Square, PA.

Cowan, P. 2014, 'Aussie Supplier Quits $51m NZ Govt Payroll Disaster', *iTnews*, 30 July, available from: www.itnews.com.au/news/aussie-supplier-quits-51m-nz-govt-payroll-disaster-390455.

Cowan, P. 2016, 'NSW's Plan to Banish IT Failures for Good', *iTnews*, 14 September, available from: www.itnews.com.au/news/nsws-plan-to-banish-it-failures-for-good-437236.

Cranefield, J. & Oliver, G. 2014, 'Yes, Minister: Satire in Information Systems Research', *Proceedings of the European Conference on Information Systems (ECIS) 2014, Tel Aviv, Israel, June 9–11, 2014*, available from: aisel.aisnet.org/ecis2014/ proceedings/track03/3.

Crawford, L.H. & Brett, C. 2001, 'Exploring the Role of the Project Sponsor', Paper, Program Management Program, University of Sydney, Sydney, available from: www.researchgate.net/publication/253751429_Exploring_the_Role_of_ the_Project_Sponsor.

Crawford, L.H. & Helm, J. 2009, 'Government and Governance: The Value of Project Management in the Public Sector', *Project Management Journal*, vol. 40, no. 1, pp. 73–87, doi.org/10.1002/pmj.20107.

Creswell, J.W. 2009, *Research Design: Qualitative, Quantitative, and Mixed Methods Approaches*, 3rd edn, SAGE Publications, New Delhi.

Crow, D. & Jones, M. 2018, 'Narratives as Tools for Influencing Policy Change', *Policy and Politics*, vol. 46, no. 2, pp. 217–234, doi.org/10.1332/03055731 8x15230061022899.

Cuervo, À., Ribeiro, D., & Roig, S. 2007, *Entrepreneurship: Concepts, Theory and Perspective*, Springer, Berlin.

Currie, W.L. & Guah, M.W. 2006, 'IT-Enabled Healthcare Delivery: The U.K. National Health Service', *Information Systems Management*, vol. 23, no. 2, pp. 7–22, doi.org/10.1201/1078.10580530/45925.23.2.20060301/92670.3.

Dacin, M.T., Ventresca, M.J., & Beal, B.D. 1999, 'The Embeddedness of Organizations: Dialogue and Directions', *Journal of Management*, vol. 25, no. 3, pp. 317–356, doi.org/10.1177/014920639902500304.

Dalcher, D. 2016, 'The Unspoken Role of Sponsors, Champions, Shapers and Influencers', *PM World Journal*, vol. V, no. IX, pp. 1–7.

Danish Board of Technology 2001, *Experiences from National IT Projects: How Can It Be Done in a Better Way?*, Danish Board of Technology, Copenhagen.

Dekker, S. & Hansén, D. 2004, 'Learning Under Pressure: The Effects of Politicization on Organizational Learning in Public Bureaucracies', *Journal of Public Administration Research and Theory*, vol. 14, no. 2, pp. 211–230, doi.org/10.1093/jopart/muh014.

Deloitte 2013, *Ministry of Education: Novopay Technical Review. Final Report*, 19 March, New Zealand Government, Wellington, available from: www.bee hive.govt.nz/sites/default/files/Novopay_Technical_Review.pdf.

Deloitte 2016, *Major Projects Leadership Academy: Transforming the Delivery of Major Government Projects*, Case Studies, Deloitte UK, London, available from: www2.deloitte.com/uk/en/pages/consulting/articles/major-projects-leadership-academy.html.

Deloitte 2017, *New Zealand Customs Service: Joint Border Management System— Lessons Learned*, November, New Zealand Customs Service, Wellington, available from: www.customs.govt.nz/globalassets/documents/tsw/jbms-lessons-learned.pdf.

Denhardt, J.V. & Denhardt, R.B. 2009, 'Building Organisational Resilience and Adaptive Management', in J. Hall & J. Reich (eds), *Handbook of Adult Resilience: Concepts, Methods and Applications*, Guilford Publications, New York, NY, pp. 333–349.

Denhardt, J.V. & Denhardt, R.B. 2011, 'Leadership', in M. Bevir (ed.), *The SAGE Handbook of Governance*, SAGE Publications, London, pp. 419–435.

Denzin, N.K. 1970, *The Research Act: A Theoretical Introduction to Sociological Methods*, Aldine, New York, NY.

Department of Corporate and Information Services (DCIS) 2017, *Annual Report 2016–17*, Northern Territory Government, Darwin, available from: dcis.nt.gov. au/__data/assets/pdf_file/0008/501488/2016-17-dcis-annual-report-full.pdf.

Department of Corporate and Information Services (DCIS) 2018, *Annual Report 2017–18*, Northern Territory Government, Darwin, available from: dcis.nt.gov. au/__data/assets/pdf_file/0007/590470/2017-18-annual-report-full.pdf.

Department of Finance (DoF) 2014, *Audit of Australian Government ICT Public Report*, December, Australian Government, Canberra, available from: s11217. pcdn.co/wp-content/uploads/2016/01/FOI-15-124-Document.pdf.

Department of Finance (DoF) 2015, *ICT Business Case Guide*, October, Australian Government, Canberra, available from: www.finance.gov.au/sites/default/files/ 2019-11/ICT_Business_Case_Guide.pdf.

Department of Finance 2019, *Gateway: Helping Your Projects Succeed … On Time, On Budget and with the Intended Benefits Realised*, Government Procurement, Government of Western Australia, Perth, available from: www.wa.gov.au/system/ files/2019-08/Gateway%20Overview%20-%20Helping%20Your%20Projects %20Succeed.pdf.

Department of Finance and Deregulation 2009, *Gateway Review: Lessons Learned Report*, 2nd edn, August, Australian Government, Canberra, available from: www. finance.gov.au/sites/default/files/2019-11/LessonsLearnedSecondEdition.pdf.

Department of Finance and Deregulation 2012, *Australian Public Service Information and Communications Technology Strategy 2012–2015*, Australian Government, Canberra, available from: itlaw.fandom.com/wiki/The_Australian_Public_ Service_Information_and_Communications_Technology_Strategy_2012-2015.

Department of Finance and Services 2012, *NSW Government ICT Strategy 2012*, NSW Government, Sydney, available from: ict-industry-reports.com.au/ wp-content/uploads/sites/4/2013/05/2012-NSW-Government-ICT-Strategy-May-2012.pdf.

Department of Finance and Services 2014, *NSW Government ICT Governance Framework for Whole of Government Investments*, November, NSW Government, Sydney, available from: docplayer.net/11993590-Nsw-government-ict-governance-framework-for-whole-of-government-investments.html.

Department of Health 2016, *Information and Communications Technology (ICT) Governance Policy*, Effective 1 July, Government of Western Australia, Perth, available from: ww2.health.wa.gov.au/~/media/Files/Corporate/ Policy-Frameworks/Information-and-Communications-Technology/Policy/ Information-and-Communications-Technology-Governance/MP1-Information-and-Communications-Technology-ICT-Governance.pdf.

Department of Infrastructure and Regional Development (DIRD) 2008, *Cost Estimation Guidance: Guidance Note 3B—Deterministic Contingency Estimation*, Australian Government, Canberra.

Department of Premier and Cabinet (DPAC) 2005, *Tasmanian Government Project Management Guidelines: Version 6.0*, March, Tasmanian Government, Hobart, available from: catalogue.nla.gov.au/Record/3578740.

Department of Premier and Cabinet (DPAC) 2008a, *Project Business Case (Medium to Large Projects): Template and Guide. Version 2.1*, April, Tasmanian Government, Hobart, available from: www.dpac.tas.gov.au/__data/assets/word_doc/0028/108964/Project_business_case_template_and_guide_for_medium_to_large_projects.docx.

Department of Premier and Cabinet (DPAC) 2008b, *Project Management Fact Sheet: Developing a Business Case. Version 1.2*, November, Tasmanian Government, Hobart, available from: www.dpac.tas.gov.au/__data/assets/pdf_file/0029/108938/Developing_a_Business_Case_Fact_Sheet.pdf.

Department of Premier and Cabinet (DPAC) 2008c, *Steering Committee Terms of Reference: Template and Guide. Version 1.1*, May, Tasmanian Government, Hobart, available from: www.dpac.tas.gov.au/__data/assets/word_doc/0033/108978/Steering_committee_terms_of_reference_template_and_guide_1.docx.

Department of Premier and Cabinet (DPAC) 2011, *Tasmanian Government Project Management Guidelines. Version 7.0*, July, Tasmanian Government, Hobart, available from: www.dpac.tas.gov.au/__data/assets/pdf_file/0029/108992/Tasmanian_Government_Project_Management_Guidelines_V7_0_July_2011_2.pdf.

Department of Premier and Cabinet (DPAC) 2013, *Tasmanian State Service Senior Executive Leadership Capability Framework*, August, Tasmanian Government, Hobart, available from: www.dpac.tas.gov.au/__data/assets/pdf_file/0022/30289/FINAL_TSS_Senior_Executive_Leadership_Capability_Framework_-_Endorsed_by_HoA_-_Signed_27-08-13.PDF.

Department of Premier and Cabinet 2014, *Victorian Government ICT Strategy 2014 to 2015*, State Government of Victoria, Melbourne, available from: silo.tips/download/victorian-government-ict-strategy-2014-to-2015.

Department of Premier and Cabinet 2016, *Information Technology Strategy: Victorian Government 2016–2020*, State of Victoria, Melbourne, available from: www.vic.gov.au/sites/default/files/2020-08/Information-Technology-Strategy-for-the-Victorian-Government-2016-2020.pdf.

Department of Premier and Cabinet 2017a, *Victorian Government Information Technology Strategy 2016–2020: 2017–2018 Action Plan*, State of Victoria, Melbourne, available from: www.vic.gov.au/information-technology-strategy-2017-18-action-plan.

Department of Premier and Cabinet 2017b, *Victorian Infrastructure Plan: Technical Report*, State of Victoria, Melbourne, available from: www.parliament.vic.gov.au/file_uploads/Technical_Report_2017_ZNxVk3Ng.pdf.

Department of the Prime Minister and Cabinet (PM&C) 2013, *Cabinet Implementation Unit Toolkit 2: Governance*, Australian Government, Canberra, accessed from: www.pmc.gov.au/sites/default/files/files/pmc/implementation-toolkit-2-governance.pdf [page discontinued].

Department of Science, Information Technology, Innovation and the Arts (DSITIA) 2013a, *Queensland Government ICT Strategy 2013–17*, State of Queensland, Brisbane, available from: cabinet.qld.gov.au/documents/2013/Jul/ICT%20Strat/Attachments/ICT%20strategy.PDF.

Department of Science, Information Technology, Innovation and the Arts (DSITIA) 2013b, *Queensland Government ICT Strategy 2013–17: Action Plan*, August, State of Queensland, Brisbane, available from: cabinet.qld.gov.au/documents/2013/Jul/ICT%20Strat/Attachments/ICT%20action%20plan.PDF.

Department of Tourism, Industry and Trade 2018, *Welcome to the Territory Incentives*, 9 November, Northern Territory Government, Darwin, available from: industry.nt.gov.au/news/2018/november/welcome-to-the-territory-incentives#:~:text=The%20'Welcome%20to%20the%20Territory,the%20high%20priority%20occupation%20list.

Department of Treasury and Finance (DTF) 2012, *Project Governance*, Investment Lifecycle and High Value/High Risk Guidelines, State of Victoria, Melbourne, available from: www.dtf.vic.gov.au/sites/default/files/2018-03/Project%20governance%20-%20Technical%20guide.doc.

Department of Treasury and Finance (DTF) 2013, *Economic Evaluation for Business Cases Technical Guidelines*, August, Investment Lifecycle and High Value/High Risk Guidelines, State of Victoria, Melbourne, available from: www.dtf.vic.gov.au/sites/default/files/2018-03/Economic%20Evaluation%20-%20Technical%20Guide.doc.

Department of Treasury and Finance (DTF) 2015, *Treasurer's Directions: Information and Communications Technology*, July, Northern Territory Government, Darwin, available from: treasury.nt.gov.au/dtf/financial-management-group/treasurers-directions.

Department of Treasury and Finance (DTF) 2018, *High Value High Risk Framework*, [Updated 4 January 2021], State of Victoria, Melbourne, available from: www.dtf.vic.gov.au/infrastructure-investment/high-value-high-risk-framework.

Department of Treasury and Finance (DTF) 2022, 'Population', *Northern Territory Economy*, [Last updated 28 June 2022], Northern Territory Government, Darwin, available from: nteconomy.nt.gov.au/population.

de Wit, A. 1988, 'Measurement of Project Success', *International Journal of Project Management*, vol. 6, no. 3, pp. 164–170, doi.org/10.1016/0263-7863(88)90043-9.

Dexter, L.A. 2006, *Elite and Specialized Interviewing. With a New Introduction by Alan Ware and Martín Sánchez-Jankowski*, ECPR Press, Colchester, UK.

Diermeier, D. & Krehbiel, K. 2003, 'Institutionalism as a Methodology', *Journal of Theoretical Politics*, vol. 15, no. 2, pp. 123–144, doi.org/10.1177/0951629803015002645.

Digital.govt.nz 2019, *Assuring Digital Government Outcomes: Assurance Guidance for Agile Delivery. Version 1.1*, October, New Zealand Government, Wellington, available from: www.digital.govt.nz/dmsdocument/115-assurance-guidance-for-agile-delivery-full/html.

Digital.govt.nz 2021, *About Digital Government*, New Zealand Government, Wellington, available from: www.digital.govt.nz/digital-government/about-digital-government/.

Digital.NSW 2021, *ICT Digital Assurance Framework Final*, January, NSW Government, Sydney, available from: www.digital.nsw.gov.au/sites/default/files/2022-12/ict-digital-assurance-framework_1.pdf.

Digital.NSW 2022a, *Agile Approach to Service Delivery*, NSW Government, Sydney, available from: www.digital.nsw.gov.au/delivery/digital-service-toolkit/resources/plan-a-project/agile-approach-to-service-delivery#:~:text=Agile%20is%20a%20form%20of,the%20right%20thing%20for%20users.

Digital.NSW 2022b, *Beyond Digital*, NSW Government, Sydney, available from: www.digital.nsw.gov.au/sites/default/files/DigitalStrategy.pdf.

Digital.NSW 2022c, *Digital Restart Fund*, NSW Government, Sydney, available from: www.digital.nsw.gov.au/transformation/digital-restart-fund.

Digital Territory 2019, 'Commence the Build Phase for the Core Clinical Systems Renewal Program', *Action Plans*, [Updated 18 May 2022], Northern Territory Government, Darwin, available from: digitalterritory.nt.gov.au/digital-government/action-plans/action-items/commence-the-build-phase-for-the-core-clinical-systems-renewal-program.

Digital Transformation Agency (DTA) 2017, *Annual Report 2016–17*, Australian Government, Canberra, available from: www.dta.gov.au/about-us/reporting-and-plans/annual-reports/annual-report-2016-17.

Digital Transformation Agency (DTA) 2018a, *Annual Report 2017–18*, Australian Government, Canberra, available from: parlinfo.aph.gov.au/parlInfo/download/publications/tabledpapers/13ea70a9-0f2e-4370-ba56-197592 e29ffe/upload_pdf/18459%20DTA%20-%20Annual%20Report%202017% C3%A2%C2%80%C2%9318-wcag%20(3).pdf;fileType=application%2F pdf#search=%22publications/tabledpape.

Digital Transformation Agency (DTA) 2018b, *Corporate Plan 2018–22*, Australian Government, Canberra, available from: www.dta.gov.au/about-us/reporting-and-plans/corporate-plans/corporate-plan-2018-22.

Digital Transformation Agency (DTA) 2018c, *Vision 2025: We Will Deliver World-Leading Digital Services for the Benefit of All Australians*, Australian Government, Canberra, available from: www.dta.gov.au/sites/default/files/files/digital-trans formation-strategy/digital-transformation-strategy.pdf.

DiMaggio, P. 1988, 'Interest and Agency in Institutional Theory', in L.G. Zucker (ed.), *Institutional Patterns and Organizations: Culture and Environment*, Ballinger Publishing, Cambridge, MA, pp. 3–21.

Dingsøyr, T., Nerur, S., Balijepally, V., & Moe, N.B. 2013, 'A Decade of Agile Methodologies: Towards Explaining Agile Software Development', *Journal of Systems and Software*, vol. 85, no. 6, pp. 1213–1221, doi.org/10.1016/j.jss. 2012.02.033.

Dinsmore, P.C., & Cabanis-Brewin, J. (eds) 2010, *The AMA Handbook of Project Management*, 3rd edn, American Management Association, New York, NY.

Dobbs, R., Pohl, H., Lin, D.-Y., Mischke, J., Garemo, N., Hexter, J., Matzinger, S., Palter, R., & Nanavatty, R. 2013, *Infrastructure Productivity: How to Save $1 Trillion a Year*, Report, 1 January, McKinsey & Company, New York, NY, available from: www.mckinsey.com/business-functions/operations/our-insights/infrastructure-productivity.

Drucker, P.F. 2008, *Concept of the Corporation*, 7th edn, Transaction Publishers, Piscataway, NJ.

Drummond, P. 2012, *Federation Flyer 36*, 23 November, New Zealand Principals' Federation, Wellington.

Dugan, J.P. 2012, *Leadership Theory: Cultivating Critical Perspectives*, Jossey-Bass, San Francisco, CA.

Duit, A. & Galaz V. 2008, 'Governance and Complexity: Emerging Issues for Governance Theory', *Governance: An International Journal of Policy, Administration, and Institutions*, vol. 21, no. 3, pp. 311–335, doi.org/10.1111/j.1468-0491.2008.00402.x.

Education Central 2013, 'The Novopay Nightmare: When Will It End?', *Education Central*, [New Zealand], 15 December, accessed from: educationcentral.co.nz/the-novopay-nightmare-when-will-it-end-2/ [page discontinued].

Education Payroll Limited (EPL) 2016, *Schools Payroll Detailed Business Case V1.00 FINAL*, 3 October, EPL, Wellington.

Education Payroll Limited (EPL) 2017, *Programme Initiation Document for Education Payroll Development Programme Implementation Phase*, 26 October, EPL, Wellington.

Education Payroll Limited (EPL) 2018, *Statement of Intent 2018–2022*, April, EPL, Wellington, available from: educationpayroll.co.nz/wp-content/uploads/2014/11/EPL-SOI_2018-WEB.pdf.

Education Payroll Limited (EPL) 2020a, *About Us*, [Online], EPL, Wellington, available from: educationpayroll.co.nz/about-us/.

Education Payroll Limited (EPL) 2020b, *Annual Report 2020*, EPL, Wellington, available from: educationpayroll.co.nz/wp-content/uploads/2020/10/EPL_Ann Rep-2020-WEB-2.pdf.

Education Payroll Limited (EPL) 2020c, *EdPay*, EPL, Wellington, available from: educationpayroll.co.nz/edpay/.

Education Payroll Limited (EPL) 2020d, 'Education Payroll Wins Internal Auditing Award', *News*, 14 January, EPL, Wellington, available from: education payroll.co.nz/education-payroll-wins-internal-auditors-new-zealand-award/#:~:text=Education%20Payroll%20has%20won%20the,IIANZ%20Chair%20James%20Rees%2DThomas.

Education Review 2013a, 'Never a Dull Moment in Education', *Education Review*, August, viewed 21 April 2020, archive.educationreview.co.nz/magazine/july-2013/never-a-dull-moment-in-education/ [page discontinued].

Education Review 2013b, 'Meeting the man heading up the Ministry', *Education Review*, August, viewed 21 April 2020, archive.educationreview.co.nz/magazine/july-2013/meeting-the-man-heading-up-the ministry/ [page discontinued].

Education Review 2013c, 'The Novopay Nightmare: When Will It End?', *Education Review*, December, viewed 21 April 2020, archive.educationreview.co.nz/magazine/december-2013/the-novopay-nightmare-when-will-it-end/ [page discontinued].

Education Review 2014, 'The Novopay Nightmare', *Education Review*, viewed 4 May 2019, archive.educationreview.co.nz/magazine/december-2013/a-collection-of-the-best-news-articles-from-the-past-2-decades/the-novopay-nightmare/

Edwards, M., Halligan, J., Horrigan, B., & Nicoll, G. 2012, *Public Sector Governance in Australia*, ANU Press, Canberra, doi.org/10.22459/psga.07.2012.

Eisenhardt, K.M. 1989, 'Building Theories from Case Study Research', *The Academy of Management Review*, vol. 14, no. 4, pp. 532–550, doi.org/10.5465/amr.1989.4308385.

Elder-Vass, D. 2010, *The Causal Power of Social Structures: Emergence, Structure and Agency*, Cambridge University Press, Cambridge, UK.

Eppel, E. 2019, *Digital Government Case Studies: Novopay*, Case Studies, Chair in Digital Government, Victoria University of Wellington, available from: www.wgtn.ac.nz/__data/assets/pdf_file/0011/1866602/digital-government-case-study-novopay-3.pdf.

Eppel, E. & Allen, B. 2020, 'Digital Government: Leadership, Innovation and Integration', in E. Berman & G. Karacaoglu (eds), *Public Policy and Governance Frontiers in New Zealand*, Emerald Publishing Limited, Melbourne, pp. 233–255, doi.org/10.1108/s2053-769720200000032032.

Espín-Sánchez, J. 2014, 'Institutional Inertia and Institutional Change', Blog, 7 July, Global Water Forum, available from: globalwaterforum.org/2014/07/07/institutional-inertia-and-institutional-change/.

Fabricius, G., & Büttgen, M. 2015, 'Project Managers' Overconfidence: How Is Risk Reflected in Anticipated Project Success?', *Business Research*, vol. 8, no. 2, pp. 239–263, doi.org/10.1007/s40685-015-0022-3.

Fagarasan, C., Popo, O., Pisla, A., & Cristea, C. 2021, 'Agile, Waterfall and Iterative Approach in Information Technology Projects', *IOP Conference Series: Material Science and Engineering*, vol. 1169, The Annual Session of Scientific Papers (IMT Oradea 2021), 27–28 May, Oradea, Romania, doi.org/10.1088/1757-899x/1169/1/012025.

Farrell, H. 2018, 'The Shared Challenges of Institutional Theories: Rational Choice, Historical Institutionalism, and Sociological Institutionalism', in J. Glückler, R. Suddaby, & R. Lenz (eds), *Knowledge and Institutions*, Knowledge and Space Vol. 13, Springer, Cham, Switzerland, pp. 23–44, doi.org/10.1007/978-3-319-75328-7_2.

Fawcett, P. & Marsh, D. 2012, 'Policy Transfer and Policy Success: The Case of the Gateway Review Process (2001–10)', *Government and Opposition*, vol. 47, no. 2, pp. 162–185, doi.org/10.1111/j.1477-7053.2011.01358.x.

Ferris, J.M. & Tang, S.Y. 1993, 'The New Institutionalism and Public Administration: An Overview', *Journal of Public Administration Research and Theory: J-PART*, vol. 3. no. 1, pp. 4–10.

Field, T., Muller, E., Lau, E., Gadriot-Renard, H., & Vergez, C. 2003, 'The Case for e-Government: Excerpts from the OECD Report "The e-Government Imperative"', *OECD Journal on Budgeting*, vol. 3, no. 1, pp. 61–96, doi.org/10.1787/budget-v3-art5-en.

Flamm, M.C. n.d., 'George Santayana (1863–1952)', *Internet Encyclopedia of Philosophy*, [Online], available from: iep.utm.edu/santayan/.

Flick, U. 2002, *An Introduction to Qualitative Research*, 2nd edn, SAGE Publications, London.

Flick, U. 2004, 'Methodology and Qualitative Research', in U. Flick, E. von Kardoff, & I. Steinke (eds), *A Companion to Qualitative Research*, SAGE Publications, London, pp. 143–184, doi.org/10.3126/njqrm.v1i0.1977.

Flick, U. 2018, 'Triangulation in Data Collection', in U. Flick (ed.), *The SAGE Handbook of Qualitative Data Collection*, SAGE Publications, London, pp. 527–544, doi.org/10.4135/9781526416070.n34.

Fligstein, N. 1997, 'Social Skill and Institutional Theory', *American Behavioural Scientist*, vol. 40, no. 4, pp. 397–405, doi.org/10.1177/0002764297040004003.

Flyvbjerg, B. 2006, 'From Nobel Prize to Project Management: Getting Risks Right', *Project Management Journal*, vol. 37, no. 3, pp. 5–15, doi.org/10.1177/875697280603700302.

Flyvbjerg, B. 2008, 'Curbing Optimism Bias and Strategic Misrepresentation in Planning: Reference Class Forecasting in Practice', *European Planning Studies*, vol. 16, no. 1, pp. 3–21, doi.org/10.1080/09654310701747936.

Flyvbjerg, B. 2013, 'Quality Control and Due Diligence in Project Management: Getting Decisions Right by Taking the Outside View', *International Journal of Project Management*, vol. 31, no. 5, pp. 760–774, doi.org/10.1016/j.ijproman. 2012.10.007.

Flyvbjerg, B. 2014, 'What You Should Know About Megaprojects and Why: An Overview', *Project Management Journal*, vol. 45, no. 2, pp. 6–19, doi.org/ 10.1002/pmj.21409.

Flyvbjerg, B. & COWI 2004, *Procedures for Dealing with Optimism Bias in Transport Planning: Guidance Document*, UK Department for Transport, London.

Flyvbjerg, B., Hon, C., & Fok, W.H. 2016a, 'Reference Class Forecasting for Hong Kong's Major Roadworks Projects', *Proceedings of the Institution of Civil Engineers: Civil Engineering*, vol. 169, no. 6(SI), pp. 17–24, doi.org/10.1680/ jcien.15.00075.

Flyvbjerg, B., Skamris Holm, M.K., & Buhl, S.L. 2005, 'How (In)accurate Are Demand Forecasts in Public Works Projects?: The Case of Transportation', *Journal of American Planning Association*, vol. 71, no. 2, pp. 131–146, doi. org/10.1080/01944360508976688.

Flyvbjerg, B., Stewart, A., & Budzier, A. 2016b, *The Oxford Olympics Study 2016: Cost and Cost Overrun at the Games*, Saïd Business School Working Paper No. 2016-20, University of Oxford, Oxford, UK, doi.org/10.2139/ssrn.2804554.

Fowler, M. 2005, 'The New Methodology', *martinfowler.com*, available from: www. martinfowler.com/articles/newMethodology.html.

Frederickson, H.G. & Smith, K.B. 2003, *The Public Administration Theory Primer*, Westview Press, Boulder, CO.

Freidson, E. 1975, *Doctoring Together: A Study of Professional Social Control*, University of Chicago Press, Chicago, IL.

Fukuyama, F. 2004, *State-Building: Governance and World Order in the 21st Century*, Cornell University Press, Ithaca, NY.

Furlong, P. & Marsh, D. 2010, 'A Skin Not a Sweater: Ontology and Epistemology in Political Science', in D. Marsh & G. Stoker (eds), *Theory and Methods in Political Science*, 3rd edn, Palgrave Macmillan, New York, NY.

Gains, F. & John, P. 2010, 'What Do Bureaucrats Like Doing? Bureaucratic Preferences in Response to Institutional Reform', *Public Administration Review*, vol. 70, no. 3, pp. 455–463, doi.org/10.1111/j.1540-6210.2010.02159.x.

Gartner 2016, 'Gartner Says Global IT Spending to Reach $3.5 Trillion in 2017', Press release, 19 October, Gartner, Orlando, FL, available from: www.gartner.com/en/newsroom/press-releases/2016-10-19-gartner-says-global-it-spending-to-reach-3-trillion-in-2017#:~:text=Driven%20by%20growth%20in%20software,software%20and%20IT%20services%20segments.

Garud, R., Hardy, C., & Maguire, S. 2007, 'Institutional Entrepreneurship as Embedded Agency: An Introduction to the Special Issue', *Organizational Studies*, vol. 28, no. 7, pp. 1055–1077, doi.org/10.1177/0170840607078958.

Gauld, R. & Goldfinch, S. 2006, *Dangerous Enthusiasms: E-Government, Computer Failure and Information System Development*, Otago University Press, Dunedin, NZ.

George, A.L. 1979, 'Case Studies and Theory Development', in P. Lauren (ed.), *Diplomacy: New Approaches in Theory, History, and Policy*, Free Press, New York, NY, pp. 43–68.

George, A.L. & Bennet, A. 2005, *Case Studies and Theory Development in Social Sciences*, MIT Press, Cambridge, MA.

Gerring, J. 2012, *Social Science Methodology: A Unified Framework*, 2nd edn, Cambridge University Press, Cambridge, UK.

Gerring, J. 2017, *Case Study Research: Principles and Practices*, Cambridge University Press, Cambridge, UK.

Gershon, P. 2008, *Review of the Australian Government's Use of Information and Communication Technology*, August, Commonwealth of Australia, Canberra, available from: ict-industry-reports.com.au/wp-content/uploads/sites/4/2013/10/2008-Review-of-Australian-Governments-Use-of-ICT-Gershon-August-2008.pdf.

Globerson, S. & Levin, N. 1987, 'Incorporating Forgetting into Learning Curves', *International Journal of Operations & Production Management*, vol. 7, no. 4, pp. 80–94, doi.org/10.1108/eb054802.

Goldfinch, S. 2007, 'Pessimism, Computer Failure, and Information Systems Development in the Public Sector', *Public Administration Review*, vol. 67, no. 5, pp. 917–929, doi.org/10.1111/j.1540-6210.2007.00778.x.

Government Project Delivery Profession (GPDP) 2021, *Project Delivery Capability Framework: For Project Delivery Professionals in Government. Version 3*, December, Infrastructure and Projects Authority, London, available from: assets.publishing.service.gov.uk/government/uploads/system/uploads/attachment_data/file/755783/PDCF.pdf.

Government of South Australia 2018, *South Australian Government ICT Strategy 2018–2021*, Government of South Australia, Adelaide, available from: www.dpc. sa.gov.au/__data/assets/pdf_file/0004/45922/sagov-ICT-strategy-2018-2021. pdf.

Graham, R.J. & Englund, R. 1994, 'Leading the change to project management', Paper presented to PMI 25th Annual Seminars and Symposium, Project Management Institute, Newtown Square, PA.

Green, S. 2005, 'Strategic Project Management: From Maturity Model to Project Leadership', *Project Management Journal*, vol. 36, no. 2, pp. 60–73.

Greene, J.C. 2007, *Mixed Methods in Social Inquiry*, Jossey-Bass, San Francisco, CA.

Grönlund, A. & Horan, T.A. 2005, 'Introducing e-Gov: History, Definitions, and Issues', *Communications of the Association for Information Systems*, vol. 15, no. 1, p. 39, doi.org/10.17705/1cais.01539.

Guida, J. & Crow, M. 2009, 'E-Government and e-Governance', in T. Unwin (ed.), *ICT4D*, Cambridge University Press, Cambridge, UK, pp. 283–320.

Hall, P. 1980, *Great Planning Disasters*, Weidenfeld & Nicolson, London.

Hall, P. & Taylor, R. 1996, 'Political Science and the Three New Institutionalisms', *Political Studies*, vol. 44, no. 5, pp. 936–957, doi.org/10.1111/j.1467-9248.1996. tb00343.x.

Hall, P.A. 1986, *Governing the Economy: The Politics of State Intervention in Britain and France*, Oxford University Press, New York, NY.

Hass, K.B. 2008, *Managing Complex Projects: A New Model*, [e-book], Berrett-Koehler Publishers, Vienna.

Hay, C. 1996, 'Structure and Agency', in D. Marsh and G. Stoker (eds), *Theory and Methods in Political Science*, Macmillan, Basingstoke, UK, pp. 83–103.

Heclo, H. 1978, 'Issue Networks and the Executive Establishments', in A. King (ed.), *The New American Political System*, American Enterprise Institute, Washington, DC, pp. 87–124.

Helm, J. & Remington, K. 2005, 'Effective Project Sponsorship: An Evaluation of the Role of the Executive Sponsor in Complex Infrastructure Projects by Senior Project Managers', *Project Management Journal*, vol. 36, no. 3, pp. 51–61, doi.org/ 10.1177/875697280503600306.

Hendry, J. 2018, 'NSW Education Finally Completes $755m, 12 Year-Long LMBR Overhaul', *iTnews*, 20 December, available from: www.itnews.com.au/news/nsw-education-finally-completes-755m-12-year-long-lmbr-overhaul-517130.

Hendry, J. 2021, 'NSW Govt IT Cost Overruns Fall by 90 Percent in Four Years', *iTnews*, 12 February, available from: www.itnews.com.au/news/nsw-govt-it-cost-overruns-fall-by-90-percent-in-four-years-560956.

Herszon, L. & Keraminiyage, K. 2014, 'Dimensions of Project Complexity and Their Impact on Cost Estimation', Paper presented at PMI Global Congress 2014—North America, Phoenix, AZ, 26 October, Project Management Institute, Newtown Square, PA, available from: www.pmi.org/learning/library/dimensions-project-complexity-impact-cost-estimation-9354.

HM Treasury 2013, *Strengthening Financial Management Capability in Government*, June, HM Treasury, London, available from: assets.publishing.service.gov.uk/government/uploads/system/uploads/attachment_data/file/209220/strengthening_financial_management_capability_in_government.pdf.

Hochschild, J.L. 2009, 'Conducting Intensive Interviews and Elite Interviews', Workshop on Interdisciplinary Standards for Systematic Qualitative Research, Harvard University, Cambridge, MA, available from: scholar.harvard.edu/jlhochschild/publications/conducting-intensive-interviews-and-elite-interviews.

Hodgkinson, S. 2019, 'Platform + Agile Experiences from the Front Lines of Public Sector Reform', *Pulse*, [LinkedIn], 11 October, available from: www.linkedin.com/pulse/platformagile-experiences-from-front-lines-public-steve-hodgkinson?articleId=6585773947894239232#comments-6585773947894239232&trk=public_profile_article_view.

Hornby, A.S. 1995, *Oxford Advanced Learner's Dictionary*, Oxford University Press, Oxford, UK.

Howlett, M. 2012, 'The Lessons of Failure: Learning and Blame Avoidance in Public Policy-Making', *International Political Science Review*, vol. 33, no. 5, pp. 539–555, doi.org/10.1177/0192512112453603.

Hughes, D.L., Dwivedi, Y.K., Rana, N.P., & Simintiras, A.C. 2016, 'Information Systems Project Failure: Analysis of Causal Links Using Interpretive Structural Modelling', *Production Planning & Control*, vol. 27, no. 16, pp. 1313–1333, doi.org/10.1080/09537287.2016.1217571.

Information Management Office (IMO) 2012, *ICT Business Case Guide*, Parliament of Australia, Canberra.

Infrastructure and Projects Authority (IPA) 2015, *Major Projects Leadership Academy (MPLA) Handbook*, UK Government, London, available from: assets.publishing. service.gov.uk/government/uploads/system/uploads/attachment_data/file/850 739/MPLA_Handbook_for_IPA_Website__2_.pdf.

Infrastructure and Projects Authority (IPA) 2018, *Annual Report on Major Projects 2017–18*, UK Government, London, available from: assets.publishing.service. gov.uk/government/uploads/system/uploads/attachment_data/file/721978/IPA_ Annual_Report_2018__2_.pdf.

Infrastructure and Projects Authority (IPA) 2020, *Major Projects Leadership Academy: MPLA Handbook*, UK Government, London, available from: assets.publishing. service.gov.uk/government/uploads/system/uploads/attachment_data/file/850 739/MPLA_Handbook_for_IPA_Website__2_.pdf.

International Centre for Complex Project Management (ICCPM) 2012, *Complex Project Manager Competency Standards. Version 4.1*, August, Department of Defence, Canberra, available from: iccpm.com/wp-content/uploads/2018/09/ CPM-Competency-Standard-V4.1.pdf.

International Project Management Association (IPMA) 2015, *IPMA Code of Ethics and Professional Conduct*, 22 January, IPMA, Amsterdam, available from: www. ipma.world/resources/ipma-code-of-ethics-and-professional-conduct/.

Jack, M. & Wevers, M. 2013, *Report of the Ministerial Inquiry into the Novopay Project*, New Zealand Government, Wellington.

James, V., Rosenhead, R., & Taylor, P. 2013, *Strategies for Project Sponsorship*, Management Concept Press, Tysons Corner, VA.

Jones, C. 2006, 'Project Sponsorship: Managing the Executive Role in Project Excellence', Paper presented at PMI Global Congress 2006—North America, Seattle, WA, 21–24 October, Project Management Institute, Newtown Square, PA, available from: www.pmi.org/learning/library/project-sponsorship-executive-project-excellence-8037.

Jones, C. 2007, *Estimating Software Costs*, 2nd edn, McGraw Hill, New York, NY.

Joslin, R. & Müller, R. 2015, 'Relationships between a Project Management Methodology and Project Success in Different Project Governance Contexts', *International Journal of Project Management*, vol. 33, no. 6, pp. 1377–1392, doi.org/10.1016/j.ijproman.2015.03.005.

Joslin, R. & Müller, R. 2016, 'The Relationship between Project Governance and Project Success', *International Journal of Project Management*, vol. 34, no. 4, pp. 613–626, doi.org/10.1016/j.ijproman.2016.01.008.

Kaarbo, J. & Beasley, R.K. 1999, 'A Practical Guide to the Comparative Case Study Method in Political Psychology', *Political Psychology*, vol. 20, no. 2, pp. 369–391, doi.org/10.1111/0162-895x.00149.

Kahneman, D. & Tversky, A. 1979, 'Prospect Theory: An Analysis of Decision under Risk', *Econometrica*, vol. 47, no. 2, pp. 263–292, doi.org/10.2307/1914185.

Katsamunska, P. 2016, 'The Concept of Governance and Public Governance Theories', *Economic Alternatives*, vol. 2, pp. 133–141.

Keall, C. 2012, 'Talent2 Boss: We're Losing Money on Novopay', *National Business Review*, [Auckland, NZ], 21 November, available from: www.nbr.co.nz/talent2-boss-were-losing-money-on-novopay/.

Keall, C. 2013, 'OIA Docs: Ministry Considered Dumping Novopay Five Months Before Launch; Evaluation Factors Revealed', *National Business Review*, [Auckland, NZ], 1 February, available from: www.nbr.co.nz/oia-docs-ministry-considered-dumping-novopay-five-months-before-launch-evaluation-factors-revealed/.

Kenny, M. 2007, 'Gender, Institutions and Power: A Critical Review', *Politics*, vol. 27, no. 2, pp. 91–100.

Kenton, W. 2022, 'Monte Carlo Simulation: History, How it Works, and 4 Key Steps', *Investopedia*, [Updated 11 August], available from: www.investopedia.com/terms/m/montecarlosimulation.asp.

Kerzner, H. & Kerzner, H.R. 2013, *Project Management: A Systems Approach to Planning, Scheduling, and Controlling*, John Wiley & Sons, Hoboken, NJ.

Kickert, W.J.M. & van der Meer, F. 2011, 'Small, Slow, and Gradual Reform: What Can Historical Institutionalism Teach Us?', *International Journal of Public Administration*, vol. 34, no. 8, pp. 475–485, doi.org/10.1080/01900692.2011.583768.

King, G., Keohane, R.O., & Verba, S. 1994, *Designing Social Inquiry: Scientific Inference in Qualitative Research*, Princeton University Press, Princeton, NJ.

Kleiner, M.M., Nickelsburg, J., & Pilarski, A.M. 2012, 'Organizational and Individual Learning and Forgetting', *ILR Review*, vol. 65, no. 1, pp. 68–81, doi.org/10.1177/001979391206500104.

Kloppenborg, T.J., Manolis, C., & Tesch, D. 2009, 'Successful Project Sponsor Behaviors During Project Initiation: An Empirical Investigation', *Journal of Managerial Issues*, vol. 21, no. 1, pp. 140–159.

Kloppenborg, T.J. & Tesch, D. 2015, 'How Executive Sponsors Influence Project Success', *MIT Sloan Management Review*, vol. 26, no. 3, pp. 27–30.

Koning, E.A. 2016, 'The Three Institutionalisms and Institutional Dynamics: Understanding Endogenous and Exogenous Change', *Journal of Public Policy*, vol. 36, no. 4, pp. 639–664, doi.org/10.1017/s0143814x15000240.

KPMG 2012, *Queensland Health: Review of the Queensland Health Payroll System*, 31 May, KPMG, Brisbane, available from: www.healthpayrollinquiry.qld.gov.au/__data/assets/pdf_file/0008/177902/KPMG_Report_dated_31_May_2012.PDF.

Ku, H.B. & Yuen-Tsang, A.W.K. 2011, 'Capacity Building', in M. Bevir (ed.), *The SAGE Handbook of Governance*, SAGE Publications, London, pp. 469–483, doi.org/10.4135/9781446200964.n30.

Kumarasingham, H. & Power, J. 2015, 'Constrained Parliamentarism: Australia and New Zealand Compared', in J. Wanna, E.A. Lindquist, & P. Marshall (eds), *New Accountabilities, New Challenges*, ANU Press, Canberra, pp. 189–206, doi.org/10.22459/nanc.04.2015.06.

Kvale, S. 2007, 'Reporting Interview Knowledge', in S. Kvale, *Doing Interviews*, SAGE Publications, London, pp. 129–135, doi.org/10.4135/9781849208963.n11.

Kwak, Y.H., Liu, M., Patanakul, P., & Zwikael, O. 2014, *Challenges and Best Practices of Managing Government Projects and Programs to the Theory and Practices*, Project Management Institute, Newtown Square, PA, available from: www.pmi.org/learning/academic-research/challenges-and-best-practices-of-managing-government-projects-and-programs.

Kwak, Y.H., Sadatsafavi, H., Walewski, J., & Williams, N.L. 2015, 'Evolution of Project Based Organization: A Case Study', *International Journal of Project Management*, vol. 33, no. 8, pp. 1652–1664, doi.org/10.1016/j.ijproman.2015.05.004.

Labuschagne, L., Cooke-Davis, T., Crawford, L., Hobbs, J.B., & Remington, K. 2006, 'Exploring the Role of the Project Sponsor', Paper presented at PMI Global Congress 2006—North America, Seattle, WA, 21–24 October, Project Management Institute, Newtown Square, PA, available from: www.pmi.org/learning/library/exploring-role-executive-project-sponsor-8107.

Laird, M. & Brennan, C. 2006, *Software Measurement and Estimation: A Practical Approach*, John Wiley & Sons, Hoboken, NJ.

Lappi, T. & Aaltonen, K. 2017, 'Project Governance in Public Sector Agile Software Projects', *International Journal of Managing Projects in Business*, vol. 10, no. 2, pp. 263–294, doi.org/10.1108/ijmpb-04-2016-0031.

Lawrence, T. 1999, 'Institutional Strategy', *Journal of Management*, vol. 25, no. 2, pp. 161–188.

Layne, K. & Lee, J. 2001, 'Developing Fully Functional E-Government: A Four Stage Model', *Government Information Quarterly*, vol. 18, no. 2, pp. 122–136, doi.org/10.1016/s0740-624x(01)00066-1.

Legislative Council Estimates Committee A 2017, *Estimates, Wednesday, 7 June 2017*, [Uncorrected proof issue], Parliament of Tasmania, Hobart, available from: www.parliament.tas.gov.au/__data/assets/pdf_file/0021/59610/lc20estimates20a20-20wednesday20720june20201720-20hidding.pdf.

Lehtinen, T.O.A., Mäntylä, M.V., Vanhanen, J., Itkonen, J., & Lassenius, C. 2014, 'Perceived Causes of Software Project Failures: An Analysis of Their Relationships', *Information and Software Technology*, vol. 56, no. 6, pp. 623–643, doi.org/10.1016/j.infsof.2014.01.015.

Leitch, C.M., Hill, F.M., & Harrison, R.T. 2009, 'The Philosophy and Practice of Interpretivist Research in Entrepreneurship: Quality, Validation, and Trust', *Organizational Research Methods*, vol. 13, no. 1, pp. 67–84, doi.org/10.1177/1094428109339839.

Levi, M.N. 1990, 'A Logic of Institutional Change', in K.S. Cook & M. Levi (eds), *The Limits of Rationality*, Chicago University Press, Chicago, IL.

Levitt, B. & March, J.G. 1988, 'Organizational Learning', *Annual Review of Sociology*, vol. 14, pp. 319–340.

Levy, J.S. 2008, 'Case Studies: Types, Designs, and Logics of Inference', *Conflict Management and Peace Science*, vol. 25, no. 1, pp. 1–18, doi.org/10.1080/07388940701860318.

Lind, H. & Brunes, F. 2014, 'Policies to Avoid Cost Overruns in Infrastructure Projects: Critical Evaluation and Recommendations', *Australasian Journal of Construction Economics and Building*, vol. 14, no. 3, pp. 74–85, doi.org/10.5130/ajceb.v14i3.4151.

Liu, L., Wehbe, G., & Sisovic, J. 2010, 'The Accuracy of Hybrid Estimating Approaches: A Case Study of an Australian State Road & Traffic Authority', *The Engineering Economist*, vol. 55, no. 3, pp. 225–245, doi.org/10.1080/0013791x.2010.502962.

Liu, X. 2018, 'Interviewing Elites: Methodological Issues Confronting a Novice', *International Journal of Qualitative Methods*, vol. 17, pp. 1–9, doi.org/10.1177/1609406918770323.

Lockett, A., Currie, G., Waring, J., Finn, R., & Martin, G. 2012, 'The Role of Institutional Entrepreneurs in Reforming Healthcare', *Social Science & Medicine*, vol. 74, no. 3, pp. 356–363, doi.org/10.1016/j.socscimed.2011.02.031.

Lowndes, V. 2002, 'Institutionalism', in D. Marsh & G. Stoker (eds), *Theory and Methods in Political Science*, 2nd edn, Palgrave Macmillan, Houndmills, UK, pp. 90–108.

Lowndes, V. 2010, 'The Institutional Approach', in D. Marsh & G. Stoker (eds), *Theory and Methods in Political Science*, 3rd edn, Palgrave, Basingstoke, UK, pp. 60–79.

Lowndes, V. 2014, 'How Are Things Done Around Here? Uncovering Institutional Rules and Their Gendered Effects', *Politics & Gender*, vol. 10, no. 4, pp. 685–691, doi.org/10.1017/s1743923x1400049x.

Lowndes, V. 2018, 'Institutionalism', in D. Marsh & G. Stoker (eds), *Theory and Methods in Political Science*, 4th edn, Palgrave, London, pp. 54–74.

Mahoney, J. 2000, 'Path Dependence in Historical Sociology', *Theory and Society*, vol. 29, no. 4, pp. 507–548.

Manuel-Navarrete, D. & Modvar, C. 2007, 'Stakeholder', in M. Bevir (ed.), *Encyclopedia of Governance*, SAGE Publications, London, pp. 918–922.

March, J.G., Friedberg, E., & Arellano, D. 2011, 'Institutions and Organizations: Differences and Linkages from Organization Theory', *Gestión y Política Publica* [*Management and Public Policy*], vol. 20, no. 2.

March, J.G. & Olsen, J.P. 1984, 'The New Institutionalism: Organizational Factors in Political Life', *American Political Science Review*, vol. 78, no. 3. pp. 734–749, doi.org/10.2307/1961840.

March, J.G. & Olsen, J.P. 2008, 'New Institutionalism', in S.A. Binder, R.A.W. Rhodes, & B.A. Rockman (eds), *The Oxford Handbook of Political Institutions*, Oxford University Press, Oxford, UK, pp. 1–19, doi.org/10.1093/oxfordhb/9780199548460.001.0001.

Marcusson, L. 2018, 'The Sponsor's Overview of an IT Project, According to IT Project Managers Opinion', *Journal of Economics and Management Sciences*, vol. 1, no. 1, pp. 65–77, doi.org/10.30560/jems.v1n1p65.

Marrs, C. 2019, 'Canada Appoints Partners to Replace Phoenix Pay System', *Global Government Forum*, 19 June, [Updated 24 September 2020], available from: www.globalgovernmentforum.com/canada-appoints-partners-to-replace-phoenix-pay-system/.

Marsh, D. 1998, *Comparing Policy Networks*, Open University Press, Buckingham, UK.

Marsh, D. & Smith, M. 2000, 'Understanding Policy Networks: Towards a Dialectical Approach', *Political Studies*, vol. 48, no. 1, pp. 4–21, doi.org/10.1111/1467-9248.00247.

Martin, D. 2011, '£12b NHS Computer System Is Scrapped … And It's All YOUR Money that Labour Poured Down the Drain', *Daily Mail*, [London], 23 September, available from: www.dailymail.co.uk/news/article-2040259/NHS-IT-project-failure-Labours-12bn-scheme-scrapped.html.

Martin, M.D. & Miller, K. 1982, 'Project Planning as the Primary Management Function', *Project Management Quarterly*, vol. 13, no. 1, pp. 31–38, available from: www.pmi.org/learning/library/project-planning-as-primary-management-function-10339.

Maxwell, J.A. 1992, 'Understanding and Validity in Qualitative Research', *Harvard Educational Review*, vol. 62, no. 3, pp. 279–300, doi.org/10.17763/haer.62.3.8323320856251826.

Maxwell, J.A. 2004, *Qualitative Research Design*, SAGE Publications, Thousand Oaks, CA.

May, K. 2019, 'Upgrade of Troubled Phoenix Could Risk Yet More Payroll Snafus for Public Servants', *National Observer*, [Vancouver, BC], 3 April, available from: www.nationalobserver.com/2019/04/03/news/upgrade-troubled-phoenix-could-risk-yet-more-payroll-snafus-public-servants.

Mayhew, C., Ridha, S., & Ahmed, M.D. 2013, 'Software Implementation: Lessons to Be Learnt from the Novopay Payroll Project', Paper presented to 26th Annual Conference of Computing & Information Technology Research & Education New Zealand, Hamilton, NZ, 6–9 October, available from: www.researchgate.net/publication/258079514_Software_Implementation_-_Lessons_to_be_learnt_from_the_Novopay_Payroll_project.

McConnell, A. 2010a, 'Policy Success, Policy Failure and Grey Areas In-Between', *Journal of Public Policy*, vol. 30, no. 3, pp. 345–362, doi.org/10.1017/s0143814x10000152.

McConnell, A. 2010b, *Understanding Policy Success: Rethinking Public Policy*, Palgrave Macmillan, Basingstoke, UK.

McConnell, A. 2015, 'What is Policy Failure? A Primer to Help Navigate the Maze', *Public Policy and Administration*, vol. 30, nos 3–4, pp. 221–242, doi.org/10.1177/0952076714565416.

McKeown, M. 2012, *Adaptability: The Art of Winning in an Age of Uncertainty*, Kogan Page, Philadelphia, PA.

McMillan, J. 1992, *Games, Strategies and Managers*, Oxford University Press, Oxford, UK.

Meckstroth, T.W. 1975, '"Most Different Systems" and "Most Similar Systems": A Study in the Logic of Comparative Inquiry', *Comparative Political Studies*, vol. 8, no. 2, pp. 132–157, doi.org/10.1177/001041407500800202.

Mertler, C.A. 2016, *Introduction to Educational Research*, SAGE Publications, Thousand Oaks, CA.

Meuleman, L. 2008, *Public Management and the Metagovernance of Hierarchies, Networks and Markets: The Feasibility of Designing and Managing Governance Style Combinations*, Springer, New York, NY.

Meyer, W.G. 2015, 'Quantifying Risk: Measuring the Invisible', Paper presented to PMI Global Congress 2015—EMEA, London, 10 October, Project Management Institute, Newtown Square, PA, available from: www.pmi.org/learning/library/quantitative-risk-assessment-methods-9929.

Meyer, W.G. 2016, 'Estimating: The Science of Uncertainty', Paper presented to PMI Global Congress 2016—EMEA, Barcelona, Spain, 13 May, Project Management Institute, Newtown Square, PA, available from: www.pmi.org/learning/library/estimating-science-uncertainty-10186.

Miles, M.B. & Huberman, A.M. 1994, *Qualitative Data Analysis: An Expanded Sources Book*, 2nd edn, SAGE Publications, Newbury Park, CA.

Ministry of Education (MoE) 2009, *Project Novopay Independent Quality Assurance Review, Stage 2 Health Check, v1.0*, New Zealand Government, Wellington, accessed from: www.education.govt.nz/assets/Documents/Ministry/Information-releases/Novopay-information-release/IQANZStage2HealthCheck.pdf [page discontinued].

Ministry of Education (MoE) 2012a, 'Novopay Briefing', Memo from Kevin Wilson to Lesley Longstone, 22 November, New Zealand Government, Wellington, available from: media.nzherald.co.nz/webcontent/document/pdf/20135/Memo NovopayBriefing22Nov12.pdf.

Ministry of Education (MoE) 2012b, *Project Initiation Document (PID) Novopay Project V3.02*, New Zealand Government, Wellington, accessed from: education.govt.nz/assets/Documents/Ministry/Information-releases/Novopay-information-release/InitiationDocProjectV3P1.pdf [page discontinued].

Ministry of Education (MoE) 2012c, 'Project Novopay Project Board Meeting Minutes, Meeting #87, 23 October 2008 to Meeting #111, 14 October 2010', New Zealand Government, Wellington, accessed from: education.govt.nz/assets/Documents/Ministry/Information-releases/Novopay-information-release/NovopayGovernanceBoardMinutesPart1.pdf [page discontinued].

Ministry of Education (MoE) 2012d, *Novo Times*, 27 July to 21 September, Issues 10–17, New Zealand Government, Wellington, accessed from: education.govt.nz/assets/Documents/Ministry/Information-releases/Novopay-information-release/Part2NovotimesIssue10to17.pdf [page discontinued].

Ministry of Education (MoE) 2012e, 'Recommendations Associated with the Outcome of the Warning Letter issued to Talent 2 on 5th April', Memo from Leanne Gibson to Anne Jackson, 19 April, New Zealand Government, Wellington.

Ministry of Education (MoE) 2012f, 'Novopay Steering Committee Meeting Minutes, Meetings 107 to 109', New Zealand Government, Wellington, accessed from: www.education.govt.nz/assets/Documents/Ministry/Information-releases/Novopay-information-release/SteeringMinutes2012PartFour.pdf [page discontinued].

Ministry of Education (MoE) 2012g, 'Novopay Steering Committee Meeting Minutes, Meetings 110 to 114', New Zealand Government, Wellington, accessed from: www.education.govt.nz/assets/Documents/Ministry/Information-releases/Novopay-information-release/SteeringMinutes2012PartFive.pdf [page discontinued].

Ministry of Education (MoE) 2012h, 'Memo to Lesley Longstone for Meeting with Talent2 on 18 September 2012', 17 September, New Zealand Government, Wellington.

Miterev, M., Mancini, M., & Turner, R. 2017, 'Towards a Design for the Project-Based Organization', *International Journal of Project Management*, vol. 35, no. 3, pp. 479–491, doi.org/10.1016/j.ijproman.2016.12.007.

Moore, S. 2015, 'IT Projects Need Less Complexity, Not More Governance', *Insights*, 17 July, Gartner, Stamford, CT, available from: www.gartner.com/smarter withgartner/it-projects-need-less-complexity-not-more-governance/#:~:text= Complexity%20leads%20to%20failure&text=Complex%20projects%20with% 20unrealistic%20goals,the%20assignment%20of%20decision%20rights%E2% 80%9D.

Moore, T. 2013, '"Worst Failure of Public Administration in this Nation": Payroll System', *Sydney Morning Herald*, 7 August, [Updated 15 August], available from: www.smh.com.au/it-pro/government-it/worst-failure-of-public-administration-in-this-nation-payroll-system-20130806-hv1cw.html.

Morris, P.W.G. 1994, *The Management of Projects*, Thomas Telford, London.

Morris, P.W.G. 1998, *Key Issues in Project Leadership: Project Management Handbook*, Jossey-Bass, San Francisco, CA.

Morse, J.M. 1991, 'Approaches to Qualitative–Quantitative Methodological Triangulation', *Nursing Research*, vol. 40, no. 2, pp. 120–123, doi.org/10.1097/00006199-199103000-00014.

Mott MacDonald 2002, *Review of Large Public Procurement in the UK*, Report for HM Treasury, July, Mott MacDonald Group, Croydon, UK, available from: www.edinburghtraminquiry.org/wp-content/uploads/2017/10/CEC02084689.pdf.

Munck af Rosenschöld, J., Rozema, J.G., & Frye-Levine, L.A. 2014, 'Institutional Inertia and Climate Change: A Review of the New Institutionalist Literature', *WIREs Climate Change*, vol. 5, no. 5, pp. 639–648, doi.org/10.1002/wcc.292.

National Business Review (NBR) 2013, 'Govt Reactivates Pre-Novopay Pay Provider as Problems Persist', *National Business Review*, [Auckland, NZ], 31 January, available from: www.nbr.co.nz/govt-reactivates-pre-novopay-pay-provider-as-problems-persist/.

Newshub 2013, 'Novopay Approved Despite Obvious Issues', *Newshub*, [NZ], 1 February, available from: www.newshub.co.nz/politics/novopay-approved-despite-obvious-issues-2013020115.

New Zealand Government 2018, *Assuring Digital Government Outcomes: All-of-Government Portfolio, Programme and Project Assurance Framework. Version 3.1*, October, New Zealand Government, Wellington, available from: www.digital.govt.nz/assets/Documents/96aog-portfolio-programme-and-project-assurance-framework-v3-2.pdf.

New Zealand Parliament 2013, '288 (2013). Clare Curran to the Minister with responsibility for Novopay', Written Questions, *Order Paper and Questions*, 30 January, New Zealand Parliament, Wellington, available from: www.parliament.nz/en/pb/order-paper-questions/written-questions/document/QWA_00288_2013/288-2013-clare-curran-to-the-minister-with-responsibility.

Nikander, P. 2012, 'Interviews as Discourse Data', in J.F. Gubrium, J.A. Holstein, A.B. Marvasti, & K.D. McKinney (eds), *The SAGE Handbook of Interview Research: The Complexity of the Craft*, SAGE Publications, Thousand Oaks, CA, pp. 397–414, doi.org/10.4135/9781452218403.n28.

North, D.C. 1990, *Institutions, Institutional Change and Economic Performance*, Cambridge University Press, Cambridge, UK.

North, D.C. 1994, *Institutional Change: A Framework of Analysis*, Working Paper, University Library of Ludwig-Maximilians-Universität München, Germany, available from: econwpa.ub.uni-muenchen.de/econ-wp/eh/papers/9412/9412 001.pdf.

NT Health 2017, *Core Clinical Systems Renewal Program (CCSRP)*, [Updated 8 February 2023], Northern Territory Government, Darwin, available from: health.nt.gov.au/professionals/core-clinical-systems-renewal-program-ccsrp.

NZ Herald 2012, 'Secretary of Education Lesley Longstone Resigns', *NZ Herald*, [Auckland], 19 December, available from: www.nzherald.co.nz/nz/news/article. cfm?c_id=1&objectid=10855074.

Office for Digital Government 2022, *South Australian Government Digital Transformation Toolkit Guide. Version 4.2*, Government of South Australia, Adelaide, available from: www.dpc.sa.gov.au/__data/assets/pdf_file/0008/46565/ Digital_Transformation_Toolkit_Guide.pdf.

Office of the Auditor-General (OAG) 2012, *Realising Benefits from Six Public Sector Technology Projects*, Discussion Paper, June, New Zealand Government, Wellington, available from: oag.parliament.nz/2012/realising-benefits/docs/ realising-benefits.pdf.

Office of the Chief Information Officer (OCIO) 2013, *Strategic ICT Feedback, Feedback on SA Connected, and the SA Government's ICT Position Paper*, Government of South Australia, Adelaide, accessed from: yoursay.sa.gov.au/ media/BAhbBlsHOgZmSSIfMjAxMy8wNi8xOS8xN180Ml8xMV8zX2Zpb GUGOgZFVA/17_42_11_3_file [page discontinued].

Office of the Commissioner for Public Employment (OCPE) 2018, *Capability Framework: NT Public Sector*, Northern Territory Government, Darwin, available from: ocpe.nt.gov.au/__data/assets/pdf_file/0014/243302/capability-framework-ntps.pdf.

Office of the Commissioner for Public Sector Employment 2022, *Executive Excellence: South Australian Leadership Academy*, Government of South Australia, Adelaide, available from: publicsector.sa.gov.au/people/leadership-development/south-australian-leadership-academy/ [page discontinued].

Office of eGovernment 2011–13, *Tasmanian Government ICT Strategy*, Department of Premier and Cabinet, Hobart, available from: nla.gov.au/nla.obj-1863483919/ view.

Office of Government Chief Information Officer (GCIO) 2016, *Digital WA: Western Australian Government—Information and Communications Technology (ICT) Strategy 2016–2020*, Government of Western Australia, Perth, available from: www.parliament.wa.gov.au/publications/tabledpapers.nsf/displaypaper/3914215afb73cc112672740b48257fd20052e83a/$file/4215.pdf.

Office of Government Commerce (OGC) 2002, *Managing Successful Projects with PRINCE2*, HM Treasury, London.

Office of Projects Victoria (OPV) 2019, *Australian Major Projects Leadership Academy*, OPV, Melbourne, available from: www.opv.vic.gov.au/System-wide-improvements/Victorian-Major-Projects-Leadership-Academy.

O'Leary, Z. 2010, *The Essential Guide to Doing Your Research Project*, SAGE Publications, London.

Oppenheimer, J.A. 2010, 'Rational Choice Theory', in M. Bevir (ed.), *Encyclopedia of Political Science*, SAGE Publications, Thousand Oaks, CA, pp. 1150–1158.

Organisation for Economic Co-operation and Development (OECD) 2001, *The Hidden Threat to e-Government: Avoiding Large Government IT Failures*, PUMA Policy Brief No. 8, March, OECD Public Management, Paris, available from: www.firma-facile.it/wp-content/uploads/1901677.pdf.

Ostrom, E. 1999, 'Institutional Rational Choice: An Assessment of the Institutional Analysis and Development Framework', in P. Sabatier (ed.), *Theories of the Policy Process*, Westview Press, Boulder, CO, pp. 35–72.

Overby, S. 2022, 'What is Outsourcing? Definitions, Benefits, Challenges, Processes, Advice', *CIO*, 25 November, available from: www.cio.com/article/2439495/outsourcing-outsourcing-definition-and-solutions.html.

Pádár, K., Pataki, B., & Sebestyén, Z. 2017, 'Bringing Project and Change Management Roles into Sync', *Journal of Organizational Change Management*, vol. 30, no. 5, pp. 797–822, doi.org/10.1108/jocm-07-2016-0128.

Parsons, C. 2007, *How to Map Arguments in Political Science*, Oxford University Press, Oxford, UK.

Pawar, B.S. & Eastman, K.K. 1997, 'The Nature and Implications of Contextual Influences of Transformational Leadership: A Conceptual Examination', *Academy of Management Review*, vol. 22, no. 1, pp. 80–109, doi.org/10.5465/amr.1997.9707180260.

Pedler, M. & Hsu, S. 2014, 'Unlearning, Critical Action Learning and Wicked Problems', *Action Learning: Research and Practice*, vol. 11, no. 3, pp. 296–310, doi.org/10.1080/14767333.2014.945897.

Peters, B.G. 2011, 'Institutional Theory', in M. Bevir (ed.), *The SAGE Handbook of Governance*, SAGE Publications, London, pp. 78–90, doi.org/10.4135/9781446200964.n6.

Peters, B.G. 2012, 'Governance as Political Theory', in D. Levi-Faur (ed.), *The Oxford Handbook of Governance*, [Online edn], Oxford University Press, Oxford, UK, doi.org/10.1093/oxfordhb/9780199560530.001.0001.

Pierson, P. 2000a, 'Increasing Returns, Path Dependence, and the Study of Politics', *American Political Science Review*, vol. 94, no. 2, pp. 251–267, doi.org/10.2307/2586011.

Pierson, P. 2000b, 'Not Just What, but *When*: Timing and Sequence in Political Processes', *Studies in American Political Development*, vol. 14, no. 1, pp. 72–92, doi.org/10.1017/s0898588x00003011.

Pierson, P. 2004, *Politics in Time: History, Institutions, and Social Analysis*, Princeton University Press, Princeton, NJ.

Pollitt, C. 2000, 'Institutional Amnesia: A Paradox of the 'Information Age'', *Prometheus*, vol. 18, no. 1, pp. 5–16, doi.org/10.1080/08109020050000627.

Potter, J. & Hepburn, A. 2012, 'Eight Challenges for Interview Researchers', in J.F. Gubrium, J.A. Holstein, A.B. Marvasti, & K.D. McKinney (eds), *The SAGE Handbook of Interview Research: The Complexity of the Craft*, SAGE Publications, Thousand Oaks, CA, pp. 555–570, doi.org/10.4135/9781452218403.n39.

PRINCE2.com 2019, 'What is PRINCE2?', *PRINCE2.com*, available from: www.prince2.com/aus/what-is-prince2.

Project Management Institute (PMI) 2011, *Practice Standard for Project Estimating*, 4th edn, Project Management Institute, Newton Square, PA.

Project Management Institute (PMI) 2012, *Executive Engagement: The Role of the Sponsor*, White Paper, Project Management Institute, Newton Square, PA, available from: www.pmi.org/-/media/pmi/documents/public/pdf/business-solutions/executive-engagement.pdf.

Project Management Institute (PMI) 2013a, *A Guide to the Project Management Body of Knowledge (PMBOK)*, 5th edn, Project Management Institute, Newton Square, PA.

Project Management Institute (PMI) 2013b, *Organizational Project Management Maturity Model (OPM3)*, 3rd edn, Project Management Institute, Newtown Square, PA.

Project Management Institute (PMI) 2014, *Navigating Complexity: A Practice Guide*, Project Management Institute, Newtown Square, PA.

Project Management Institute (PMI) 2017, *Code of Ethics and Professional Conduct*, Project Management Institute, Newtown Square, PA, available from: www.pmi.org/about/ethics/code.

Project Management Institute (PMI) 2018, *Pulse of the Profession 2018*, Project Management Institute, Newtown Square, PA, available from: www.pmi.org/learning/thought-leadership/pulse/pulse-of-the-profession-2018.

Project Management Institute (PMI) 2019, *Standards & Publications*, Project Management Institute, Newtown Square, PA, available from: www.pmi.org/pmbok-guide-standards.

Public Accounts Committee 2014, *Management of ICT Projects by Government Agencies*, Legislative Assembly of the Northern Territory, Darwin.

Public Sector Commission (PSC) 2017, *Information and Communications Technology Capability Framework*, Government of Western Australia, Perth.

Public Service Commission (PSC) 2013, *The NSW Public Sector Capability Framework*, NSW Public Service Commission, Sydney.

Public Service Commission (PSC) 2019, *Occupation Specific Capability Sets*, NSW Public Service Commission, Sydney, available from: www.psc.nsw.gov.au/workforce-management/capability-framework/occupation-specific-capability-sets.

Public Service Commission (PSC) 2020, *The NSW Public Sector Capability Framework. Version 2:2020*, NSW Public Service Commission, Sydney, available from: www.psc.nsw.gov.au/sites/default/files/2020-11/capability_framework_v2_2020.pdf.

Queensland Government Chief Information Office (QGCIO) 2018a, *ICT Skills Framework*, Queensland Government, Brisbane, accessed from: www.qgcio.qld.gov.au/information-on/workforce-planning/ict-skills-framework [page discontinued].

Queensland Government Chief Information Office (QGCIO) 2018b, *Program and Project Assurance Framework. V3.0.0*, November, Queensland Government, Brisbane, available from: www.qgcio.qld.gov.au/documents/program-and-project-assurance-framework.

Queensland Government Chief Information Office (QGCIO) 2019, *ICT (Definition)*, Queensland Government, Brisbane, accessed from: www.qgcio.qld.gov.au/publications/qgcio-glossary/ict-definition [page discontinued].

Queensland Government Customer and Digital Group (QGCDG) 2018, *Portfolio, Program and Project Management Policy. v3.0.0*, Queensland Government, Brisbane, available from: www.qgcio.qld.gov.au/documents/portfolio-program-and-project-management-policy.

Queensland Public Service Commission (QPSC) 2009, *QPS Capability and Leadership Framework*, January, Queensland Government, Brisbane, available from: www.forgov.qld.gov.au/__data/assets/pdf_file/0025/182824/capability-leadership-framework.pdf.

Queensland Treasury 2015, *Project Assessment Framework: Business Case Development*, July, State of Queensland, Brisbane, available from: s3.treasury.qld.gov.au/files/paf-business-case-development.pdf.

Queensland Treasury Corporation (QTC) 2019, *Project Management*, QTC, Brisbane, accessed from: clients.qtc.com.au/education/workshops/project-management/ [page discontinued].

Raaschelders, J.C.N. 2011, 'The Future of the Study of Public Administration: Embedding Research Object and Methodology in Epistemology and Ontology', *Public Administration Review*, vol. 71, no. 6, pp. 916–924, doi.org/10.1111/j.1540-6210.2011.02433.x.

Radio New Zealand (RNZ) 2013, 'Deputy Secretary Resigns Over Novopay', *Radio New Zealand*, 11 June, available from: www.rnz.co.nz/news/national/137392/deputy-secretary-resigns-over-novopay.

Red Hat Software 2020, *Red Hat Innovation Awards*, Red Hat Software, Raleigh, NC, available from: www.redhat.com/en/success-stories/innovation-awards.

Reinecke, I. 2011, *Implementing the ICT Strategic Vision: A Report for the Secretary of the Commonwealth Department of Finance and Deregulation on the Draft ICT Strategic Vision*, May, Australian Government, Canberra, available from: studylib.net/doc/17794755/implementing-the-ict-strategic-vision.

Remler, D.K. & Van Ryzin, G.G. 2011, *Research Methods in Practice: Strategies for Description and Causation*, SAGE Publications, London.

Ribbers, P.M.A. & Schoo, K.-C. 2002, 'Program Management and Complexity of ERP Implementations', *Engineering Management Journal*, vol. 14, no. 2, pp. 45–52, doi.org/10.1080/10429247.2002.11415162.

Richards, D. 1996, 'Elite Interviewing: Approaches and Pitfalls', *Politics*, vol. 16, no. 3, pp. 199–204, doi.org/10.1111/j.1467-9256.1996.tb00039.x.

Richardson, J. 2012, 'New Governance or Old Governance? A Policy Style Perspective', in D. Levi-Faur (ed.), *The Oxford Handbook of Governance*, [Online edn], Oxford University Press, Oxford, UK, doi.org/10.1093/oxfordhb/9780199560530.001.0001.

Rigg, C. 2016, 'Conscious Unlearning, Unconscious Unlearning and Forgetfulness: A Plea to Record Our Action Learning Experiences', *Action Learning: Research and Practice*, vol. 13, no. 3, pp. 199–200, doi.org/10.1080/14767333.2016.1220173.

Rolstadås, A. & Schiefloe, P.M. 2017, 'Modelling Project Complexity', *International Journal of Managing Projects in Business*, vol. 10, no. 2, pp. 295–314, doi.org/10.1108/ijmpb-02-2016-0015.

Rosenthal, G. 2018, *Interpretive Social Research: An Introduction*, Göttingen University Press, Göttingen, Germany.

Rothstein, B. 1996, 'Political Institutions: An Overview', in R.E. Gordon and H.D. Klingemann (eds), *A New Handbook of Political Science*, Oxford University Press, Oxford, UK, pp. 133–166, doi.org/10.1093/0198294719.003.0004.

Rothstein, B. 2012, 'Good Governance', in D. Levi-Faur (ed.), *The Oxford Handbook of Governance*, [Online edn], Oxford University Press, Oxford, UK, doi.org/10.1093/oxfordhb/9780199560530.001.0001.

Rothstein, B. & Teorell, J. 2008, 'What is Quality of Government? A Theory of Impartial Government Institutions', *Governance*, vol. 21, pp. 165–190, doi.org/10.1111/j.1468-0491.2008.00391.x.

Roulston, K. 2013, 'Analysing Interviews', in U. Flick (ed.), *The SAGE Handbook of Qualitative Data Analysis*, SAGE Publications, London, pp. 297–312, doi.org/10.4135/9781446282243.n20.

Royal Academy of Engineering & British Computer Society (BCS) 2004, *The Challenges of Complex IT Projects*, Royal Academy of Engineering, London.

Royce, W.W. 1970, 'Managing the Development of Large Software Systems', in *Proceedings of IEEE WESCon*, vol. 26, Institute of Electrical and Electronics Engineers, Piscataway, NJ, pp. 328–388.

Sabot, E.C. 1999, 'Dr Jekyl, Mr H(I)de: The Contrasting Face of Elites at Interview', *Geoforum*, vol. 30, no. 4, pp. 329–335, doi.org/10.1016/s0016-7185(99)00023-8.

Saïd Business School (SBS) 2019a, *Major Projects Leadership Academy*, Saïd Business School, University of Oxford, Oxford, UK, available from: www.sbs.ox.ac.uk/programmes/custom-executive-education/major-projects-leadership-academy.

Saïd Business School (SBS) 2019b, *Orchestrating Major Projects: A Programme for Director Generals*, Saïd Business School, University of Oxford, Oxford, UK, available from: www.sbs.ox.ac.uk/programmes/custom-executive-education/orchestrating-major-projects-programme-director-generals.

SA Office of the Chief Information Officer 2013, *South Australia Connected: Ready for the Future*, Position Paper, 27 March, Government of South Australia, Adelaide, available from: apo.org.au/sites/default/files/resource-files/2013-03/apo-nid33480.pdf.

Schibi, O. & Lee, C. 2015, 'Project Sponsorship: Senior Management's Role in the Successful Outcome of Projects', Paper presented to PMI Global Congress 2015–EMEA, London, 10 October, Project Management Institute, Newtown Square, PA, available from: www.pmi.org/learning/library/importance-of-project-sponsorship-9946.

Schmidt, V.A. 2008, 'Discursive Institutionalism: The Explanatory Power of Ideas and Discourse', *Annual Review of Political Science*, vol. 11, pp. 303–326, doi.org/10.1146/annurev.polisci.11.060606.135342.

Schmidt, V.A. 2010, 'Taking Ideas and Discourse Seriously: Explaining Change through Discursive Institutionalism as the Fourth "New Institutionalism"', *European Political Science Review*, vol. 2, no. 1, pp. 1–25, doi.org/10.1017/s175577390999021x.

Schmidt, V.A. 2011, 'Discursive Institutionalism', in B. Badie, D. Berg-Schlosser, & L. Morlino (eds), *International Encyclopedia of Political Science*, SAGE Publications, Thousand Oaks, CA, pp. 684–686, doi.org/10.4135/9781412994163.

Schmidt, V.A. 2014, 'Institutionalism', in M.T. Gibbons, D. Coole, E. Ellis, & K. Ferguson (eds), *Encyclopedia of Political Thought*, John Wiley & Sons, Hoboken, NJ, pp. 1–4, available from: www.researchgate.net/publication/313505827_Institutionalism.

Schneider, V. 2012, 'Governance and Complexity', in D. Levi-Faur (ed.), *The Oxford Handbook of Governance*, [Online edn], Oxford University Press, Oxford, UK, doi.org/10.1093/oxfordhb/9780199560530.001.0001.

Schwaber, K. 2004, *Agile Project Management with Scrum*, Microsoft Press, Redmond, WA.

Scott, W.R. 1995, *Institutions and Organizations*, SAGE Publications, Thousand Oaks, CA.

Scott, W.R. 2005, 'Institutional Theory', in G. Ritzer (ed.), *Encyclopedia of Social Theory*, SAGE Publications, Thousand Oaks, CA, pp. 409–414.

Scott, W.R. 2014, *Institutions and Organisations: Ideas, Interests and Identities*, 4th edn, SAGE Publications, Los Angeles, CA.

Seawright, J. & Collier, D. 2010, 'Glossary', in H.E. Brady & D. Collier (eds), *Rethinking Social Inquiry*, 2nd edn, Rowman & Littlefield, Lanham, MD, pp. 313–359.

Se Eun, L. 2018, 'Gershon Review Still Posing Questions for Feds', *Intermedium*, 18 June, available from: www.intermedium.com.au/article/gershon-review-still-posing-questions-feds.

Senate Economics References Committee 2016, *2016 Census: Issues of Trust*, November, Parliament of Australia, Canberra, available from: www.aph.gov.au/parliamentary_business/committees/senate/economics/2016census/report.

Senate Finance and Public Administration References Committee 2018a, *Digital Delivery of Government Services*, Report, 27 June, Parliament of Australia, Canberra, available from: www.aph.gov.au/Parliamentary_Business/Committees/Senate/Finance_and_Public_Administration/digitaldelivery/Report/.

Senate Finance and Public Administration References Committee 2018b, 'Committee Views and Recommendations', in *Digital Delivery of Government Services*, Report, 27 June, Parliament of Australia, Canberra, available from: www.aph.gov.au/Parliamentary_Business/Committees/Senate/Finance_and_Public_Administration/digitaldelivery/Report/c01.

Senate Finance and Public Administration References Committee 2018c, 'Background and Context', in *Digital Delivery of Government Services*, Report, 27 June, Parliament of Australia, Canberra, available from: www.aph.gov.au/Parliamentary_Business/Committees/Senate/Finance_and_Public_Administration/digitaldelivery/Report/.

Senate Finance and Public Administration References Committee 2018d, 'Whole-of-Government Issues', in *Digital Delivery of Government Services*, Report, 27 June, Parliament of Australia, Canberra, available from: www.aph.gov.au/Parliamentary_Business/Committees/Senate/Finance_and_Public_Administration/digitaldelivery/Report/.

SFIA Foundation 2018, *SFIA 7*, SFIA Foundation, London, available from: sfia-online.org/en/legacy-sfia/sfia-7.

Sharpe, W. 2007, 'The Gateway Review Process in Victoria', in J. Wanna (ed.), *Improving Implementation: Organisational Change and Project Management*, ANU Press, Canberra, pp. 199–218, doi.org/10.22459/ii.02.2007.17.

Shenhar, A. & Dvir, D. 2007, *Reinventing Project Management: The Diamond Approach to Successful Growth and Innovation*, Harvard Business Review Press, Cambridge, MA.

Shergold, P. 2015, *Learning from Failure: Why Large Government Policy Initiatives Have Gone So Badly Wrong in the Past and How the Chances of Success in the Future Can be Improved*, Report, 12 August, Australian Public Service Commission, Canberra.

Shore, B. 2005, 'Failure Rates in Global IS Projects and the Leadership Challenge', *Journal of Global Information Technology Management*, vol. 8, no. 3, pp. 1–5, doi.org/10.1080/1097198x.2005.10856399.

Siemiatycki, M. 2015, *Cost Overruns in Infrastructure Projects: Patterns, Causes and Cures*, IMFG Perspectives Paper No. 11, Institute on Municipal Finance and Governance, University of Toronto, Toronto, ON.

Skarbek, D. 2020, 'Qualitative Research Methods for Institutional Analysis', *Journal of Institutional Economics*, vol. 16, no. 4, pp. 409–422, doi.org/10.1017/s174413741900078x.

Small, F. 2000, *Ministerial Inquiry into INCIS*, 13 October, Report for New Zealand Government, Wellington, available from: www.cs.auckland.ac.nz/courses/compsci230s1c/lectures/clark/INCIS%20inquiry.pdf.

Small, V. 2013, 'Novopay Claims Major Education Ministry Scalp', *Stuff*, [Wellington], 11 June, available from: www.stuff.co.nz/ipad-editors-picks/8782110/Novopay-claims-major-Education-Ministry-scalp.

Smith, K. 2007, 'Organizational Learning', in M. Bevir (ed.), *Encyclopedia of Governance*, SAGE Publications, London, pp. 643–644.

Sorensen, A. 2015, 'Taking Path Dependence Seriously: An Historical Institutionalist Research Agenda in Planning History', *Planning Perspectives*, vol. 30, no. 1, pp. 17–38, doi.org/10.1080/02665433.2013.874299.

South Australian Executive Service (SAES) 2019, *SAES Competency Framework*, Government of South Australia, Adelaide, available from: www.publicsector.sa.gov.au/__data/assets/pdf_file/0020/211673/SAES-Competency-Framework.pdf.

Standing, C., Guilfoyle, A., Lin, C., & Love, P.E.D. 2006, 'The Attribution of Success and Failure in IT Projects', *Industrial Management & Data Systems*, vol. 106, no. 8, pp. 1148–1165, doi.org/10.1108/02635570610710809.

Standish Group 2014, *Big Bang Boom*, The Standish Group International, Boston, MA, available from: www.standishgroup.com/sample_research_files/BigBang Boom.pdf.

Standish Group 2015, *Chaos Report 2015*, The Standish Group International, Boston, MA, available from: www.standishgroup.com/sample_research_files/CHAOS Report2015-Final.pdf.

Starik, M. & Rands, G.P. 1995, 'Weaving an Integrated Web: Multilevel and Multisystem Perspectives of Ecologically Sustainable Organizations', *Academy of Management Review*, vol. 20, no. 4, pp. 908–935, doi.org/10.5465/amr.1995. 9512280025.

Stark, A. 2019, 'Explaining Institutional Amnesia in Government', *Governance*, vol. 32, no. 1, pp. 143–158, doi.org/10.1111/gove.12364.

Stark, A. & Head, B. 2019, 'Institutional Amnesia and Public Policy', *Journal of European Public Policy*, vol. 26, no. 10, pp. 1521–1539, doi.org/10.1080/ 13501763.2018.1535612.

State Services Commission (SSC) 2011, *Gateway Reviews: Lessons Learned Report*, July, SSC, Wellington, available from: treasury.govt.nz/sites/default/files/2015- 04/gateway-lessons-learned-report-jul11.pdf.

State Services Commission (SSC) 2013, *Gateway Review: Lessons Learned Report*, December, SSC, Wellington, available from: treasury.govt.nz/sites/default/files/ 2015-04/gateway-lessons-learned-report-dec13.pdf.

State Services Commission (SSC) 2016, *Expanded Guide to the Leadership Success Profile*, July, SSC, Wellington, available from: pdf4pro.com/cdn/expanded- guide-to-the-leadership-success-2417eb.pdf.

Steinmo, S. 2015, 'Institutionalism', in J.D. Wright (ed.), *International Encyclopedia of the Social & Behavioural Sciences*, 2nd edn, Elsevier, Amsterdam, pp. 181–185.

Stoica, R. & Brouse, P. 2013, 'IT Project Failure: A Proposed Four-Phased Adaptive Multi-Method Approach', *Procedia Computer Science*, vol. 16, pp. 728–736, doi.org/10.1016/j.procs.2013.01.076.

Stoker, G. 1998, 'Governance as Theory: Five Propositions', *International Social Science Journal*, vol. 50, no. 155, pp. 17–28, doi.org/10.1111/1468-2451. 00106.

Streeck, W. & Thelen, K. 2005, 'Introduction: Institutional Change in Advanced Political Economies', in W. Streeck & K. Thelen (eds), *Beyond Continuity: Institutional Change in Advanced Political Economies*, Oxford University Press, Oxford, UK, pp. 1–39.

Stretton, A. 1994, 'A Short History of Project Management. Part One: The 1950s and 60s', *The Australian Project Manager*, vol. 14, pp. 36–37.

Sullivan, H., Williams, P., & Jeffares, S. 2012, 'Leadership for Collaboration', *Public Management Review*, vol. 14, no. 1, pp. 41–66, doi.org/10.1080/14719037.2011.589617.

Sutcliffe, K. & Vogus, T.J. 2003, 'Organizing for Resilience', in K.S. Cameron, J.E. Dutton, & R.E. Quinn (eds), *Positive Organisational Scholarship*, Berrett-Koehler Publishers, San Francisco, CA, pp. 94–110.

Swan, J., Scarbrough, H., & Newell, S. 2010, 'Why Don't (Or Do) Organizations Learn from Projects?', *Management Learning*, vol. 41, no. 3, pp. 325–344, doi.org/10.1177/1350507609357003.

Swann, D. 2015, 'Government IT Spending Set to Hit $6.2bn', *The Australian: Business Review*, 19 May, available from: www.theaustralian.com.au/business/business-spectator/government-it-spending-set-to-hit-62bn/news-story/0b0c990f3c478aef25900dacb1292775.

Synergy International Ltd 2001, *Guidelines for Managing and Monitoring Major IT Projects*, Prepared for the State Services Commission (SSC) & The Treasury, New Zealand Government, Wellington, available from: kiwiwiki.co.nz/pmwiki/uploads/Technology/Professional/2001-it-guidelines.pdf.

Tatnall, A., Davey, B., Wickramasinghe, N., & Dakich, E. 2013, 'Major eGovernment Projects in Health, Education and Transport in Victoria', in *BLED 2013 Proceedings*, 26th Bled eConference: eTrust: eInnovation: Challenges and Impacts for Individuals, Organizations and Society, Bled, Slovenia, 9–13 June.

Thelen, K. 1999, 'Historical Institutionalism in Comparative Politics', *Annual Review of Political Science*, vol. 2, pp. 369–404, doi.org/10.1146/annurev.polisci.2.1.369.

Thelen, K. 2004, *How Institutions Evolve: The Political Economy of Skills in Germany, Britain, the United States and Japan*, Cambridge University Press, Cambridge, UK, doi.org/10.1007/s11615-005-0266-1.

Thesing, T., Feldman, C., & Burchardt, M. 2021, 'Agile Versus Waterfall Project Management: Decision Model for Selecting the Appropriate Approach to a Project', *Procedia Computer Science*, vol. 181, pp. 746–756, doi.org/10.1016/j.procs.2021.01.227.

The Treasury 2015, *Better Business Cases: Guide to Developing the Programme Business Case*, 30 September, New Zealand Government, Wellington, available from: www.treasury.govt.nz/sites/default/files/2015-04/bbc-prgbus-gd.pdf.

The Treasury 2017, *New Zealand Gateway Reviews: Lessons Learned Report 2017*, Fourth Lessons Learned Report: New Zealand Gateway Reviews 151-200, New Zealand Government, Wellington, available from: treasury.govt.nz/sites/default/files/2018-03/gateway-lessons-learned-report-jul17.pdf.

The Treasury 2019, *Better Business Cases (BBC)*, [Last updated 19 October 2022], New Zealand Government, Wellington, available from: treasury.govt.nz/information-and-services/state-sector-leadership/investment-management/better-business-cases-bbc.

The Treasury 2020, *Investment Review Report for Education Payroll Limited, Operational & Benefits Realisation Review*, New Zealand Government, Wellington.

The Treasury 2021, *Investment Logic Mapping*, [Last updated 23 November], New Zealand Government, Wellington, available from: treasury.govt.nz/information-and-services/state-sector-leadership/investment-management/better-business-cases-bbc/bbc-methods-and-tools/investment-logic-mapping.

Thiry, M. 2007, 'Creating Project-based Organizations to Deliver Value', Paper presented to PMI Global Congress 2007–Asia Pacific, Hong Kong, 31 January, Project Management Institute, Newtown Square, PA, available from: www.pmi.org/learning/library/project-based-organizations-deliver-value-7330.

Thiry, M. & Deguire, M. 2007, 'Recent Developments in Project-Based Organisations', *International Journal of Project Management*, vol. 25, no. 7, pp. 649–658, doi.org/10.1016/j.ijproman.2007.02.001.

Thomas, G. & Fernández, W. 2008, 'Success in IT Projects: A Matter of Definition?', *International Journal of Project Management*, vol. 26, no. 7, pp. 733–742, doi.org/10.1016/j.ijproman.2008.06.003.

Thomke, S. & Reinertsen, D. 1998, 'Agile Product Development: Managing Development Flexibility in Uncertain Environments', *California Management Review*, vol. 41, no. 1, pp. 8–30, doi.org/10.2307/41165973.

Thomson, A.M. & Perry, J.L. 2006, 'Collaboration Processes: Inside the Black Box', *Public Administration Review*, vol. 66, no. 1, pp. 20–32, doi.org/10.1111/j.1540-6210.2006.00663.x.

Thorn, P. & McMahon, J. 2013, *Review of Lessons Learned from State Services Commission's Role in the Ministry of Education's Novopay Project*, Report for State Services Commission, 15 February, Caravel Group (NZ) Limited, Wellington, available from: www.publicservice.govt.nz/assets/DirectoryFile/Caravel-Group-Review-SSC-role-Novopay.pdf.

Thummadi, B.V. & Lyytinen, K. 2020, 'How Much Method-in-Use Matters? A Case Study of Agile and Waterfall Software Projects and Their Design Routine Variation', *Journal of the Association for Information Systems*, vol. 21, no. 4, pp. 864–900, doi.org/10.17705/1jais.00623.

Timney, M.M. 1996, 'Institutionalism and Public Administration or "I'm from Government and I'm Here to Help"', *Administrative Theory & Praxis*, vol. 18, no. 2, pp. 101–107.

Touran, A. & Lopez, R. 2006, 'Modeling Cost Escalation in Large Infrastructure Projects', *Journal of Construction Engineering Management*, vol. 132, no. 8, pp. 853–860, doi.org/10.1061/(asce)0733-9364(2006)132:8(853).

Turner, J.R. 1993, *The Handbook of Project-Based Management*, McGraw-Hill, Maidenhead, UK.

Turner, J.R. & Xue, Y. 2018, 'On the Success of Megaprojects', *International Journal of Managing Projects in Business*, vol. 11, no. 3, pp. 783–805, doi.org/10.1108/ijmpb-06-2017-0062.

Ulriksen, G.-H., Pedersen, R., & Ellingsen, G. 2016, 'Establishing ICT Governance for Regional Information Infrastructures in Healthcare', in *2016 49th Hawaii International Conference on System Sciences (HICSS)*, Koloa, HI, pp. 5137–5146, doi.org/10.1109/hicss.2016.636.

Vance, A. & Chapman, K. 2013, 'Novopay System Twice Delayed', *Stuff*, [Wellington], 1 February, available from: www.stuff.co.nz/national/politics/8250237/Novopay-system-twice-delayed.

Van Evera, S. 1997, *Guide to Methods for Students of Political Science*, Cornell University Press, Ithaca, NY.

Van Keersbergen, K. & Van Waarden, F. 2004, '"Governance" as a Bridge between Disciplines: Cross-Disciplinary Inspiration Regarding Shifts in Governance and Problems of Governability, Accountability and Legitimacy', *European Journal of Political Research*, vol. 43, no. 2, pp. 143–171, doi.org/10.1111/j.1475-6765.2004.00149.x.

Van Wart, M. 2003, 'Public Sector Leadership Theory: An Assessment', *Public Administration Review*, vol. 63, no. 2, pp. 214–228, doi.org/10.1111/1540-6210.00281.

Victoria Police 2016, *Victoria Police Capability Plan 2016–25: Capability Framework*, Victoria Police, Melbourne, available from: www.police.vic.gov.au/capability-plan [page discontinued].

Victorian Auditor-General's Office (VAGO) 2008, *Investing Smarter in Public Sector ICT*, VAGO, Melbourne, available from: www.audit.vic.gov.au/sites/default/files/20080730-ICT-BPG.pdf.

Victorian Auditor-General's Office (VAGO) 2012, *Managing Major Projects*, Victorian Auditor-General's Report 2012-13:07, October, VAGO, Melbourne, available from: www.audit.vic.gov.au/sites/default/files/20121010-Major-Projects.pdf.

Victorian Auditor-General's Office (VAGO) 2013, *Planning, Delivery and Benefits Realisation of Major Asset Investment: The Gateway Review Process*, Victorian Auditor-General's Report 2012-13:28, May, VAGO, Melbourne, available from: www.parliament.vic.gov.au/file_uploads/20130508-Gateway-Review-Process_y6Khg9hf.pdf.

Victorian Government 2019, *Project Governance Executive Program*, [Reviewed 16 February 2021], State Government of Victoria, Melbourne, available from: www.vic.gov.au/digital-capability-uplift.

Victorian Government CIO Council 2015, *Selecting a Project Management Methodology: Guideline*, 1 July, State Government of Victoria, Melbourne, available from: www.vic.gov.au/sites/default/files/2019-08/PM-GUIDE-01-Project-management-methodology-selection-guideline.pdf.

Victorian Ombudsman 2011, *Own Motion Investigation into ICT-Enabled Projects*, November, Victorian Ombudsman, Melbourne, available from: www.vgls.vic.gov.au/client/en_AU/search/asset/1267225/0.

Victorian Ombudsman 2012, *The Victorian Ombudsman's Investigation into ICT-Enabled Projects*, Victorian Ombudsman, Melbourne, available from: www.publicsector.sa.gov.au/South-Australian-Leadership-Academy/executive-excellence.

Victorian Public Sector Commission (VPSC) 2015, *VPS Human Resources Capability Framework*, VPSC, Melbourne, available from: vpsc.vic.gov.au/wp-content/pdf-download.php?postid=173064.

Volden, G.H. & Andersen, B. 2018, 'The Hierarchy of Public Project Governance Frameworks: An Empirical Study of Principles and Practices in Norwegian Ministries and Agencies', *International Journal of Managing Projects in Business*, vol. 11, no. 1, pp. 174–197, doi.org/10.1108/ijmpb-04-2017-0040.

Wachs, M. 1990, 'Ethics and Advocacy in Forecasting for Public Policy', *Business & Professional Ethics Journal*, vol. 9, nos 1–2, pp. 141–157, doi.org/10.5840/bpej199091/215.

Wanna, J. (ed.) 2007, *Improving Implementation: Organisational Change and Project Management*, ANU Press, Canberra, doi.org/10.22459/II.02.2007.

Wanna, J. 2021, 'Delivering Public Policy Programs to Senior Executives in Government: The Australia and New Zealand School of Government 2002–18', in T. Mercer, R. Ayres, B. Head, & J. Wanna (eds), *Learning Policy, Doing Policy: Interactions between Public Policy Theory, Practice and Teaching*, ANU Press, Canberra, pp. 83–106, doi.org/10.22459/LPDP.2021.04.

Wateridge, J. 1998, 'How Can IS/IT Projects Be Measured for Success?', *International Journal of Project Management*, vol. 16, no. 1, pp. 59–63, doi.org/10.1016/s0263-7863(97)00022-7.

Whiteford, P. 2020, 'Robodebt was a Fiasco with a Cost We Have Yet to Fully Appreciate', *The Conversation*, 16 November, available from: theconversation.com/robodebt-was-a-fiasco-with-a-cost-we-have-yet-to-fully-appreciate-150169.

Williams, T. & Samset, K. 2010, 'Issues in Front-End Decision Making on Projects', *Project Management Journal*, vol. 41, no. 2, pp. 90–109, doi.org/10.1002/pmj.20160.

Zwikael, O. 2009, 'The Relative Importance of the PMBOK Guide's Nine Knowledge Areas during Project Planning', *Project Management Journal*, vol. 40, no. 4, pp. 94–103, doi.org/10.1002/pmj.20116.

Zwikael, O. & Meredith, J.R. 2018, 'Who's Who in the Project Zoo? The Ten Core Project Roles', *International Journal of Operations and Production Management*, vol. 38, no. 2, pp. 474–492, doi.org/10.1108/ijopm-05-2017-0274.

Zwikael, O. & Smyrk, J. 2012, 'A General Framework for Gauging the Performance of Initiatives to Enhance Organizational Value', *British Journal of Management*, vol. 23, no. S1, pp. S6–S22, doi.org/10.1111/j.1467-8551.2012.00823.x.

Zwikael, O. & Smyrk, J. 2015, 'Project Governance: Balancing Control and Trust in Dealing with Risk', *International Journal of Project Management*, vol. 33, no. 4, pp. 852–862, doi.org/10.1016/j.ijproman.2014.10.012.

www.ingramcontent.com/pod-product-compliance
Lightning Source LLC
Chambersburg PA
CBHW060025030426
42334CB00019B/2183